Second Edition

Microcomputers for Engineers and Scientists

Glenn A. Gibson

Yu-cheng Liu

University of Texas at El Paso
El Paso, Texas

PRENTICE-HALL, INC., Englewood Cliffs, New Jersey 07632

Library of Congress Cataloging-in-Publication Data

GIBSON, GLENN A.
  Microcomputers for engineers and scientists.

  Includes bibliographies and index.
  1. Microcomputers. 2. Microprocessors.
  I. Liu, Yu-cheng. II. Title.
  QA76.5.G49 1987   004.16   86-30320
  ISBN 0-13-580366-7

Editorial/production supervision and
  interior design: Mary Jo Stanley
Cover design: 20/20 Services, Inc.
Manufacturing buyer: Rhett Conklin

The following figures were taken from
Microcomputer Systems: The 8086/8088 Family,
2nd Edition, by Yu-cheng Liu and Glenn A.
Gibson, © 1986, and have been reprinted or
altered and reprinted by permission of
Prentice-Hall, Inc.: 6-36, 6-37, 6-40, 7-1, 7-2,
7-6, 10-11, 10-12, 10-15, 10-22, 10-24, 10-25,
10-27, 10-28, 10-30, 10-31, 10-33, 10-35, 10-36,
10-37, 10-39, 10-40, 10-41, 11-13, 11-14.

ISBN 0-13-580366-7 025

PRENTICE-HALL INTERNATIONAL (UK) LIMITED, *London*
PRENTICE-HALL OF AUSTRALIA PTY. LIMITED, *Sydney*
PRENTICE-HALL CANADA INC., *Toronto*
PRENTICE-HALL HISPANOAMERICANA, S.A., *Mexico*
PRENTICE-HALL OF INDIA PRIVATE LIMITED, *New Delhi*
PRENTICE-HALL OF JAPAN, INC., *Tokyo*
PRENTICE-HALL OF SOUTHEAST ASIA PTE. LTD., *Singapore*
EDITORA PRENTICE-HALL DO BRASIL, LTDA., *Rio de Janeiro*

To Our Parents

Horace James Gibson   *Hsiao-sheng Liu*
Maggie Case Gibson   *Hsi-cheng Liu*

Contents

Preface

Recent advances in microelectronics brought about by very large scale integration (VLSI) have made it possible to put a powerful computer into a single integrated circuit package. Because so much electronic circuitry is available in small, inexpensive, and highly reliable microelectronic packages that are capable of performing complex tasks, the number of uses to which this new technology can be applied has increased dramatically. Therefore, if our ability to use new circuitry is to stay within striking distance of our ability to produce inexpensive circuitry with ever-increasing complexity, we must efficiently disseminate the necessary information to a broad base of potential users. Fortunately, the building-block nature of these microelectronic packages makes it possible for engineers and scientists with only a limited understanding of electronic circuitry to include them in their designs.

Just what information is sufficient and how it should be made available is much debated. This book represents an attempt made by two computer engineers to solve this problem in digital electronics applications that are complicated enough to justify the use of microprocessors. The book is designed for scientists and engineers who wish to acquire an overall knowledge of microcomputers and for hardware designers who need to understand microcomputer programming. This book could be used for two types of a one-semester course. One would not assume a knowledge of logical design and would cover the first ten chapters. The other would assume a background in logical design and would include Chapter 1, perhaps Chapter 2, and Chapters 5 through 12. The only prerequisites to understanding the material presented here is a technically oriented aptitude, an elementary understanding of electricity, a general familiarity with computers, and knowledge of at least one high-level programming language (e.g., Fortran or BASIC).

This book concentrates on 8-bit microprocessors. Although single-chip 16-

bit and 32-bit microprocessors are now available, this book considers only the smaller 8-bit processors and primarily examines the Intel 8085. The main reason for studying 8-bit processors in a first course on microcomputer design is that they are more easily understood but still demonstrate the more important features of small computer systems. The 8-bit processors are still widely used and are likely to remain that way for the foreseeable future. Their larger successors have more processing power than is needed for many applications and, for these applications, there is no justification for the increased expense of the processor and the associated increase in supporting electronics.

The Intel 8085 was chosen as the principal example in our discussions because of its popularity in designing small systems. The Zilog Z80 and Motorola MC6809 processors are also examined and comparisons are made with the 8085. For those interested in the 16-bit processors, the book *Microcomputer Systems: The 8086/ 8088 Family*, 2nd Edition, which is also by Liu and Gibson, and published by Prentice-Hall, is recommended. Some of the material in this second edition, material that is mutually applicable, was taken from that book.

In writing this text, it has been assumed that, in order to include a microprocessor effectively in a design, the designer should not only understand how to put the microelectronic packages together but should have some knowledge of their structure so that he or she will know their capabilities and limitations. With this in mind, the first five chapters explain the salient points of microcomputer architecture, the formats used in storing data inside a computer, and the principles underlying the design of logic circuits. Chapter 5 surveys the important microcomputer architectural features and serves as an introduction to Chapters 6 through 12. Chapters 6, 7, and 8 discuss microcomputer programming, the effects architecture has on programming, and the trade-offs to be considered in writing a program. Chapters 9 through 11 consider hardware topics, including bus structure and timing, interface design, and memory module design. Chapter 12 discusses the available systems for aiding in the development of both the hardware and software needed for an application. Three appendices summarize the instruction sets of the Intel 8085, Zilog Z80, and Motorola MC6809, respectively.

There is a considerable amount of jargon associated with computers, much of it being rather fuzzily defined. This is unfortunate and no solution is offered here. However, in order to read computer manuals, texts, technical articles and so on, it is necessary to become familiar with the general meaning of this jargon. The authors have attempted to determine the common usage definitions of most important terms and, when stating these definitions, have italicized the terms being defined. These terms also appear in the index so that they can be easily referenced.

As with the first edition, the authors would like to acknowledge the cooperation of the Electrical Engineering Department at the University of Texas at El Paso during the preparation of the second edition. Also, Glenn Gibson would like to thank the Electrical and Electronics Engineering Departments at the University of Auckland, where he visited for a year, for giving him the time to complete this revision.

Chapter 1

Introduction
to Computers

A *digital computer* is an electronic machine capable of quickly performing complex calculations by means of stored instructions and data. It internally represents numbers and its own instructions in terms of combinations of distinct states and stores information in either electronic or magnetic devices. Digital computers are capable of performing a wide variety of tasks. They can be used to compile, correlate, sort, merge, and store data as well as perform calculations. For this reason digital computers are often called general purpose.

A digital computer is different from a calculator in that it is capable of operating according to instructions that are stored within the computer, whereas a calculator must be given instructions on a step-by-step basis. By this definition a programmable calculator is a computer, something that many computer people would argue is not quite true. This distinction has been chosen here because it permits a fairly clear defining line that provides some clarification of the subject matter to be presented.

Historically, digital computers have been categorized according to size using the words *large, medium, minicomputer,* and *microcomputer.* The defining lines between these categories is somewhat blurred and, with the recent advances in microelectronics, have become almost meaningless. A *microcomputer* is a digital computer whose processing circuitry is embedded in a single, small surface called an *integrated circuit* (*IC*), or *chip*. Within the last few years, microcomputers have become so powerful that they have made the word *minicomputer* obsolete. The size of a computer has come to imply more about the number, speed, and capacity of its peripherals and mass storage devices than the power of its processor.

The principal advantages of microcomputers are their low cost and the amount of circuitry contained on a single component. The latter provides a modularity that allows a wider variety of designers, some of whom may have a limited understanding of computers, to incorporate them into their designs. It is microcomputers that this book is about.

1-1 THE GENERAL ORGANIZATION OF COMPUTERS

Despite the fact that the evolution of computers has resulted in an extensive range of sizes and applications and that considerable time has been spent reconfiguring the basic components of a computer, the simple diagram in Fig. 1-1 still provides a good starting point for discussions of computer organization. As indicated by this figure, the four fundamental components of a computer are its *memory, central processing unit* (*CPU*), *mass storage subsystem,* and *input/output* (*I/O*) *subsystem.* The purpose of the memory is to store both the instructions that dictate the operations of the computer and the data being operated on. The CPU controls the decoding and execution of the instructions. The mass storage subsystem stores large quantities of all types of information over extended periods, and the input/ output subsystem gives the external world a means of communicating with the computer. Although mass storage is a form of memory, programs and data must be transferred to the computer's main memory before they can be executed or operated on. This is because it takes the CPU much longer to retrieve information from mass storage than from main memory.

The diagram shows all of the components connected to a common line that represents a set of conductors referred to as the *system bus.* It is over this set of conductors that all information that is transmitted from one component to another must travel.

The CPU is divided into two major parts, one part being responsible for the overall control of the system and for retrieving and decoding the instructions and the other part, called the *arithmetic/logic unit* (*ALU*), being responsible for the arithmetic and logical operations. Because the CPU performs several functions, it is usually broken down even further (see Chapter 5). The CPU in a microcomputer system is called the *microprocessor unit* (*MPU*).

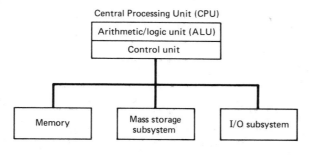

Figure 1-1 Simplified block diagram of a computer.

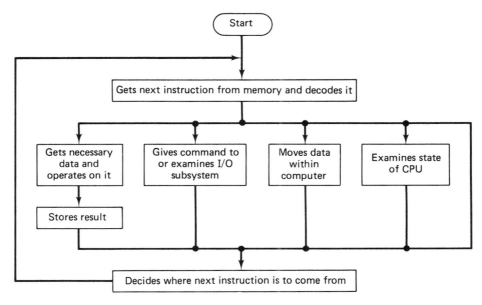

Figure 1-2   Flowchart of a computer's operation.

The operation of a computer proceeds as shown in Fig. 1-2. The CPU brings an instruction in from memory, decodes it, brings in the required data, operates on the data if necessary, dispenses the results to the proper locations, and decides where in memory it is to go to get the next instruction. As shown in the figure, once the computer has decoded the instruction, it will take different paths in executing the instruction, depending on the type of the instruction. Some instructions will perform calculations, some will give commands to or examine the status of the I/O subsystem, some will simply move data around, and others will only decide where the next instruction is to come from, perhaps basing the decision on the current state of the computer.

From the definition of a digital computer, it is seen that its distinguishing characteristic is that it stores and manipulates information as combinations of states. Each element within the computer is capable of assuming M states and by grouping the elements into sets of n each, M^n different combinations, i.e., different pieces of information, can be represented by each set. It should be evident that the designer's selection of M, n, and the number of sets is basic. It turns out that M is dictated by the present state of technology and is 2. The parameter n is normally 8, and even for simple applications, the number of sets would usually be in the tens of thousands. For some of today's applications the computer must contain billions of elements. This means that each element must be extremely reliable; otherwise, thousands of elements could be malfunctioning at any given time and the computer's results would be worthless.

There are two reasons why 2 is the best value for *M*. First, an element that can take on only two distinct states requires very few electronic components (transistors, diodes, resistors, etc.), and even though a larger value of *M* would decrease the number of elements, it would increase the number of electronic components. Second, because the properties of electronic components change with age and because there is always some noise (extraneous electromagnetic signals) within electronic circuits, it is much easier to identify reliably one of two states than it is to identify one of a greater number of states. Electronic circuits are much more stable and much less susceptible to noise when they are operated in their extreme states, and normally there are only two such states in a given circuit.

1-2 MICROCOMPUTER APPLICATIONS

The information stored in each element of a binary machine is called a *bit*. The applications for which a computer is suitable are strongly related to the maximum number of bits that can be included in its memory and the speed with which its CPU can operate on these bits. Speed is very much dependent on the number of

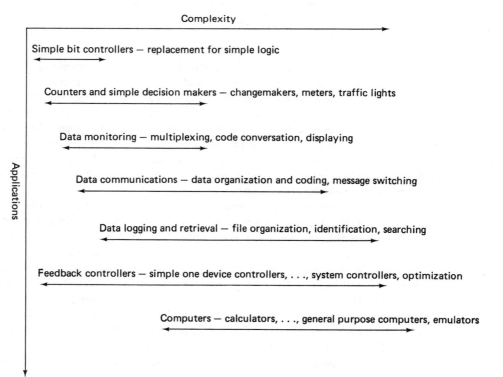

Figure 1-3 Microcomputer applications.

bits that can be transferred over the system bus at one time and the number of bits that can be involved in a single arithmetic or logical operation. Accordingly, microprocessors have been put into 8-bit, 16-bit, and 32-bit classifications, with those in the 32-bit class being 10 to 50 times as fast as those in the 8-bit class.

The popular 8-bit microcomputers can have as many as 0.5 million bits in their memories and add two nine-digit integers in approximately 20 μs. On the other hand, the newer 32-bit microprocessors have maximum memory sizes of more than 100 million bits and can add nine-digit numbers in less than 1 μs. Applications that require high speed also tend to demand large memories.

Figure 1-3 illustrates the types of microcomputer applications and their ranges of complexity. Some applications that require only simple bit controllers can be satisfied with a single microprocessor chip; they are shown toward the left side of the figure. The complexity increases as one moves toward the right side of the figure. The more complicated multibit controllers appear next, followed by such applications as data monitoring, data logging, communications controllers, and feedback controllers. Finally, appearing at the bottom are the applications in which a microcomputer is used in place of a large computer. The slower 8-bit microprocessors are used primarily for the applications at the top of the figure, and 16- and 32-bit processors are needed for replacing large, general purpose computers. However, many single-user personal computers are based on 8-bit processors.

1-2-1 Example: A Microcomputer Warning Device

Consider a chemical process in which it is necessary to maintain the temperature and pressure inside a vessel within a certain area, as shown in Fig. 1-4. If the temperature/pressure combination wanders outside this area, it is necessary to alert the operator by lighting a lamp and sounding a horn. Figure 1-5 shows a block diagram of a microprocessor-based system capable of performing the required task. Assuming that the temperature/pressure pairs that describe the perimeter of the area are stored in memory, the system would operate by periodically reading in the temperature and pressure, comparing the current pressure against the pressure limits for the current temperature using the perimeter table, and giving warning signals if the pressure is outside these limits. This application could be easily implemented with an 8-bit microprocessor.

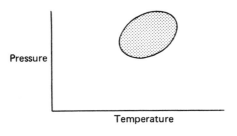

Figure 1-4 Permissible temperatures and pressures for the warning system example.

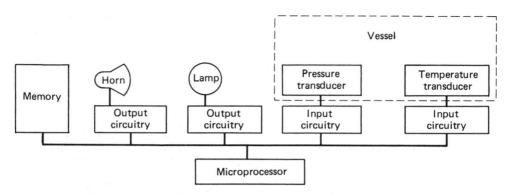

Figure 1-5   Design of the microcomputer-based warning system.

One of the major advantages of the proposed system is its flexibility.   If a different perimeter is needed, one would need only change the contents of memory, or perhaps change the memory module itself, since it would probably consist of a single, inexpensive chip.   The system could easily be expanded to monitor several vessels by adding the necessary transducers and input circuitry for each vessel, a separate light and associated output circuitry for each vessel, and an expanded program.   If the flexibility of changing the program or perimeter separately is desired, one may choose to put the program and perimeter data in separate memory chips.

1-2-2 Example: An Automobile Ignition System

The optimal time to ignite the fuel mixture in a cylinder of an automobile engine depends on the following six quantities:

1. Inlet-air temperature
2. Crankshaft position
3. Intake-manifold vacuum
4. Engine temperature
5. Throttle position
6. Rate of change of throttle position

The optimization criterion in this example would be some weighted combination that would tend to minimize fuel consumption and exhaust pollutants and maximize performance.   Once the criterion is established, optimal control theory could be used to produce an algorithm for determining the output timing from the input variables listed above.   Such algorithms are much too complicated to implement by the electromechanical means used in the past.   What is needed is a high-speed computational element with storage capability (i.e., a computer).

A block diagram of a computerized ignition system is shown in Fig. 1-6. This is a classic example of a computer application that was not economically feasible before the development of microelectronics. In this system the input variables are read periodically and used by the optimization algorithm to predict the precise time to ignite the fuel mixture. The memory not only can be used to store the current information but, depending on the complexity of the algorithm, could also store past readings of the input variables. Changing the system so that it could be used on a different engine would require parameter changes in the algorithm and could be accomplished simply by replacing a memory chip. As with the previous example, an 8-bit processor would probably be sufficient.

1-2-3 Example: A Rocket Feedback Control System

Suppose that a rocket's sensors are able to measure the distance between it and a target and the planar X-Y deviation of the target from the rocket's line of flight. Once again optimal control theory could be used to find an algorithm that would use the input variables to produce outputs to the rocket's control surfaces. Figure 1-7 shows a block diagram of an air-to-surface rocket's control system in which two control surfaces have been assumed. Past as well as current information could be used to predict the relative position of the rocket to the target. This would be particularly important if the target were moving. Because of the rocket's high velocity, this application would require the speed of a 16-bit or perhaps a 32-bit microprocessor.

1-2-4 Example: An Automated Retailing System

There has been considerable progress recently toward the automation of retail sales. Figure 1-8 illustrates a simplified system in which several sales stations, including microcomputers, are connected to a central accounting and inventory computer. Figure 1-8a shows the overall layout and Fig. 1-8b shows a block

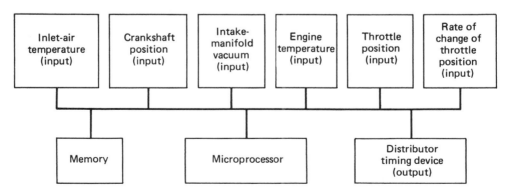

Figure 1-6   Block diagram of an automobile ignition timing system.

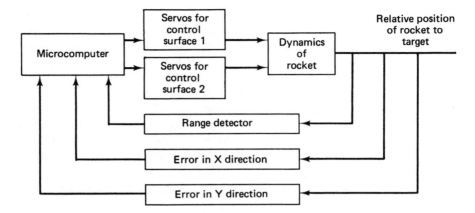

Figure 1-7   Block diagram of an air-to-surface missile's control system.

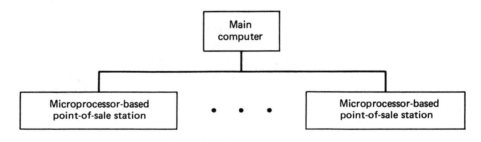

(a) Overall layout

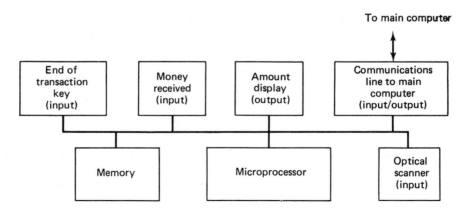

(b) Point-of-sales station

Figure 1-8   Automated retail accounting and inventory system.

diagram of a point-of-sales station. Each station is equipped with an optical scanner for reading the identifying Universal Product Code, an End of Transaction key, a device for inputting the exact amount received from the customer, a lighted display for registering the cost of each item and the customer's change, and a communication device for transmitting information to and receiving information from the main computer.

The system would execute a transaction as follows:

1. An item would be passed over the optical scanner and the scanner's output would be read by the microprocessor.
2. The microprocessor would convert the scanner output into an inventory number and send the inventory number to the main computer.
3. The main computer would find the price of the item in its pricing table, send the price to the sales station, report the sale to its accounting system, and deduct the item from the inventory records.
4. The sales station microcomputer would indicate the cost of the item on the amount display and add the price to the customer's total cost.
5. If another item is passed over the scanner, steps 1 through 4 are repeated; if the End of Transaction key is depressed, step 6 is executed.
6. The total is momentarily indicated on the amount display, the tax is computed and momentarily indicated, and then the final total is displayed.
7. The cashier keys in the exact amount received from the customer, and the change to be taken from the cash register is displayed.
8. The total price, total tax, and final total are sent to the main computer's accounting routine and the sales station is reinitialized for the next transaction.

Obvious additions to this system would be scales for weighing certain grocery items and an automatic change and/or stamp dispenser. Changes in the tax laws or in the system itself could be accommodated by reprogramming the sales station. This, incidentally, could be done through the main computer by making the changes using a terminal attached to the main computer and then sending the updated programs to the sales stations via the communication link. The point-of-sales stations could be designed around 8-bit processors, but the central computer would probably be a 32-bit facility.

1-3 HARDWARE AND SOFTWARE HIERARCHIES

A computer system's *hardware* is its electrical and mechanical parts; its *software* is the programs used to direct its operation. A system must have both to operate, and the design of both must be part of the overall design effort. A system's hardware and software and their associated design work fall into well-defined hierarchies.

The primary factor contributing to the hierarchical structure of computer hardware design is the binary nature of its elements. A large portion of a computer is a composite of two-state elements that can be implemented using the logic gates and bistable devices discussed in Chapter 3. These elements have inputs and outputs that at any given time can take on only one of two possible values, and their input/output relationships can be easily defined in terms of tables and timing diagrams. The internal design of these devices is more or less independent of the design of the modules that are constructed from them. The hardware design hierarchy is shown in Fig. 1-9 and consists of the electronic design of the logic gates, bistable devices, and other logical devices; the logical design of modules treating the logic gates and other devices as basic building blocks; the piecing together of the modules to form major subsystems; and the final organization of the overall system from its subsystems. The key product of the system design phase is usually a block diagram similar to those included in the previous examples.

An introduction to logical design is given in Chapters 3 and 4 and the various aspects of microprocessor-based subsystem and system design are discussed in Chapters 5 and 9 through 12.

For the most part the microcomputer designer does not need to do the design work at the electronic level. Current technology permits the production of thousands of elements on a single integrated circuit chip, and it is the manufacturer of these chips who is responsible for their internal circuitry. When including a chip in a system, the user need only understand the signals that must be applied to its inputs and taken from its outputs. Most of the logical design is also done by the chip manufacturer; however, a substantial amount of it must be done while putting the chips together.

The software design hierarchy shown in Fig. 1-10 is surprisingly similar to that of the hardware. The machine (or binary) language level consists of telling the computer what to do in its own language, in terms of two-state combinations, and is analogous to the electronic level in hardware design. Just as most of the electronic design is isolated from the user by the chip manufacturer, most of the

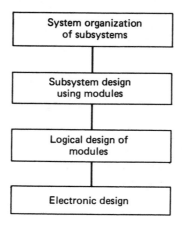

Figure 1-9 Hardware design hierarchy.

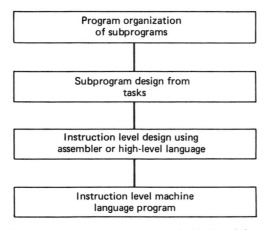

Figure 1-10 Software design hierarchy.

machine language programming is isolated from the user by the computer manufacturer. All computer manufacturers, including microcomputer manufacturers, make available to the user programs that translate strings of alphanumeric characters into machine language. These programs permit the computer itself, or perhaps another computer, to generate the machine language instructions. The input to a translating program is called *source code*. If the source code is structurally very similar to the machine language but differs only in form, it is called an assembler language program and the translating program is called an *assembler*. Some translating programs are written so that the source code bears no resemblance to the machine language they output, but is such that the source code is closer to languages used by people (e.g., the English language). In such cases, the inputs are referred to as high-level (or advanced) language programs, and the translating program is called a *compiler or interpreter*. Just as most hardware design is done at the logical level or above, most software design is done using a translator (although this is not quite as true of microcomputers as it is of larger computers).

Software design is normally accomplished by dividing the project into tasks and subtasks, writing the program segments needed to perform the subtasks and putting them together to form subprograms, and then joining the subprograms together to form the overall software package. Once the program has been written, an assembler or compiler can be used to translate it into machine language. Chapters 6 through 8 and 12 consider microcomputer programming in detail, with Chapter 7 concentrating on subprogram design.

1-4 THE STATE OF THE ART

Progress in building and applying computers has proceeded in six major directions:

1. Software
2. Input/output
3. Mass storage

4. Memories
5. Processors
6. Communications

The last five are hardware-related and are associated with the four areas depicted in Fig. 1-1. Although there were substantial gains in software in the 1950s and early 1960s, this area was relatively inactive during the late 1960s and early 1970s. However, the rapid advances in hardware development have brought about renewed activity in software. This activity has been fostered by areas such as software engineering, computer networking, distributed processing, and multi-processor architectures.

Of the hardware areas, advances in the input/output area have been the least impressive. While speeds have increased and costs have dropped, the changes have not had the impact that microelectronics has caused in the other areas. New developments in noncontact printing are having a significant effect, however. Mass storage devices that involve mechanical movement, such as magnetic tape drives and disks, have experienced modest gains, primarily as a result of improved head design and alignment. Some improvements in controllability have been realized through microelectronics.

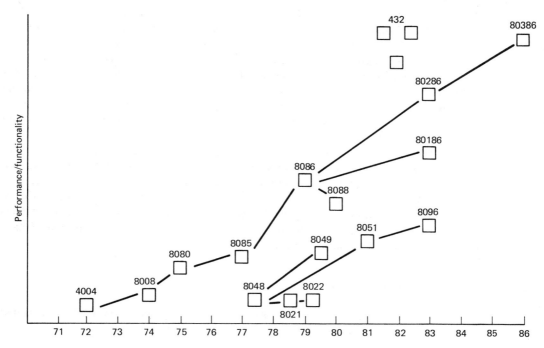

Figure 1-11 Intel family of microprocessors. (Modified Intel drawing; reprinted by permission of Intel Corporation. Copyright 1985.)

The greatest and most publicized advances have been made in those areas that depend on the miniaturization of electronic circuitry: electronic mass storage, memory, processors, and communication equipment. These improvements are centered on the ability to put more and more circuitry on a single chip and the increased speed with which the activity on a given chip takes place. For example, when designing a processor, the possibility of putting more circuitry on a single chip makes available several choices. The designer could increase the power of the processor by allowing it to operate on more bits at a time or could put more of the system circuitry on the processor chip and thereby reduce the total number of electronic devices in the system. The latter would not only simplify the original design but would make the system more reliable. Increasing the speed of the processor is also an option but, unfortunately, the speed and amount of circuitry that can be put on a chip are inversely related (i.e., the higher the speed, the less the circuitry). Therefore, a technological advance tends to permit improved speed or more dense circuitry or moderate amounts of both.

As an example, consider the growth of the Intel family of microprocessors (see Fig. 1-11). This family has expanded from the original 4-bit 4000 series bit controller chips to the 32-bit 386 and its supporting devices. The 8008, 8080, and 8085 represent the progression of 8-bit processors, with each new device including more circuitry and being more flexible. The 8086 begins the 16-bit sequence of processors that includes the 186 and 286. The 386 is Intel's entry into single-chip 32-bit processors and has the processing capability of what was considered to be a fairly large computer during the mid-1970s. This succession clearly shows the improvement in microelectronic technology over the last 15 years. Also shown is the 432 multichip processor set and a second family of microprocessors designed for controller applications. This second family grew out of the 8-bit 8048 and includes the advanced 16-bit 8096 controller.

Chapter 2

Data Formats

There are several formats a computer can use to store the information it is to operate on, but because a computer is binary in nature, all these formats must be patterns of 1's and 0's. These formats fall into two major categories. The first of these categories consists of the three formats, called *number formats*, that are used to store only numbers. The reason there are three such formats is that no single format has the versatility needed to cover all situations efficiently. The advantages and disadvantages of these formats will become apparent as they are discussed below. The second category consists of those formats that are used to store both numbers and characters, including the alphabetic characters, and are called *alphanumeric codes*.

The formats may be summarized as follows:

1. Number formats
   a. Integer (or, more generally, fixed point)
   b. Floating point (or real)
   c. Binary-coded decimal (BCD) (or decimal)
2. Alphanumeric codes.

This chapter considers each format in order and, for the number formats, discusses the algorithms for carrying out the arithmetic operations.

2-1 THE INTEGER FORMAT

It should be emphasized at the outset that the definition of a number has nothing to do with the symbology used to represent it. Numbers are abstract mathematical entities that are defined from fundamental assumptions called postulates. Historically, several systems have been employed to write these numbers. The discussion in this section will be restricted to nonnegative integers and will open by describing the usual way of representing them (i.e., using decimal digits).

From elementary arithmetic it is known that any nonnegative integer may be written in the form

$$a_n 10^n + a_{n-1} 10^{n-1} + \ldots + a_1 10^1 + a_0 10^0$$

$$= a_n 10^n + a_{n-1} 10^{n-1} + \ldots + a_1 10 + a_0$$

where a_n, a_{n-1}, $\ldots$, a_1, a_0 are integers in the range 0 through 9. Normally, the powers of 10 and the plus signs are deleted, leaving the abbreviated form

$$a_n a_{n-1} \ldots a_1 a_0$$

The integers a_n, $\ldots$, a_0 are called *digits* and the notation is further facilitated by using single symbols to represent them. There must be 10 of these symbols and the standard symbols used for these integers are, of course, 0, 1, $\ldots$, 8, 9. As an example, the number

$$6 \times 10^3 + 2 \times 10^2 + 3 \times 10 + 5$$

is conventionally written 6235. Although the algorithms for performing the arithmetic operations are derived using the expanded form, once they are known they may also be reduced so that the powers of 10 and the plus signs need not appear. As a result, the expanded form never appears in ordinary arithmetic.

The question is: Can the same notation be applied to the 1/0 combinations that the computer is required to use? The restriction is that only two symbols are available because the computer is limited to two-state combinations. Ten symbols were required in the foregoing notation because powers of 10 were used. Could powers of 2 be used? The answer is "yes"; in fact, powers of any positive integer greater than 1 could be employed as long as an equal number of symbols is available. The general form is

$$a_n x^n + \ldots + a_1 x + a_0$$

where the positive integer x is called the *base* (or *radix*). If the base is 10, the resulting notational system us called the *decimal number system* and the associated arithmetic is referred to as *base 10 arithmetic*. If the base is 2, the notational system is called the *binary number system* and the associated arithmetic is referred to as *base 2 arithmetic*. The digits in the binary number system are sometimes called *bits* and the standard two symbols used to represent the bits are 0 and 1. An example of a binary number is

$$1 \times 2^3 + 0 \times 2^2 + 1 \times 2 + 1 = 1011$$

There are two other number systems that frequently appear in computer-related discussions: the *octal number system* (*base 8*) and the *hexadecimal number system* (*base 16*). The commonly used number bases and their symbols are summarized in Fig. 2-1. The binary equivalents of the decimal, octal, and hexadecimal numbers are given in parentheses. Note that for the hexadecimal system, symbols beyond those utilized by the decimal number system must be found to represent the integers 10 through 15. Because they conform to our writing habits, the letters A through F have been chosen to fill this need. (Unfortunately, these choices sometimes lead to ambiguities.)

Although the computer cannot work directly with the numbers in the octal and hexadecimal systems, these systems have a simple relationship to the binary system that is useful in reducing notation. In the binary example above, a sequence of four digits was needed to represent the number eleven. Eleven would be written with only two digits (13) in octal and only one digit (B) in hexadecimal. The savings in digits is even more pronounced as the integers get larger.

It is seen from Fig. 2-1 that, where possible, the same symbols are used in all four number systems. This leads to the obvious problem of determining which system is being used to represent a number. Is 1101 the integer thirteen or the integer one thousand one hundred and one? If a discussion is centered on a single number system and that system is easily understood from the context, there is no difficulty; but if several systems are mixed in a discussion, the need to extend the

Binary (Base 2)	Octal (Base 8)	Decimal (Base 10)	Hexadecimal (Base 16)
0	0 (000)	0 (0000)	0 (0000)
1	1 (001)	1 (0001)	1 (0001)
	2 (010)	2 (0010)	2 (0010)
	3 (011)	3 (0011)	3 (0011)
	4 (100)	4 (0100)	4 (0100)
	5 (101)	5 (0101)	5 (0101)
	6 (110)	6 (0110)	6 (0110)
	7 (111)	7 (0111)	7 (0111)
		8 (1000)	8 (1000)
		9 (1001)	9 (1001)
			A (1010)
			B (1011)
			C (1100)
			D (1101)
			E (1110)
			F (1111)

Note: Binary equivalents are given in parentheses.

Figure 2-1 Commonly used number systems.

$$2^0 = 1$$
$$2^1 = 2$$
$$2^2 = 4$$
$$2^3 = 8$$
$$2^4 = 16$$
$$2^5 = 32$$
$$2^6 = 64$$
$$2^7 = 128$$
$$2^8 = 256$$
$$2^9 = 512$$
$$2^{10} = 1024$$

Figure 2-2   Powers of 2 from 0 to 10.

notation so that it designates the base is apparent.   The most common method of denoting the base is to subscript the number with the base written in decimal; for example, 1101_2 would indicate the integer thirteen and 1101_{10} would indicate one thousand one hundred and one.   If no subscript is given, the intended base should be evident from the context.

Because people think in terms of decimal numbers and computers work with binary numbers, there is an immediate need to convert numbers from one system to another.   First consider the conversion from binary to decimal.   This is accomplished by using the decimal system to carry out the computation indicated by the expression

$$a_n 2^n + a_{n-1} 2^{n-1} + \ldots + a_1 2 + a_0$$

One way of performing this computation is simply to compute the necessary powers of 2 and sum those whose coefficients are 1.   Figure 2-2 is a tabulation of the powers of 2 from 0 to 10.   (These numbers will be referenced frequently and should be memorized.)   The decimal equivalent of the binary number 110101 can be found as follows:

$$1 \times 2^5 + 1 \times 2^4 + 0 \times 2^3 + 1 \times 2^2 + 0 \times 2 + 1$$
$$= 32 + 16 + 0 + 4 + 0 + 1 = 53_{10}$$

A more systematic way of performing the same computation is to use *Horner's rule*, which states that

$$a_n x^n + a_{n-1} x^{n-1} + \ldots + a_1 x + a_0 = ((\ldots(a_n x + a_{n-1})x \ldots)x + a_1)x + a_0$$

For example

$$1 \times 2^5 + 1 \times 2^4 + 0 \times 2^3 + 1 \times 2^2 + 0 \times 2 + 1$$
$$= ((((1 \times 2 + 1)2 + 0)2 + 1)2 + 0)2 + 1$$

This suggests the procedure

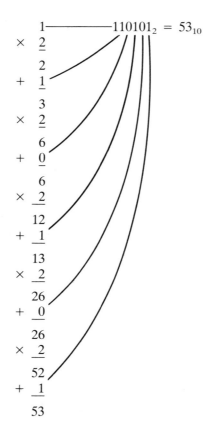

$$
\begin{array}{rl}
 & 1 \underline{\hspace{3em}} 110101_2 = 53_{10} \\
\times & 2 \\
\hline
 & 2 \\
+ & 1 \\
\hline
 & 3 \\
\times & 2 \\
\hline
 & 6 \\
+ & 0 \\
\hline
 & 6 \\
\times & 2 \\
\hline
 & 12 \\
+ & 1 \\
\hline
 & 13 \\
\times & 2 \\
\hline
 & 26 \\
+ & 0 \\
\hline
 & 26 \\
\times & 2 \\
\hline
 & 52 \\
+ & 1 \\
\hline
 & 53
\end{array}
$$

Horner's rule can also be used to find the binary equivalent of a decimal number.   To understand how this is done, note that

$$\frac{((\,.\,.\,.\,(a_n x + a_{n-1})x\,.\,.\,.\,)x + a_1)x + a_0}{x} = (\,.\,.\,.(a_n x + a_{n-1})x\,.\,.\,.\,)x + a_1 + \frac{a_0}{x}$$

The quantity

$$(\,.\,.\,.(a_n x\ +\ a_{n-1})x\,.\,.\,.\,)x\ +\ a_1$$

is the quotient and a_0 is the remainder.   By repeating the operation on the quotient, the equation

$$\frac{(\,.\,.\,.(a_n x\ +\ a_{n-1})x\,.\,.\,.\,)x\ +\ a_1}{x} = (\,.\,.\,.(a_n x\ +\ a_{n-1})x\,.\,.\,.\,)x\ +\ a_2\ +\ \frac{a_1}{x}$$

is obtained.   This time, a_1 is the remainder.   Clearly, repeated divisions will successively produce the coefficients a_0 through a_n. The method is demonstrated as follows:

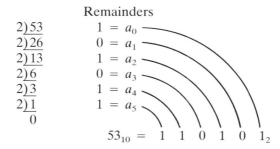

To convert from octal to binary, it is necessary only to convert each digit and then place the resulting bit combinations side by side as follows:

This procedure is justified by the equation

$$7 \times 8^2 + 5 \times 8 + 2 = (1 \times 2^2 + 1 \times 2 + 1)2^6 + (1 \times 2^2 + 0 \times 2 + 1)2^3$$
$$+ (0 \times 2^2 + 1 \times 2 + 0)$$
$$= 1 \times 2^8 + 1 \times 2^7 + 1 \times 2^6 + 1 \times 2^5 + 0 \times 2^4$$
$$+ 1 \times 2^3 + 0 \times 2^2 + 1 \times 2 + 0$$

To convert from binary to octal it is simply a matter of grouping the bits by threes and converting each group to its octal equivalent; for example

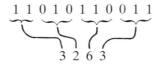

The conversions between binary and hexadecimal can be performed similarly, except that the grouping is done by fours instead of threes:

The algorithms for carrying out the arithmetic operations in the binary number system are the same as those used in the decimal number system but are somewhat easier to execute because of the simplicity of the addition and multiplication tables.

```
        0    1
   ─────────────
   0 │  0    1
   1 │  1    10
```

(a) Addition

```
        0    1
   ─────────────
   0 │  0    0
   1 │  0    1
```

(b) Multiplication

Figure 2-3   Addition and multiplication tables for the binary number system.

These tables are given in Fig. 2-3.   An example of each of the four operations is given in Fig. 2-4; each example is accompanied by the equivalent decimal calculation.   Carrying, borrowing, and shifting are done exactly the same way as if the operands were decimal numbers.   Note that multiplication involves only shifting and adding because multiplication by a single bit is a matter of writing an intermediate result (multiplication by 1) or shifting without writing the intermediate result (multiplication by 0).   Similarly, division consists of shifting and subtracting.

Performing the arithmetic operations in octal is more difficult than in decimal because people are generally unfamiliar with the octal addition and multiplication tables.   In hexadecimal, they are even more difficult to perform because these tables are so large.   Although it is worthwhile to learn how to add and subtract in these number systems, very few people learn how to multiply or divide in them. If a product or quotient is needed, one can convert the operands to the decimal system, perform the operation, and then convert the result back to the original system.

Because the storage capacity of a computer's memory and control circuitry is finite, it is necessary to group the bits it operates on into finite sequences.   This means that once the size of a group of bits is decided upon, there are only a finite

```
   110101        53              101101        45
  + 10010       +18            − 100110       −38
  ───────       ───            ────────       ───
  1000111        71               111          7
```

(a) Addition   (b) Subtraction

```
     10110      22                10001      17
   × 1011      ×11          110)1100110    6)102
   ───────     ───              110          6
     10110      22              ─────        ──
    10110       22              00110        42
   10110       ───               110         42
  ─────────    242             ─────        ──
  11110010                         0          0
```

(c) Multiplication   (d) Division

Figure 2-4   Examples of the four arithmetic operations using both binary and decimal arithmetic.

number of integers that can be represented by the group. If there are n bits in a group, the number of possible combinations of 0's and 1's is 2^n. If the bits are used to represent nonnegative integers, the integers 0 through $2^n - 1$ can be represented (e.g., 8 bits can represent the integers 0 through 255).

Quite often the groups are large and n may be 24, 32, 64, and so on. There are tables available that give these high powers of 2 exactly, but it is usually not necessary that they be known exactly. Normally, one needs only an estimate of the powers of 2 greater than 10, and such an estimate can be quickly obtained from Fig. 2-2 and the approximation

$$2^{10} = 1024 \approx 10^3$$

To see how this is done, suppose that an approximation of 2^{36} is desired. Then

$$2^{36} = 2^6 \times 2^{30} = 2^6 \times (2^{10})^3 \approx 2^6 \times (10^3)^3 = 64 \text{ billion}$$

One undesirable aspect of the finiteness of the groups of bits is that the result of an operation may not fit into the number of bits reserved for it. When this is the case, an *overflow* is said to occur. The magnitude of the result of an addition or subtraction (assuming negative integers, which are discussed in the next section, are possible) may require one more bit than either of the operands, and the product of two numbers may require twice as many bits as is reserved for the number being multiplied. Although the division of two integers never yields a quotient that needs more bits than is reserved for the dividend, it is usually desirable also to store the remainder. Therefore, to conserve space and minimize the circuitry, it is common to reserve a fewer number of bits for the quotient than would be needed to accommodate all possible cases. The end result is that all four arithmetic operations may cause overflows and the size of the bit groupings is an important consideration when designing a computer.

2-2 NEGATIVE INTEGERS AND 2'S COMPLEMENT

Until now only nonnegative integers have been considered. Normally, a negative number is written by writing its magnitude and then placing a minus sign to the left of the magnitude. However, a computer element can take on only one of two states and they are associated with 0 and 1, so a minus sign must be represented by a 0 or 1. Therefore, if a number is to be stored in n bits, the most obvious format is to place the magnitude in the $n - 1$ rightmost bits and let the left bit indicate the sign. When this is done it is conventional to represent + by 0 and − by 1 and the format is called the *sign-magnitude format*. Note that in the sign-magnitude format a distinction is made between $+0$ and -0. The range of integers that can be expressed in a group of 8 bits is from $-(2^7 - 1) = -127$ to $2^7 - 1 = 127$, with one bit being reserved to indicate the sign.

Although the sign-magnitude format is easy to understand, a different format permits a much simpler arithmetic/logic unit design. Once again the decimal system will be reverted to for introducing a fundamental concept. Suppose that the numbers -1000 to 999 are of interest and let x represent an arbitrary number in this range. The *four-digit 10's complement* of x is defined to be

$$10^4 - x$$

For example, if $x = 0572$, the 10's complement of x is

$$10000 - 572 = 9428$$

Now let the 10's complement of a number be used to represent its negative. Because the 10's complement of the 10's complement of x, that is, $10^4 - (10^4 - x)$ is x, this scheme for storing negative numbers clearly satisfies the fundamental property

$$-(-x) = x$$

Provided that only the four least significant digits of the result are saved, the scheme also accommodates the standard algorithm for addition.

As an example, consider the addition of 0557 and

$$-328 = 10^4 - 328 = 9672$$

The sum is

$$
\begin{array}{r}
0557 \\
+ \ 9672 \\
\hline
1 \quad 0229 \\
\end{array}
$$
$$\text{lost} \nearrow$$

but the 1 on the left is lost, leaving only 0229, which is the correct answer. Now suppose that 0557 is to be added to

$$-725 = 10^4 - 725 = 9275$$

The sum is

$$
\begin{array}{r}
0557 \\
+ \ 9275 \\
\hline
9832 \\
\end{array}
$$

The 9 in the most significant digit indicates that the sum is negative. If the magnitude is wanted, the 10's complement (the negative) of the sum must be taken:

$$10^4 - 9832 = 0168$$

Therefore, the sum is a negative number whose magnitude is 0168.

When using the 10's complement, the most significant digit must be reserved to indicate the sign, leaving only three digits for the magnitude. There is one exception: there is no ambiguity in letting 9000 represent the four-digit number -1000, but if the most significant digit being nonzero is to mean the sign is negative, then $+1000$ is not acceptable. Consequently, the range is from -1000 to 999.

As opposed to the sign-magnitude format, there is only one way to represent a 0. On the other hand, there is a negative number, -1000, whose absolute value cannot be represented.

Subtraction is performed by taking the negative, the 10's complement, and adding. Unfortunately, multiplication and division cannot be carried out directly. For these operations the magnitudes must be operated on and then the sign must be assigned or special algorithms are needed.

Now consider the binary number system and define the *n-bit 2's complement* of x to be $2^n - x$. All that has been said regarding four-digit 10's-complement arithmetic applies to n-bit 2's-complement arithmetic; however, in working with the 2's-complement format, there is an additional simplification that permits one to find the 2's complement of a number immediately. Let

$$2^n - x - 1$$

be defined as the *n-bit 1's complement* of x. Obviously, the 2's complement is the 1's complement plus 1. The following example with $n = 8$ shows that the 1's complement can be obtained by simply interchanging the 1's and 0's:

$$\begin{array}{r} 1\ 1\ 1\ 1\ 1\ 1\ 1\ 1 \\ -\ 1\ 0\ 1\ 0\ 1\ 1\ 0\ 1 \\ \hline 0\ 1\ 0\ 1\ 0\ 0\ 1\ 0 \end{array}$$

Therefore, the 2's complement can be found by interchanging the 1's and 0's and adding 1.

Subtraction can be performed by interchanging the 1's and 0's in the subtrahend, adding 1, and adding the result to the minuend. For example, if

$$01101010 - 01011011$$

is to be found, the procedure is

$$\begin{array}{r} 01011011 \longrightarrow 10100100 \\ +\ \underline{\qquad\qquad 1} \\ 10100101 \\ 01101010 \\ 1\ \ \overline{00001111} \end{array}$$

lost $\nearrow$

After discarding the ninth bit, the correct answer 00001111 is obtained.

Regardless of the format used to represent negative numbers, the concept of overflow is changed slightly; it is no longer a carry from the most significant bit. (Hereafter, most significant bit will be abbreviated MSB and least significant bit will be abbreviated LSB.) Recall that in 2's-complement arithmetic, a carry from the MSB is commonplace and is of no consequence. With regard to 2's-complement arithmetic, it can be shown that an addition overflow has occurred only when both operands are of the same sign and the result has the opposite sign, and a subtraction overflow has occurred only when the operands are of opposite signs and the difference has the same sign as the subtrahend.   (Overflows of these types are discussed further in Chapter 6.)

2-3 FIXED-POINT FORMATS

To be able to work only with integers would clearly be too restrictive, and a means of storing and manipulating numbers with fractional parts is needed.   There are two approaches to solving this problem, the fixed-point approach, which is considered here, and the floating-point approach, which is explained in the next section. If the data being operated on are such that the number of figures to the right of the decimal point is always the same, then the *fixed-point format* is usually adopted. The word *fixed* refers to the fact that the decimal point has the same position throughout the set of numbers being manipulated.   An example of this situation is in accounting, where there are always two places to the right of the decimal point.

From the computer's standpoint there is no difference between fixed-point arithmetic and integer arithmetic.   Because the computer can store only 1's and 0's, it has no means of storing a decimal point within a number.   It is up to the programmer to keep track of where the decimal point is and adjust the instructions accordingly.   Fixed-point arithmetic is really a matter of scaling.   The number being manipulated is not the true number, but the true number multiplied by a factor called the *scale factor*.   In the accounting example one would simply adjust the instructions to operate on cents instead of dollars, keeping in mind that there should be a decimal point two places from the right.   The scale factor in this example is 100.

As with any scaling problem, there is no difficulty in adding or subtracting— the sum or difference will have the same number of places to the right of the decimal point as the numbers being added or subtracted.   Multiplication, however, doubles the number of places to the right of the decimal point, and the programmer is faced with eliminating the extra digits or remembering that they are there and writing instructions to fit the situation.   If integer division is applied to two numbers with the same scale factor, the scale factor cancels and the quotient is unscaled. Therefore, if the original scaling is to be retained, the dividend should be multiplied by the scale factor before the division is performed.

Although the scale factor can be any number, the implication here has been that it is a power of 10.   Because of the binary nature of computers, it is often more convenient to use a power of 2.   To understand better the use of a decimal point and extend its usage to the binary number system, consider the origin of decimal fractions.   It is known that any positive real number can be written as accurately as desired using an expression of the form

$$a_n 10^n + \ldots + a_1 10 + a_0 + a_{-1} 10^{-1} + \ldots + a_{-m} 10^{-m}$$

where $a_n, \ldots, a_1, a_0, a_{-1}, \ldots, a_{-m}$ are decimal digits and m is large enough to satisfy the required accuracy. As in the discussion regarding integers, this expression is written in the abbreviated form obtained by writing the digits side by side. Because m is indeterminate, one modification is needed, however, to divide the string of digits into its integral and fractional parts. This is done by placing a period, the decimal point, between the a_0 and a_{-1} digits. For example

$$6 \times 10^2 + 3 \times 10 + 1 + 2 \times 10^{-1} + 5 \times 10^{-2}$$

is written 631.25.

The base, of course, does not have to be 10; it can be any integer. Using this notation

$$1 \times 2^2 + 0 \times 2 + 1 + 1 \times 2^{-1} + 1 \times 2^{-2}$$

is written 101.11. In this example, the digits to the right of the decimal point multiply negative powers of 2 ($\frac{1}{2}$, $\frac{1}{4}$, etc.) instead of negative powers of 10. As before, the decimal equivalent of a number can be found by adding those powers of 2 with coefficients of 1; for example

$$101.11 = 4 + 0 + 1 + 0.5 + 0.25 = 5.75$$

If a decimal number with a fraction is given, the binary equivalent of the integer portion can be found in the usual manner. The binary equivalent of the fraction can be found by assuming that the fraction is in the form

$$a_{-1}2^{-1} + \ldots + a_{-m}2^{-m}$$

and successively multiplying by 2. The first multiplication gives

$$a_{-1} + a_{-2}2^{-1} + \ldots + a_{-m}2^{-m+1}$$

Thus the integer part of the product is a_{-1}. A multiplication of

$$a_{-2}2^{-1} + \ldots + a_{-m}2^{-m+1}$$

by 2 produces a_{-2}, and so on. For example, the integer part of 3.6875 is 11 and the fractional part is found as follows:

$$
\begin{array}{cccc}
0.6875 & 0.375 & 0.75 & 0.5 \\
\times \quad 2 & \times \quad 2 & \times \quad 2 & \times \quad 2 \\
\hline
1.3750 & 0.750 & 1.5 & 1.0 \leftarrow \text{stop,} \\
& & & \text{fraction} \\
& & & \text{is zero}
\end{array}
$$

$$a_{-1} = 1 \qquad a_{-2} = 0 \qquad a_{-3} = 1 \qquad a_{-4} = 1$$

Therefore

$$3.6875_{10} = 11.1011_2$$

The algorithms for performing the arithmetic operations are the same regardless of the base. Just as in decimal arithmetic, the decimal point is moved by multiplying by the appropriate power of the base; for example

$$101.11 = 10111 \times 2^{-2} = 0.10111 \times 2^3$$

The reason it is convenient to assign a scale factor that is a power of 2 is that this fixes the decimal point within the binary number. If the scale factor is 2^3, the decimal point is always 3 bits to the left of the right side of the number. A change in the scale factor by a power of 2 merely moves the decimal point to right or left. A multiplication of the scale factor by 2^{-4} corresponds to moving the decimal point four places to the right.

2-4 FLOATING-POINT FORMATS

Scientists and engineers must frequently use both very large and very small numbers in a single calculation, and in order to avoid writing numerous trailing and leading 0's, they write the numbers in the form

$$\text{fraction} \times \text{base}^{\text{exponent}}$$

where the base is usually 10. For example,

leading zeros

$$0.\overbrace{00000}^{}351 = 0.351 \times 10^{-5}$$

trailing zeros

$$625\overbrace{000}^{} = 0.625 \times 10^6$$

(The fraction is sometimes called the *significand* and the exponent is sometimes called the *characteristic*.) When a number is written in this form, it is said to be written in *scientific notation*. Numbers written in scientific notation can easily be manipulated using the well-known laws of exponents. If two numbers are being added or subtracted, they must have the same exponent; if they are being multiplied, the exponents are added; and if they are being divided, the exponent of the divisor is subtracted from the exponent of the dividend.

A *floating-point format* is a format for storing numbers given in scientific notation inside the computer. To define a floating-point format, one must designate the following:

1. The base
2. The number of bits reserved for the exponent
3. The number of bits reserved for the fraction
4. The method for storing the sign and magnitude of the exponent

5. The method for storing the sign and magnitude of the fraction
6. The order in which the two signs and two magnitudes are to appear

The combinations of choices made with regard to these six items are extremely varied, and the combination chosen for a given computer depends, at least in part, on its hardware design. Some computers have built-in circuitry that is capable of performing the arithmetic operations on numbers in floating-point format directly. Most 8-bit microcomputers do not have such hardware, but most 32-bit microcomputers have floating-point circuitry. If a computer has floating-point circuitry, the floating-point format is fixed by the hardware designer. Otherwise, the floating-point operations must be accomplished step by step using the computer's integer instructions, and the floating-point format is determined by the programmer. Even in the latter case, however, the programmer would need to take the hardware characteristics of the computer into account.

A representative floating-point format is shown in Fig. 2-5. Although a base must be chosen, it never actually appears in the format, and once chosen, it is fixed. Bases are always powers of 2 and typical bases are 2, 8, and 16. Regardless of whether the sign-magnitude format or 2's-complement format is used to store the exponent and fraction, 1 bit will be needed for each sign; therefore, the total number of bits is $N + M + 2$, where N and M are the numbers of bits reserved for the magnitudes of the exponent and fraction, respectively.

There is no way in which all the numbers in the real system can be designated using a fixed format. Therefore, designers must do the best they can with the finite systems they have available. The two primary decisions they must make are with regard to

1. The resolution that the system must be able to accommodate
2. The largest and smallest nonzero magnitudes that the system must be capable of handling

The first of these decisions is related to the number of bits reserved for the magnitude of the fraction. The second is related to the size of the base and the largest and smallest possible values the exponent can attain, this value being determined by the number of bits reserved for the magnitude of the exponent.

If there are M bits for storing the magnitude of the fraction, there are 2^M combinations that can be used for designating the numbers between 0 and 1. The resolution, or spacing between consecutive points, in the fraction is therefore 2^{-M}. For $M = 23$, the resolution is

$$2^{-23} = (\tfrac{1}{8})(2^{-20}) \approx (\tfrac{1}{8})(10^{-3})^2 \approx 10^{-7}$$

If a number is specified to one-half part in 10^{-k}, it is said to be *accurate to k significant figures* (or the *precision is k significant figures*). If the fraction is rounded before it is truncated and $M = 23$, the magnitude of the part of the fraction that

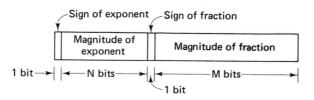

Figure 2-5 Typical floating-point format.

is deleted cannot exceed 2^{-24}, and the ratio of the error to the fraction cannot exceed

$$\frac{2^{-24}}{F} = \frac{\frac{1}{16}(10^{-3})^2}{F} \approx \frac{10^{-7}}{F}$$

where F is the magnitude of the fraction. Therefore, for F near 1, the accuracy is to approximately seven significant figures.

Usually, not all bit combinations are used to specify the fraction because the number of leading 0's is minimized by adjusting the exponent. Because the number F in the preceding paragraph needed to be near 1 in order to maintain the significant figures of accuracy, leading 0's have the desirable feature of decreasing accuracy. The process of minimizing the number of leading 0's is called *normalization*. Usually, the result of an operation is normalized before it is stored so that all numbers are stored in their normalized form.

If the base is 2, there will be no leading 0's and only those combinations in which the MSB is 1 can occur. A fraction such as 0.001×2^4 would be normalized to 0.1×2^2. If the base is $16 = 2^4$, the decimal point must be moved four places at a time and as many as three leading 0's can occur. For example, the reduction

$$0.000001 \times 16^3 = 0.01 \times 16^2$$

is possible, but a further decrease in the exponent would move the decimal point to the right of the 1, and this is not normally permissible. From these examples it is seen that as the base gets larger, the number of possible leading 0's increases, providing an argument for keeping the base small.

If a base of 2 is assumed, the largest number that can be stored using a floating-point format is approximately

$$2^{2^N - 1}$$

If $N = 7$, the largest number is approximately

$$2^{127} = 2^7(2^{10})^{12} \approx 128 \times 10^{36} \approx 10^{38}$$

This may seem like a very large number, but for some applications it may not be large enough. Whenever an operation results in a number that is so large that the maximum size of the exponent is exceeded, an *exponent overflow* is said to occur. There is a trade-off between the amount of space that is sacrificed to store the exponent and the largest number that can result without an exponent overflow. The size of the largest possible number can also be increased by increasing the base; for example

$$16^{127} = 2^{508} \approx 256 \times 10^{150}$$

but, as discussed above, this introduces leading 0's.

Another problem related to having a limited size for N is that of the size of the smallest nonzero magnitude that can be stored. Again assume that the base is 2 and that $N = 7$. After normalization the smallest fraction is $\frac{1}{2}$; therefore, the smallest number that can be stored is

$$\tfrac{1}{2} \times 2^{-2N} = \tfrac{1}{2} \times 2^{-128} = 2^{-129} \approx \left(\tfrac{1}{512}\right)(10^{-36}) \approx 10^{-38}$$

This is a small number, but smallness is relative. As with the maximum size discussed above, it may not be small enough for some applications. If during the course of an operation, the sign of the exponent is negative and the magnitude becomes too large, an *exponent underflow* is said to occur. The usual action taken to process an exponent underflow is simply to set the number to zero, but this is not always the case. (Note that this could cause a subsequent division to result in a "divide by 0" fault.)

It has been stated that the fraction and the exponent can be stored using either the sign-magnitude or the 2's-complement format; but there is a third format that is frequently employed for storing the exponent. This format is obtained by adding a number, called the *offset*, to the exponent before storing it. If $N + 1$ bits are reserved for the exponent (including sign), the offset chosen is usually 2^N and the format is called the *excess 2^N format*. For $N = 7$ the offset is $2^7 = 128 = 10000000_2$ and the format is called the excess 128 format. When using an excess format the exponent is obtained from the quantity simply by subtracting the offset. In excess 128 format, the stored number $01111110_2 = 126$ implies that the exponent is -2. It should be noted that in excess 2^N format a 1 in the MSB indicates a positive exponent and a 0 indicates a negative exponent. This is opposite from either the sign-magnitude or the 2's-complement notation.

To bring together the ideas presented above, the bit combination for storing the decimal number -13.6875 in the format shown in Fig. 2-6 will be considered. Upon converting the number to binary, the number -1101.1011_2 is obtained, and putting the binary form into scientific notation produces the result -0.11011011×2^4. The exponent in excess 128 format is

$$128 + 4 = 132 = 10000100_2$$

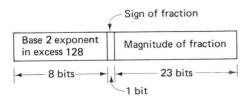

Figure 2-6 Typical 32-bit floating-point format.

and the desired bit combination is

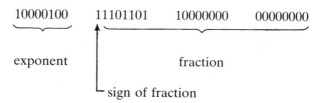

The bit combination in hexadecimal is 84ED8000.

As an example of reversing the foregoing process, suppose that the bit combination corresponding to the hexadecimal number 7E5C0000 represents a number in the floating-point format shown in Fig. 2-6 and that the decimal number is desired. Subtracting 80_{16} from $7E_{16}$ gives the exponent -2. Therefore, the number in binary is

$$0.10111 \times 2^{-2} = 0.0010111$$

The decimal equivalent of this binary number is

$$0.125 + 0.03125 + 0.015625 + 0.0078125 = 0.1796875$$

A trick that is often used takes advantage of the fact that if the base is 2, the bit to the immediate right of the decimal point is always 1. Because it is always 1, there is no information lost if it is not stored, and a 24-bit fraction can be stored in 23 bits. This does complicate the manipulation of the fraction slightly and the extra bit of precision may not be worth it if the floating-point arithmetic must be programmed. On the other hand, if hardware is designed to perform the floating-point arithmetic, the amount of extra circuitry required would be small and probably worth the improved performance.

The floating-point software developed by Intel for use on its 8085 uses this idea, but also places the decimal so that the number stored is always of the form

$$\pm 1.\text{fraction} \times 2^{\text{exponent}}$$

and then does not store the 1. The complete format is shown in Fig. 2-7. Note that the offset in the exponent is 127 instead of 128, but the range is still approximately 10^{-38} to 10^{38}. For example, the integer 1.25 would be stored as follows:

$$\text{Sign} = 0 \qquad \text{Exponent} = 01111111 \qquad \text{Fraction} = 010 \ldots 000$$

$$001111111010 \ldots 000 = 3FA00000$$

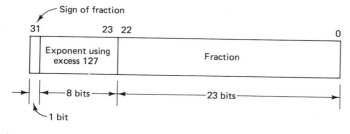

Figure 2-7 Intel's floating-point format for an 8085.

The arithmetic operations on numbers in floating-point format are carried out in steps. If the operands are not in their normalized form, they should first be put into that form; this is called the *prenormalization step*. (Prenormalization is not necessary if numbers are always stored in their normalized form.) Because two numbers in floating-point format must have the same exponent before they are added or subtracted, the decimal point associated with the fraction having the smaller exponent must be shifted to the left until the exponents are equal. This is called the *alignment step* and is combined with the prenormalization step (if prenormalization is necessary). Finally, any of the arithmetic operations may produce an unnormalized result and the usual procedure is always to normalize the result; this is called the *postnormalization step* (or, simply, the *normalization step*). Although alignment is not required during the multiplication and division operations, if an excess format is used, one must perform the addition or subtraction of the exponents in such a way that the offset is included exactly once in the exponent of the result.

Assume the format given in Fig. 2-6 and consider the following addition and multiplication examples (hexadecimal is used to reduce the notation):

Example 1:
$$
\begin{array}{ll}
\ 826013\text{AC} & \text{Alignment} \qquad\ 826013\text{AC} \\
+\ \underline{8040\text{AB}04} & \longrightarrow \qquad +\ \underline{82102\text{AC}1} \\
& 82703\text{E}6\text{D}
\end{array}
$$

No normalization required

Example 2:
$$
\begin{array}{ll}
\ 83600000 \\
+\ \underline{83\text{C}00000} & \text{No alignment necessary} \\
\ 83200000 \\
\ \ \downarrow & \text{Normalization} \\
\ 82400000
\end{array}
$$

Example 3:
$$
\begin{array}{llll}
\ 82600000 & & \text{Exponent} & \ 82 \\
\times\ \underline{85\text{D}00000} & & \text{calculation} & +\ \underline{85} \\
\ 87\text{BC}0000 & & & \ 107 \\
& & & -\ \underline{80} \\
\ \ \ \downarrow \qquad \text{Normalization} & & & \ 87 \\
86\text{F}80000
\end{array}
$$

On an 8085, example 2 is equivalent to
$$
\begin{array}{l}
\ 40\text{C}00000 \\
+\ \underline{\text{C}0800000} \\
\ 40\text{C}00000 \\
\ \ \ \downarrow \qquad \text{Normalization} \\
40000000
\end{array}
$$

2-5 BCD FORMATS

The third format for storing numbers is obtained by placing the 4-bit binary equivalents of the decimal digits side by side.   A format of this type is called a *binary-
coded-decimal (BCD) format* (or a *decimal format*).   Negative numbers can be
stored in either 10's-complement or sign-magnitude format.   Because only ten of
the sixteen 4-bit combinations are needed to represent the decimal digits, any two
of the remaining combinations can be used to represent the plus and minus signs.
The 4-bit combination representing the sign can appear either to the left or to the
right of the combinations representing the digits.   The sign is most often placed
after the digits, the reason being that the arithmetic operations are executed beginning with the low-order digit, and the sign must be known before execution
begins.

Figure 2-8 shows a typical BCD format.   Using this format, the number
$-34,159$ would be stored as

$$0011 \quad 0100 \quad 0001 \quad 0101 \quad 1001 \quad 1101$$

Although one of the remaining bit combinations could represent a decimal point,
the usual procedure is to assume the fixed-point approach.   This means that the
decimal point is implicit and it is up to the programmer to keep track of it.

Some large computers have built-in BCD hardware to perform BCD arithmetic directly, but microcomputers do not usually have such hardware, and BCD
arithmetic must be programmed.   Most microcomputers do, however, have a special instruction that supplements the integer addition instruction so that the two
instructions together will perform a BCD addition.   For the 8085, this instruction
is explained in detail in Chapter 6.   Some have a similar instruction to aid BCD
subtraction.

Nothing can be done in a BCD format that could not be done in the integer
format, and vice versa; and one might wonder why they are both considered.   The
reason BCD formats are considered is that most input and output are done in an
alphanumeric code and most alphanumeric codes contain the binary equivalents
of the decimal digits as the low-order 4 bits.   Therefore, an alphanumeric string
can easily be converted to a BCD string.   On the other hand, because the computer
is a binary device, it is more difficult to design the circuitry needed to perform
BCD arithmetic.   Also, the integer format makes much more efficient use of the
storage space.   Only the numbers -999 to 999 could be stored in 16 bits if a sign-
magnitude BCD format is used, but the numbers $-32,768$ to 32,767 could be stored

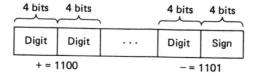

Figure 2-8   Typical decimal format.

in the same space in the integer format. Therefore, applications that involve a lot of input and output tend to stay with the BCD format, but those that involve a lot of computations convert the incoming code to binary, perform the calculations, and reconvert the results for outputting. This is discussed further in Chapter 8.

2-6 *ALPHANUMERIC CODES*

An *alphanumeric code* is an assignment of bit combinations to the letters of the alphabet, the decimal digits 0 through 9, punctuation marks, and several special characters, such as $ and #. There are a variety of alphanumeric codes, but only two are prominent. They are the *Extended Binary-Coded-Decimal Interchange Code (EBCDIC)* used by IBM and the *American Standard Code for Information Interchange (ASCII)* used by most other manufacturers. The ASCII code will be assumed in this book; it is given in Fig. 2-9.

The number of bits in a code is called its *length*. If the length is L bits, then 2^L is the maximum number of characters that can be represented by the code. The ASCII code has a length of seven and therefore can represent 128 characters. As seen from Fig. 2-9, it includes not only printing characters such as the upper- and lowercase letters, the decimal digits, and several punctuation marks and special symbols, but also a variety of nonprinting characters, including space, carriage return (CR), line feed (LF), and form feed (FF) for formatting and others that are associated with the control keys found on a standard terminal. The control keys provide the user with a means of giving special commands to the computer, such as "terminate the current program," "log me off," "delete the previous character," "end of transmission" (EOT), "end of file" (EOF—for formatting files, and so on. So that a string of decimal digits in ASCII can easily be converted to a string of digits in BCD format, the low-order 4 bits of the digits are the binary equivalents of the decimal digits.

The bit combination that consists of all 0's is called the *null character* and causes no action and gives no command; it simply takes up the space of a character in a character string. Because characters are transmitted one at a time, the null character is normally used as a means of inserting a time delay. For example, to guarantee that a mechanical terminal has time to execute its return after a CR character has been received, a string of several null characters can be inserted following the CR character. In particular, note that neither the space character nor the decimal digit 0 corresponds to the bit combination consisting of all 0's.

Upon examination of the ASCII code, it is seen that the lower a letter is in the alphabet, the lower is its numeric value. Therefore, not only does A have a lower numeric value than B, but the string ABE has a lower numeric value than ANN when each string is considered as a single positive binary number. This means that ordinary subtraction can determine which of two character strings is first in the alphabetical order.

ASCII Char.	Hex. Code	Control Character	ASCII Char.	Hex. Code	Control Character	ASCII Char.	Hex. Code	Control Character
NUL	00	Null	+	2B		V	56	
SOH	01	Start heading	,	2C		W	57	
STX	02	Start text	–	2D		X	58	
ETX	03	End text	.	2E		Y	59	
EOT	04	End transmission	/	2F		Z	5A	
ENQ	05	Inquiry	0	30		[	5B	
ACK	06	Acknowledgment	1	31		\	5C	
BEL	07	Bell	2	32		]	5D	
BS	08	Backspace	3	33		^	5E	
HT	09	Horizontal tab	4	34		_	5F	
LF	0A	Line feed	5	35		`	60	
VT	0B	Vertical tab	6	36		a	61	
FF	0C	Form feed	7	37		b	62	
CR	0D	Carriage return	8	38		c	63	
SO	0E	Shift out	9	39		d	64	
SI	0F	Shift in	:	3A		e	65	
DLE	10	Data link escape	;	3B		f	66	
DC1	11	Device control 1	<	3C		g	67	
DC2	12	Device control 2	=	3D		h	68	
DC3	13	Device control 3	>	3E		i	69	
DC4	14	Device control 4	?	3F		j	6A	
NAK	15	Neg. acknowledge	@	40		k	6B	
SYN	16	Synchronous/Idle	A	41		l	6C	
ETB	17	End trans. block	B	42		m	6D	
CAN	18	Cancel data	C	43		n	6E	
EM	19	End of medium	D	44		o	6F	
SUB	1A	Start special seq.	E	45		p	70	
ESC	1B	Escape	F	46		q	71	
FS	1C	File separator	G	47		r	72	
GS	1D	Group separator	H	48		s	73	
RS	1E	Record separator	I	49		t	74	
US	1F	Unit separator	J	4A		u	75	
SP	20	Space	K	4B		v	76	
!	21		L	4C		w	77	
"	22		M	4D		x	78	
#	23		N	4E		y	79	
$	24		O	4F		z	7A	
%	25		P	50		{	7B	
&	26		Q	51				7C	
'	27		R	52		}	7D	
(	28		S	53		~	7E	
)	29		T	54		DEL	7F	Delete–rubout
*	2A		U	55				

Figure 2-9   ASCII code.

BIBLIOGRAPHY

1. BORDEN, WILLIAM, JR., *How to Buy and Use Minicomputers and Microcomputers* (Indianapolis, Ind.: Howard W. Sams & Co., 1976).
2. STRUBLE, GEORGE, *Assembler Language Programming: The IBM System 360/370*, 2nd ed. (Reading, Mass.: Addison-Wesley, 1975).

EXERCISES

1. Find the binary, octal, and hexadecimal equivalents of the following decimal numbers:
   (a) 10   (b) 72
   (c) 156   (d) 651
   (e) 1257   (f) 53,626
2. Find the decimal equivalents of the following numbers:
   (a) 1011_2 (b) 11011010_2
   (c) 735_8 (d) 3251_8
   (e) $A5_{16}$ (f) $7A3F_{16}$
3. Let $A = 1011_2$, $B = 101_2$, $C = 1111101_2$, and $D = 11001_2$ and perform the following calculations in binary arithmetic:
   (a) $C + D$ (b) $D - A$
   (c) AB (d) C/D
   (e) $(C + D)/B$ (f) C/A
   (g) CD (h) $AB + C$
4. Let $A = BA41_{16}$, $B = A429_{16}$, and $C = 14AF_{16}$ and perform the following calculations in hexadecimal:
   (a) $A + B$ (b) $A - B$
   (c) $A + C$ (d) $A - C$
   (e) $B + C$ (f) $A + B - C$
5. Find the 8-bit 2's complement of $A = 01001011_2$, $B = 11011010_2$, and $C = 00101101_2$. Carry out the following operations using the 2's-complement format. Perform the subtractions by adding the negatives of the subtrahends. Note the overflows.
   (a) $A + B$ (b) $A - B$
   (c) $A - C$ (d) $C - A$
   (e) $B - C$ (f) $B + C - A$
6. Find the binary equivalent of the following decimal numbers to eight decimal places:
   (a) 3.625   (b) 0.1
   (c) 525.03125   (d) 1.05
7. What is the approximate range of signed integers that can be stored in 64 bits?
8. Assume the format shown in Fig. 2-6 and find the bit combinations corresponding to the following decimal numbers (write your answers in hexadecimal):
   (a) 2.5   (b) -3.0625
   (c) 25.7265625   (d) 0.0078125
   (e) -151.0625 (f) 0.1
   Repeat this exercise assuming the 8085 format shown in Fig. 2-7.
9. Repeat Exercise 8 assuming that the base is 16 instead of 2.

10. Assume that the following hexadecimal numbers represent floating-point numbers stored in the format shown in Fig. 2-6 and find their decimal equivalents:

(a) 82480000   (b) 7FC80000

(c) 82600000   (d) 85F00000

(e) 77FE0000   (f) 805A136B

(g) Add the numbers in part (a) and (d). (First align the operands by making their exponents equal.)

(h) Subtract the number in part (a) from the number in part (c) and normalize the result.

(i) Multiply the numbers in parts (a) and (c) and normalize the result. (Add the exponents but include the offset only once; then multiply the fractions and normalize.)

Repeat this exercise assuming the 8085 format shown in Fig. 2-7.

11. Determine the approximate smallest (normalized) nonzero magnitude, largest magnitude, and resolution (in significant figures) associated with the following format:

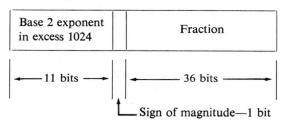

12. Repeat Exercise 11 assuming base 16 for the exponent instead of base 2, and assume the worst case with regard to leading 0's when computing the resolution in significant figures.

13. Assume the BCD format shown in Fig. 2-8 and find the bit combinations corresponding to the following numbers:

(a) 325   (b) −3

(c) −7,265,172   (d) 59,721

14. Find the binary equivalents of the numbers given in Exercise 13 and compare the numbers of bits needed to store these numbers in the BCD and integer formats, respectively.

15. Extend the ASCII code to 8 bits by adding a 0 to the left of each character and find the bit combinations needed to store the character strings given below. Give your answers in hexadecimal notation. (*Caution:* Do not overlook the spaces, periods, carriage returns, line feeds, etc.)

(a) JOE JONES   (b) DOE, JOHN

(c) −3.157   (d) DUN (SIC)

(e) ANN LAT
    315 JET ST.

16. Compare the bit combinations corresponding to the following four-character ASCII character strings (fill out with *trailing* spaces where necessary) and put them in ascending order using binary arithmetic:

ANN   BOY   BOAT   CAN   BB

Chapter 3

Combinational Logic

As mentioned previously, for reasons of reliability and modularity, digital computers are based on electronic components whose inputs and outputs are, at any point in time, in one of two possible states. These two states could be two voltage levels, two current levels, or forward and reverse magnetic field directions. Except for data storage and transmission, the two states are almost always voltage levels, and this is the type of circuitry that will be considered in the present chapter. Just what the voltage levels are is not important; they differ from computer to computer, and may differ from one section to the next within a single computer. However, if two sections use different pairs of voltage levels, care must be taken to interface the two sections properly. Within each section one voltage level can arbitrarily be denoted by 1 and the other by 0. If the higher voltage is associated with 1, the circuitry is said to be based on *positive logic*; if the lower voltage is associated with 1, it is said to be based on *negative logic.*

A variable that can take on two states (i.e., a 0 or 1) is called a *logical variable.* An electronic circuit such as the one in Fig. 3-1, whose inputs and outputs can be described by logical variables, is called a *logical network.* There are two principal

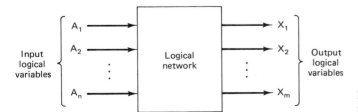

Figure 3-1 Definition of a logical network.

categories of logical networks: combinational networks and sequential networks. The difference between them is that for *combinational networks* the outputs depend only on the current inputs, but for a *sequential network* the outputs may depend on the current state of the network as well as the inputs. Also, timing is a much more important consideration in sequential networks than in their combinational counterparts; thus combinational networks tend to be significantly simpler to design. For this reason, we will examine combinational networks in this chapter and defer discussion of sequential networks until Chapter 4.

This chapter introduces the most fundamental logical networks, logic gates, and then discusses that area of mathematics used to model two-state systems, Boolean algebra. The remaining sections study the logical network design process and design tools and include several important combinational networks and design approaches.

3-1 LOGIC GATES

A *logic gate* is a combinational network with only one output. Because logic gates have only one output, and each input and the output can assume only one of two states, there is a natural relationship between the study of logic gates and the study of elementary two-value logic. Two-value logic is a discipline that concerns statements, called tf-statements, that are either true or false and do not allow for judgment. For example, either x is equal to y or x is not equal to y. On the other hand, the statement

x is nearly equal to y

is not a tf-statement, since it depends on judgment. If a tf-statement is true, it is said to have a truth value "true"; if it is false, its truth value is "false." Tf-statements are used as conditions in control transfer statements (e.g., IF statements) in computer programming.

A tf-statement can be made to take on the opposite truth value (i.e., is negated) by prefacing it with the phrase "it is not true that. . . ." For example

It is not true that x is proportional to y

is true if

x is proportional to y

is false, and is false if the latter statement is true.

Simple tf-statements can be combined to form complex tf-statements called composites by using words called *connectives*. When this is done, each connective must have associated with it a set of rules, called a *truth table,* that specifies the truth value of the composite for all possible combinations of truth values for the statements making up the composite. The two most common connectives are "and" and "or." The truth tables for negation and the connectives "and" and

A	Not A
F	T
T	F

(a) Negation

A	B	A and B
F	F	F
F	T	F
T	F	F
T	T	T

(b) The "and" connective

A	B	A or B
F	F	F
F	T	T
T	F	T
T	T	T

(c) The "or" connective

Figure 3-2 The truth tables that define logical negation and the "and" and "or" connectives.

"or" are shown in Fig. 3-2. In these truth tables, T represents true, F represents false, and A and B represent arbitrary tf-statements. It is seen that a composite formed using the connective "and" is true only if both parts are true, and one formed using connective "or" is false only if both parts are false. The statement

$$x > 0 \quad \text{and} \quad y < x$$

is true only if

$$x > 0$$

and

$$y < x$$

are both true. On the other hand

$$x > 0 \quad \text{or} \quad y < x$$

is false only if

$$x > 0$$

and

$$y < x$$

are both false.

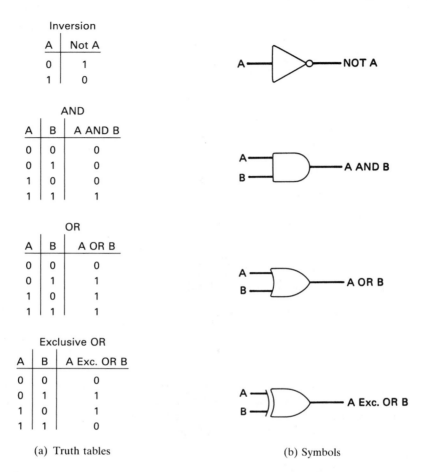

(a) Truth tables   (b) Symbols

Figure 3-3 Truth tables and symbols for the inverter, AND, OR, and exclusive OR gates.

By associating

1. The 0 state with false
2. The 1 state with true
3. Logic gates with connectives

a direct analogy can be drawn between logic gates and composite tf-statements in which the states of the inputs correspond to the truth values of the simple tf-statements, and the state of the output corresponds to the truth value of the composite. The most common logic gates are the *inverter* (or *NOT*), the *AND*,

and the *OR*, which are analogous to the logical operations negation, "and," and "or," respectively.   The defining rules for logic gates are also tabulated using truth tables, although 0's and 1's are normally used in place of the F's and T's.   Another popular logic gate is the "*exclusive OR*," which has an output of 0 if both inputs are the same and an output of 1 if they are different.   The truth tables for the inverter, AND, OR, and exclusive OR gates are shown in Fig. 3-3a and the symbols used to represent them are shown in Fig. 3-3b.   The letters A and B represent arbitrary logical input variables.

It is seen from Fig. 3-3 that the inverter has one input and the other three gates have two inputs.   Although the inverter and exclusive OR gates can have only the numbers of inputs shown, the AND and OR gates can easily be generalized to any number of inputs.   For the generalized AND, the output is 1 only if all the inputs are 1, and for the generalized OR the output is 0 only if all the inputs are 0.

By following an AND gate with an inverter, one can obtain another commonly used gate called a *NAND* gate (an abbreviation for not AND).   Similarly, a *NOR* gate is obtained by following an OR gate with an inverter.   The truth tables and symbols for NAND and NOR gates are shown in Fig. 3-4.   Note that the symbols for NAND and NOR are the same as those for AND and OR except there is a small circle at the output.   It is generally true in logic gate symbology that if an inverter is combined with another logic gate, the presence of the inverter is indicated simply by placing a small circle at the affected input or output.

Just as AND's and OR's can be extended to more than two inputs, so can

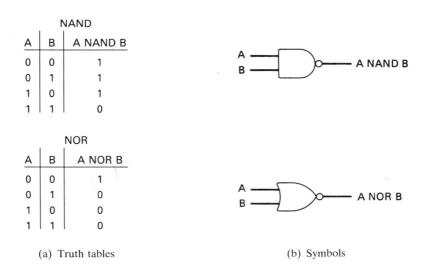

(a) Truth tables   (b) Symbols

Figure 3-4   Truth tables and symbols for the NAND and NOR gates.

NAND's and NOR's.   In general, a NAND gate has a 0 output only if all its inputs are 1, and a NOR gate has a 1 output only if all its inputs are 0.

Clearly, complex logic gates can be built by combining several of the elementary logic gates discussed above.   Suppose a logic gate is needed that has four inputs, which are denoted A, B, C, and D, and is such that the output is 1 only if both A and B are 1 and either C or D is 1.   Figure 3-5a shows a logic gate made from two AND gates and one OR gate that meets these requirements.   Figure 3-5b gives the truth table for the composite gate shown in Fig. 3-5a.

When constructing logic networks from the elementary gates indicated above, it is apparent that several configurations of the elementary gates may have the same input/output characteristics; that is, each combination of input states produces

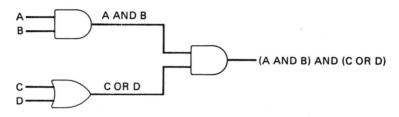

(a) Logic diagram

A	B	C	D	A AND B	C OR D	(A AND B) AND (C OR D)
0	0	0	0	0	0	0
0	0	0	1	0	1	0
0	0	1	0	0	1	0
0	0	1	1	0	1	0
0	1	0	0	0	0	0
0	1	0	1	0	1	0
0	1	1	0	0	1	0
0	1	1	1	0	1	0
1	0	0	0	0	0	0
1	0	0	1	0	1	0
1	0	1	0	0	1	0
1	0	1	1	0	1	0
1	1	0	0	1	0	0
1	1	0	1	1	1	1
1	1	1	0	1	1	1
1	1	1	1	1	1	1

(b) Truth table

Figure 3-5 Logic gate consisting of more than one elementary gate.

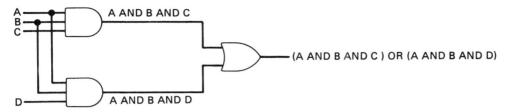

(a) Logic diagram

A	B	C	D	A AND B AND C	A AND B AND D	(A AND B AND C) OR (A AND B AND D)
0	0	0	0	0	0	0
0	0	0	1	0	0	0
0	0	1	0	0	0	0
0	0	1	1	0	0	0
0	1	0	0	0	0	0
0	1	0	1	0	0	0
0	1	1	0	0	0	0
0	1	1	1	0	0	0
1	0	0	0	0	0	0
1	0	0	1	0	0	0
1	0	1	0	0	0	0
1	0	1	1	0	0	0
1	1	0	0	0	0	0
1	1	0	1	0	1	1
1	1	1	0	1	0	1
1	1	1	1	1	1	1

(b) Truth table

Figure 3-6   Logic network that is equivalent to the one in Fig. 3-5.

the same output states.   The logic gate diagrammed in Fig. 3-6a has the same input/output characteristics as the gate shown in Fig. 3-5a.   Two logic networks that have the same input/output characteristics are said to be *equivalent*.   The most straightforward way of showing that two networks are equivalent is to compare their truth tables.   Figure 3-6b gives the truth table corresponding to the configuration shown in Fig. 3-6a.   By writing the input combinations in the same order as they appear in Fig. 3-5a, equivalence can be established by observing that the output columns in the two truth tables are identical.   Another method for proving equivalence is to use Boolean algebra, the topic of Section 3-3.

One simple but important equivalence is that an inverter cascaded with an inverter is equivalent to no gate at all.   This is shown by noting that the first and last columns in the following truth table are the same:

A	NOT A	NOT (NOT A)
0	1	0
1	0	1

In general, an odd number of cascaded inverters is equivalent to a single inverter, and an even number is equivalent to no gate.

Once it is recognized that several logic networks are equivalent with respect to the circuitry connected to them, the immediate question is: Which network requires the smallest number of elementary gates or is the most economical in some other sense? The answer to this question has been the object of considerable

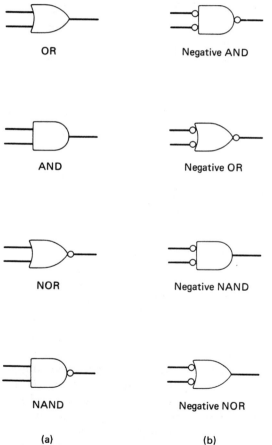

OR	Negative AND
AND	Negative OR
NOR	Negative NAND
NAND	Negative NOR
(a)	(b)
(a) Positive logic	(b) Negative logic

Figure 3-7 Summary of the elementary positive and negative logic gates. (The positive logic gates in the left column are equivalent to the corresponding negative gates in the right column.)

research that is generally classified as *logic minimization*. Logical minimization will enter into the design discussions given later, and a description of an important minimization tool is included in Section 3-6.

In the foregoing discussion an inverter was cascaded to the outputs of the AND and OR gates to form the NAND and NOR gates. One might naturally be interested in the gates formed by cascading inverters with the inputs to the elementary gates. If inverters are placed at the inputs to a NAND gate, the following truth table results:

A	B	NOT A	NOT B	(NOT A) NAND (NOT B)
0	0	1	1	0
0	1	1	0	1
1	0	0	1	1
1	1	0	0	1

Note that the two leftmost columns and the rightmost column are identical to those given in the truth table for the OR gate. Therefore, an equivalent for the OR gate has been found. Similarly, the NOR, AND, and OR gates with inverters at their inputs are equivalent to the AND, NOR, and NAND gates, respectively (the proofs are requested in Exercise 1). These equivalents are shown side by side in Fig. 3-7.

It sometimes happens that when studying some areas of a computer's circuitry, it is useful to assign the state 1 to the lower voltage and 0 to the higher voltage. In other words, these areas are to be treated in terms of negative logic. Note that if the 0's and 1's are interchanged in the truth table for an AND gate whose inputs and output have all been inverted, the resulting truth table is that of an AND gate without the inversions. Therefore, the gate shown in the upper right-hand corner of Fig. 3-7 is called a *negative AND gate*. The other elementary negative logic gates are also shown in the right-hand column of this figure.

3-2 MULTIPLEXERS

As an example, let us consider a simple but important logic network, called a *multiplexer* (or *data selector*), which is capable of selecting a single set of data inputs from a number of sets of inputs. A simple multiplexer that has a single output is such that its inputs are divided into two groups. One group of inputs, the *control group*, serves to select which of the inputs in the other group, called the *data group*, is passed through to the output. The simplest type of multiplexer is shown in Fig. 3-8a. This multiplexer has one control input and two data inputs. As seen from its truth table, the output is equal to data input A if the control input $P = 0$, and is equal to data input B if $P = 1$. Because this multiplexer reduces two data inputs to a single output, it is referred to as a 2-to-1 multiplexer.

| Control | Data | | Output |
P	A	B	X
0	0	0	0
0	0	1	0
0	1	0	1
0	1	1	1
1	0	0	0
1	0	1	1
1	1	0	0
1	1	1	1

Figure 3-8 A 2-to-1 multiplexer.

This example also illustrates the gatelike property of logic gates. For a two-input AND gate, one of the inputs can be viewed as if it opens and closes the gate for the other input. If P and B are applied to an AND gate and $P = 0$, then the gate is closed and the output is 0 regardless of the state of the B input. If $P = 1$, then the gate is open and the output is equal to the input. An OR gate is different in that when $P = 1$ the gate is closed and the output is always 1 regardless of the input. But when $P = 0$, the output is the same as the B input. For the 2-to-1 multiplexer shown in Fig. 3-8, NOT P opens and closes the AND gate for the A input and P opens and closes it for the B input. Therefore, exactly one gate is open at a time. In this example, the OR gate simply combines the outputs of the two AND gates so that exactly one of the inputs is reflected in the output.

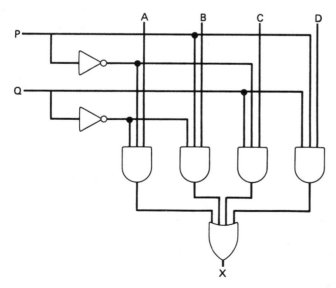

Figure 3-9 A 4-to-1 multiplexer.

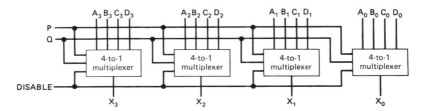

Figure 3-10 A quad 4-to-1 multiplexer.

A logical network that would cause exactly one set of inputs, say, $A_1, \ldots,$ A_n or $B_1, \ldots, B_n$, to be passed through to the outputs could be obtained by placing several 2-to-1 multiplexers side by side and controlling them with a single P input (see Exercise 2).

Figure 3-9 shows a 4-to-1 multiplexer that selects exactly one of four inputs. Because four distinct control possibilities are needed to choose one out of four, two inputs (which can produce one of the possible controls 00, 01, 10, or 11) are required.   Clearly, for an n-to-1 multiplexer, the inequality

$$2^k \geqq n$$

where k is the number of control lines, must be satisfied.

Figure 3-10 shows a quad 4-to-1 (four inputs per set and four sets) multiplexer that is constructed by placing four 4-to-1 multiplexers in parallel.   This multiplexer includes a common variation that allows the multiplexer to be turned off (disabled). When the disable line is 1, the multiplexer outputs are 0 regardless of the inputs. (In Exercise 11, the reader is asked to incorporate the disable feature into the detailed logical design of a multiplexer.)

3-3 BOOLEAN ALGEBRA

As more and more logic gates are added, highly complex logic networks can be constructed: networks that have multiple outputs and are capable of performing binary addition, subtraction, multiplication, and division, as well as other complicated bit manipulations.   If a design requires only a few logic gates, such as the multiplexers discussed above, intuition is all that is needed to effect a design. However, as the requirements become more complicated, intuition becomes hopelessly inadequate and mathematics is needed to maintain order in the reasoning process.   The area of mathematics that is used to model logical networks is called Boolean algebra.

Boolean algebra is a mathematical structure that consists of the set containing only 0 and 1, the unary operation *complementation* (or *negation*), and the binary operations *addition* and *multiplication*.   The tables defining complementation, multiplication, and addition are given in Fig. 3-11.   Complementation is indicated by placing a bar over the quantity being complemented.   Addition and multiplication

A	$\overline{A}$
0	1
1	0

(a) Complementation (or negation)

A	B	AB
0	0	0
0	1	0
1	0	0
1	1	1

(b) Multiplication

A	B	A + B
0	0	0
0	1	1
1	0	1
1	1	1

(c) Addition

A	B	A $\oplus$ B
0	0	0
0	1	1
1	0	1
1	1	0

(d) Exclusive OR

Figure 3-11 Defining tables for the Boolean algebra operations.

are denoted in the usual manner. (Subtraction and division are not defined in Boolean algebra.) Another operation that is not included in the basic Boolean algebra structure but has proved to be quite useful is the one that corresponds to the exclusive OR gate. The symbol used to represent this operation is $\oplus$ and its defining table is given in Fig. 3-11d.

The similarity between the tables in Fig. 3-11 and those defining the inverter, AND, OR, and exclusive OR gates is obvious. In fact, it is generally true that the logical truth tables in the previous sections and the tables used in detailing Boolean operations have the same appearance. For this reason, both types of tables are called truth tables.

From the definitions it is seen that the Boolean expressions $\overline{A}$, AB, and $A + B$ model the inverter, AND, and OR gates. The following tables show that $\overline{AB}$ and $\overline{A + B}$, respectively, model the NAND and NOR gates.

A	B	AB	$\overline{AB}$
0	0	0	1
0	1	0	1
1	0	0	1
1	1	1	0

A	B	A + B	$\overline{A + B}$
0	0	0	1
0	1	1	0
1	0	1	0
1	1	1	0

From these simple models of the elementary gates it is easy to find Boolean models (or expressions) of more complex logic networks. The Boolean expression describing the gate in Fig. 3-5a is $AB(C + D)$. (The reader should verify that this expression has the same truth table as the one given in Fig. 3-5b.) Figure 3-12 shows a still more complicated logic network with more than one output. Note

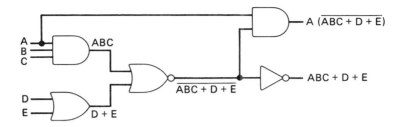

Figure 3-12 Logic network with more than one output and the Boolean expressions needed to describe it.

that there is a Boolean expression for describing each of the outputs in terms of the inputs.

Just as in other areas of mathematics, it is useful to establish the validity of certain basic propositions and then use these propositions as stepping stones when proving more complex relationships.   What needs to be shown in Boolean algebra is equivalence between some of the fundamental expressions.   The primary means of establishing these equivalences is, of course, the truth table.   Once an equivalence has been proven, however, it can be used to show other equivalences.

As an example, suppose that

$$A(B + C) = AB + AC$$

is to be verified.   This is done by constructing the following truth table and noting that the fifth and eighth columns are identical:

A	B	C	B + C	A(B + C)	AB	AC	AB + AC
0	0	0	0	0	0	0	0
0	0	1	1	0	0	0	0
0	1	0	1	0	0	0	0
0	1	1	1	0	0	0	0
1	0	0	0	0	0	0	0
1	0	1	1	1	0	1	1
1	1	0	1	1	1	0	1
1	1	1	1	1	1	1	1

Also, it is clear from the symmetry of the defining truth table for multiplication that

$$AB = BA$$

By applying these two equivalences as follows

$$(B + C)A = A(B + C) = AB + AC = BA + CA$$

the equivalence

$$(B + C)A = BA + CA$$

is proved without resorting to a truth table. These and several other equivalences are given in Fig. 3-13. Their proofs are left to the reader. (See Exercise 4.)

As a word of caution, equivalence in Boolean algebra is not the same as equality in the algebra of real numbers. This is because subtraction and division are not defined. In the algebra of real numbers, quite often a quantity is eliminated from both sides of an equation by subtracting it from both sides or by dividing it

$$A = \overline{\overline{A}}$$

$$AA = A$$

$$A + A = A$$

$$A \cdot 0 = 0$$

$$A + 0 = A$$

$$A \cdot 1 = A$$

$$A + 1 = 1$$

$$A \cdot \overline{A} = 0$$

$$A + \overline{A} = 1$$

$AB = BA$	Commutative law for multiplication
$A + B = B + A$	Commutative law for addition
$(AB)C = A(BC)$	Associative law for multiplication
$A + (B + C) = (A + B) + C$	Associative law for addition
$A(B + C) = AB + AC$	Left distributive law
$(B + C)A = BA + CA$	Right distributive law
$\overline{A + B} = \overline{A}\,\overline{B}$	De Morgan's laws.
$\overline{AB} = \overline{A} + \overline{B}$	

$$AB + A\overline{B} = A$$

$$A + AB = A$$

$$(A + \overline{B})B = AB$$

$$(A + B)(A + \overline{B}) = A$$

$$(A + B)(A + C) = A + BC$$

$$A(A + B) = A$$

$$A\overline{B} + B = A + B$$

$$\overline{A}B + A\overline{B} = A \oplus B$$

$$\overline{AB}(A + B) = A \oplus B$$

Figure 3-13 Some of the equivalences most frequently used in reducing Boolean expressions.

into both sides. To demonstrate that this cannot be done in Boolean algebra, consider the equivalence

$$C = C + C$$

This does not imply that the logical variable C must always be zero (i.e., $C = 0$).

3-4 A PARALLEL BINARY ADDER/SUBTRACTER

A very good example of the application of logical design is the logic gate implementation of a binary adder/subtracter network. The truth table needed for designing a 1-bit adder is given in Fig. 3-14a. One-bit adders are called *half adders*. In this table A_0 and B_0 are the bits being added. S_0 is the LSB of the sum, and C_1 is the MSB of the sum. The expression for C_1 and S_0 are

$$C_1 = A_0 B_0$$

$$S_1 = \overline{A}_0 B_0 + A_0 \overline{B}_0 = \overline{A_0 B_0} \, (A_0 + B_0)$$

A network that corresponds to these expressions is shown in Fig. 3-14b.

A_0	B_0	C_1	S_0
0	0	0	0
0	1	0	1
1	0	0	1
1	1	1	0

(a) Truth table

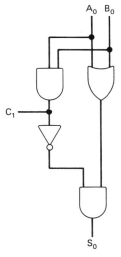

(b) Logic diagram

Figure 3-14 Logic gate implementation of a half adder.

Two-bit addition can be accomplished by placing two adding networks in parallel (i.e., side by side). However, 2-bit addition is more complex because addition of the higher-order bit must take into account a possible carry from the low-order sum. Let the inputs to the high-order adder network be A_1, B_1, and C_1, where C_1 is the carry from the low-order sum. An adder that includes a carry input from a lower-order sum is called a *full adder*. The truth table for a full adder is given in Fig. 3-15a. From the truth table it is seen that when $A_1 = 0$, the output C_2 is B_1C_1 and S_1 is $B_1 \oplus C_1$. When $A_1 = 1$, C_2 is $B_1 + C_1$ and S_1 is

A_1	B_1	C_1	C_2	S_1
0	0	0	0	0
0	0	1	0	1
0	1	0	0	1
0	1	1	1	0
1	0	0	0	1
1	0	1	1	0
1	1	0	1	0
1	1	1	1	1

(a) Truth table for full adder

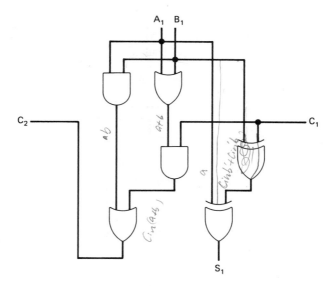

(b) Full adder

Figure 3-15 Design of an adder.

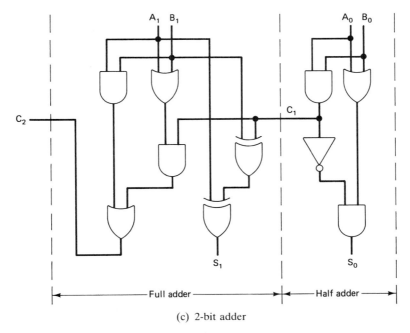

(c) 2-bit adder

Figure 3-15 Continued.

$\overline{B_1 \oplus C_1}$. Therefore, using the equivalences in Fig. 3-13, we get

$$C_2 = \overline{A}_1 B_1 C_1 + A_1 (B_1 + C_1)$$

$$= \overline{A}_1 B_1 C_1 + A_1 B_1 + A_1 C_1$$

$$= A_1 B_1 + C_1 (\overline{A}_1 B_1 + A_1)$$

$$= A_1 B_1 + C_1 (A_1 + B_1)$$

$$S_1 = \overline{A}_1 (B_1 \oplus C_1) + A_1 (\overline{B_1 \oplus C_1})$$

$$= A_1 \oplus (B_1 \oplus C_1)$$

The logic diagram for a full adder corresponding to these expressions is given in Fig. 3-15b; a logic network that combines a half adder and full adder to produce 2-bit addition is given in Fig. 3-15c. Clearly, n-bit addition could be obtained by putting n-2 more full adders in parallel on the left.

To design a 2's-complement subtracter, one need only modify an adder by inverting all the bits in the subtrahend before they are input to the respective full adders and then add a 1 to the result. An easy way to add the 1 is to replace the half adder on the right with a full adder and set its input carry bit to 1. Figure 3-16 shows a network that is capable of performing either an addition or subtraction. This network would function by applying the operands . . . $A_1 A_0$ and . . . $B_1 B_0$ to

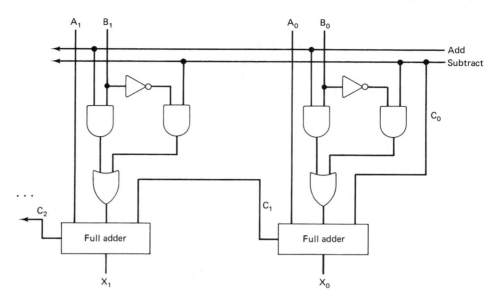

Figure 3-16 Parallel adder/subtracter network.

the inputs and then applying a 1 to the "add" line if an addition is desired, or a 1 to the "subtract" line if a subtraction (with . . . B_1B_0 as the subtrahend) is desired.

3-5 DIGITAL DESIGN PROCESS

In general, mathematical modeling is used to optimize a design, predict the results that will occur from various situations, or determine the important factors related to the feasibility or economics of the system being modeled. The modeling procedure is to

1. Find the mathematical model for the given system.
2. Use the model to make the necessary simplifications, predictions, and so on.
3. Determine the final design of the system from the final form of the model.

In the case at hand, modeling is used in the design of logic networks as follows:

1. Determine all the input/output relationships that must be true for the network being designed and put them into a convenient tabular form.
2. Use the table resulting from step 1 to find a Boolean expression for each output that relates the inputs to that output.
3. Simplify, or perhaps optimize, the expressions resulting from step 2.

Figure 3-17 Conversions needed during the design process.

4. Use the expressions resulting from step 3 to develop the desired logic diagrams.

If only a modification of an existing design is desired, steps 1 and 2 could be replaced with:

Find the Boolean expressions for the outputs of the given network.

In the preceding discussion, three design aids have been introduced: truth tables, Boolean expressions, and logic diagrams. Because truth tables are primarily used to originally define a logical network, Boolean expressions are needed for minimization, and logic diagrams are needed actually to put the network together, a designer must be able to convert from one form of a network's description to another. In particular, a designer must be able to perform the conversions shown in Fig. 3-17.

As a tabular listing of the outputs for all possible inputs, a truth table serves as the definition of the network to be designed. It can normally be obtained from a precise statement of what the network is to do. For example, suppose that a three-input network is needed that will output a 1 if the majority of inputs is 1 and, otherwise, it is to output a 0. In other words, if X is the output and A, B, and C are the inputs, then

$$X = 0 \text{ if none or exactly one input is 1}$$

$$X = 1 \text{ if any two or all three inputs are 1}$$

This statement can be easily used to obtain the truth table:

A	B	C	X
0	0	0	0
0	0	1	0
0	1	0	0
0	1	1	1
1	0	0	0
1	0	1	1
1	1	0	1
1	1	1	1

Once the truth table is established, a Boolean expression for each output is needed, i.e., a truth table to Boolean expression conversion must be made. There are two approaches to this problem.   The first uses the facts that

1. A product is 1 if and only if all of its factors are 1.
2. A sum is 1 if and only if at least one of its terms is 1.

Therefore, a Boolean expression for an output can be derived from a truth table by forming a product for each row for which the output is 1 and then adding these products.   Again, considering the voting example above, we will first examine the fourth row in the truth table and note that $X_3 = \overline{A}BC$ is 1 if and only if $A = 0$, $B = 1$, and $C = 1$.   For the sixth, seventh, and eighth rows

$$X_5 = A\overline{B}C \text{ is 1 if and only if } A = 1, B = 0, \text{ and } C = 1$$

$$X_6 = AB\overline{C} \text{ is 1 if and only if } A = 1, B = 1, \text{ and } C = 0$$

$$X_7 = ABC \text{ is 1 if and only if } A = 1, B = 1, \text{ and } C = 1$$

Also

$$X = X_3 + X_5 + X_6 + X_7 = \overline{A}BC + A\overline{B}C + AB\overline{C} + ABC$$

is 1 if and only if at least one of the variables X_3, X_5, X_6, and X_7 is 1.   Any combination of values for A, B, and C other than those given in the definitions of X_3, X_5, X_6, and X_7 will cause all of the terms in the output X to be 0 and thus will cause X to be 0.   An expression such as the one given for X in this example is called a *sum of products*.

Alternatively, the output expression could have been based on

1. A sum is 0 if and only if all of its terms are 0.
2. A product is 0 if and only if at least one of its factors is 0.

In this case, a sum is formed for each row for which the output is 0 and then these sums are multiplied.   For the voting example, note that

$$X_0 = A + B + C \text{ is 0 if and only if } A = 0, B = 0, \text{ and } C = 0$$

$$X_1 = A + B + \overline{C} \text{ is 0 if and only if } A = 0, B = 0, \text{ and } C = 1$$

$$X_2 = A + \overline{B} + C \text{ is 0 if and only if } A = 0, B = 1, \text{ and } C = 0$$

$$X_4 = \overline{A} + B + C \text{ is 0 if and only if } A = 1, B = 0, \text{ and } C = 0$$

Therefore

$$X = X_0X_1X_2X_3 = (A + B + C)(A + B + \overline{C})(A + \overline{B} + C)(\overline{A} + B + C)$$

is 0 if and only if at least one of the variables X_0, X_1, X_2, and X_4 is 0.   The *product of sums* solution is, of course, equivalent to the sum of products solution obtained above.

The reverse conversion for getting a truth table from a Boolean expression can be accomplished by finding the value of the output expression for each possible input and noting these values in the truth table. This could possibly be done more quickly by establishing columns in the table that contain values for intermediate subexpressions. Figure 3-18 gives a truth table that defines

$$X = \overline{A}D + B + C\overline{D}$$

$$Y = (\overline{A} + C)(C + D)$$

After having found the desired output columns (the seventh and tenth columns), the designer could redraw the truth table without the intermediate columns (the fifth, sixth, eighth, and ninth columns).

Finding the logic diagram that corresponds to a given Boolean expression is the easiest of the conversions shown in Fig. 3-17. It is simply a matter of drawing the gates that represent the operations in the expression and then connecting them together. For example, the diagram in Fig. 3-19a can be obtained from

$$(A\overline{B} + D)\,\overline{C} + BD$$

by scanning the expression from left to right and drawing the gate symbols as the scanning takes place. Then, by noting the variables involved in the operations, the gate symbols can be connected together.

For complex expressions, a more systematic approach may be required. By using the distributive law to multiply out the expression to obtain a sum of products, one could then form the logic diagram by complementing all variables whose

A	B	C	D	$\overline{A}D$	$C\overline{D}$	$X = \overline{A}D + B + C\overline{D}$	$\overline{A} + C$	$C + D$	$Y = (\overline{A} + C)(C + D)$
0	0	0	0	0	0	0	1	0	0
0	0	0	1	1	0	1	1	1	1
0	0	1	0	0	1	1	1	1	1
0	0	1	1	1	0	1	1	1	1
0	1	0	0	0	0	1	1	0	0
0	1	0	1	1	0	1	1	1	1
0	1	1	0	0	1	1	1	1	1
0	1	1	1	1	0	1	1	1	1
1	0	0	0	0	0	0	0	0	0
1	0	0	1	0	0	0	0	1	0
1	0	1	0	0	1	1	1	1	1
1	0	1	1	0	0	0	1	1	1
1	1	0	0	0	0	1	0	0	0
1	1	0	1	0	0	1	0	1	0
1	1	1	0	0	1	1	1	1	1
1	1	1	1	0	0	1	1	1	1

Figure 3-18   Obtaining a truth table from Boolean expressions.

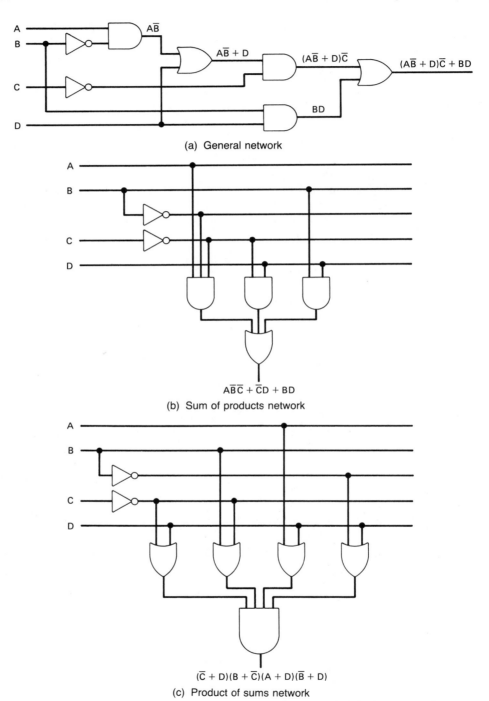

(a) General network

(b) Sum of products network

(c) Product of sums network

Figure 3-19   Equivalent logic diagrams corresponding to a typical Boolean expression.

complements appear in the expression, draw a row of AND gates to get the products, and use an OR gate to get the sum.   Using the same expression as in the above example, we get

$$(A\overline{B} + D)\,\overline{C} + BD = A\overline{B}\overline{C} + \overline{C}D + BD$$

which corresponds to the diagram in Fig. 3-19b.

A similar systematic approach consists of factoring the expression to get a product of sums.   Once again, consider the expression

$$(A\overline{B} + D)\,\overline{C} + BD = (\overline{C} + D)\,(B + \overline{C})\,(A + D)\,(\overline{B} + D)$$

Fig. 3-19c can be obtained by complementing the necessary variables, using OR gates to implement the sums, and then using an AND gate to produce the output.

The design of the voting network discussed at the beginning of this section could be completed by simplifying the output as follows:

$$\overline{A}BC + A\overline{B}C + AB\overline{C} + ABC = \overline{A}BC + ABC + A\overline{B}C + ABC + AB\overline{C} + ABC$$

$$= (\overline{A} + A)\,BC + (\overline{B} + B)\,AC + (\overline{C} + C)\,AB$$

$$= BC + AC + AB$$

$$= A\,(B + C) + BC$$

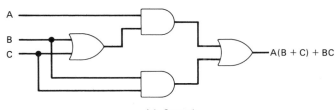

(a) General

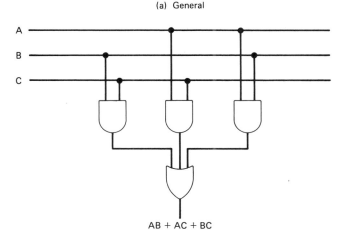

AB + AC + BC

(b) Sum of products

Figure 3-20   Voting network designs.

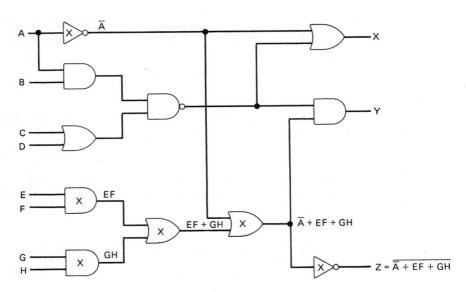

Figure 3-21   Finding the Boolean expression for an output by tracing backward to find the contributing gates.

The first equality is justified because an existing term (in particular, *ABC*) can be repeated as many times as desired without changing the value of the expression. Two equivalent logic diagrams for implementing the voting network are shown in Fig. 3-20.

     The reverse conversion, that of obtaining an output Boolean expression from a logic diagram, is also very straightforward. It can be accomplished by tracing backward from the output to determine all gates that contribute to the output and then moving forward and finding the Boolean expressions for the outputs of these gates. This is demonstrated in Fig. 3-21.

3-6 *MINIMIZATION USING KARNAUGH MAPS*

At this point it is clear that one of the principal problems confronting a digital designer is that of reducing a Boolean expression, thereby permitting it to be implemented using fewer gates. The purpose of this section is to describe a design tool, called a *Karnaugh map*, that permits such reduction by visual inspection. Before we introduce Karnaugh maps, however, a few preliminary definitions are needed. As we have seen, there are two standard Boolean expressions that can be obtained for an output in an arbitrary truth table: the sum of products expression and the product of sums expression. The occurrence of a variable or its complement in an expression is called a *literal*, and a term in a sum of products that includes a literal for every input is called a *minterm*. Similarly, a sum in a product of sums that includes a literal for every input is called a *maxterm*. For example, if A, B, and C are the inputs, then in

$$A\overline{B}C + \overline{A}BC + A\overline{C}$$

$A\overline{B}C$ and $\overline{A}BC$ are minterms and $A\overline{C}$ is not a minterm. For

$$(\overline{A} + B + \overline{C}) (A + \overline{B} + \overline{C}) (\overline{A} + C)$$

$\overline{A} + B + \overline{C}$ and $A + \overline{B} + \overline{C}$ are maxterms, but $\overline{A} + C$ is not.

A Karnaugh map is nothing more than a truth table for a single output that is organized in a special way. It consists of an array of squares, such as those in Fig. 3-22, where each square corresponds to a row in the truth table. The symbol(s) at the top indicates the variable(s) associated with the columns and the symbol(s) on the left indicates the variable(s) associated with the rows. The value of the output for each input is put in the corresponding square, as shown in Fig. 3-23. Therefore, for each 1 in the Karnaugh map, there is a minterm in the output's sum of products expression, and for each 0 there is a maxterm in the product of sums expression. From either the truth table or the Karnaugh map, the following output expressions could be produced immediately

$$X = ABC + AB\overline{C} + \overline{A}BC$$

$$= (A + B + C) (A + B + \overline{C}) (A + \overline{B} + C) (\overline{A} + B + C) (\overline{A} + B + \overline{C})$$

Minimization of expressions using Karnaugh maps is based on the fact that if S is a sum of a subset of the minterms and

$$S = PQ$$

where Q consists of all possible combinations of a subset of the inputs, then

$$S = P$$

This is so because if Q consists of all possible combinations of a subset of the inputs, then $Q = 1$. The reason a Karnaugh map helps simplify an expression is

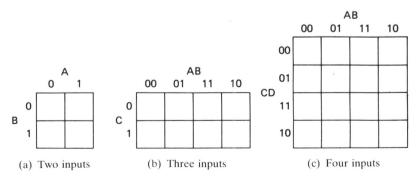

(a) Two inputs   (b) Three inputs   (c) Four inputs

Figure 3-22   Examples of Karnaugh map constructions.

A	B	C	X
0	0	0	0
0	0	1	0
0	1	0	0
0	1	1	1
1	0	0	0
1	0	1	0
1	1	0	1
1	1	1	1

AB

C	00	01	11	10
0	0	0	1	0
1	0	1	1	0

$$X = ABC + AB\overline{C} + \overline{A}BC$$

Figure 3-23 Truth table and its associated Karnaugh map.

that its rows and columns are arranged so that all possible combinations of the various subsets of inputs are adjacent, thus making it easy to spot such combinations.

In the example shown in Fig. 3-23 the 1's appearing in the 11 column correspond to the minterms $AB\overline{C}$ and ABC. The sum of these terms can be factored as follows:

$$AB\overline{C} + ABC = AB(\overline{C} + C) = AB$$

The two 1's in the bottom row correspond to the minterms $\overline{A}BC$ and ABC, and

$$\overline{A}BC + ABC = (\overline{A} + A)BC = BC$$

These groupings are indicated in Fig. 3-24a and result in

$$X = ABC + AB\overline{C} + \overline{A}BC$$
$$= ABC + AB\overline{C} + ABC + \overline{A}BC$$
$$= AB + BC$$

Note that because $P + P = P$, a minterm, i.e., a 1 in the map, may be used in as many groupings as desired.

Because a sum of all combinations of one variable consists of two terms, of two variables consists of four terms, of three variables consists of eight terms, etc., the designer must look for adjacent groups that include 2^n, $n = 1, 2, \ldots$, ones. The larger the grouping, the greater the reduction in the number of literals and minterms. If the Karnaugh map of Y is as shown in Fig. 3-24b, then

$$Y = \overline{A}\,\overline{B}\,\overline{C} + \overline{A}\,\overline{B}C + \overline{A}B\overline{C} + \overline{A}BC + ABC$$
$$= \overline{A}(\overline{B}\,\overline{C} + \overline{B}C + B\overline{C} + BC) + BC(A + \overline{A})$$
$$= \overline{A} + BC$$

The products that correspond to maximum groupings are called *prime implicants*.

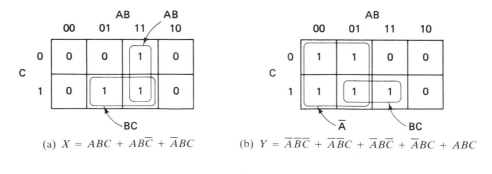

(a) $X = ABC + AB\overline{C} + \overline{A}BC$ (b) $Y = \overline{A}\,\overline{B}\,\overline{C} + \overline{A}\,\overline{B}C + \overline{A}B\overline{C} + \overline{A}BC + ABC$

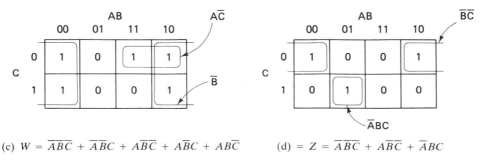

(c) $W = \overline{A}\,\overline{B}\,\overline{C} + \overline{A}\,\overline{B}C + A\overline{B}\,\overline{C} + A\overline{B}C + AB\overline{C}$ (d) $= Z = \overline{A}\,\overline{B}\,\overline{C} + A\overline{B}\,\overline{C} + \overline{A}BC$

Figure 3-24   Minimization of three-variable outputs.

A three-variable Karnaugh map should be considered to be a cylinder with the left column being adjacent to the right column.   Therefore, if the map for W is as shown in Fig. 3-24c, then the prime implicants are $\overline{B}$ and $A\overline{C}$, and

$$W = \overline{B} + A\overline{C}$$

A fourth example is given in Fig. 3-24d.   In this example the prime implicants are $\overline{B}\,\overline{C}$ and $\overline{A}BC$, and

$$Z = \overline{B}\,\overline{C} + \overline{A}BC$$

Note that in all of the above examples the variables that do not change in a grouping are the variables that appear in the corresponding prime implicant.

A Karnaugh map of a four-variable output is shown in Fig. 3-25a.   The prime implicants are $A\overline{B}$, $A\overline{C}D$, and $\overline{A}B\overline{C}$, and

$$X = A\overline{B} + A\overline{C}D + \overline{A}B\overline{C}$$

The minterm $AB\overline{C}D$ could also be covered by $B\overline{C}D$; therefore, it is also true that

$$X = A\overline{B} + B\overline{C}D + \overline{A}B\overline{C}$$

and it is seen that the prime implicants used in the final expression are not unique.

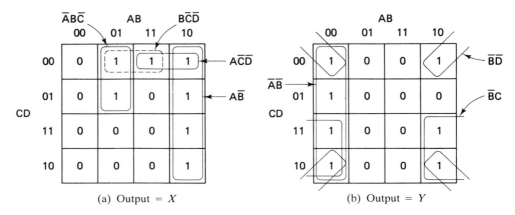

(a) Output $= X$ (b) Output $= Y$

Figure 3-25   Examples of four-variable outputs.

For purposes of adjacency the four-variable Karnaugh map is to be considered as a doughnut-shaped surface that is formed by first attaching the top to the bottom to obtain a cylinder and then attaching the left and right ends to obtain a doughnut shape.   When this is done, the top is adjacent to the bottom, the left side is adjacent to the right side, and the four corners are adjacent.   To demonstrate these relationships let us consider the example shown in Fig. 3-25b.   The output for this map is found to be

$$Y = \overline{B}\overline{D} + \overline{B}C + \overline{A}\overline{B}$$

In this example, note that the minterm $\overline{A}\overline{B}C\overline{D}$ was not picked up by simply adding it to the others; it was covered by forming a grouping of four even though only one 1 was left to be included.   Thus, only two literals were required in the third term instead of four.   Once again it is emphasized that the larger the groupings the better.

Karnaugh maps can also be used for attacking problems involving five or six inputs.   For these cases multiple four-input maps are used, as shown in Fig. 3-26. So that adjacencies can be used to find prime implicants, the four-input maps should be viewed as if they are in a stack.   For the six-variable case the $E = F = 0$ map should be on top followed by the $E = 0$, $F = 1$ map, the $E = F = 1$ map and the $E = 1$, $F = 0$ map, respectively.   The top and bottom maps are considered to be adjacent.   The output indicated by the five-variable map shown in Fig. 3-27 is

$$X = \overline{A}D\overline{E} + ABD + ADE$$

As an example of a complete network design using a Karnaugh map, let us consider the problem of developing a network that will compare the binary numbers $A = A_2A_1A_0$ and $B = B_2B_1B_0$ and output a 1 if $B>A$.   The Karnaugh map

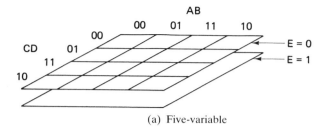

(a) Five-variable

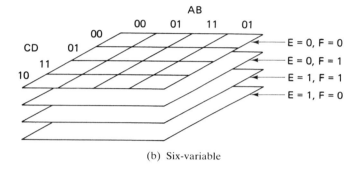

(b) Six-variable

Figure 3-26 Construction of five- and six-variable maps.

describing the network is given in Fig. 3-28a.   From this map we get

$$X = \overline{A}_2B_2 + \overline{A}_2\overline{A}_1B_1 + B_2\overline{A}_1B_1 + \overline{A}_2\overline{A}_1\overline{A}_0B_0 + B_2\overline{A}_1\overline{A}_0B_0$$
$$+ \overline{A}_2\overline{A}_0B_1B_0 + B_2\overline{A}_0B_1B_0$$
$$= \overline{A}_2B_2 + \overline{A}_2(\overline{A}_1B_1 + \overline{A}_1\overline{A}_0B_0 + \overline{A}_0B_1B_0)$$
$$+ B_2(\overline{A}_1B_1 + \overline{A}_1\overline{A}_0B_0 + \overline{A}_0B_1B_0)$$

A network for implementing the comparator is shown in Fig. 3-28b.

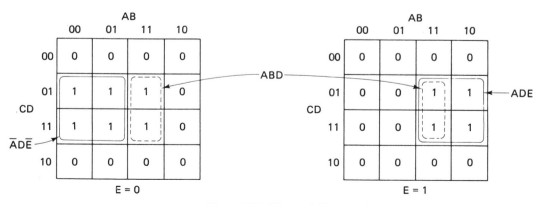

Figure 3-27 Five-variable example.

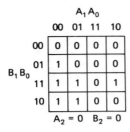

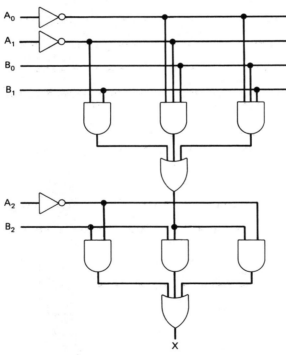

(a) Karnaugh map

X

(b) Logic diagram

Figure 3-28   Design of a 3-bit comparator.

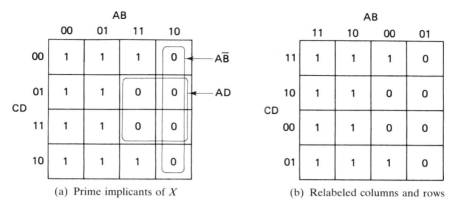

(a) Prime implicants of X (b) Relabeled columns and rows

Figure 3-29   Example of finding a product of sums.

Our ability to visualize only three dimensions and the fact that only two variables may be associated with each dimension limit the use of Karnaugh maps when working with more than six inputs.   Although they can be used to help solve problems involving more than six variables, the use of adjacencies to spot the prime implicants is limited to only six variables at a time.

In order to arrive at a product of sums we note that the Karnaugh map of $\overline{X}$ is obtained by interchanging the ones and zeros in the Karnaugh map of X.   Then the sum of products expression for $\overline{X}$ is found and DeMorgan's laws are used to complement $\overline{X}$ to obtain X as a product of sums.   For example, let the Karnaugh map for X be the one shown in Fig. 3-29a.   By finding prime implicants using groups of zeros it is seen that

$$\overline{X} = A\overline{B} + AD$$

Therefore

$$X = \overline{\overline{X}} = \overline{A\overline{B} + AD} = (\overline{A\overline{B}})(\overline{AD}) = (\overline{A} + B)(\overline{A} + \overline{D})$$

By interchanging the ones and zeros in the column and row labels as shown in Fig. 3-29b and interchanging the use of the ANDs and ORs

$$X = (\overline{A} + B)(\overline{A} + \overline{D})$$

could have been obtained directly.

Finally, because for some designs some input combinations cannot occur, the outputs corresponding to these combinations are optional.   These combinations may be chosen to be either one or zero as is convenient to the minimization process.   They are represented by X's in the Karnaugh map and may or may not be included in the prime implicants.   For the output whose map is shown in Fig. 3-30, it is useful to include the minterm $A\overline{B}C\overline{D}$ in a prime implicant, but it is not useful to

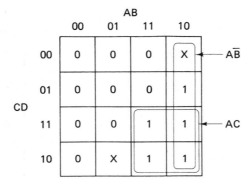

Figure 3-30 Map with optional minterms.

include the minterm $\overline{A}BC\overline{D}$ in a prime implicant. The minimized output function is

$$X = A\overline{B} + AC$$

As a final example, suppose that a network is needed that will output a 1 at X if and only if the binary number $A_3A_2A_1A_0$ is greater than 0 and less than 4. Also, suppose that it is known that because the inputs are controlled by a rotary switch, at most one input can be 1 at any given time, except one switch position will allow all inputs to be 1. The needed Karnaugh map is in Fig. 3-31. A sum of products solution is

$$X = \overline{A}_3A_0 + \overline{A}_3A_1 = \overline{A}_3(A_0 + A_1)$$

By grouping the 0's it is seen that the product of sums solution is the same, i.e.

$$X = \overline{\overline{X}} = \overline{A_3 + \overline{A}_1\overline{A}_0} = \overline{A}_3(A_1 + A_0)$$

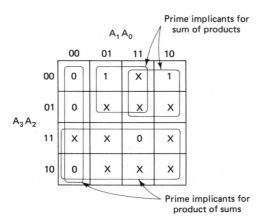

Figure 3-31 Rotary switch example.

3-7 CODE CONVERTERS

So far, adder/subtracter, voting, and comparator networks have been developed as examples of combinational network design, and all of them are important to computer design. Two other combinational networks that are quite often present in one or more places within a computer system are considered in this section and Section 3-8. As before, they will also serve as design examples.

The data in a computer system may take on several different forms. In fact, as the data pass from one part of the system to another, they may change forms several times. A terminal, for example, may receive its information from the keys in one form, immediately convert it to another before transmitting it to the computer, and then the computer may convert it to yet another form before using it. Electronic circuitry whose sole purpose is to convert data from one format to another is called a *code converter*. Sometimes the data format is changed only for the purpose of transmitting the data over a communications link or for recording it on a storage medium, such as a diskette. When this is the case, the code converter

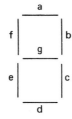

(a) Seven-segment display

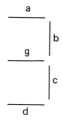

(b) A 3 on a seven-segment display

A_3	A_2	A_1	A_0	a	b	c	d	e	f	g
0	0	0	0	1	1	1	1	1	1	0
0	0	0	1	0	1	1	0	0	0	0
0	0	1	0	1	1	0	1	1	0	1
0	0	1	1	1	1	1	1	0	0	1
0	1	0	0	0	1	1	0	0	1	1
0	1	0	1	1	0	1	1	0	1	1
0	1	1	0	0	0	1	1	1	1	1
0	1	1	1	1	1	1	0	0	0	0
1	0	0	0	1	1	1	1	1	1	1
1	0	0	1	1	1	1	0	0	1	1

(c) Truth table for defining the conversion

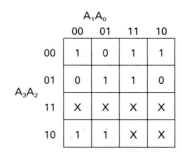

X—output is optional

(d) Karnaugh map for output *a*

Figure 3-32   Seven-segment display and the defining truth table for the BCD-to-seven-segment code converter.

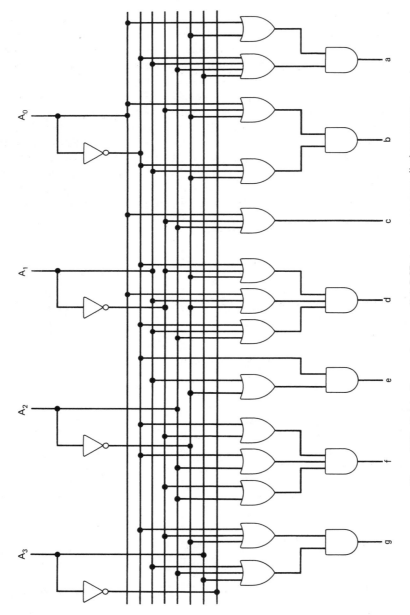

Figure 3-33 Logic diagram for a one-digit BCD-to-seven-segment display converter.

is called an *encoder*, and the converter at the receiving end or for reading from the medium is called a *decoder*.

Let us consider the problem of changing a single BCD digit into the signals needed to light the seven-segment display given in Fig. 3-32a. Fig. 3-32b shows what a 3 would look like on the display, Fig. 3-32c summarizes the outputs to the various segments for all possible inputs, and Fig. 3-32d gives the Karnaugh map for segment *a*. In this map, *X*'s are used to indicate the input combinations that should never occur. The complete BCD to seven-segment converter design is given in Fig. 3-33. Verification of the outputs is requested in Exercise 24.

3-8 ERROR DETECTION AND CORRECTION

When transmitting or storing data, there is always a chance that an error will occur due to electromagnetic noise or physical damage to the storage medium. If an error should occur, it is, of course, highly desirable that it be detected or possibly even corrected. Therefore, if data are to be transmitted more than a very short distance or are to be stored, they should include some type of error-protection scheme. The only way of providing data with error protection is to build in some form of redundancy.

The primary disadvantages in having redundancy are that when transmitting data, it either increases the number of lines and associated circuitry or it increases the time required to send the data, and when storing data it increases the complexity of the storage device and decreases the storage capacity. It has been theoretically determined that, if the data consist of n bits, in order to detect and correct one erroneous bit the number of extra bits r must satisfy the inequality

$$2^r - 1 \geq n + r$$

Another bit will permit 2 erroneous bits to be detected, although only the occurrence of one error can be corrected. Bounds also exist for the detection and correction of higher numbers of bits, but a discussion of these bounds is beyond the scope of this book.

By far the most prevalent type of error protection is single-bit detection. This can be attained by adding only one bit to the data. This bit is called the *parity bit* and it is set according to one of the following two rules:

EVEN PARITY—The parity bit is set if there is an odd number of 1's in the data bits; otherwise, it is cleared. Therefore, the total number of 1's is even.

ODD PARITY—The parity bit is set if there is an even number of 1's in the data; otherwise, it is cleared. Therefore, the total number of 1's is odd.

The standard nine-track magnetic tape unit employs this type of detection scheme. The tracks are spread laterally across the tape, and eight of the nine tracks contain data bits; the ninth track contains the parity bit and it is set according

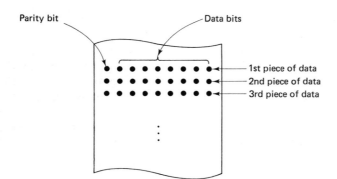

Parity bit   Data bits

1st piece of data
2nd piece of data
3rd piece of data

Figure 3-34 Distribution of information on a nine-track magnetic tape.

to either the even-parity rule or the odd-parity rule. (Clearly, the type of parity chosen would be used throughout a tape.) The distribution of data on a nine-track tape is shown in Fig. 3-34. In this figure a dot indicates either a 1 or a 0. If the tape is damaged after the data along with its parity bits have been stored on it, the probability that at least one of the parity bits in the damaged area will reflect the wrong number of 1's is extremely high. Therefore, when the tape is read, the error-detection circuitry can sense the erroneous data and alert the computer to the problem. In addition to the lateral detection method discussed here, most magnetic tape units also have a longitudinal error-detection scheme incorporated into their design. Thus the chance of detecting an error is increased even more.

Once it has been decided to utilize error detection and/or correction in storing or transmitting data, the necessary circuitry for generating the redundant bits and then later checking them must be designed. As an example, suppose that even

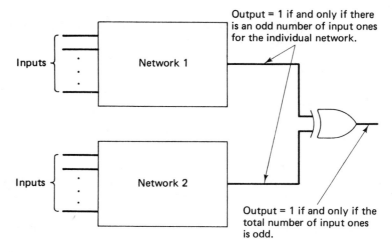

Output = 1 if and only if there is an odd number of input ones for the individual network.

Inputs { Network 1

Inputs { Network 2

Output = 1 if and only if the total number of input ones is odd.

Figure 3-35 Basic relationships used in designing even- and odd-parity networks.

parity is to be used.   Before proceeding with the design, consider the situation depicted in Fig. 3-35.   If, as illustrated in this figure, two networks having the property

> The output is 1 if and only if there
> is an odd number of input 1's.

are connected to the inputs of an exclusive OR gate, it can be shown simply by considering the four possible cases that the resulting overall network will also have this property.   Because an exclusive OR gate has this property, an even-parity bit for 4-bit data can be generated by implementing the logic diagram shown in Fig. 3-36a.   The corresponding 5-bit error-detection network is given in Fig. 3-36b. These networks could be easily extended to accommodate any number of data bits. For odd parity, the same logic network could be used except than an inverter must be placed in the parity output of both the generator and the detector.

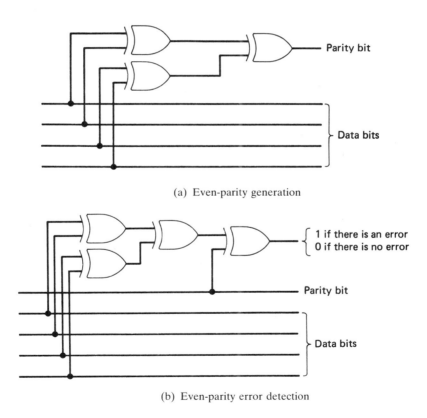

(a) Even-parity generation

(b) Even-parity error detection

Figure 3-36   Logic networks for generating even parity and detecting even-parity errors for 4-bit data.

3-9 ROMs AND PLAs

One approach to manufacturing combinational networks is to start with a design that is equivalent to the one in Fig. 3-37 and then construct the desired network by leaving out certain connections. This allows all networks with the same numbers of inputs and outputs to be made using the same uniform pattern. This uniformity permits a large number of gates to be put in a single IC. Actually, the components in the circuits would not resemble AND and OR gates, but would only have the same effect as the logic diagram shown in Fig. 3-37.

There are two basic types of networks that use this approach, read-only memories (ROMs) and programmed logic arrays (PLAs). A ROM would, in

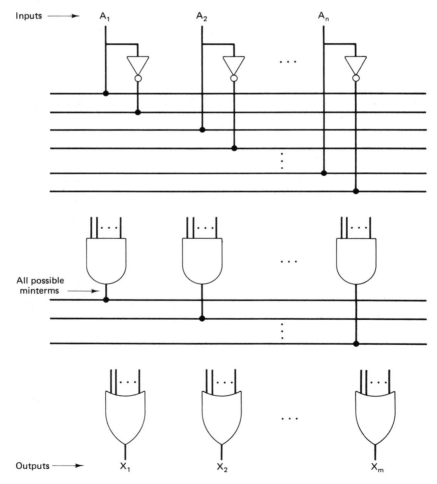

Figure 3-37 Basic construction of ROMs and PLAs.

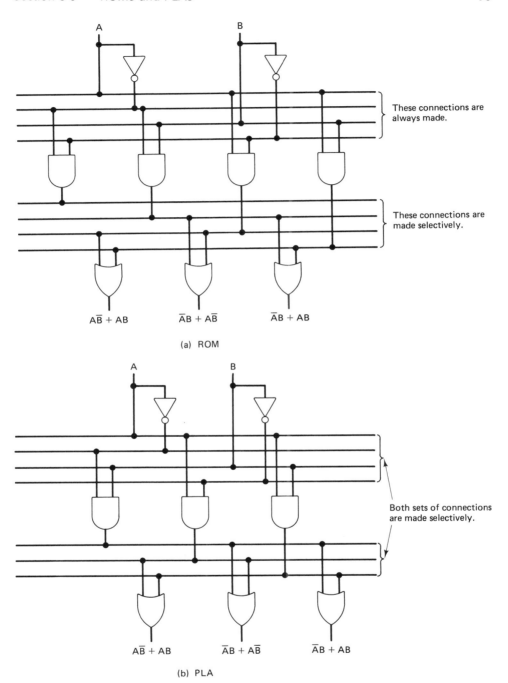

(a) ROM

(b) PLA

Figure 3-38 ROM and PLA examples.

effect, produce all possible products of the inputs (i.e., all possible minterms), and each output would be obtained by disconnecting the OR inputs from the AND gates whose minterms are not to be included in the output. A two-input, three-output ROM is shown in Fig. 3-38a. Because a 1 in an output column of a truth table corresponds to the presence of a minterm and a 0 to its absence, the connections and disconnections can be thought of as permanently storing 1's and 0's in the network—hence the name memory. "Read-only" is due to the fact that once the disconnections are made, they cannot be changed. ROMs are more often used as computer memories than as combinational networks and are discussed further in Chapter 5. It will be seen that when a ROM is used as a memory, the inputs are the memory's address and the outputs are the contents of the address.

A PLA is similar to a ROM, but takes advantage of the fact that some minterms will not be needed in any of the outputs. Therefore, for an n-input network, there is no need to have 2^n AND gates. However, this means that there must be a way of selecting which minterms are to be generated, i.e., a way of selectively connecting the AND gate inputs as well as the OR gate inputs. For a PLA the maximum number of minterms that can be used in all outputs is determined by the number of AND gates it contains and, as with a ROM, the maximum number of outputs would be the number of OR gates. A three-AND gate PLA implementation of the ROM network in Fig. 3-38a is given in Fig. 3-38b.

A third way of constructing combinational networks without connecting together individual AND and OR gates is to use multiplexers. This approach is outlined in Exercise 31.

BIBLIOGRAPHY

1. MALMSTADT, HOWARD V., CHRISTIE G. ENKE, and STANLEY R. CROUCH, *Electronic Measurements for Scientists* (Menlo Park, Calif.: W. A. Benjamin, 1974).

2. MARCUS, MITCHELL P., *Switching Circuits for Engineers*, 2nd ed. (Englewood Cliffs, N.J.: Prentice-Hall, 1967).

3. HILL, FREDRICK J., and GERALD R. PETERSON, *Introduction to Switching Theory and Logical Design*, 3rd ed. (New York: John Wiley, 1981).

4. ROTH, CHARLES H., *Fundamentals of Logical Design* (St. Paul, Minn.: West Publishing Co., 1975).

5. HILBURN, JOHN L., and PAUL M. JULICH, *Microcomputers/Microprocessors: Hardware, Software, and Applications*, (Englewood Cliffs, N.J.: Prentice-Hall, 1976).

6. BARNA, ARPAD, and DAN I. PORAT, *Integrated Circuits in Digital Electronics* (New York: John Wiley, 1973).

EXERCISES

1. Show that the NOR, AND, and OR gates with inverters at their inputs are equivalent to AND, NOR, and NAND gates, respectively.

2. Design a multiplexer that selects one of two sets of four input variables to be passed through to four outputs.

3. A network that directs an input to two or more possible outputs is called a demultiplexer. Design a one-input, two-output (1-to-2) demultiplexer; a 1-to-4 demultiplexer.

4. Verify the equivalences given in Fig. 3-13.

5. Find the Boolean expression and a truth table for each of the outputs in the accompanying logic diagram.

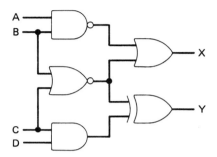

6. Simplify the output expressions found in Exercise 5 using the equivalences given in Fig. 3-13 and redraw the logic diagram using the simplified expressions.

7. Using the equivalences in Fig. 3-13, simplify the following Boolean expressions and then draw a logic diagram for each of the simplified expressions:
   (a) $(A + \overline{B} + AB)(A + \overline{B})\overline{A}B$
   (b) $(A + \overline{B} + A\overline{B})(AB + \overline{A}C + BC)$
   (c) $(A + \overline{BC})A(C + B\overline{C} + \overline{B}C)$
   (d) $A\overline{B}C + A\overline{B}C + \overline{A}BC + \overline{A}\overline{B}C + \overline{A}\overline{B}\overline{C}$
   (e) $(A + B + C)(A + \overline{B} + C)(A + B + \overline{C})(\overline{A} + \overline{B} + C)$

8. Prove the following equivalences:
   (a) $AB + A\overline{B}C = A(B + C)$
   (b) $(A + B)(A + \overline{B} + C) = (A + B)(A + C)$
   (c) $AB + \overline{A}C + BC = AB + \overline{A}C$
   (d) $(X + Y)(\overline{X} + Z)(Y + Z) = (X + Y)(\overline{X} + Z)$

9. Given the following truth table, use both the sum of products method and the product of sums method to find Boolean expressions for each output:

A	B	C	X	Y	Z
0	0	0	1	0	0
0	0	1	0	1	1
0	1	0	0	1	1
0	1	1	0	0	1
1	0	0	1	0	1
1	0	1	0	0	1
1	1	0	0	0	1
1	1	1	0	0	0

Simplify each of the expressions obtained and draw a diagram of a logic network having the specified input/output relationships.

10. Given the network shown, find Boolean expressions for the outputs, simplify these expressions, and then draw an equivalent network using the simplified expressions.

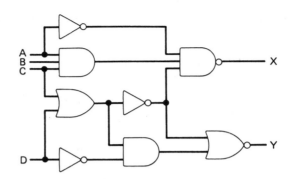

11. Give a complete truth table, the Boolean expressions of the outputs, and a logical design of a dual 2-to-1 multiplexer with a disable feature.

12. Design a four-input voting network that outputs a 0 if the vote is a tie or there are more 0 inputs than 1 inputs.

13. It will be seen in Chapter 6 that an adder/subtracter circuit is sometimes needed that will add a carry or subtract a borrow from the MSB of a previous addition or subtraction. Modify Fig. 3-16 so that the carry input of the LSB's full adder is added if addition is being performed and is subtracted if subtraction is being performed.

14. Find the Karnaugh maps for
(a) $AB\overline{C} + \overline{A}BC + A\overline{B}\overline{C} + \overline{A}B\overline{C}$
(b) $A\overline{B}C\overline{D} + \overline{A}\overline{B}CD + ABCD + \overline{A}BCD + \overline{A}B\overline{C}\overline{D} + \overline{A}B\overline{C}\overline{D}$
(c) $\overline{A}BCD\overline{E} + \overline{A}BC\overline{D}E + \overline{A}\overline{B}CDE + \overline{A}BC\overline{D}\overline{E} + \overline{A}\overline{B}C\overline{D}\dot{E} + \overline{A}BC\overline{D}E$

15. Find the minimized sum of products for

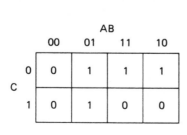

(a)

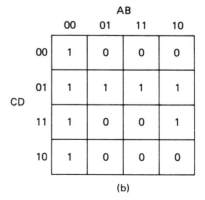

(b)

	AB 00	01	11	10
CD 00	0	0	1	1
01	0	1	1	1
11	0	1	1	1
10	0	0	0	1

E = 0

	AB 00	01	11	10
CD 00	0	0	0	1
01	1	0	1	1
11	1	0	1	1
10	0	0	0	1

E = 1

(c)

16. Find the minimized product of sums for the maps given in Exercise 15.

17. Given the following truth table, use Karnaugh maps to find a simplified logic network that has A, B, and C as its inputs and X and Y as its outputs:

A	B	C	X	Y
0	0	0	0	0
0	0	1	0	0
0	1	0	1	0
0	1	1	0	1
1	0	0	0	0
1	0	1	0	0
1	1	0	1	1
1	1	1	1	1

(Note that a Karnaugh map of XY could have been used to find the prime implicant that is common to both X and Y.)

18. Find a minimized sum of products expression for the output whose map is

	AB 00	01	11	10
CD 00	1	0	0	X
01	0	0	0	0
11	X	1	1	X
10	1	1	1	1

19. Find a minimized product of sums expression for the map given in Exercise 18.
20. Because two Karnaugh maps are identical if and only if the mapped expressions are equal, maps can be used to show equality. Use a Karnaugh map to prove the following equality:

$$A\overline{C} + BC = A\overline{C} + AB + BC$$

21. Design a logic network that will take the 4-bit 2's complement of a number.
22. Find a logic diagram such as the one in Fig. 3-19b for each of the following (use an AND gate for each term and OR the terms):

$$X = ABC + ABC$$

$$Y = A\overline{B} + ABC + \overline{A}\overline{B}\overline{C}$$

$$Z = A + \overline{A}B\overline{C} + A\overline{B}C$$

23. Use a logic network such as the one in Fig. 3-19c to implement the following input/output relationships:

$$X = (A + \overline{B} + C)(A + C)(B + C)$$

$$Y = (\overline{A} + B + \overline{C})(A + \overline{B} + C)(\overline{A} + B + C)$$

$$Z = (A + B)(\overline{A} + \overline{B} + C)(\overline{A} + B + \overline{C})$$

24. Verify that the outputs in Fig. 3-33 are correct.
25. Use the sum of products method to design a logic network that will convert the ASCII code for the letters A, B, and C to form likenesses of these letters on a seven-segment display. (Note that only the lower 2 bits of the ASCII code need to be used.)
26. Design a 6-bit odd-parity generator and a corresponding detector.
27. Devise a scheme that uses three extra lines to provide 1-bit error correction for two data lines. Define the scheme in terms of a truth table and explain why a bit can always be corrected if it is assumed that only 1 bit can be wrong. Keep in mind that errors can also occur in the extra bits. (*Hint:* Perform simple parity checking on different combinations of lines.)
28. How many extra bits must be present to permit single error correction if there are 8 data bits?
29. Use AND and OR gates to design a three-input, four-output ROM whose outputs are

$$W = \overline{A}B + A\overline{B} \qquad\qquad X = A\overline{B}C + AB$$

$$Y = A\overline{B}C + A\overline{C} \qquad\qquad Z = A\overline{B}C + \overline{A}B + AC$$

30. Implement the outputs in Exercise 29 as a six AND gate PLA.
31. Any three-variable output function can be implemented with a 4-to-1 multiplexer by using the following procedure:
    1. Assume the input variables are A, B, and C and let A and B be the two control inputs.
    2. Let D_3, D_2, D_1, and D_0 be the data inputs. Each A and B input combination corresponds to two rows of the truth table. The table and multiplexer are shown as follows.

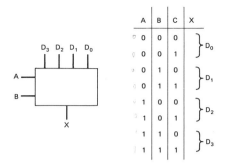

A	B	C	X
0	0	0	$\left.\begin{array}{c} \\ \\ \end{array}\right\} D_0$
0	0	1	
0	1	0	$\left.\begin{array}{c} \\ \\ \end{array}\right\} D_1$
0	1	1	
1	0	0	$\left.\begin{array}{c} \\ \\ \end{array}\right\} D_2$
1	0	1	
1	1	0	$\left.\begin{array}{c} \\ \\ \end{array}\right\} D_3$
1	1	1	

Assign D_0 according to the output combination for the first two rows using the following rules:

$$\left.\begin{array}{c} 0 \\ 0 \end{array}\right\} D_0 = 0 \qquad \left.\begin{array}{c} 0 \\ 1 \end{array}\right\} D_0 = C \qquad \left.\begin{array}{c} 1 \\ 0 \end{array}\right\} D_0 = \overline{C} \qquad \left.\begin{array}{c} 1 \\ 1 \end{array}\right\} D_0 = 1$$

Similarly, D_1 can be assigned using the third and fourth rows, etc. Use the procedure to implement

$$X = A\overline{B}C + AB\overline{C} + \overline{A}\,\overline{B}\,\overline{C}.$$

32. Discuss the use of an 8-to-1 multiplexer in implementing a four-variable output function.

Chapter 4

Sequential Logic and Computer Circuits

In Chapter 3 the discussion centered on networks whose outputs depend only on the current inputs. In contrast, there are networks, called *sequential networks*, that depend on their past histories as well as their current inputs. A simple counting circuit is a good example of a sequential network. Not only would its output depend on the input signal that causes the output to increment, but the output would also depend on the current count that was determined by past inputs. A memory circuit for holding a single datum is another example. A past set of inputs would be stored until they are needed, at which time a control input would be used to cause the contents of the memory circuit to be applied to the outputs.

In sequential networks, the variable time takes on a significant role, whereas combinational networks are considered to be time independent. It is usually necessary to define a sequential network according to its inputs and outputs over a period of time instead of simply noting the input/output relationships in a truth table that ignores time. The chief aid employed in examining the time-dependent aspects of a sequential network is called a *timing diagram*. A typical timing diagram is shown in Fig. 4-1. In this figure A and B are the inputs and X and Y are the outputs.

Time is measured horizontally, but the actual time scale is normally not given. This is because the time between events is usually not known or is not important; only the order in which events occur is relevant. If a time is important, it is specified as shown in the diagram for the Y output. The vertical scale consists of two values, with the higher value corresponding to state 1 and the lower value to state 0. In the figure, A begins in the 0 state and B and X begin in the 1 state. The transition of A to the 1 state does not change the X output, but the subsequent

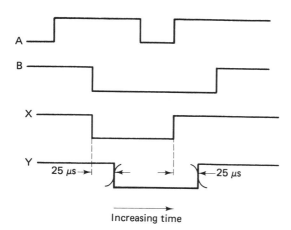

A

B

X

Y

$25\ \mu s$ $25\ \mu s$

Increasing time   **Figure 4-1** Typical timing diagram.

transition of B from 1 to 0 causes X to change to 0. The change of A from 1 to 0 does not affect X, but the following transition of A causes X to change to 1. The output Y is shown to change states 25 μS after a change in X.

Sometimes the current state of a variable is unimportant and the timing diagram is to indicate only a change of state. The S-shaped curves superimposed on the timing diagram for Y imply that the state of Y at a particular time is unknown, but regardless of the current state a change will take place at the indicated point. If the current state is 0, the state will become 1, and vice versa.

Many sequential networks need to be synchronized by a time standard called a *clock*. A clock is a circuit that generates an evenly spaced train of pulses. The time between consecutive pulses is called its *period*, and the number of pulses per second (the reciprocal of the period) is called its *frequency*. The output of a clock is illustrated graphically in Fig. 4-2. Although this figure shows the amount of time the clock is 1 to be exactly half of the period, this is not always the case. This amount divided by the period and expressed as a percentage is called the clock's *duty cycle*. Quite often a clock's duty cycle must fall within a specified range (e.g., the clock for an Intel 8088 requires a duty cycle of at least 33 percent).

This chapter introduces the fundamental sequential circuits, called flip-flops, and uses these circuits with the gates discussed in Chapter 3 to build a variety of computer-related circuits. Section 4-6 introduces the more important sequential network design tools. Although space does not permit a thorough discussion of timing problems and their associated design considerations, some of these problems are pointed out and classified in Sections 4-7 and 4-8. The last two sections are concerned with special electronic devices that are needed in connecting computer components together.

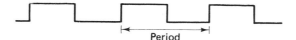

Period   **Figure 4-2** Typical clock output.

4-1 FLIP-FLOPS AND LATCHES

A primary component necessary to the construction of a computer is a device capable of storing information. Such components are called *memory devices* and, because computers are of a two-state nature, computer memory devices are called *bistable devices*. As the name implies, a bistable device is one that can assume either of two possible states and will maintain its current state until an external excitation causes it to change states. (The use of the word *memory* here is generic, and is not to be confused with the specific usage regarding a "computer's memory.") The most common electronic bistable devices are called *flip-flops*, and the most common types of flip-flops are the R-S, J-K, T, and D types.

4-1-1 R-S Flip-Flops

The most fundamental flip-flop is the *reset-set (R-S) flip-flop*. Figure 4-3a shows a logic diagram for an R-S flip-flop, and Fig. 4-3b shows its defining table. The R-S flip-flop has three inputs and two outputs. One of the inputs is denoted by C and is often a clock input that synchronizes the action of the flip-flop with its surrounding network. Therefore, C is sometimes called the clock input. The input designated R is the reset input and the one designated S is the set input. The two outputs are always in opposite states from each other and are denoted Q and $\overline{Q}$. Because both the R and S inputs are ANDed with the clock, they have no effect on the state of the flip-flop while the clock is in state 0. In this case, if

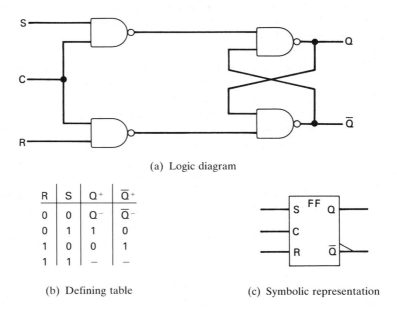

(a) Logic diagram

R	S	Q^+	$\overline{Q}^+$
0	0	Q^-	$\overline{Q}^-$
0	1	1	0
1	0	0	1
1	1	–	–

(b) Defining table

(c) Symbolic representation

Figure 4-3   Definition of an R-S flip-flop and the symbol used to represent it.

$Q = 1$, the output $\overline{Q} = 0$ and this causes Q to be maintained at 1. Hence, the network is stable. Similarly, if $\overline{Q} = 1$, then $Q = 0$ and this causes $\overline{Q}$ to be maintained at 1. Once again the network is stable. If the clock is raised to 1, the network will not change if $R = S = 0$, will take on the state $Q = 0$ and $\overline{Q} = 1$ if $R = 1$ and $S = 0$, and will take on the state $Q = 1$ and $\overline{Q} = 0$ if $R = 0$ and $S = 1$.

Because changes in the output states cannot occur while the clock is in its 0 state, for defining purposes the most significant changes occur when there is a clock transition. Therefore, tables for flip-flops must indicate the output states just prior to and just after a change in the clock input, assuming that the other inputs are held constant during this time. The table in Fig. 4-3b gives the outputs that result from applying three of the possible four input states while the clock changes from 0 to 1.

If R and S are both 1, then $Q = \overline{Q} = 1$, but this is not considered to be a useful combination of inputs, and therefore the entry made in the truth table has not been specified. The superscript $-$ on the outputs Q and $\overline{Q}$ indicates the outputs just prior to the clock becoming a 1, and the superscript $+$ indicates the outputs just after the clock becomes 1. The values for R and S are those that exist when the clock switches from 0 to 1. There are several similar symbols used to represent an R-S flip-flop; the one that will be used in this book is shown in Fig. 4-3c.

While the clock is high (i.e., in state 1), the outputs will follow the changes in the inputs. During the times that R and S are both 0, no changes in the outputs will take place. However, if S is pulsed, Q will be *set* (become 1), regardless of its previous state, and $\overline{Q}$ will be *cleared* (become zero). Conversely, if R is pulsed, Q will be cleared, or *reset*, and $\overline{Q}$ will become 1. A representative timing diagram for an R-S flip-flop is shown in Fig. 4-4.

If the clock input is a constant one, the outputs will follow the changes in inputs at all times. When this is the case, the C input terminal is usually deleted from the R-S flip-flop symbol shown in Fig. 4-3c.

The R-S flip-flop discussed above uses the C input to determine whether or not the inputs are to be recognized, and is called an *R-S latch*. It is often desirable

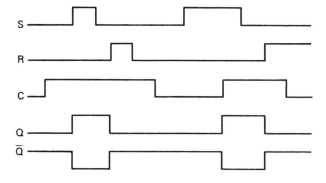

Figure 4-4   Typical timing diagram for an R-S flip-flop.

to have a flip-flop change states only at the very beginning (or the very end) of a clock pulse. Such flip-flops are called *edge-triggered flip-flops*. A change from 0 to 1 is called a *positive transition* and the positive transition of the clock pulse is called the *leading edge* of the pulse. A change of 1 to 0 is called a *negative transition* and the negative transition of a clock pulse is called its *trailing edge*. If the logic diagram shown in Fig. 4-3 is modified by inverting the clock signal and then using this signal as third inputs to the input NAND gates, the resulting network is as shown in Fig. 4-5. As will be discussed later, logic gates do not react instantaneously; therefore, both the C input and the output of the inverter will momentarily be 1. This will cause the outputs of the input NAND gates to reflect the R and S inputs only during the very beginning of the clock pulse. An R-S flip-flop of this type is called a *positive edge-triggered R-S flip-flop*. By adding an inverter to the clock input, a flip-flop whose outputs change only during the trailing edge of the clock pulse is obtained. The result is a *negative edge-triggered R-S flip-flop*.

4-1-2 J-K Flip-Flops

A *J-K flip-flop* is an R-S flip-flop that has been modified by feeding the outputs back and ANDing them with the inputs as shown in Fig. 4-6a. This produces the input-output relationship defined by the table in Fig. 4-6b. The only difference between this table and the one that defines the R-S flip-flop is that the $C = J = K = 1$ combination is meaningful and results in the output states being reversed. The symbol used to represent a J-K flip-flop is given in Fig. 4-6c. The J-K flip-flop shown must be constructed from an edge-triggered R-S flip-flop; otherwise the $C = J = K = 1$ state would be unstable. Although J-K flip-flops that are not edge-triggered could be made, they are not often used.

One important modification to the J-K flip-flop is called a *master-slave J-K flip-flop* and is shown in Fig. 4-7a. This flip-flop provides its output at the trailing edge (the same as a negative edge-triggered J-K flip-flop) but, by properly adjusting the trigger levels on the master and slave, the slave can be disconnected from the master while the master is being set and the master can be disconnected from its

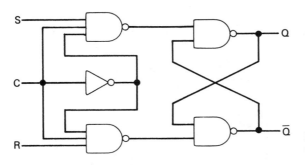

Figure 4-5 Logic diagram of a positive edge-triggered flip-flop.

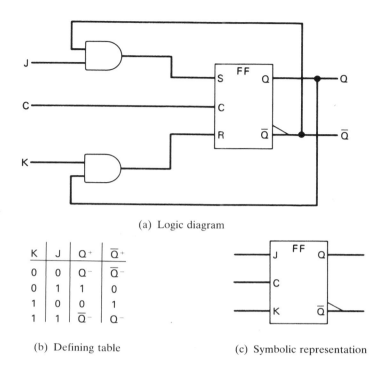

(a) Logic diagram

K	J	Q⁺	Q̄⁺
0	0	Q^-	$\bar{Q}^-$
0	1	1	0
1	0	0	1
1	1	$\bar{Q}^-$	Q^-

(b) Defining table   (c) Symbolic representation

Figure 4-6   Definition of a J-K flip-flop and its symbolic representation.

inputs while the slave is being set.   Figure 4-7b gives a timing diagram that illustrates the timing sequence.   The slopes in the clock signal have been exaggerated so that the trigger-level differences can be shown.   With a simple J-K flip-flop, an input transition while it is being triggered can cause the output to be temporarily unstable. The isolation of the master from the slave while the master is being set eliminates this problem and guarantees a clean switching action at the output.

4-1-3 T Flip-Flops

A *toggle flip-flop* (*T flip-flop*) is a flip-flop that has only one input and whose output states are reversed each time the input is pulsed.   Figure 4-8a gives a logic diagram for a T flip-flop.   In the figure the R-S flip-flop symbol must represent an edge-triggered flip-flop; if the flip-flop were not edge-triggered, the network would be unstable.   Figure 4-8b gives the defining table for the T flip-flop, and Fig. 4-8c shows the symbol used to represent it.   As will be seen later, T flip-flops are frequently used in the design of counters.   A T flip-flop could be obtained from a J-K flip-flop by permanently applying 1's to the J and K inputs (see Exercise 5).

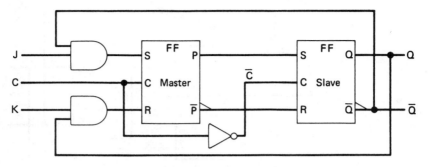

(a) Logic diagram for the master-slave J-K flip-flop

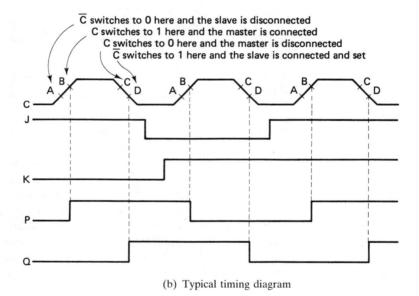

(b) Typical timing diagram

Figure 4-7 Master-slave J-K flip-flop and a representative timing diagram.

4-1-4 D Flip-Flops

A *data flip-flop* (*D flip-flop*) has two inputs, a clock input and an input labeled D, which is such that the Q output is equal to the D input whenever the clock input is set to 1, and is otherwise not affected by the D input. It is easily constructed from an R-S flip-flop by letting D be the S input and connecting R to D through an inverter. A logic diagram for a D flip-flop is given in Fig. 4-9a; its defining table is given in Fig. 4-9b, and the symbol used to represent it is shown in Fig.

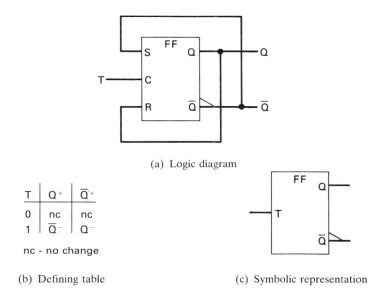

(a) Logic diagram

T	Q^+	$\overline{Q}^+$
0	nc	nc
1	$\overline{Q}^-$	Q^-

nc - no change

(b) Defining table   (c) Symbolic representation

Figure 4-8   Definition of a T flip-flop and the symbol used to represent it.

4-9c. D flip-flops are used in a variety of sequential network designs, including register designs.

A D flip-flop can be of the edge-triggered type, but if it is not, the clock controls whether or not the Q output follows the D input.   When this is the case, a D flip-flop is called a *D latch*.

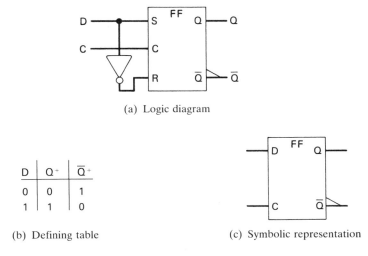

(a) Logic diagram

D	Q^+	$\overline{Q}^+$
0	0	1
1	1	0

(b) Defining table   (c) Symbolic representation

Figure 4-9   Definition of a D flip-flop and the symbol used to represent it.

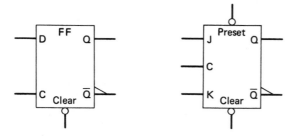

(a) Symbolic
representation of
a D flip-flop with
a Clear input

(b) Symbolic
representation of
a J-K flip-flop
with Clear and
Preset inputs

Figure 4-10 Symbol changes
corresponding to the Clear and Preset
inputs.

4-1-5 Clear and Preset Inputs

A common variation on a flip-flop is to provide it with an input that can clear and/ or an input that can set the output Q, regardless of the state of the other inputs. Fig. 4-10a gives the symbolic representation of a D flip-flop with the clear feature, and Fig. 4-10b shows the symbolic representation of a J-K flip-flop that incorporates both variations. In both figures the Clear input is used to clear Q, and in Fig. 4-10b the Preset input is used to set Q. The inverters (small circles) shown at these inputs reflect the normal usage in which these inputs are of a negative logic nature; that is, a 0 input will initiate the action instead of a 1 input.

4-2 REGISTERS

Thus far, only the single-bit storage capacity of a single flip-flop has been considered. Obviously, any number of flip-flops could be placed in parallel to form several bits of storage. When this is done, the resulting network is called a *register*. Figure 4-11 illustrates a 4-bit register constructed from four D flip-flops. The common clock input Load permits new information to be loaded, and the common Read line and associated AND gates provide a controlled readout mechanism. (Note that the clock input does not come from a clock, but from a control line.) Registers are used anywhere within a computer where it is necessary to store a group of bits. Some of the places where registers are needed are discussed in Chapter 5.

4-3 SHIFT REGISTERS AND DATA TRANSMISSION

Frequently, it is necessary to shift the bits in a register either to the left or right. A register that is capable of performing this function is, naturally enough, called a *shift register*. Shift registers are classified according to their inputs and outputs.

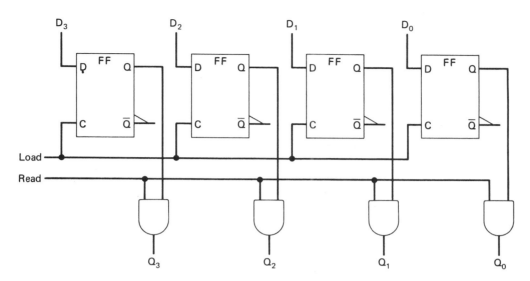

Figure 4-11   Four-bit register.

Both the input and the output may be classified as serial or as parallel. A *serial* input is one for which the input arrives 1 bit at a time, and each time a bit arrives the register is shifted by one to accommodate the new bit. A *parallel* input is one for which the inputs are all loaded at the same time, such as they are for the 4-bit nonshifting register shown in Fig. 4-11. Serial and parallel outputs are similarly defined.

One of the most important applications of shift registers is in converting between types of data communications. Most computer systems include two types of binary data transmission. One type consists of sending the 1's and 0's representing a piece of data, hereafter called a *character*, over the required number of lines simultaneously. If an 8-bit character were to be sent, the voltage levels corresponding to the 1's and 0's would simply be applied to eight different lines at the same time. This is called *parallel data transmission*. Usually, the number of lines employed in parallel transmission is greater than the number of data bits. The extra lines are control lines that are used by the transmitting device to signal the receiving device when data are ready to be read, and by the receiving device to signal the transmitting device that the data have been read. The passing back and forth of signals on the control lines during a transmission is called *handshaking*. Sometimes one of the control lines is used to transmit clock pulses and the timing of all other signals is controlled by these pulses. When this is done, the data transmission is said to be *synchronous*. A transmission that is not controlled by a common clock signal is said to be *asynchronous*.

The second type of transmission is more complicated. In this case the data are sent over a single line in sequential fashion. For each character the transmitter and receiver must divide the period of time used to transmit the data into subin-

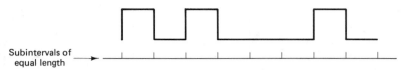

Subintervals of equal length

Figure 4-12   Timing diagram of an ASCII coded E as it is being transmitted serially.

tervals, one subinterval for each data bit.   An 8-bit character would occupy eight sub-intervals.   This is called *serial data transmission*.   A timing diagram showing how an ASCII coded letter E would appear as it is being transmitted serially is shown in Fig. 4-12.   Once again, control lines may be used for handshaking or synchronization.   Serial transmission is often made over a single pair of lines and the beginning and end of transmissions are marked by special bits.   One very common kind of serial transmission is considered in detail in Chapter 10.

The obvious advantage of parallel transmission is that, because several bits can be sent simultaneously, higher information transfer rates can be attained.   The disadvantage is that more wires (or communication channels) are needed than with serial transmission.   Conseqeuntly, whenever distance is a factor, serial communication is most often chosen; but if the transfer rate must be high, parallel communication may be required.

Because a computer system usually includes both types of data communications, it must also include a means of converting from one type to the other.   Figure 4-13a shows a serial input/parallel output 4-bit shift register that could be used as a serial-to-parallel code converter, and Fig. 4-13b gives a parallel input/serial output shift register that could be used as a 4-bit parallel-to serial converter.   The flip-flops in both figures must be edge-triggered.   In Fig. 4-13a it is assumed that a negative logic Reset precedes each data character, thus clearing the shift register.   Then each clock pulse loads a data bit until the register is full.   After the 4-bit character has been loaded, it can be read from the parallel output lines D_0 through D_3.   In Fig. 4-13b, once the data are made available at input lines D_3 through D_0, they can be loaded into the shift register by applying a Load signal.   Then four clock pulses can be used to cause the 4-bit character to appear sequentially at the output.   Because a zero is applied to the leftmost flip-flop, the register will be cleared by the readout operation and thereby made ready for the next input. Also, clearing can be done by applying a reset signal.

Within the CPU of a computer, several registers are needed to provide temporary storage while the various operations are being carried out.   Many of these operations, such as multiplication and division, require shifting.   Because high information-transfer rates are always needed within the CPU, all modern computers use parallel input/parallel output shift registers.   Figure 4-14 shows a 4-bit register capable of shifting left or right.   This register is loaded the same way as the one shown in Fig. 4-13b and read the same way as the one shown in Fig. 4-11.   Its current contents can be shifted left by applying a 1 to the Left shift line and right by applying a 1 to the Right shift line.   The D flip-flops must be positive edge-

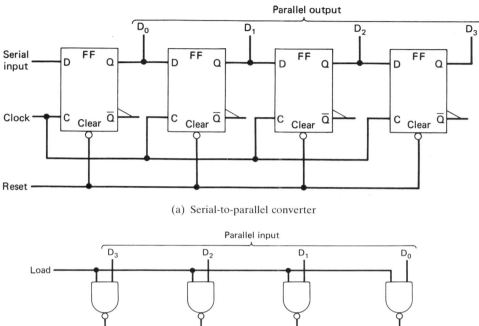

(a) Serial-to-parallel converter

(b) Parallel-to-serial converter

Figure 4-13 Sequential networks for converting between serial and parallel binary data transmissions.

triggered to avoid indefinite results and to guarantee exactly one shift for each pulse on a shift line. Also, pulses should not be applied to both the Left shift and Right shift lines at the same time.

The positive edge-triggering of the flip-flops shown in this figure could cause problems because this forces the design to be arranged so that the D inputs to the flip-flops must be stabilized before the C input is sensed. The problem is easily overcome by placing a delay device in the C input line. Delay devices and timing problems are discussed in Section 4-7.

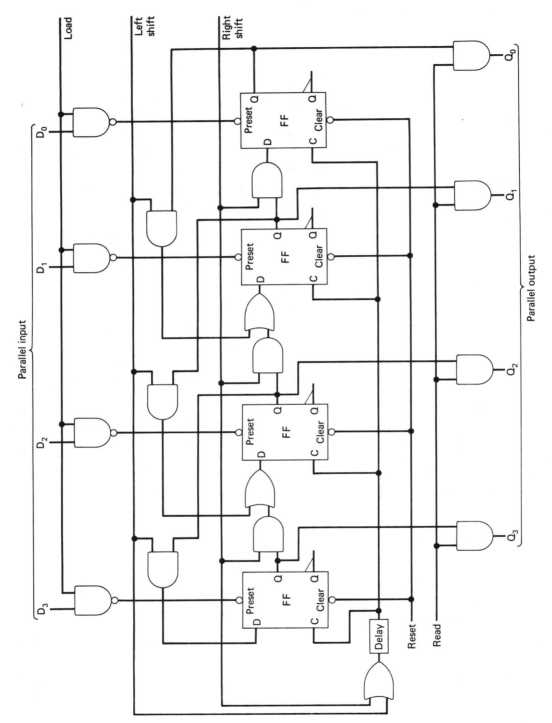

Figure 4-14 Logic diagram for a register that can shift either left or right.

A left shift will cause the leftmost bit to be lost and the right bit to be replaced with a 0.   A right shift will cause the rightmost bit to be lost and the left bit to be replaced with a 0.   An important variation of this network is obtained by connecting the output of the rightmost flip-flop to the input of the left flip-flop through an AND with a Rotate line.   Then, by setting the Rotate line to 1 before applying a Right shift signal, the rightmost bit can be rotated into the left bit.   By similarly connecting the output of the leftmost flip-flop to the input of the right flip-flop, the Rotate and Left shift lines could be used to get a rotation in the other direction. These modifications are left to the reader.   (See Exercise 6.)

4-4 COUNTERS AND FREQUENCY DIVIDERS

Another important type of sequential network is one that can count in binary.   A *binary counter* is used to count and store the number of pulses arriving at its input. If the pulses are evenly spaced with a known period, a counter can be used as a timer whose resolution is one-half this period.   Conversely, if the period is unknown but the total time over which the counting takes place is known, the counter can be used to measure the frequency of the input.   When a counter is used for the latter purpose, it is called a *frequency counter*.   Figure 4-15a shows a 4-bit counter capable of counting from 0000 through 1111 (0 through 15).   The T flip-flops are negatively edge-triggered and, therefore, the incrementing takes place on the trailing edge of the input pulses.   Incrementing at the leading edge could be obtained by putting an inverter at the input to the first T flip-flop.

The Enable input provides a means of turning the counting process on and off, and the Reset input provides a means of clearing the entire register.   Note that the sixteenth pulse has the same effect as the Reset input: it will clear all 4 bits.   However, if the output of the MSB were used as an input to another 4-bit counter, the sixteenth pulse would cause the LSB in the second counter to be set. Thus counters having a small number of bits can easily be cascaded to produce a counter with a large number of bits.

A counter can also be used to produce a pulse train with a lower frequency. Figure 4-15b gives the timing diagram of the input and the outputs of the four flip-flops.   From this figure it is seen that the outputs of the first, second, third, and fourth flip-flops have respective frequencies that are one-half, one-fourth, one-eighth, and one-sixteenth that of the input.   By selecting one of these outputs, a clock with a frequency that is only a fraction of the input frequency is obtained. When a counter is used in this way, it is called a *frequency divider*.

By designing external circuitry to reset when 1001 is incremented, one can construct a counter that will output a 1 to the next counter and cause a reset after the tenth input pulse.   Such a 4-bit counter is called a *decade counter*, and a logic diagram of a decade counter is given in Fig. 4-16.   Note that this design includes an inverter at the first T input so that the incrementing is initiated by the leading edge of the input pulse.

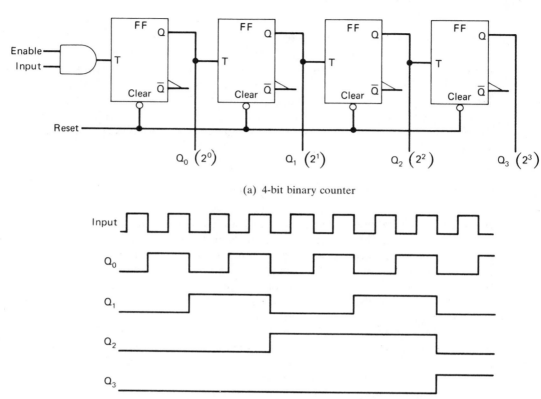

(a) 4-bit binary counter

(b) Timing diagram for the input and the outputs

Figure 4-15 Four-bit binary counter and the associated timing diagram showing the timing relationships between the input and the various outputs.

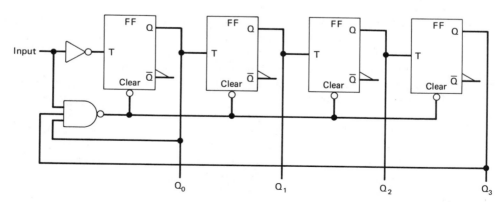

Figure 4-16 Decade counter.

4-5 MONOSTABLE MULTIVIBRATORS

A flip-flop is such that its output Q is set to 1 whenever the proper inputs are applied and will maintain the 1 state until the inputs dictate that it be reset to 0. In some designs it is necessary that the 1 output be maintained only a short period of time and then automatically return to 0. This could be accomplished by connecting to the output of the flip-flop a device that outputs a pulse whenever a 1 is applied to its input. A device of this type is called a *monostable multivibrator* and is denoted by the symbol shown in Fig. 4-17a. A small circle at the input of this symbol is used to indicate that a pulse is triggered by a negative transition. A small circle at the output indicates that the output pulse is negative going.

Figure 4-17b shows a logic diagram for a simple monostable multivibrator that is triggered by a positive transition and outputs a positive pulse. When T goes to 1, the output of the left gate goes to 0. Because the voltage across the capacitor cannot change instantaneously, the input to the right inverter must also be 0, hence its output must go to 1. As the capacitor charges through resistor R, the input to the right inverter once again approaches 1. When this input reaches the voltage level that causes the inverter to switch, the output state will again go to 0. This will cause the output of the left gate to return to 1 whenever the T input goes to 0, and will cause the capacitor to discharge. The width of the output

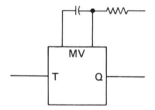

(a) Symbolic representation

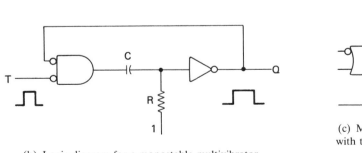

(b) Logic diagram for a monostable multivibrator

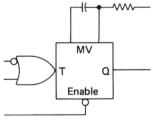

(c) Monostable multivibrator with two inputs and an enable pin

Figure 4-17   Monostable multivibrator design and the symbols for representing monostable multivibrators.

pulse will be proportional to the product $(R + R_0)C$, where R_0 is the output resistance of the left gate.

The input pulse may return to 0 at any time after the output pulse is initiated; it does not need to wait until the output pulse is complete. However, the capacitor must have time to discharge completely before the next input pulse occurs, because a residual charge on the capacitor will shorten the output pulse. Generally, the capacitor is considered to be completely discharged after $4(R + R_0)C$ seconds.

Frequently, monostable multivibrator designs are more complicated than the one shown and provide more flexibility in adjusting the ratio of pulse width to time between pulses. Other common features include an inverted enable pin, which can be used to turn the multivibrator on or off, and a second input, which allows the output pulse to be triggered by either a positive transition or a negative transition, according to which input is used. The symbol for indicating a monostable multivibrator with these features is shown in Fig. 4-17c. Some multivibrators also have two outputs that provide both positive and negative pulses.

4-6 SEQUENTIAL NETWORK DESIGN AIDS

As with combinational networks, as sequential networks become more complex, design aids are needed to analyze and design them. However, because timing becomes an important factor when working with sequential networks, the use of design aids and algorithms is not as straightforward. As a result, a complete discussion of the sequential network design procedures cannot be given here, but it is useful to introduce some basic concepts associated with sequential design. More thorough discussions can be found in the bibliography at the end of the chapter.

The design of a sequential network is primarily based on the states of the networks. A *state* is determined by a 0–1 combination of the outputs of the flip-flops in the network. If a network contains n flip-flops, then the theoretically possible number of states would be 2^n. However, the actual number of states that the network can be in may be less because the construction of the network may not allow some output combinations to occur. If m is the number of states that can occur, then

$$2^n \geqq m$$

Each state is assigned a unique 0–1 combination of the outputs of the flip-flops.

Since a sequential network depends on its current state as well as its inputs, a truth table cannot adequately describe it. Two tables are needed, one called the *state table*, which indicates the new states as a function of the inputs and current state, and one called the *output table*, which gives the outputs as a function of the current state. Typical state and output tables that assume two inputs A and B, five states S_0, S_1, S_2, S_3, and S_4, and three outputs X, Y, and Z are shown in Figs. 4-18a and 4-18b. In Fig. 4-18a the states are listed in the column on the left and

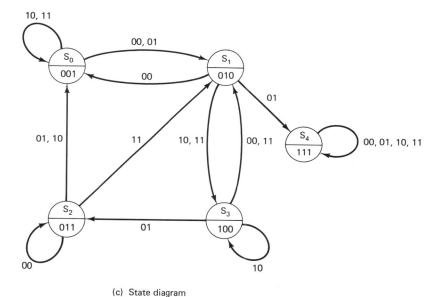

AB	00	01	11	10
S_0	S_1	S_1	S_0	S_0
S_1	S_0	S_4	S_3	S_3
S_2	S_2	S_0	S_1	S_0
S_3	S_1	S_2	S_1	S_3
S_4	S_4	S_4	S_4	S_4

(a) State table

	X	Y	Z
S_0	0	0	1
S_1	0	1	0
S_2	0	1	1
S_3	1	0	0
S_4	1	1	1

(b) Output table

(c) State diagram

Figure 4-18 Principal sequential network design aids.

the possible inputs are listed across the top.   The table entries are the new states after the inputs take effect.   The entry in the second column and third row indicates that if the current state is S_2 and the input is 01, then the new state will be S_0.   In Fig. 4-18b the leftmost column gives the states and the remaining columns give the corresponding outputs.   Note that neither of these tables gives the assignments of the states to the flip-flop outputs and this would need to be done separately.   For example, assuming three flip-flops, S_0 could be assigned 010, S_1 could be assigned 011, and so on.   Only five of the possible 3-bit combinations would be used, but two flip-flops would be insufficient if five states are required because $2^2 \leqq 5$.

The information in the state and output tables can be combined into a single graphics display, as shown in Fig. 4-18c.   A display such as this is called a *state diagram*.   The circles represent the states and the notation inside the circles gives the symbol for the state and the corresponding output.   The arrows represent the

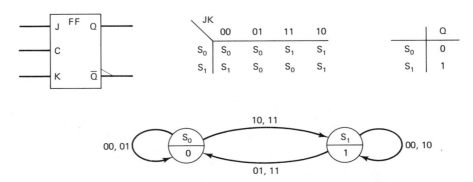

Figure 4-19 Description of a J-K flip-flop using a state table, an output table, and a state diagram.

transitions between the states, and the 0–1 combinations next to the arrows indicate all input combinations that initiate the transitions (e.g., if the current state is S_2, both 01 and 10 would cause a transition to S_0).

The state table, output table, and state diagram of a network consisting of only a J-K flip-flop are shown in Fig. 4-19. S_0 corresponds to $Q = 0$ and S_1 to $Q = 1$. The clock input to the network is not considered an input to the network but simply a signal to initiate the transitions. This is normally the case.

Figure 4-20 shows a more complicated network involving logic gates as well as J-K flip-flops. Also given in the figure are the corresponding Boolean expressions for the inputs to the flip-flops, the state table, the output table, and the state diagram. The state assignments that are assumed are $S_0 = 00$, $S_1 = 01$, $S_2 = 11$, and $S_3 = 10$ where the first bit corresponds to the upper flip-flop and the second bit to the lower flip-flop. It is seen from the state diagram that this network

Sequences through the outputs 00, 01, 11, and 10 as clock pulses arrive while $A = 1$.

Has no change of output if $A = B = 0$ when a clock pulse arrives.

Resets the output to 00 if $A = 0$ and $B = 1$ when there is a clock pulse.

A code that is ordered such that only 1 bit changes with each increment through the code is called a *Gray code*. The network in Fig. 4-19 is an example of a Gray code generator.

Note that the analysis of this network proceeds by first finding the input expressions for the flip-flops, then deriving the state and output tables, and finally drawing the state diagram. On the other hand, the design of a sequential network would tend to follow the reverse of this procedure, with the state diagram being developed first. The state diagram could then be used to define the state and output tables, which, in turn, could be used to develop the flip-flop inputs and the logic diagram.

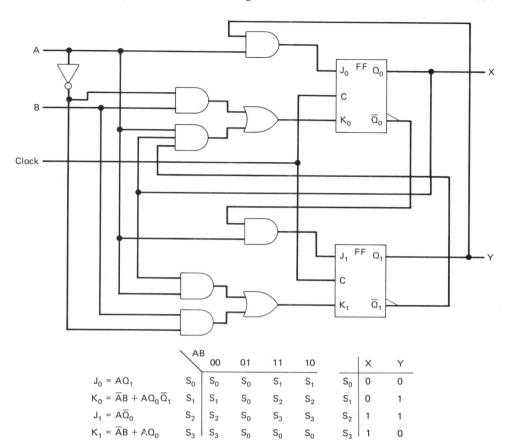

	AB					X	Y
		00	01	11	10		
$J_0 = AQ_1$	S_0	S_0	S_0	S_1	S_1	S_0	0	0
$K_0 = \overline{A}B + AQ_0\overline{Q}_1$	S_1	S_1	S_0	S_2	S_2	S_1	0	1
$J_1 = A\overline{Q}_0$	S_2	S_2	S_0	S_3	S_3	S_2	1	1
$K_1 = \overline{A}B + AQ_0$	S_3	S_3	S_0	S_0	S_0	S_3	1	0

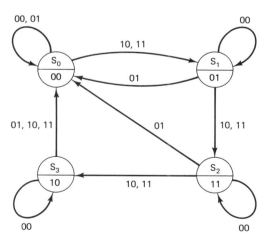

Figure 4-20   Analysis of a Gray code generator.

AB	00	01	11	10
S_0	$S_0/0$	$S_0/0$	$S_1/0$	$S_1/0$
S_1	$S_1/0$	$S_0/0$	$S_2/1$	$S_2/1$
S_2	$S_2/0$	$S_0/0$	$S_3/0$	$S_3/0$
S_3	$S_3/0$	$S_0/0$	$S_0/1$	$S_0/1$

(a) State/transition output table

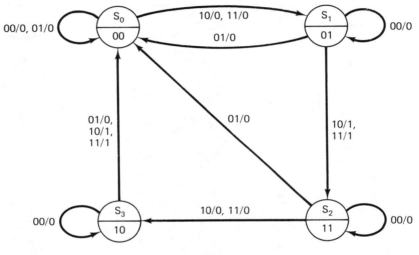

(b) State diagram

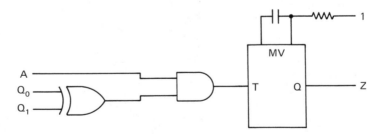

(c) Added logic for transition output

Figure 4-21 Modified Gray code generator.

Important variations of the state table and diagram are needed when some of the outputs are caused by certain combinations of the current states and inputs. These outputs are called *transition outputs*. For example, suppose that a Gray code generator is wanted that outputs a pause at Z whenever there is an increment from 01 to 11 or from 10 to 00 while $A = 1$. The required modifications to the state table and diagram and logic diagram given in Fig. 4-20 are shown in Fig. 4-21. The pulse could be produced by ANDing A and the exclusive OR of Q_0 and Q_1 and applying the output to a monostable multivibrator. It is assumed that inputs are applied long enough before the clock pulse that causes the change of state so that the monostable multivibrator will be activated.

There could be several transition outputs that depend on the current state, and the inputs and these outputs could even change more than once between clock pulses to reflect changes in the inputs. However, the above example represents the normal case in which only one change of inputs would occur between clock pulses.

4-7 DELAYS

No electronic circuits react instantaneously, and consequently, all such circuits, including logic gates and flip-flops, have delays associated with them. The length of these delays depends on the resistances and capacitances built into the circuits. Sometimes these inherent delays are undesirable, but other times they are needed. Sometimes if the natural delays are not sufficient, special circuits, called *delay devices*, are included in a design for the sole purpose of creating a delay of a particular length. For example, a delay device was required in the shift register design in Fig. 4-14 so that the D inputs to the flip-flops would have time to stabilize before the clock input is applied.

For a delay device, the output is the same as the input except that the output occurs at a later time than the input. The amount of delay is referred to as the delay time. Figure 4-22a gives the symbol for a delay device, and Fig. 4-22b shows how such a device could be constructed from inverters. The amount of time it takes for a logic gate's or flip-flop's output to reflect its input(s) is called its *switching time*. Therefore, if $2n$ inverters are used to build a delay device, then the delay time of the device is $2n$ times the switching time of the inverters. If an odd number of inverters are used, the output is not only delayed but is also inverted. Adjustable

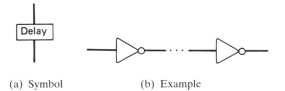

(a) Symbol   (b) Example

Figure 4-22 Symbol for a delay device and an example showing how one could be constructed from inverters.

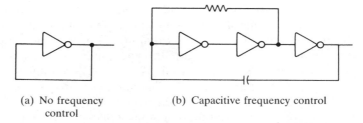

(a) No frequency
   control

(b) Capacitive frequency control

Figure 4-23   Clock designs using inverters and feedback.

delays can be obtained by including a variable resistor-capacitor circuit in the delay
device's design.

Figure 4-23a shows how a clock could be made by using the delay of a simple
inverter. If the output of the inverter is initially 0, the feedback will cause the
input to also be 0. Therefore, the inverter will switch and the output will become
1. This 1 will be fed back and the inverter will again switch, causing the output
to become 0 once again. This action will continue indefinitely and the output will
be a pulse train whose period is twice the switching time of the inverter. Figure
4-23b shows a slightly more complicated clock in which the time required to charge
the capacitor determines the period. Although the clocks in Fig. 4-23 could be
used in some applications, they may be deficient in two areas: (1) their frequency
may drift (change slightly with time), and (2) their waveshape may not be sharp
enough. For those applications that need improvement in these areas, a more
sophisticated design that includes a crystal oscillator may be required.

When logic gates and/or flip-flops are cascaded (i.e., placed so that the output
of one provides the input to the next) the delays produce an effect known as *ripple*.
A good example of ripple is seen by examining the counter design in Fig. 4-15.
Here the final output is not present until the effect of the input has had time to
ripple through all four of the T flip-flops. The ripple time would be four times
the switching time of a T flip-flop.

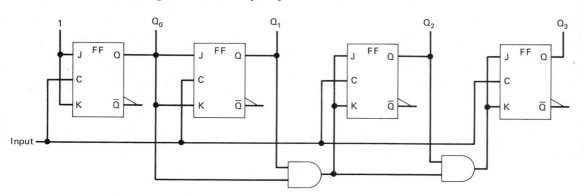

Figure 4-24   Synchronous counter.

Because the switching time of a single gate or flip-flop is usually only a few nanoseconds, cascading four such devices would seldom cause any difficulties. But if a counter that will count to one million is wanted, then 20 flip-flops must be cascaded and this could cause a problem. To lessen or eliminate ripple, various carry-forward techniques are used. For the counter example, the design could be improved by using J-K flip-flops and adding AND gates, as shown in Fig. 4-24. In this design, some outputs are carried forward so that the third and fourth outputs will be established sooner. Because all of the flip-flops receive the input at the same time, this circuit is known as a *synchronous counter*.

4-8 *TIMING CONSIDERATIONS*

Because of the time element, the design of sequential networks is much more difficult than that of combinational networks. There are many reasons for this, and there are many approaches to solving timing-related problems. Although these problems have been thoroughly studied and appropriate design techniques exist, a complete discussion of these problems and design techniques would be too long to include here. Consequently, we must be content with considering the major problem classifications.

Many timing problems are solved by controlling all flip-flops in the network with a clock and designing the network in such a way that the values of the states and outputs are only important when the leading (or trailing) edge of the clock pulse arrives. The states and outputs can change during the intervening time without being noticed. Networks such as this are known as *synchronous networks* because they are synchronized by the clock. Other networks are said to be *asynchronous*. Synchronizing a network allows spurious intermediate activity to settle out before the next transition is allowed, thus making the next transition predictable. However, the clock's period must be long enough to guarantee that all unintended states and outputs have passed.

Unfortunately, few networks can be completely synchronized, and it is necessary for us to consider some of the consequences of having asynchronous areas within a design. Figure 4-25 demonstrates a class of problems called *races*. If more than one flip-flop is to change at the same time, a race exists because the switching times of the flip-flops may differ even if they are of the same construction. A *noncritical race* is one in which the final outcome is not in doubt, even though there may be unintended states before it is achieved.

The network in Fig. 4-25a is an example of a noncritical race. Suppose that initially $A = X = Y = 0$ and the flip-flops are positive edge-triggered. Depending on which flip-flop reacts faster, the next state could be $X = 0$, $Y = 1$ or $X = 1$, $Y = 0$, but in any case the final state would be $X = Y = 1$.

Figure 4-25b shows a network containing a *critical race*. If both D flip-flops are latches, the J-K flip-flop is negative edge-triggered, and $A = B = X$ are initially 0 while Enable is held at 1, then a simultaneous change of A and B to 1 may or

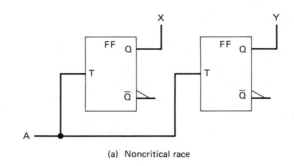

(a) Noncritical race

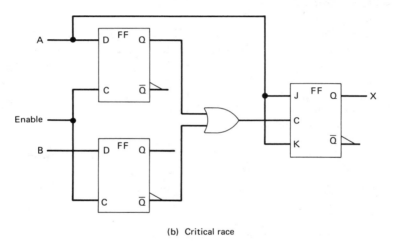

(b) Critical race

Figure 4-25 Sequential networks that contain races.

may not cause X to become 1. If the upper D latch reacts faster than the lower, then the C input to the J-K flip-flop would not change and X would remain at 0. Otherwise, C would briefly become 0 and the negative transition would cause X to become 1.

Figure 4-26a shows a different situation in which a problem arises because the switching time of a gate momentarily causes its inputs not to be reflected at its output. Such problems are called *hazards*. For the network shown in the figure, suppose that $X = A = 0$, $B = C = 1$, the T flip-flop is negative edge-triggered, and that A changes to 1. Then X will change to 1 if the upper gate is faster than the lower gate; otherwise, it will remain at 0.

A hazard that involves the change of only a single input can be easily eliminated by adding redundant gates. To see how this is done, the Karnaugh map of the combinational part of the network in Fig. 4-26a is given in Fig. 4-26b. The hazard is due to the uncertainty associated with the transition between the prime implicants $\overline{A}B$ and AC. This uncertainty could be eliminated by adding the redundant prime implicant BC, which would force at least one input to the OR gate to be 1 at all times, thus guaranteeing that this gate's output would be held constant at 1.   A network that includes the new prime implicant is shown in Fig. 4-26c.

If two inputs are allowed to change simultaneously, there may still be a problem even when the prime implicants overlap.   To see this, consider the network in Fig. 4-27a.   In this case, if $A = B = 1$ and $C = 0$ and there is a change to $A = B = C = 0$, then the transition would follow one of the paths indicated by the arrows in Fig. 4-27b.   Depending on which path is taken, X would change or not change.

The last timing problem that we will consider can occur in any electronic circuit.   It is due to the fact that a signal does not travel down a wire (or conducting surface) instantaneously.   There is a *propagation delay* between the time a signal is applied at one end of a wire and the time it is seen at the other end.   The length of this delay is clearly dependent on the length of the wire, but it is also dependent

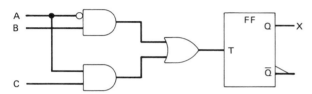

(a) Network with hazard

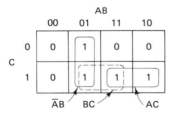

(b) Karnaugh map

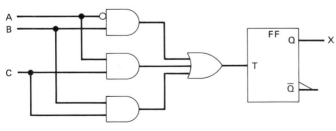

(c) Network without hazard

Figure 4-26 Example showing a hazard and how it can be eliminated.

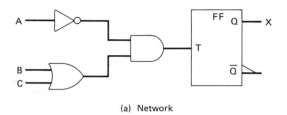

(a) Network

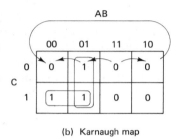

(b) Karnaugh map

Figure 4-27 Example demonstrating the difficulty associated with changing two inputs simultaneously.

on such things as the wire's position relative to other conductors. This means that two wires of the same length may have slightly different propagation delays. This is called *skew*. Propagation delays and skew are most likely to produce undesirable effects when cables (or other sets of conductors) are used to connect computer components together. Problems associated with propagation delay and skew are usually overcome by adding handshaking signals or by intentionally inserting a delay at the receiving end of the cable whose delay time is longer than any possible skew.

4-9 OUTPUT DEVICES

In discussing the overall layout of a computer system in Chapter 1, we saw that a microcomputer communicates with its memory and I/O devices through a multi-conductor cable called a bus. But most logic gates are made so that their outputs can only serve as inputs to other logic gates or digital circuits with reasonably high input impedance. Their outputs cannot be connected to the same piece of conducting material (such as a conductor in a bus) because, if one logic gate were to output a 1 while another is outputting a 0, the gate whose output is 1 would be damaged by the current caused by the voltage difference between the 1 and 0 outputs. This dilemma, which is illustrated in Fig. 4-28, prompts the question:

> How can the output of two devices be connected to a common bus so that they can take turns sending information to the computer?

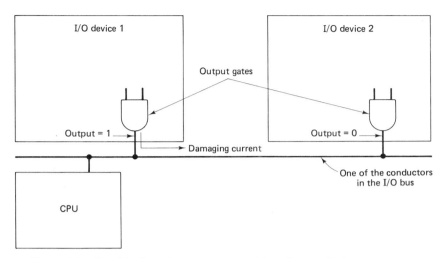

Figure 4-28 Possibly damaging current caused by tying two logic gate outputs together.

The answer lies in providing special components that will serve as buffers between the logic network of a device and the common conductor in the bus. The two most common logic gates that can have their outputs connected together are the tristate gate and the wire-ORed gate.

4-9-1 *Tristate Gates*

A *tristate gate* is a gate that has two inputs and one output but whose output can take on any one of three possible states: a 0, a 1, or a state that effectively disconnects the output. The latter output state is called the *high-impedance state* (or *floating state*). One of the inputs, called the *control input*, determines whether or not the output is in its high-impedance state (disconnected); if it is a 1, the output is connected, and if it is a 0, the output is disconnected. The other input determines whether the output is a 0 or a 1 when the output is connected. Figures 4-29a and 4-29b give the defining table and symbolic representation of a tristate gate, respectively. Most tristate gates also perform an inversion; they are called *tristate inverters* and are represented by adding a small circle to the output of the gate symbol.

It should be clear how tristate gates can be used to circumvent the problem described above. The tristate gates serve as the needed buffer and their outputs are disconnected until a device needs to output data to the bus. When a device is given control of the bus, it applies a 1 to the control inputs of its tristate gates and thereby connects its outputs to the bus. It must be made certain, however, that the design is such that no two devices can be given control of the bus at the same time.

Control	Input	Output
0	0	Disconnected
0	1	Disconnected
1	0	0
1	1	1

(a) Defining table

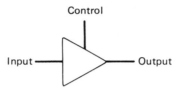

(b) Symbolic representation

Figure 4-29 Defining table and symbol for a tristate gate.

4-9-2 Wire-ORed Gates

A *wire-ORed gate* or *open collector gate* is nothing more than a specially designed gate that is such that its output can be directly tied to the outputs of other wire-ORed gates without any of the gates being damaged.   The state at the common point is 1 if all the gate outputs would normally be 1; otherwise, it is 0 (for this reason, some designers prefer the term *wire-ANDed*).   Such gates require that a resistor, called a *pull-up resistor*, be placed between the common output and the state 1 voltage.   If the common point is a bus conductor, the capacitance of the conductor and the resistance of the pull-up resistor form an *RC* circuit that lengthens the time it takes the output to change states.   Whether or not the increased time is significant depends on the length of the conductor, its capacitance per unit length, the resistance of the pull-up resistor (which is determined by the number of gates connected to the bus conductor), and the speed with which the output must react in order to operate satisfactorily.   In most microcomputer systems the switching time of the output is not that critical, but when it is inconvenient to use pull-up resistors or timing is a factor, tristate devices should be used.

Most often a wire-ORed connection is indicated by simply connecting the outputs together, as shown in Fig. 4-30a, but such a connection is sometimes emphasized by using the symbol shown in Fig. 4-30b.   (Verification of the outputs given in these figures is requested in Exercise 20.) In the latter case the pull-up resistor need not be shown.   Figure 4-30a shows how two signals, *A* and *B*, that are to be ORed can be output to a common conductor and then retrieved in such a way that the overall result is $A + B$.   Figure 4-30b shows another often used configuration.   The reason these configurations are typical is because the design of a wire-ORed gate is simplified if it includes an inversion.   As seen from these figures, by again inverting the signal as it is taken from the bus, the output is a sum (thus justifying the term *wire-ORed*).

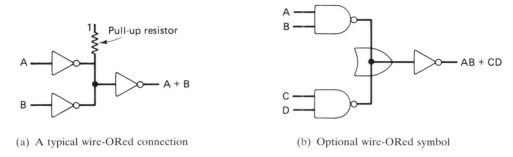

(a) A typical wire-ORed connection   (b) Optional wire-ORed symbol

Figure 4-30 Typical wire-ORed connections.

4-10 *DRIVERS*

Because most logic gates are made of very small transistors that are closely packed onto IC chips, anywhere from a few gates to thousands of gates can be put on a single chip.   There are several advantages to this miniaturization, but there is also one major disadvantage.   Because the transistors are so densely packed, the design must be such that each transistor will operate with moderate voltages and very small currents; otherwise, the electric fields and/or the amount of heat generated within the chip would be intolerable.   This means that only small currents can be obtained from the output pins.   Also, the output voltage will be limited to the voltages of state 0 and state 1.   If the outputs of one chip are to be used only as inputs to another chip, there is no problem because only small input currents will be needed and the required input voltages will be the same as those being output (assuming the chips are compatible).   On the other hand, if an output needs to control a device that needs a greater current or a different voltage, such as a lighted display or relay, an amplifying circuit must be placed between the chip output and the device.   Such circuits are called *drivers* or *repower gates* and will be indicated in logic diagrams by a rectangle enclosing the word "Driver."   For example, the BCD-to-seven segment converter given in Fig. 3-33 may, depending on the power requirements of the lighted displays, need drivers connected to outputs *a* through *g*.   Figure 4-31 shows how the output of a logic network could be connected to a relay.

Special note should be made of a very common type of logic called transistor-transistor logic (TTL).   For TTL logic the 0 and 1 states correspond to approxi-

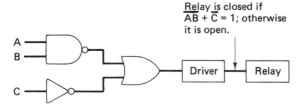

Figure 4-31 Typical application of a driver.

mately 0 and 5 volts, respectively.   If the states of a binary signal or logic device are these voltage levels, the signal or device is said to be *TTL-compatible*.

BIBLIOGRAPHY

1. SLOAN, M. E., *Computer Hardware and Organization* (Palo Alto, Calif.: Science Research Associates, Inc., 1976).
2. MANO, M. MORRIS, *Digital Logic & Computer Design* (Englewood Cliffs, N.J.: Prentice-Hall, 1979).
3. MARCUS, MITCHELL P., *Switching Circuits for Engineers,* 2nd ed.   (Englewood Cliffs, N.J.: Prentice-Hall, 1967).
4. ROTH, CHARLES H., *Fundamentals of Logic Design* (St. Paul, Minn.: West Publishing Co., 1975).
5. WIATROWSKI, CLAUDE A., and CHARLES H. HOUSE, *Logic Circuits and Microcomputer Systems* (New York: McGraw-Hill, 1980).
6. HILL, FREDERICK J., and GERALD R. PETERSON, *Digital Logic and Microprocessors* (New York: John Wiley, 1984).
7. HALL, DOUGLAS V., *Microprocessors and Digital Systems* (New York: McGraw-Hill, 1980).

EXERCISES

1. Sketch the timing diagram for all inputs and outputs of an R-S flip-flop given that initially $R = S = C = Q = 0$ and the following sequence of events:

$$R = 1, \quad C = 1, \quad R = 0, \quad S = 1, \quad C = 0, \quad S = 0, \quad C = 1,$$

$$R = 1, \quad R = 0, \quad S = 1, \quad S = 0, \quad C = 0$$

2. Given the accompanying timing diagram, indicate the corresponding sequence of events. (This problem is the reverse of Problem 1.)

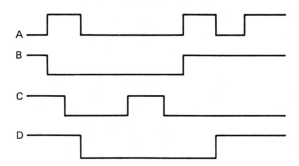

3. For all points in the logic diagram of the positive edge-triggered R-S flip-flop shown in Fig. 4-5, indicate the states for all three R and S input combinations at the following times during a clock pulse (assume that $Q = 0$ initially):

(a) Just before C becomes 1.

(b) Just after C becomes 1 but before $\overline{C}$ goes to 0.

(c) Just after $\overline{C}$ goes to 0.

(d) Just after C goes to 0 but before $\overline{C}$ becomes 1.

(e) Just after $\overline{C}$ becomes 1.

Also, for each of the three cases, draw a timing diagram showing R, S, C, and Q.

4. For all points in the master-slave logic diagram shown in Fig. 4-7a, note the states just after each event in the following sequence has occurred (assume that initially $J = K = R = S = C = P = Q = 0$):

$$J = 1, \quad K = 1, \quad C = 1, \quad J = 0, \quad C = 0, \quad K = 0, \quad J = 1, \quad C = 1,$$

$$C = 0, \quad J = 0, \quad K = 1$$

Also, draw the timing diagram corresponding to this sequence. The diagram is to show the states of C, J, K, P, and Q.

5. Show that a T flip-flop can be constructed from a J-K flip-flop by connecting its J and K inputs to 1.

6. Modify the shift register in Fig. 4-14 to include the right and left rotate features.

7. Design a 4-bit counter that will count backward.

8. Both decade counters with BCD outputs and BCD-to-seven segment code converters are available on single chips. By using appropriately labeled blocks to represent these two types of logic networks, design a three-decimal digit counter with a seven-segment readout. In addition to the decade counters and the BCD-to-seven segment converters, the design should include a means of turning the counting process on and off, clearing the counter, and turning the display signals on and off while the counter continues to operate.

9. What simple sequential device could be used to provide a 1 output if an odd number of pulses has been applied to its input and a 0 if an even number has been applied? How could this device be used to detect parity errors in serially received data?

10. Design a comparator that has two sets of four inputs each and will set a D latch if both sets are the same and will otherwise reset the latch.

11. Assume that an inverter, a NAND gate, and a J-K flip-flop are cascaded and that their propagation delays are approximately 10, 15, and 30 nS, respectively. If the given delays are accurate to within 10 percent, what are the overall minimum and maximum delays?

12. Give the state and output tables and the state diagram for an edge-triggered D flip-flop. For a T flip-flop.

13. For the illustrated network

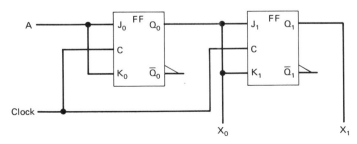

find Boolean expressions for the control inputs to the flip-flops and determine the state table, output table, and state diagram that describe the network.

14. Draw the logic diagram for a network that is described by the following state diagram:

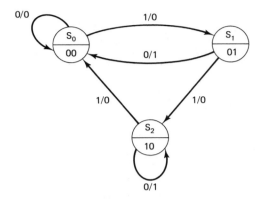

15. Assume a 10 nS delay per gate and the adder design shown in Fig. 3-15b, and determine the total delay time due to ripple of a 16-bit adder.

16. Assume an 8 nS delay per gate and a 12 nS delay per flip-flop and that four 4-bit counters such as those shown in Fig. 4-15 are cascaded together. Determine the total delay time due to ripple. Resolve the problem assuming the synchronous counter in Fig. 4-24.

17. Give examples (other than those in Fig. 4-25) of networks containing critical and non-critical races.

18. Add a redundant gate to the following network that will eliminate the hazard.

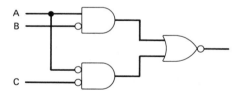

19. Suppose that A and B are connected to the D and C inputs, respectively, of a positive edge-triggered D flip-flop using two long wires. What would happen if B has a greater propagation delay than A and 1 is applied to A and B simultaneously? Give a possible remedy.

20. Use truth tables to verify the outputs shown in Fig. 4-30.

Chapter 5

Introduction
to Microcomputer
Architecture

The *architecture* of a computer is the general layout of its major components, the principal features of these components, and how they are connected together. The purpose of this chapter is to examine those architectural features that are important enough that they are used in classifying computers with regard to their architecture. This chapter is not intended to complete; rather, it *serves only as an introduction to the remaining chapters*. The discussion will center on microcomputers, but much of it applies to larger computers as well.

Figure 5-1 depicts the overall architecture of a typical microcomputer system. The components shown in the figure are the central processing unit (CPU), timing circuitry, memory, input/output (I/O) subsystem, bus control logic, and system bus. In a microcomputer the CPU is a microprocessor and is often referred to as the *microprocessor unit* (*MPU*). Its purpose is to decode the instructions and use them to control the activity within the system. It also performs all arithmetic and logical computations. The timing circuitry, or *clock*, is needed to synchronize the activity within the microprocessor and the bus control logic. For many recent microprocessors, the timing circuitry, except for the oscillator, is included in the same integrated circuit as the processing circuitry.

The *main memory*, or simply *memory*, is used to store both the data and instructions that are currently being used. It is normally broken into several modules, with each module containing several thousand locations. Each location may contain part or all of a datum or instruction and is associated with an identifier called a *memory address* (or, simply, an *address*). The CPU does its work by successively inputting, or *fetching*, instructions from memory and carrying out the tasks dictated by them.

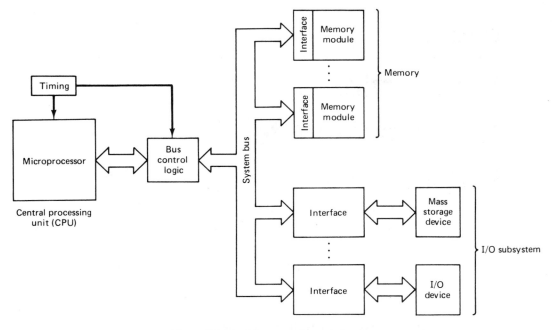

Figure 5-1 Architecture of a typical microprocessor.

The I/O subsystem may consist of a variety of devices for communicating with the external world and for storing large quantities of information. Keyboards, light pens, and analog to digital (A/D) converters are examples of input equipment, CRT monitors, and line printers, plotters, and digital to analog (D/A) converters are output devices. Some devices, such as terminals, provide both input and output capabilities. Computer components for permanently storing programs and data are referred to as *mass storage units*. The more popular types of mass storage equipment are magnetic tape and disk units, but recent technology has made available magnetic bubble memories (MBMs). Although a mass storage unit may be used to store both programs and data, programs must be transferred to memory before they are executed, and data must be in memory before they can be operated on by a program.

The *system bus* is a set of conductors that connects the CPU to its memory and I/O devices. It is over these conductors, which may be wires in a cable or lines on a printed circuit (PC) board, that all information must travel. Exactly how information is transmitted over the bus is determined by the bus's specifications. Normally, the bus conductors are separated into three groups:

1. The data lines for transmitting the information
2. The address lines, which indicate where the information is to come from or is to be placed
3. The control lines, which regulate the activity on the bus

The signals on the bus must be coordinated with the signals created by the various components connected to the bus. The circuitry needed to connect the bus to a device is called an *interface*, and the *bus control logic* is the interface to the CPU. Most manufacturers provide a variety of IC devices for facilitating the design of interfaces and the bus control logic. Depending on the complexity of the system, the bus control logic may be partially or totally contained in the CPU IC.

Memory interfaces consist primarily of the logic needed to decode the address of the memory location being accessed and to buffer the data onto or off of the bus, and of the circuitry to perform memory reads or writes. I/O interfaces may be quite simple or very complex. All I/O interfaces must be capable of buffering data onto and/or off of the system bus, receiving commands from the CPU, and transmitting status information from their associated devices to the CPU. In addition, those connected to mass storage units must be capable of communicating directly with memory and this requires them to have the ability to control the system bus. The communication between an I/O interface and the data bus is accomplished through registers which are referred to as *I/O ports*.

Section 5-1 introduces the important parts of the CPU, and the next three sections discuss the memory, the I/O and mass storage subsystem, and the system bus, respectively. Section 5-5 briefly considers the CPU architecture of three popular microprocessors—the Intel 8085, the Zilog Z80, and the Motorola MC6809. Section 5-6 considers machine language programming, and the last section discusses why microprocessor families have evolved.

5-1 THE CPU

From our experience with high-level languages, it is seen that a CPU must facilitate working with

1. Assignments and arithmetic expressions
2. Unconditional branches
3. Conditional branches and relational and logical expressions
4. Looping
5. Arrays and other data structures
6. Subroutines
7. I/O

A typical CPU architecture that is designed to accommodate these features is given in Fig. 5-2. It includes a control unit, and possibly a control memory, for decoding and carrying out the instructions, a set of working registers for helping with the addressing and computational tasks, an arithmetic/logic unit (ALU) for executing the arithmetic and logical operations, and a bus control section for handling communications with the bus.

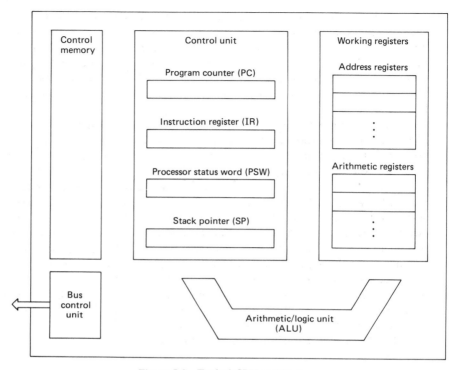

Figure 5-2 Typical CPU architecture.

The control unit normally contains the following registers:

PROGRAM COUNTER (PC)—This register holds the address of the main memory
location from which the next instruction will be fetched.

INSTRUCTION REGISTER (IR)—This register receives the instruction as it is brought
in from main memory and holds it while it is decoded and executed.

PROCESSOR STATUS WORD (PSW)—This may not be a register but a collection of
individual flip-flops called *condition flags*, or simply flags. As far as a user
is concerned, these flags are used to indicate the current state of the CPU
and the important characteristics of the results of the previous instruction.
The number and purpose of these flags will vary from one computer to the
next, but typically they are used to indicate a zero result, a negative result,
a carry, an overflow, and so on.

STACK POINTER (SP)—Most microcomputers utilize something called a *stack*. A
stack normally consists of a portion of main memory. It is used for temporarily storing important information while subroutines or service routines
are being executed. Most stacks are last-in, first-out (LIFO) stacks; that is,
the last information put onto the stack is the first to be retrieved from the
stack. The top of the stack is the last information put onto the stack. The
stack pointer points to (i.e., holds the address of) the top of the stack.

Just as with high-level language programs, unless a branch instruction is encountered, a machine-level program is executed in sequence. The IR is used to hold the current instruction and the PC is used to hold the address of the next instruction. When the present instruction has completed its execution, the address in the PC is placed on the address bus, the memory places the next instruction on the data bus, and the CPU inputs the instruction to the IR. While this instruction is decoded, its length in bytes is determined and the PC is incremented by the length so that the PC will point to the next instruction. When the execution of this instruction is completed, the contents of the PC are placed on the address bus, and the cycle is repeated.

Unconditional branch instructions permit the normal sequencing to be altered by replacing the contents of the PC with an address determined by the branch instruction. Conditional branch instructions may replace the contents of the PC or increment these contents, depending on the results of the previous instructions, i.e., the current state of the processor as determined by the previous instructions. The current state of the processor is stored in a register called the *processor status word* (*PSW*). The PSW contains bits that indicate such things as whether the previous arithmetic operations produced a positive, negative, or zero result. For example, if a "subtract" instruction is followed by a "branch on zero" instruction, then the branch will be taken if the PSW indicates that the subtraction resulted in a zero. If the PSW shows that the subtraction produced a nonzero result, the branch will not be taken. When a branch is taken, a new sequence of instructions begins at the address to which the branch is made. A flowchart illustrating the sequencing of instructions within a computer is given in Fig. 5-3.

Looping is normally performed using conditional branch instructions, although some microprocessors have instructions that combine counting and/or testing with the conditional branching. Most loops, such as a Fortran DO-loop, involve incrementing or decrementing a counter and repeating the loop until the counter reaches a limit. Each time the counter is changed, the result is compared with the limit, the PSW is set accordingly, and the branch is taken or not taken depending on the contents of the PSW.

The sequencing involved in a subroutine call is shown in Fig. 5-4 and requires a special form of branching. As with other branching, a subroutine call also causes the contents of the PC to be replaced by the address being branched to, but it must also save the current contents of the PC, which is the *return address*. The return branch instruction must be capable of restoring the return address to the PC so that the main program can continue in sequence once the subroutine is complete. In addition to saving the return address, it is usually necessary to temporarily store other information, such as the contents of the working registers, while the subroutine is executing. This is so because the subroutine might otherwise destroy the original contents of these registers and they may be needed when the return is made to the main program. It will be seen later that this information is normally stored on the stack.

If a CPU includes a control memory, then the control memory is used to hold a set of instructions called *microcode*. Some microcomputers are constructed so

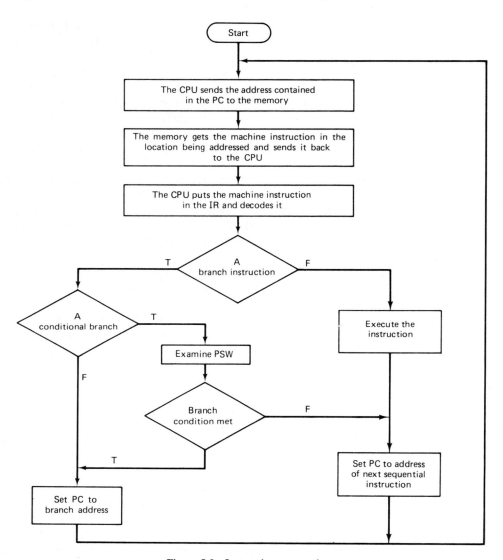

Figure 5-3 Instruction sequencing.

that it is possible to program them at two different levels. The first level consists of instructions that are capable of performing only the most elemental operations within the computer; they are called the *microinstructions* of the computer. The microinstructions are grouped together to form the more useful operations, which are normally referred to as the *macroinstructions* (or simply *instructions*). If the CPU architecture is based on a control memory, the macroinstruction in the instruction register will direct the control unit to the sequence of microcode that corresponds to that instruction, and the control unit will control the execution of these microinstructions. If the control memory is on a separate chip, it is possible for users to develop their own macroinstruction set by programming this memory. Such programming is called microprogramming and will not be considered in this book.

Not all CPUs execute their instructions by using microcode taken from control memory; instead, they use circuitry that completely decodes the instructions. The presence or absence of control memory will not be important in this book, because microprogramming will not be considered. It will be assumed that if microcode exists, it cannot be changed by the user and, therefore, the machine-level instruction set of the computer (move, add, subtract, and so on) will be considered to be "fixed." Machine-level instructions are discussed in detail in Section 5-6.

All computers contain a certain number of working resisters, which fall into one or both of the following categories:

ACCUMULATORS OR ARITHMETIC REGISTERS—Registers that serve as a scratch pad
   for arithmetic and logical operations.
ADDRESS REGISTERS—Registers that aid in addressing data and instructions in main
   memory.

A register that can perform either of these functions with equal facility is called a *general purpose register*.

The address group is used for making the addressing of data more flexible. A datum being operated on by an instruction may be part of the instruction, its address may be part of the instruction, it may be in a register, its address may be in a register, or its address may be the sum of part of the instruction and the contents of one or more registers. Sometimes when a register is used the instruction simply indicates the register that contains the address, but other times the address determination is more complicated. For example, when accessing elements of an array the address of an element is composed of two parts, a *base address*, which is the address of the first element in the array, and an *offset*. Because one often

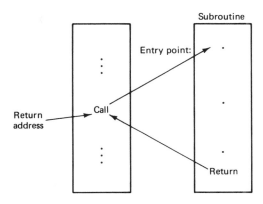

Figure 5-4 Subroutine call.

needs to index through an array, it is helpful if the offset can be easily incremented. Therefore, the address of an array element is frequently computed by adding two registers together, one that contains the base address and is called a *base register* and one that contains the offset and is called an *index register*. A two-dimensional array offers a slightly more complex situation that requires the additon of a base, a column offset, and a displacement. This normally involves the sum of part of the instruction (the displacement), a base register, and an index register. Base registers are also used to relocate programs and blocks of data within memory.

Arithmetic registers are for temporarily holding the operands and results of the arithmetic operations. Because transfers over the system bus are the primary limiting factor with regard to speed, accessing a register is much faster than accessing memory. Therefore, if several operations must be performed on a set of data, it is better to input the data to the arithmetic registers, do the necessary calculations, and return the result to memory than it is to work directly from memory. The tendency is that the more arithmetic registers a CPU contains, the faster it can execute its computations.

The number of bits in a working register is called its *width*. For an address register, the width determines the maximum address or offset that the register can be used to store. The width of a computer's arithmetic registers is normally the number of bits that a single arithmetic or logical instruction can operate on (e.g., if the arithmetic registers are 8 bits wide, then an add instruction could only add two 8-bit quantities). Many microprocessors with 8-bit arithmetic registers also have arithmetic/logic instructions that use the registers in pairs, thereby permitting 16-bit operations.

Some manufacturers use the width of the arithmetic registers to classify their microprocessors as 8-bit, 16-bit, and so on, but others use the number of lines in the system bus that are used for transmitting data. The microprocessors discussed in this book are considered 8-bit processors, both because their basic arithmetic register width is 8 and the number of data lines is 8.

The *arithmetic/logic unit* (*ALU*) performs arithmetic and logical operations on the contents of the working registers, the program counter, and/or locations in main memory, and stores the results in the place indicated by the instruction, usually in an accumulator. It also sets or clears the appropriate flags.

The *bus control unit* is used to coordinate the CPU's activities with those of the external world. In microcomputers some of the control functions, such as external interrupts, may be controlled by separate chips in the external bus control logic. Just how much of this circuitry must be outside the microprocessor chip depends on the system. Interrupts and bus control are treated in detail in Chapter 9.

Although there are many variations of CPU architecture, this discussion has summarized the operation and major parts of microprocessors in general. The purpose of this section has been to give the reader an overview that will help with further study of microprocessors.

The various parts of the CPU are, of course, made up of combinational and sequential networks such as those discussed in Chapters 3 and 4. These networks would be embedded in the surface of the CPU's IC chip. The registers in the control unit and ALU and the working registers could be constructed such as those shown in Fig. 4-11 or 4-14. The ALU would need to include add/subtract circuitry similar to that given in Figs. 3-15 and 3-16. The PC could be designed either as a counter (as in Figs. 4-16 and 4-24) that could be loaded with an arbitrary value (in case there is a branch) or as a register associated with a network that could add instruction lengths to the register. If a control memory is present, the various macroinstructions would need to address different points in the microcode and this would require a decoder. If a control memory is not present, decode logic would still be needed, but it would have to be combined with sequential logic that could cause different actions to be taken as the execution of the instruction progresses (e.g., an add instruction would need to retrieve the first operand, then the second operand, initiate the addition, and store the result.) (Exercises 1 through 6 request example CPU-related designs.)

5-2 MEMORY

All memory locations and I/O registers are, of course, composed of bits, but because single bits contain very little information they are grouped together to form *bytes* and *words*. Because characters are normally 7 or 8 bits long and because computers work more naturally with powers of 2, bytes almost always consist of 8 bits. Words may consist of 2, 3, or 4 bytes, depending on the computer and its system bus structure.

Each byte has an identifying address associated with it, and when a byte is to be accessed its address is transmitted to the appropriate interface via the address lines. Addresses are composed of bit combinations and the set of all possible combinations for a given situation is called an *address space*. Some computers have two address spaces, while others use a single address space to access all memory locations and I/O registers. If there are separate memory and I/O address spaces, then some of the control lines must be used in conjunction with the address lines to determine which space is being accessed. Because the memory is divided into modules, some of the high-order bits in a memory address are used to select the module and the remaining (low-order) bits are used to identify the byte (or word) within the module. Similarly, an interface is identified by the high-order bits in an I/O address and the register within the interface is selected by the 2 or 3 low-order bits. The overall organization of memory and I/O registers and how they are addressed are summarized in Fig. 5-5.

The number of possible bits in an address determines the size of an address space. If an address is n bits wide, then there are 2^n possible addresses (0 through $2^n - 1$). The number of address lines in the system bus dictates the size of the memory (or possibly the combined memory and I/O) space. A total of n address lines would imply a maximum memory (or overall memory and I/O) capacity of

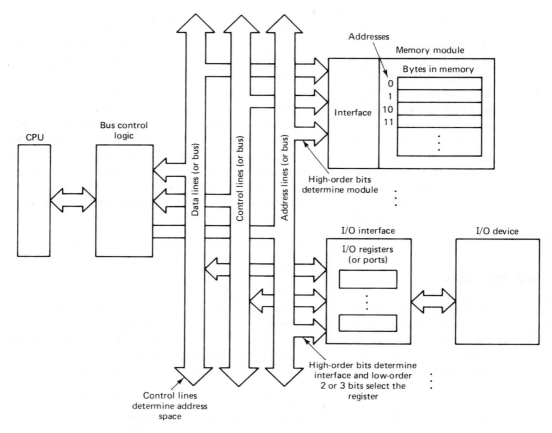

Figure 5-5 Memory and I/O register organization.

2^n bytes.   Sixteen address lines would imply a capacity of

$$2^{16} = 2^6 (2^{10}) = 64K \text{ bytes}$$

When there are 2 bytes in a word there is some question as to which byte address is to be used to identify the word.   Also, it is sometimes necessary to comment about a specific bit in a byte or word.   Throughout this book the address of a word is the address of its low-order, or low-address, byte.   The bits are numbered with 0 being assigned to the least significant bit (LSB).   In a byte the most significant bit (MSB) is numbered 7 and in a word the MSB is numbered 15.   These conventions are summarized in Fig. 5-6.

There are several ways of classifying memory.   One way is according to whether or not it can retain its contents while its power is turned off.   A memory that can do so is said to be *nonvolatile*; otherwise, it is said to be *volatile*.   Whether or not a memory is volatile is particularly important if it contains instructions, because if it is volatile, these instructions will be lost every time the computer is shut down and will have to be reloaded each time the computer is brought up. This is intolerable in most microcomputer applications. Even worse, if all of the computer's memory is either volatile or memory that can only be read from (and not written into), there is no possibility of recovering from a power failure, since the program counter, processor status, or other register contents are volatile and there is no place to store them. The best known type of nonvolatile memory is magnetic core (or, simply, core) memory. The most widely used volatile memory is MOS memory.

Memories are also classified according to their read/write capabilities and, in this regard, fall into the two major categories discussed below.

5-2-1 Read-Only Memory

Read-only memory (*ROM*) can, as its name implies, only be read. Once its contents are set, they can be changed only by special equipment. There are basically four types of ROMs, the four types being distinguished by the way in which their contents are set. Setting the contents of a memory is sometimes called programming, but should not be confused with the programming (i.e., the generation of instruction sequences) discussed in the succeeding chapters. In one type of ROM the contents are determined by a masking operation that is performed while the chip is being manufactured. Such chips cannot be altered by the user and are referred to simply as ROMs. The contents of the second type can, if the proper equipment is available, be set by the user. They are called programmable-read-only memories. Once a memory of this type is programmed, its contents can never be changed. The third and fourth types not only can be programmed by the user, but by using special equipment can be reprogrammed many times. They are called erasable-programmable-read-only memories and electrically alterable-programmable-read-only memories. Obviously, all ROMs are nonvolatile.

When designing a microcomputer for a particular application, there is often a set of instructions and/or constants that need not be altered after the computer is installed. Such information is usually stored in a ROM. The irreversible nature of ROMs may be highly desirable in some applications where an accidental change in an instruction or other memory contents could cause disastrous results. In addition, their simpler construction, which primarily involves diodes, permits higher

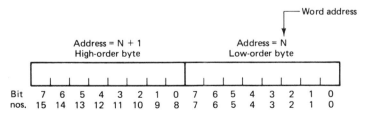

Figure 5-6 Address and bit numbering conventions.

bit densities, lower power consumption, and higher speeds. For these reasons control memories are ROMs.

Programmable-read-only memory (PROM) is read-only memory that can be programmed by the user. Usually PROMs are constructed of diode matrices implanted in IC chips. By using the external pins, selected diodes can be "burned" or "blown," thus causing the diode matrix to be permanently programmed.

Erasable-programmable-read-only memory (EPROM) is read-only memory that can be reprogrammed by using special equipment. EPROMs are programmed by charge injection, and once programmed the charge distribution is maintained until it is disturbed by some external energy source such as an ultraviolet light. The external energy source causes the charge to be redistributed to its natural state, thus destroying the old memory contents. The EPROM can then be reprogrammed. EPROMs are used primarily during the development and testing stages of a design and are replaced with ROMs or PROMs once the design is complete. EPROMs are considered nonvolatile but can lose their contents with age.

Electrically alterable-programmable-read-only memory (EAPROM) is read-only memory that is electrically reprogrammable. It is programmed by applying an address to several of its pins and then applying a write voltage to a write pin, just as PROMs are programmed, but an EAPROM program is not permanent. An EAPROM primarily differs from an EPROM in that, when used with properly designed read/write circuitry, it can be reprogrammed by a computer.

5-2-2 Random-Access Memory

Random-access memory (RAM) is the name commonly used for memory that can be both read from and written into (read/write). The prefix random-access is really a misnomer, because ROMs are also random-access memories. *Random access* means that all locations can be accessed with equal ease, but the use of the term has become corrupted and, with regard to memory, has come to mean read/write. Some applications in which the computer is being used as a simple controller may not require the use of RAM, but most applications involve inputting and storing more data than can be held in the CPU registers. If this is the case, RAM is needed to store the data while they are being operated on. For reasons of operative reliability, low cost, and flexibility, most designs include both ROM and RAM memory.

5-3 I/O DEVICES AND INTERFACES

There are a wide variety of peripheral (or I/O) devices that are connected to microcomputers. Typical peripheral devices are terminals, liquid crystal diode (LCD) and cathode ray tube (CRT) display monitors, diskettes, analog to digital (A/D) converters, digital to analog (D/A) converters, digital I/O devices, cassette tapes or diskette devices, printers, and plotters.

The wide range of microcomputer applications means that the peripherals used on microcomputer systems can vary radically from one system to another. A microcomputer used as a controller may include only a microprocessor and sufficient electronics to input and output single bits in a serial fashion. A slightly more complicated application would be in a data acquisition system that requires parallel inputs from A/D converters and/or digital input devices. If data monitoring is required, D/A converters, digital output, and/or a terminal could be needed. Data logging might require a plotter or printer.

All data transfer, except that which is done inside the CPU, is done over one or more buses. All I/O devices and main memory must somehow be connected to these buses. If there is more than one bus, one is primarily used for memory and the others are for peripherals. In a single-bus architecture, the same bus is used for both memory and I/O transfers. The more complicated structures are predominant in larger computers, but the popular microcomputers have single-bus structures, and it is these microcomputers that will be considered in this book.

Memory and peripherals are connected to these buses through interfaces and controllers. The definitions of these terms are somewhat nebulous and they are sometimes used interchangeably. For our purposes, a *controller* is the circuitry that is needed to initiate the commands given a device and to sense the status of the device. It is often an integral part of the peripheral. An *interface* is the circuitry needed to connect the peripheral and its control circuitry to the appropriate bus. The interface must perform some combination of the following functions:

1. Make the peripheral's status available to the computer.
2. Provide buffer storage for data being input from the peripheral into the computer.
3. Relay commands from the computer to the peripheral.
4. Provide buffer storage for data being output from the computer to peripheral.
5. Signal the computer when an operation is complete.
6. Signal the computer when an error has occurred during an operation.
7. Pack several bits into bytes or words for input and unpack them for output.

Data transfers between an I/O or mass storage device and the CPU or memory can be categorized according to amount as follows:

BYTE OR WORD TRANSFERS—A transfer in which only one byte or word of information is moved by a given computer command. A terminal is an example of a device that is normally capable of only this type of transfer.

BLOCK TRANSFERS—A transfer in which a whole block of information is moved by a single computer command. Such transfers take place between the peripheral device and memory and are called *direct memory accesses* (*DMAs*). To accomplish a block transfer, the device's interface must be used in conjunction with something called a DMA controller that can address memory directly without intervention by the CPU. A disk is an example of a device that uses

DMA. Most devices that require high transfer rates are DMA devices because the CPU may not be able to move the information as fast as it comes in or must be made available (e.g., as fast as it passes under the read head or must be received by the write head of a disk drive). When DMA capability is available, it usually has priority over all other bus activity. DMA not only makes fast data movement possible but also permits the CPU to·continue its processing as the transfer takes place.

The types of transfers that an I/O or mass storage device is capable of performing are determined by the nature of the design of its interface. Many interfaces are designed to perform both types of transfers. A/D converters sometimes need to perform block transfers when the data rate is high, but may need to use byte transfer to the CPU when the data rate is low. (Note that block transfers cannot move information into the CPU.)

5-4 SYSTEM BUS

As mentioned in the previous section, a computer may have one bus that is used primarily for memory and others for peripherals, or it may have only one bus that is used for both purposes. If there is only one external bus, it is usually referred to as the *system bus*. In any case, the lines in the bus can be classified as described below. Figure 5-5 illustrates the salient features of a system bus.

DATA LINES—These are the lines used by the information that is being moved. When communicating with memory this information may be either data or instructions. When communicating with an I/O or mass storage device, the information may be data, device status or commands, or other information. The number of data lines in a bus determines the number of bits that can be transferred simultaneously, and therefore has a direct bearing on the speed with which information can be moved. As mentioned in Section 5-1, the number of data lines is sometimes used to classify a microcomputer as being an 8-bit, 16-bit, or 32-bit computer.

ADDRESS LINES—As we have seen, each memory location or interface register has associated with it a unique bit combination called an *address*. The address lines are used to transmit the bit combinations that are decoded as addresses by the interfaces connected to the bus. In the case of a memory module, each byte has its own address and the memory interface is designed to recognize all the addresses of the bytes in its memory. Although several memory modules can be connected to the same bus, no two bytes can have the same address. Usually, a memory system is designed so that the top few bits of an address serve to select the module and the remaining bits are used to find a particular location within the module. If I/O devices share a bus with memory, some of the addresses must be reserved for their interface registers. Each register must have its own address, and an interface must be able to recognize the addresses of all its registers. Once a memory or device interface recognizes one of its addresses, it either inputs the information on the data lines and transmits it to the proper place, or it retrieves the necessary data and puts them on the data lines. As mentioned in Section 5-2, the number of bits used to specify an address determines the set of all possible addresses.

In some computers the address lines and the data lines may be the same. In this situation the addresses and data must alternately use the lines, and the CPU and interfaces must be designed to coordinate this more complicated bus activity.

CONTROL LINES—Regardless of the bus arrangement being used, a certain amount of control information must be passed back and forth among the CPU, the memory modules, and the device interfaces. The communication of this information is a form of handshaking. The information includes some combination of the following:

1. *Requests for bus usage,* which are made by the DMA controllers connected to the bus
2. *Grants for bus usage,* which are given by the CPU according to a predetermined priority scheme
3. *Interrupt signals,* which indicate that external events require attention from the CPU
4. *Timing signals* for coordinating the data and address transfers made on the bus
5. *Parity signals* for indicating data transfer errors
6. Signals for indicating malfunctions or power loss

The arrangement of these control lines varies considerably from one microcomputer design to the next. Because the buses must communicate with the microprocessor chip, a detailed description of the pin assignments of this chip will tell a designer what is available in the way of CPU control signals.

Only an overview of the bus structure has been given here. A thorough examination of the concepts touched on above is given in Chapter 9.

5-5 EXAMPLE CPUs

Some of the architectural features described above will now be examined for a few of the more popular 8-bit microprocessors: the Intel 8085, the Zilog Z80, and the Motorola MC6809. The discussions will be concerned primarily with those CPU components that a programmer might need to know. These components constitute what is called the *programming model* of the CPU.

5-5-1 The Intel 8085

Figure 5-7 is a programming model of the 8085 microprocessor. It is seen from this diagram that the 8085 is an 8-bit processor with six general purpose registers (identified by the letters B, C, D, E, H, and L), which are 8 bits each and are associated in pairs, one 8-bit accumulator (denoted by A), a 16-bit stack pointer,

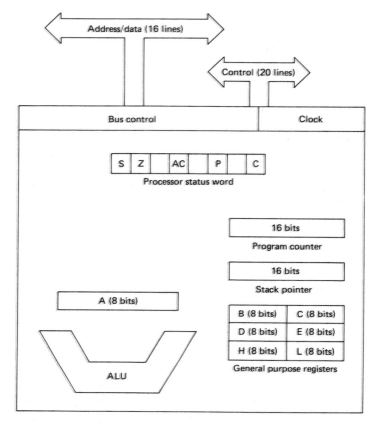

Figure 5-7   Programming model of the Intel 8085 microprocessor.

a 16-bit program counter, and a program status word with five flags.   Much of the necessary bus control circuitry is part of the CPU chip but it must be supplemented with external circuitry.   The system timing pulses are generated internally using an external oscillator.

As discussed previously, the PSW flags indicate important things about past results and are used primarily to decide whether or not conditional branches should be taken.   The flags for the 8085 are the following:

ZERO (Z)—If the result of the operation is zero, this flag is set; otherwise, it is cleared.

SIGN (S)—If the sign of the result is negative (i.e., bit 7 of the result is set), this flag is set; otherwise, it is cleared.

PARITY (P)—If the sum of the bits in the result is even, this flag is set; otherwise, it is cleared.

CARRY (C)—If an addition resulted in a carry from the high-order bit, or if a subtraction or comparison resulted in a borrow, this flag is set; otherwise, it is cleared.   It is cleared by the logical operations and set or cleared by the rotate instructions as indicated by their definitions.

AUXILIARY CARRY (AC)—If the operation caused a carry from bit 3 to bit 4, this flag is set; otherwise, it is cleared.   This flag is affected by the arithmetic and logical operations as described in the individual instruction definitions.   It is used primarily for BCD arithmetic (see Section 6-4-2).

Figure 5-8 shows the 8085 pin assignments.   It is a 40-pin chip with pins for

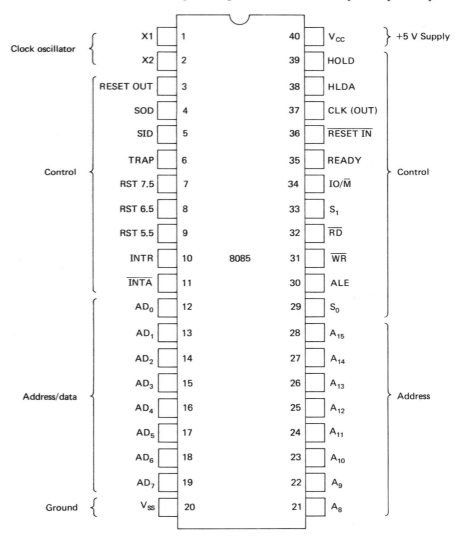

Figure 5-8   Pin assignments for the 8085 microprocessor.

16 address/data lines, 20 control lines, 2 oscillator lines, 1 supply voltage, and a ground.   From the pin assignments it is seen that

1. The addresses and data share the same bus lines and, therefore, must take turns using these lines (i.e., must be time multiplexed).
2. One 8-bit byte of data can be transmitted at a time.
3. The address space is 0 to $2^{16} - 1$.
4. An external oscillator, but not an external clock, is needed.
5. Only a $+5$ V supply voltage is needed.
6. There are 20 control signals to be understood before one can connect the 8085 into a design.

When addresses and data share the same lines, the address must be sent out first and then the data must be sent or received.   This complicates the design of the external bus control circuitry and requires careful timing and that an external latch register be used to hold the address throughout a transfer.

5-5-2 The Zilog Z80

Figure 5-9 shows a programming model of the Zilog Z80, a microprocessor that can be thought of as an enhanced version of the Intel 8080.   It is an 8-bit processor that contains two 16-bit index registers, a 16-bit stack pointer, a 16-bit program counter, two 8-bit special purpose registers, and two identical sets of registers. Each of these sets contains an 8-bit accumulator, a processor status word with six flags, and six general purpose registers that can be used singly or in pairs.   The primary bus control circuitry is part of the CPU chip but may be supplemented with external circuitry.   A separate clock must provide the timing pulses.

The flags for the Z80 are the same as those of the 8085 except that the parity flag becomes the parity/overflow flag and is set differently, depending on the instruction.   For input and logical operations, it is set according to even parity as on the 8085.   An arithmetic operation causes it to be set to 1 if there is a 2's-complement signed overflow; otherwise, it is cleared.   The N flag is 1 during a subtract operation and is 0 during an add, but is for internal use and is not accessible to a program.   The H is for half-carry and is the same as the 8085's AC flag.

Figure 5-10 gives the external connections to the Z80.   It is a 40-pin chip with 8 data lines, 16 address lines, 13 control lines, 1 clock line, 1 supply voltage, and a ground.   Examination of the figure shows that

1. Addresses and data use separate sets of lines and do not need to be time-multiplexed.
2. One 8-bit byte of data can be transmitted at a time.
3. The address space is 0 to $2^{16} - 1$.
4. An external clock is required.

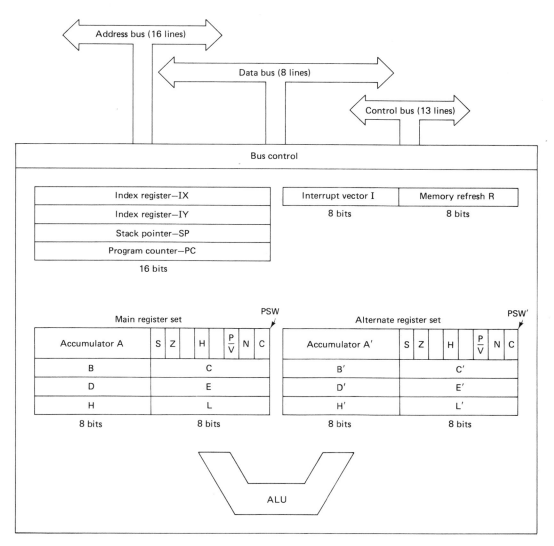

Figure 5-9   Programming model of the Zilog Z80 microprocessor.

5. Only a single supply voltage of +5 V is needed.
6. There are 13 control signals to be understood before one can connect the Z80 into a design.

5-5-3 The Motorola MC6809

A programming model for the Motorola MC6809 is shown in Fig. 5-11. It is an 8-bit microprocessor that contains two 16-bit index registers, an 8-bit page register for addressing, a 16-bit program counter, two 16-bit stack pointers (one for a user

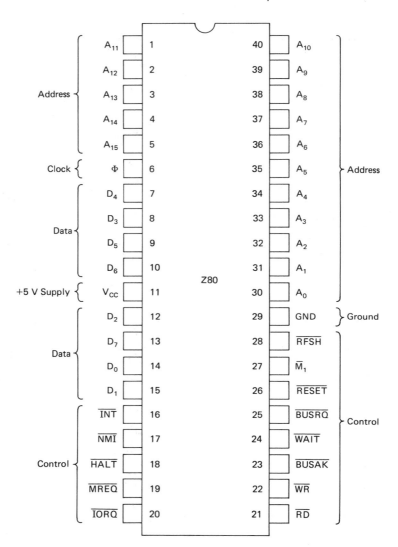

Figure 5-10 Pin assignments for the Zilog Z80 microprocessor.

stack and one for a system stack), two 8-bit accumulators that can be used as a pair to form one 16-bit accumulator, and a PSW with eight flags. Some of the bus control circuitry is internal, but may be supported by external circuitry.

The Z and C flags are the same as on the 8085, and the N and H flags are the same as the 8085's S and AC flags, respectively. The overflow (V) flag is set to 1 if a 2's-complement signed arithmetic operation produces an overflow; otherwise, it is cleared. The other three flags are for interrupt control. (Interrupts are introduced in Chapter 8.)

As shown in Fig. 5-12, the MC6809 is a 40-pin chip with 8 data pins, 16 address pins, 12 control pins, 2 oscillator pins, a $+5$ V supply pin, and a ground. From the figure it is seen that

1. Addresses and data use separate sets of lines.
2. One 8-bit byte of data can be transmitted at a time.
3. The address space is 0 to $2^{16} - 1$.
4. The clock is internal and only an oscillator signal must be externally supplied.
5. Only a single supply voltage of $+5$ V is needed.
6. There are 12 control signals that must be understood before one can connect the MC6809 into a design.

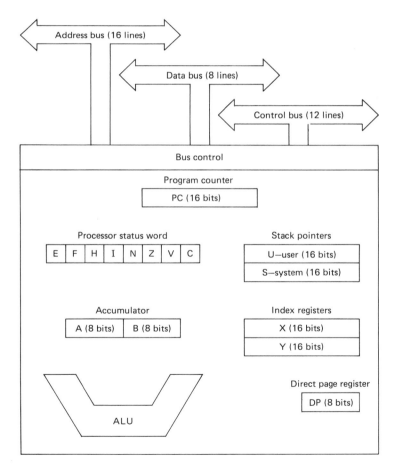

Figure 5-11 Programming model for the Motorola MC6809 microprocessor.

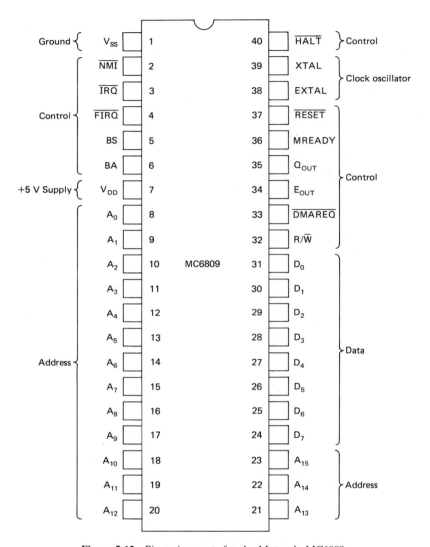

Figure 5-12 Pin assignments for the Motorola MC6809.

5-6 *MACHINE LANGUAGE INSTRUCTIONS*

At the time they are executed by the computer, all instructions are made up of a
sequence of bytes, each byte being a combination of 1's and 0's. By examining
these 0–1 combinations, the CPU's decode logic, and perhaps its control memory,
is able to direct the computer through a sequence of operations that will carry out
the instruction. Because the instructions in their 0–1 form can be directly understood by the computer, they are called *machine language instructions*. These

instructions execute the most elementary operations that a programmer can perform. They are the macroinstructions that were discussed at the beginning of the chapter. Other forms of programs, assembler language and high-level language programs, must be reduced to their machine language forms using assemblers and compilers before they can be executed.

All computers must be able to perform the following types of operations:

1. Move information from memory to the CPU, and vice versa.
2. Perform arithmetic and logical operations.
3. Operate on individual bits as well as bytes and words.
4. Execute branches, including unconditional and conditional branches and subroutine calls and returns.
5. Perform looping.
6. Communicate with I/O and mass storage devices.

It is not necessary that these actions be done by single instructions, but there must exist combinations of instructions that can carry them out.

A typical sequence of instructions would be one that would

1. Move the contents of a memory location into a CPU register.
2. Add this register to the contents of a second memory location and replace the register contents with the sum.
3. Compare the sum with 100 and set the sign and zero flags in the PSW accordingly.
4. Examine the zero flag and branch to step 6 if it is set; otherwise, continue in sequence by executing step 5.
5. Subtract 10 from the sum and put the difference back into the CPU register.
6. Move the contents of the CPU register to a third memory location.

Most 8-bit microprocessors would require one instruction for each of these steps.

5-6-1 *Instruction Formats*

The arrangement of an instruction with respect to assigning meaning to its various groups of bits is called its *format*. That portion of an instruction that specifies what the instruction does is called its *operation code* (or *op code*). Any address or piece of data that is needed by an instruction in order to complete its execution is called an *operand*. An instruction consists of its operation code and a number of operands.

To be completely flexible, an instruction could require as many as four operands. For example, an addition instruction could involve the two numbers being added, the result, and the address of the next instruction. If a byte is 8 bits long and it requires 16 bits to specify an address, then an instruction requiring four operands would occupy 8 bytes of memory plus whatever is needed to store its op code. In addition, if the memory has only eight data lines, it would require at least nine memory accesses to fetch the instruction. If maximum flexibility were used as the primary criterion in designing an instruction set, the result would be a computer that is both slow and wasteful with regard to memory space. Therefore, most computers are designed so that no more than two operands are needed by any single instruction. This is accomplished by

1. Permitting only branch instructions to include the address of the next instruction; for all others the next instruction will be taken from the memory locations following the instruction being executed. (It is because of this rule that branch instructions are needed.)
2. Using the location of one of the data items being operated on to store the result (e.g., using the location of the addend to store the sum).

A further reduction in the number of bits needed to specify the operands is obtained by having either or both contained in the CPU registers. In this case the saving results from the fact that it takes only a few bits to designate a register address.

Some instructions require only one operand and are called *single-operand instructions*. Those requiring two operands are called *double-operand instructions*. If there are two operands, one of them is usually altered by the instruction while the other is left unchanged. Because information is only taken from one of the locations, that location is called the *source*; the location that is changed is called the *destination*. For example, in executing an instruction that moves data from one location to another, the location from which the data are being taken is the source and the location that receives the data is the destination. Also, in executing an "add" instruction, the augend is normally only used by the instruction and is therefore the source operand. The addend location is used to store the result and is the destination operand. Sometimes the operand in a single-operand instruction is referred to as the source or destination, depending on whether or not it is altered by the instruction.

The possible ways for locating and accessing an operand are the addressing modes (e.g., including the address in the instruction, getting it from a register, indexing, and so on). If a computer designer includes in a design a number of addressing modes, he or she must reserve bits in the instruction format for designating the addressing mode for each operand. If eight addressing modes have been decided upon, 3 bits are needed to indicate each mode. Although a variety of addressing modes may permit greater versatility in utilizing the CPU registers, thereby reducing the number of memory accesses, the advantages are partially offset by the number of bits needed to specify the modes.

Virtually all instruction formats reserve the first bits of the instruction for at least part of the op code, but beyond this the formats vary considerably from one computer to the next. The remaining bits must designate the operands or their locations and consequently are used for combinations of modes, register addresses, memory addresses, relative addresses, and immediate operands. Typically, instructions vary in length from 1 byte to 3 or 6 bytes. A few representative 8085 instruction formats are shown in Fig. 5-13. Three of them are for moving data and the other is for branching.

A great deal of information about a microcomputer can be obtained by examining its instruction formats. In fact, in designing a microcomputer, virtually all of its dominant characteristics must be known before the instruction formats are decided upon. These characteristics include the number and types of working registers, the number and types of addressing modes, the bus structure, the maximum number of interface registers permitted on the I/O bus, the maximum memory capacity, the word and byte sizes, the CPU structure, and the number and types of instructions. In the planning process the designer must decide on how many

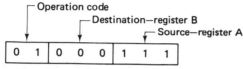

(a) Register to register transfer

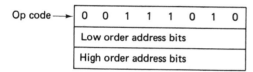

(b) Load accumulator from memory

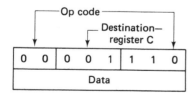

(c) Transfer of immediate data to register

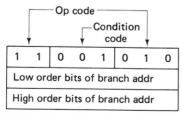

(d) Conditional branch on zero result

Figure 5-13 Representative Intel 8085 machine language instructions.

bits it takes to uniquely specify an operation, a memory operand, a register operand, an I/O interface register, an immediate operand, and an addressing mode.

5-6-2 Addressing and Addressing Modes

In order to communicate with their various components, all computers must have some means of identifying the individual external memory locations, CPU registers, and I/O interface registers. This is done by assigning each of these storage units an address (i.e., a unique bit combination). Just how many bits are in the combination will, of course, determine the total number of units that can be differentiated. A computer will have separate address spaces for its memory and its CPU register set and will sometimes have a separate space for its I/O interface registers. This means that there would be two or three storage units with address 0; one memory location, one CPU register, and perhaps one I/O device register. Which of the two or three locations is intended would have to be determined by the instruction.

    CPU Register Address Space. Typically, there are from 4 to 32 CPU registers that need to be identified, and to differentiate among the registers requires 2 to 5 bits.

    Memory Address Space. As we have seen, the maximum number of memory storage units a computer can have is 2^n, where n is the number of bits needed to designate an address. Most 8-bit microcomputers are designed to use 16 bits to designate a memory address. Therefore, the maximum amount of memory would be 2^{16} bytes.

    The main memory in some microcomputers is divided into *pages*. When this is done, the lower bits, typically 8 to 10 bits, are used to designate the position within the page specified by the higher bits. For example, the higher 6 bits could be used to specify one of 64 pages and the lower 10 bits would then specify one of the 1024 bytes within a page. The segmentation of memory into pages is used in certain types of addressing schemes; these schemes are discussed below. When paging is used, the *base page* is the page beginning with memory address zero. The *current page* is the page that includes the address currently contained in the program counter.

    I/O Interface Registers. Frequently, the addresses of the I/O interface registers are in the same address space as memory, but sometimes they have a separate address space. When they have a separate space, it typically includes 2^8 to 2^{16} addresses. If the I/O registers are in the memory address space, the memory system must be designed so that it will not accept those addresses given to the I/O interface registers.

    Because there are up to three different address spaces and memory is used to store both instructions and data, all computers include a variety of addressing modes for accessing their various storage locations. The more important addressing modes are defined below. A given microcomputer is designed to implement some combination of these modes. These definitions are not standard and the terminology may vary from one manual to the next, but the definitions given here are representative of the popular usage of these phrases.

IMMEDIATE—Information is said to be immediate if it is part of the instruction; therefore, no addressing is needed to get the information.

DIRECT ADDRESSING—The address specified is part of the instruction.

REGISTER ADDRESSING—A form of direct addressing in which the operand is in a register and the register's address is part of the instruction.

INDIRECT (or DEFERRED) ADDRESSING—The address is in the location whose address is specified as part of the instruction. This location may be either a register, in which case the phrase *register indirect addressing* is used, or a memory location. Some computers are designed to have several or even an indeterminant number of deferrals; that is, one location refers to another location, which, in turn, refers to another location, and so on, with each reference being a *level of deferral.*

BASE ADDRESSING—The address is formed by adding the contents of a memory location or register to a number, called a *displacement*, that is part of the instruction. Base addressing may be used in conjunction with indirect addressing. It is primarily used in referencing arrays or in relocating a program within memory.

INDEXING—Indexing is the process of incrementing or decrementing an address as the computer sequences through a set of consecutive or evenly spaced addresses. This is normally done by successively changing an address that is stored in a register, called an *index register*, that can be conveniently incremented or decremented. Some 16-bit microcomputers, such as the Intel 8086, permit simultaneous base addressing and indexing, for which the final address is the sum of a base address, an index, and perhaps a displacement. Indexing is used primarily to sequentially address elements in arrays.

AUTOINCREMENTING/AUTODECREMENTING—A form of indexing in which the index is automatically incremented (or decremented) by the instruction.

PAGE ADDRESSING—A form of addressing in which the specified address is formed from a page address, which determines the high-order bits of the address, and a displacement, which determines the low-order bits. The page address normally comes from a special register called the *page address register.*

RELATIVE (or PC) ADDRESSING—The address is the sum of a number and the current contents of the program counter. The number is the address of the operand relative to the current instruction and is usually a part of the instruction, but may be contained in a working register.

An addressing scheme may include modes that are combinations of those defined above (e.g., indirect relative addressing).

5-7 *MICROPROCESSOR FAMILIES*

As technology improves, manufacturers are able to put more and more logic into single integrated circuits. Being able to put more logic into an IC permits a single-chip microprocessor's capabilities to be expanded in several directions. The principal ways a microprocessor's capabilities can be extended are by

Enhancing the instruction set and, perhaps, providing more addressing modes.

Increasing the size of the working registers and the number of bits that can be involved in arithmetic operations. This allows single instructions to operate on larger ranges of numbers.

Increasing the number of lines in the data bus, which makes it possible to transfer more data to or from memory with each access.

Increasing the number of lines in the address bus, thus increasing the size of the address space.

Including more bus control logic and, perhaps, interfacing logic on the microprocessor chip. This reduces the amount of external logic needed and simplifies the design of the bus control logic and interfaces (see Chapters 9 and 10).

Improving the processor's ability to manage memory, something that is needed for multiprogramming applications.

Being able to improve continually single-chip microprocessors has led to the creation of microprocessor families such as the Intel family shown in Fig. 5-14. The growth shown in this figure has proceeded from the 4004, which could operate on only 4 bits at a time, to the 386, which includes 32-bit operations, a 32-bit data bus, a 32-bit address bus and, therefore, a 16M byte address space, and memory management.

In examining a family such as this, it is important to note that more powerful is not always better. Although the 4-bit 4004 and Intel's earlier 8-bit microprocessors are now obsolete, Intel's 8085 and its competitors are still widely used and are likely to be used for some time to come. The reason for this is twofold. First, the 16-bit 8086 and 32-bit 386 are much more expensive and, second, they have more pins and, consequently, require more external bus control logic. Together, these factors can substantially increase the cost of a design, and many applications do not require the extra capabilities. Matching the microprocessor to the application is an important part of the design. There is no point in having the speed of an 8086 designed into a simple controller, such as a traffic-light controller, or putting the multiprogramming capability of a 386 into a personal computer that is going to be used by only one person.

This book will concentrate on 8-bit microprocessors. The reason for this is not only because they are used in numerous small computers and other digital applications but also because their designs are easier to understand and can be explained in a first course on microcomputers. On the other hand, the fundamental

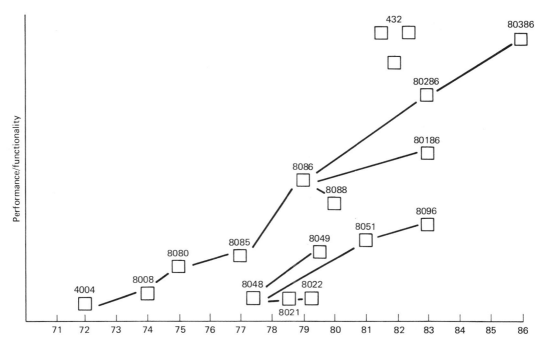

Figure 5-14   Intel family of microprocessors.   (Modified and reprinted by permission of Intel Corporation.   Copyright 1982.)

principles used in constructing 8-bit microcomputers are the same as are employed in 16-bit and 32-bit systems.   For more information on the Intel 8086/8088/186/286 microprocessors, the reader should refer to reference 1 in the Bibliography.

BIBLIOGRAPHY

1. Liu, Yu-cheng, and Glenn A. Gibson, *Microcomputer Systems: The 8086/8088 Family*, 2nd ed.   (Englewood Cliffs, N.J.: Prentice-Hall, 1986).
2. *The MCS 80/85 Family Users Manual* (Santa Clara, Calif.: Intel Corporation, 1983).
3. Hayes, John P., *Computer Architecture and Organization* (New York: McGraw-Hill, 1978).
4. Uffenbeck, John, *Microcomputers and Microprocessors: The 8080, 8085, and Z-80* (Englewood Cliffs, N.J.: Prentice-Hall, 1985).
5. Andrews, Michael, *Programming Microprocessor Interfaces for Control and Instrumentation* (Englewood Cliffs, N.J.: Prentice-Hall, 1982).
6. Short, Kenneth L., *Microprocessors and Programmed Logic* (Englewood Cliffs, N.J.: Prentice-Hall, 1981).
7. Rafiquzzaman, Mohamed, *Microcomputer Theory and Applications* (New York: John Wiley, 1982).

EXERCISES

1. Suppose that a computer's instructions can be 1, 2, or 3 bytes long and the PC contains 16 bits. Use 4-bit adders, 4-bit registers made with edge-triggered D flip-flops having clear inputs, and the necessary gates to design the PC. Assume that the only inputs are B_1 and B_0, which indicate the length of the instruction, a reset input, and a clock input.

2. Extend the solution to Exercise 1 to include a Load input, which is 1 when a branch instruction is executed, and inputs A_{15} through A_0, which make up the new address.

3. Design the network needed to drive the Load input given in Exercise 2. Assume that the PSW contains a Z (zero) bit and an M (minus) bit, all instructions contain a bit F that is 1 if and only if it is a branch instruction, and branch instructions contain a bit G that indicates whether the branch is conditional or unconditional and bits C_1 and C_0 that indicate the type of condition. The network is to output a 1 to Load if one of the following is true:
   (a) There is an unconditional branch.
   (b) $C_1 = C_0 = 0$ and $Z = 0$.
   (c) $C_1 = 0$, $C_0 = 1$, and $Z = 1$.
   (d) $C_1 = 1$, $C_0 = 0$, and $M = 1$.
   (e) $C_1 = C_0 = 1$ and $M = 0$.
   In all other cases a 0 is to be applied to Load.

4. Design a network with inputs A, B, C, and Clock and outputs X and Y. If, when the first clock pulse arrives, $A = B = 0$, then X is to be set to C and Y to 0 when the second clock pulse arrives. On the other hand, if $A = B = 1$, X is to be set to 0 and Y to C. For the case for which $A = 0$ and $B = 1$, X is to be 0 and Y is to be 1 and when $A = 1$ and $B = 0$, X is to be 1 and Y is to be 0.

5. Consider a CPU with four registers, each of which is constructed of an 8-bit latch such as the one shown here. If a signal is applied to STROBE, the inputs D_7–D_0 will be latched and if a signal is applied to OE, the contents of the latch will be output to Q_7–Q_0. Design the control circuitry needed to move the contents of any one of these registers to any other of these registers. The circuitry is to receive from the instruction decode logic the inputs MOVE REG, S_1 and S_0 (the source register's address), and D_1 and D_0 (the destination register's address). It is to output the signals $STROBE_3$–$STROBE_0$ and OE_3–OE_0. Also show how the latches would be connected together by an internal bus.

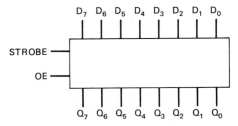

6. Suppose that an I/O interface contains four registers that have four consecutive 8-bit addresses in the I/O address space. The lowest address is to be divisible by 4 and is to be selected by the 6 high-order address bits. Each register is to latch its data inputs

when it receives a signal on its LOAD pin.   Design the address decode logic that is needed to load an addressed register.   The logic is to include a set of six switches, a comparator that outputs a 1 if its two sets of six inputs match, and other logic whose inputs are from a memory-I/O select line (that is 0 for I/O), the two lower-order address lines, and the comparator's output, and whose outputs are the four LOAD lines.

7. Using your intuition, briefly describe the principal advantages and disadvantages of having a greater number of pins on a microprocessor chip.

8. Suppose a computer is designed so that its basic unit of information is 12 bits in length and the instructions reserve 3 bits for each address mode, 4 bits for each register address, 24 bits for each memory address, and 8 bits for each I/O address.   Determine the following.

   (a) Number of address modes
   (b) Number of registers
   (c) Memory capacity and memory address space
   (d) Number of I/O addresses
   (e) Range of integers that can be stored in single precision using the 2's-complement format
   (f) Range of integers that can be stored in double precision
   (g) Range of BCD integers that can be stored in two words in 10's-complement format
   (h) Approximate range of floating-point numbers if 12 bits are reserved for the exponent and the exponent is stored using a base of 2 and the 2's-complement format
   (i) Approximate precision in significant figures if 24 bits are reserved for storing the fraction

Chapter 6

Assembler Language Programming

Although machine language instructions are the only ones that a computer can decode directly, there are other ways of programming a computer. One could write a program using a high-level language, such as Fortran or Pascal, and then use a compiler to translate its statements into machine language instructions. This kind of programming tends to divorce the programmer from the intricacies of the machine, but limits the programmer's control over exactly what happens within the machine. An alternative is to write a program using *assembler language instructions* and a translator, called an *assembler*, to convert them into machine language instructions. Unlike high-level language statements, there is an assembler language instruction for each machine language instruction, thereby giving the programmer the control he or she would have using machine language.

Other than machine language code, assembler language code is the most primitive form a program can assume. There are two types of statements in an assembler language. There are *instructions*, which are translated into machine instructions by the assembler, and *directives*, which give directions to the assembler during the assembly process but are not translated into machine instructions.

Although each assembler language instruction produces only one machine language instruction, assembler language instructions are easier to write because acronyms, called *mnemonics*, indicate the type of instruction, and character strings, called *symbols* or *identifiers*, represent addresses and perhaps numbers. A typical assembler instruction

ADD   A,M

adds the contents of a memory location to register A.   The abbreviation ADD is the instruction mnemonic.   An example of a directive is

COST: DS   1

which causes the assembler to reserve a byte and associate the symbol COST with the byte, but does not result in a machine language instruction.

A simple program segment for an Intel 8085 microprocessor that adds the two numbers in the memory locations represented by NUM1 and NUM2 and puts the result in the accumulator (register A) is

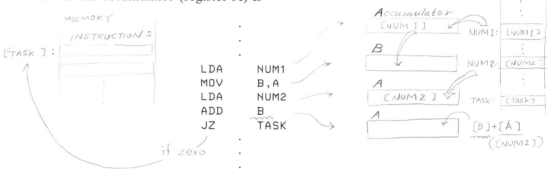

The first instruction transfers one of the numbers into the accumulator, the second instruction transfers the number from the accumulator to the working register denoted by B, and the third transfers the second number from memory into the accumulator (the first number that was in the accumulator has now been replaced by the second number).   The fourth instruction adds the two numbers and replaces the contents of the accumulator with the sum.   The last instruction causes the next instruction to be brought in from memory location TASK if the result was 0; otherwise, the next instruction will be brought in from the memory location following the JZ instruction.

There are several important points that become evident through this example. Three of the most important points are

1. Most instructions involve movement of information from one part of the computer system to another.   This implies there is a need to differentiate among the locations within the system so that they can be uniquely specified in a way that the computer understands.

2. Computers are not generally capable of operating on entities within the system in a completely flexible manner.   For example, in the Intel 8085 one of the numbers being added must be the accumulator at the time the ADD instruction is given.   Therefore, many transfers within a computer serve only to put the information into the proper place before operating on it.

3. Some instructions are solely for determining where the next instruction is to be found.

The discussion presented in this chapter considers these and other basic points in detail.

The basic operations performed by any computer can be categorized as shown below. Because of their limited size, 8-bit microprocessors do not usually have a sufficient instruction repertoire to be able to perform each of these operations with just one instruction. In this and the next two chapters we examine how these operations are normally accomplished by 8-bit microprocessors.

TRANSFER—Between registers, between memory and the registers, and between memory locations.

INDEXING AND COUNTING—Incrementing and decrementing.

ARITHMETIC—Addition, subtraction, multiplication, division, and negation. They fall into three types:

1. Integer (or fixed-point)
2. Floating-point
3. BCD (or decimal)

BRANCHING—Ordinarily instructions are taken from consecutive memory locations; however, it is sometimes necessary to jump out of the ordinary sequence of code. The branching instructions perform this function. They fall into three main categories:

1. *Unconditional branching*, in which the branch will be taken regardless of the state of the CPU.
2. *Conditional branching*, which is made or not made according to some combination of the PSW flags. This is sometimes done with a combination of a skip, which means to skip the next instruction, followed by an unconditional branch.
3. *Subroutine branches and returns*. A return address is stored by the branch and the return branch uses this address. They may be either conditional or unconditional. (Subroutines are discussed in Section 7-3.)

LOOPING—A combination of incrementing or decrementing, comparing, testing, and branching, the purpose being to execute repetitively a program segment.

SHIFT AND ROTATE—Shift right, shift left, rotate right, rotate left, and multiple word (or byte) shifts and rotates.

LOGICAL—OR, AND, exclusive OR, and complementation.

STACK MANIPULATION—For putting things on and taking them off the stack. (See Section 7-2.)

I/O COMMUNICATION AND TRANSFER—For initiating and performing I/O data transfers, testing the I/O status, giving I/O commands, and so on. (See Chapter 8.)

The features that are available in high-level languages must also be available in assembler languages, even though a single high-level language statement may require several assembler statements to implement it. In addition to including ways of performing branches, loops, I/O, arithmetic operations, and assignments, an assembler needs to provide the equivalents of preassignment, storage allocation, naming of constants, commenting, structuring data, calling procedures, statement functions, and global labeling.

Regardless of the level of the language in which programs are written, programs involve inputting, processing, and outputting. Complex programs may require an intermixing of these functions, as illustrated by the diagram in Fig. 6-1a, but simple programs tend to perform them in sequence, as shown in Fig. 6-1b. This chapter concentrates on simple programs with the inputting, processing, and outputting being performed in order. Because I/O programming is not introduced until Chapter 8, the input and output code will not be given in the examples, but its presence, as well as that of another code, will be indicated by comments. The purpose of this chapter is to provide all the material needed to write relatively complex single-module input-process-output programs that are complete, except for the exclusion of the I/O code.

Because an assembler is nothing more than a translating program, the format and syntax of the instructions and directives depend on how the assembler is written, not on the computer. The assembler assumed in the examples in this book is the ASM-85 assembler designed by Intel. It is representative of 8085 assemblers, and its major features are representative of assemblers in general. For reasons of clarity, some of the seldom used features of the ASM-85 assembler will not be

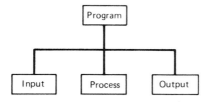

(a) Intermixing I/O with processing

(b) Sequential input-process-output

Figure 6-1   General program structures.

presented.   For programming details, one should refer to the assembler language manual for the system being used.

This chapter will proceed by first exploring the assembler language instruction format and the memory allocation and definition directives.   Then Sections 6-2 through 6-9 define and discuss the 8085's transfer, arithmetic, branching, logical, shift and rotate, and flag manipulation instructions, with Section 6-6 describing how incrementing, comparing, and conditional branching can be used to produce looping.   Section 6-10 considers some commonly used directives that make assembler language easier to use, Section 6-11 describes the assembly process, and Section 6-12 considers instruction timing.   The last two sections discuss the assembler languages for the Zilog Z80 and Motorola MC6809 microprocessors.   By considering the extra address registers and modes available in these microprocessors, these sections provide contrasting examples to the 8085 examples given in the earlier sections.

6-1 ASSEMBLER INSTRUCTION FORMAT

The general format of an assembler instruction is

```
Label:     Mnemonic     Operand,Operand        ;Remarks
```

where the inclusion of spaces is arbitrary, except that at least one space must be inserted if no space would lead to an ambiguity (e.g., between the mnemonic and first operand).   Also, there can be no spaces within a mnemonic or symbol.   *Label* is a symbol that is assigned the address of the first byte of the instruction in which it appears.   The presence of a label in an instruction is optional, but, if present, the label provides a symbolic name that can be used in branch instructions to branch to the instruction.   If there is no label, then the colon must be deleted. All instructions must contain a mnemonic.   The presence of the operands depends on the instruction.   Some instructions have no operands, some have one, and some have two.   If there are two operands, they are separated by a comma.   The *Remarks* field is for documenting the program and may contain any combination of characters.   It is optional, and if it is deleted the semicolon may also be deleted. A remark may appear on a line by itself, provided that the first character on the line is a semicolon.   Figure 6-2 shows the details of a typical assembler language

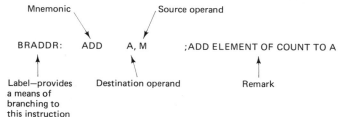

Figure 6-2   Representative assembler language instruction.

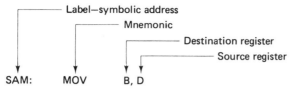

(a) Register to register transfer

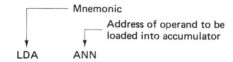

(b) Load accumulator from memory

(c) Transfer of immediate operand to register

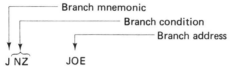

(d) Conditional branch on nonzero result

Figure 6-3   Representative Intel 8085 assembler language instructions.

instruction.   Figure 6-3 gives the assembler language instructions corresponding to the machine language instructions given in Fig. 5-13.

An assembler language instruction usually has an operand for each machine language instruction operand and the notation for each operand must be sufficient to indicate the operand's addressing mode.   If there are two operands, the destination operand appears first and the source operand second.   When an operand is a word in memory the low-order byte of the word will have the lower address and the high-order byte the higher address—e.g., if the symbol COST is used as a word operand, then COST is associated with the low-order byte and COST+1 with the high-order byte.

For the examples in this book, an assembler language operand appears as an expression made up of one or more of the following concatenated together:

LABEL—A symbol that represents the first byte of an instruction or datum.

CONSTANT—A number whose base is indicated by a suffix as follows:

B—binary

D—decimal

O—octal

H—hexadecimal

The default is decimal. The first digit in a hexadecimal number must be 0 through 9; therefore, if the most significant digit is a letter (A–F), then it must be prefixed with a 0. Examples are

$$1011_2 = 1011B$$

$$223_{10} = 223D = 223$$

$$B25A_{16} = 0B25AH$$

STRING CONSTANT—A character string enclosed in single quotes (''').
ARITHMETIC OPERATORS—The operators "+", "−", "*", and "/".
NAME—A symbol that represents a constant, string constant, or expression (see Section 6-10).

A symbol must be six or fewer characters in length and begin with a letter, a question mark, or an @ sign. An expression that does not include a label can be evaluated by the assembler to produce a number. Such an expression is called a *constant expression*. Three instructions with operands that are more than a simple variable, constant, or label are shown in Fig. 6-4.

Each 8085 instruction will be defined and discussed in detail before it is used. For convenience in referencing these instructions, they are summarized in Appendix

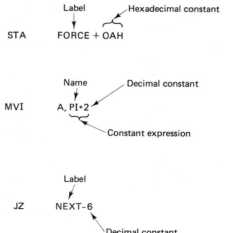

Figure 6-4 Instructions with expressions for operands.

accumulator	Register A
addr	16–bit address quantity
data	8–bit data quantity
data 16	16–bit data quantity
byte 2	The second byte of the instruction
byte 3	The third byte of the instruction
port	8–bit address of an I/O device
r, r1, r2	One of the registers A, B, C, D, E, H, L
DDD, SSS	The bit pattern designating one of the registers A, B, C, D, E, H, L (DDD = destination, SSS = source):
NNN	The binary representation 000 through 111 for restart number 0 through 7 respectively.
CCC	Condition flags:

Z	-	Zero,
S	-	Sign,
P	-	Parity,
C	-	Carry,
AC	-	Auxilliary Carry

( )	The contents of the memory location or registers enclosed in the parentheses.
←	"Is transferred to"
∧	Logical AND
∀	Exclusive OR
V	Inclusive OR
+	Addition
−	Two's complement subtraction
*	Multiplication
↔	"Is exchanged with"
—	The one's complement (e.g., ($\overline{A}$))
n	The restart number 0 through 7

Figure 6-5 Symbols and abbreviations used in the 8085 instruction definitions. (Reprinted by permission of Intel Corporation.)

A.   Figure 6-5 defines the abbreviations and symbols that appear in the instruction definitions.   (Many of the same abbreviations, symbols, formats, and so on, are more or less standard and are used in manuals published by other manufacturers.) In particular, note that if a memory location or register is indicated inside parentheses, its contents are to be assumed, not the location or register itself.   The meaning of these symbols will become clearer as the instructions are used in the examples given below.   As shown in Fig. 6-6, each instruction definition will be formatted as follows:

1. The assembler format, consisting of the instruction mnemonic and operand field, is printed on the left side of the first line.
2. The name of the instruction is enclosed in parentheses on the right side of the first line.

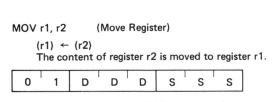

MOV r1, r2   (Move Register)

(r1) ← (r2)
The content of register r2 is moved to register r1.

0	1	D	D	D	S	S	S

Addressing: register
Flags: none

Figure 6-6 Example of an 8085 instruction definition.

3. The next line(s) contains a symbolic description of the operation of the instruction.

4. This is followed by a narrative description of the operation of the instruction.

5. The following line(s) contains the binary fields and patterns that make up the machine instruction.

6. The last two lines contain information about the execution of the instruction.

The Intel 8085 has a byte length of 8 bits and all instructions are 1, 2, or 3 bytes long. Those instructions that involve only register or register indirect addressing are 1 byte long; those involving I/O or immediate operands are 2 or 3 bytes long.

As seen in Chapter 5, there are seven working registers in the 8085; they are denoted A, B, C, D, E, H, and L. Their register addresses are given in Fig. 6-7 together with other register-related information. Except for the accumulator (register A), the registers are sometimes considered in the pairs BC, DE, and HL. Note that both registers in these pairs have the same higher 2 bits in their register addresses. When referencing a register pair, only these two bits are used. The 16-bit stack pointer is addressed as a register pair using the pair address 11. It is sometimes necessary to refer to a single bit in a register or memory location. This is done by numbering the bits 7 through 0 from left to right and referring to the bit by its number.

As mentioned in the introduction, besides instructions an assembler language must include directives, which *direct* the assembler during the assembly process. Before we present assembler language examples, it is necessary to introduce the directives for reserving memory locations, assigning these locations to labels, and perhaps filling them with data. ASM-85 has three directives for satisfying these needs and all three have the format:

```
Label:      Mnemonic        Operand, ..., Operand
```

where *Label* is optional and *Mnemonic* is DS, DB, or DW.

The DS (define storage) directive is used only for reserving memory and perhaps assigning a label to the first byte of the reserved area. It can include only one operand and that operand must be a constant expression whose value indicates the number of bytes to be reserved. An example of a DS directive is

```
ARRAY:     DS     20
```

which reserves 20 bytes and assigns the label ARRAY to the byte with the lowest address.

The DB (define byte) directive can be used to put values into, or *preassign* values to, memory locations as well as reserve space and assign labels. It serves the same purpose as the DATA statement in Fortran. It can include up to eight

rp   One of the register pairs:

    B represents the B C pair with B as the high-order register and C as the low-order register;

    D represents the D E pair with D as the high-order register and E as the low-order register;

    H represents the H L pair with H as the high-order register and L as the low-order register;

    SP represents the 16-bit stack pointer register.

RP   The bit pattern designating one of the register pairs B, D, H, SP:

Register Addr. (DDD or SSS)	Register Name
000	B
001	C
010	D
011	E
100	H
101	L
111	A

rh   The first (high-order) register of a designated register pair.

rl   The second (low-order) register of a designated register pair.

PC   16-bit program counter register (PCH and PCL are used to refer to the high-order and low-order 8-bits respectively).

SP   16-bit stack pointer register (SPH and SPL are used to refer to the high-order and low-order 8-bits respectively).

r_m Bit m of the register r (bits are number 7 through 0 from left to right).

Register Pair Address (RP)	Register Pair
00	BC
01	DE
10	HL
11	SP (One 16 bit register)

Figure 6-7 Register and register pair addresses and the register abbreviations used in the instruction definitions. (Reprinted by permission of Intel Corporation. Copyright 1983.)

operands, with each operand being a string constant with no more than 128 characters or a constant expression that evaluates to a 2's complement number from − 128 to 127.   The values of the operands are put in consecutive bytes of memory in the order in which they appear.   For string constants the first character in the string is put in the first byte reserved for the string and so on.   For example

```
DATA:    DB      14H,'ABC',01101000B
```

would reserve 5 bytes, associate the label DATA with the first byte, and fill the 5 bytes as shown in Fig. 6-8a.   (Throughout this book all memory location contents and addresses will be in hexadecimal unless noted otherwise.)

The DW directive is similar to the DB directive except that it reserves words instead of bytes.   Each of its possible eight operands must be a label or a constant expression that evaluates to a 16-bit number, or a string of one or two characters. The low-order byte of the word is stored in the lower byte address and the high-order byte in the higher byte address.   For example

```
PTABLE:    DW      TASK1,TASK2,092AH
```

where TASK1 and TASK2 are labels, reserves three words (6 bytes), associates PTABLE with the first byte in the first word, and fills the words with the addresses of TASK1 and TASK2 and the number 092AH, respectively.   The contents of the reserved memory locations are given in Fig. 6-8b, which assumes that the labels TASK1 and TASK2 have been assigned to the memory locations 2010 and 108C, respectively.

6-2 TRANSFER INSTRUCTIONS

In a high-level language such as Fortran, only memory to memory transfers can be made using assignment statements of the form

$$X = Y$$

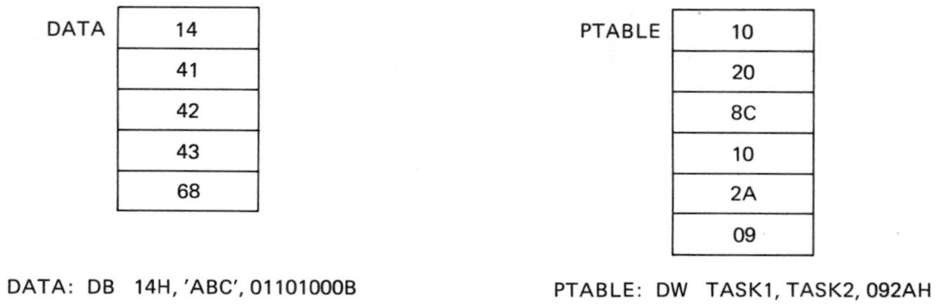

DATA: DB 14H, 'ABC', 01101000B

(a) DB

PTABLE: DW TASK1, TASK2, 092AH

(b) DW

Figure 6-8   Examples of DB and DW directives.

LHLD addr   (Load H and L direct)

(L) ← ((Byte 3) (byte 2))
(H) ← ((byte 3) (byte 2) + 1)
The content of the memory location, whose address
is specified in byte 2 and byte 3 of the instruction, is
moved to register L. The content of the memory
location at the succeeding address is moved to
register H.

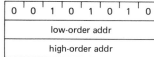

Addressing: direct
Flags: none

LXI rp, data 16   (Load register pair immediate)

(rh) ← (byte 3),
(rl) ← (byte 2)
Byte 3 of the instruction is moved into the high-order
register (rh) of the register pair rp. Byte 2 of the
instruction is moved into the low-order register (rl) of
the register pair rp.

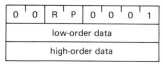

Addressing: immediate
Flags: none

SHLD addr   (Store H and L direct)

((byte 3) (byte 2)) ← (L)
((byte 3) (byte 2) + 1) ← (H)
The content of register L is moved to the memory
location whose address is specified in byte 2 and
byte 3. The content of register H is moved to the
succeeding memory location.

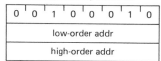

Addressing: direct
Flags: none

XCHG   (Exchange H and L with D and E)

(H) ⟷ (D)
(L) ⟷ (E)
The contents of registers H and L are exchanged with
the contents of registers D and E.

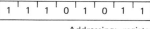

Addressing: register
Flags: none

Figure 6-9 Word transfer instructions. (Reprinted by permission of Intel Corporation.
Copyright 1983.)

which causes the contents of Y to be transferred to X. In assembler and machine
language the programmer has complete control of movement of data between
memory and the CPU registers. It is possible to move a datum between registers,
between memory and a register, or between memory locations. Some of these
moves, particularly the latter, may require more than one assembler instruction
but can be performed in a sequence of two or three instructions.

The 8085 includes 13 transfer instructions, four of which can move an entire
word and are defined in Fig. 6-9. The LHLD instruction causes a word to be
taken from memory and put into the HL register pair. The address of the byte
put into L, which is considered to be the low-order byte, is specified by the second
and third bytes of the instruction with the second byte containing the low-order
part of the address. The byte put into H is taken from the next memory location.
SHLD is similar to LHLD, except that the transfer is in the opposite direction,
from the HL pair to memory. The LXI instruction transfers the second and third
bytes of the instruction into the HL pair, with the second byte (the low-order byte)
being put into L. XCHG exchanges the contents of the HL pair with those of the
DE pair. It is needed whenever two addresses are being used. One can be stored
in the HL pair and the other in the DE pair, and XCHG can be used to change
from one address to the other easily, depending on which is needed next.

It is no accident that all of the word transfer instructions involve the HL pair. It will be seen shortly that this pair is primarily used for holding addresses, and addresses are one word long. The HL pair could, however, be used for storing data, in which case these instructions would be used to manipulate 16-bit data.

The other nine transfer instructions move only one byte at a time. They are defined in Fig. 6-10. Note that three of them—the MOV and MVI instructions that involve memory, employ register indirect addressing through the HL pair (i.e., the HL pair contains the address) and two of the others, the LDAX and STAX instructions—use register indirect addressing through the BC or DE pair. The other MOV and MVI instructions involve only registers and immediate data (i.e., data that are included in the instruction). LDA uses direct addressing (in which the address is part of the instruction) to move a byte from memory to the accumulator (A register). STA is the same as LDA except that the transfer is in the opposite direction.

Figure 6-11 shows three ways of putting the constant $1D_{16}$ into register B. The left side of the figure shows the code and the right side illustrates the actions taken. The first two sequences of code assume the constant is in X, which is associated with the address 01A0. The third approach lets the constant be immediate data in the second byte of the MVI instruction. Although this approach requires only one instruction, it is less flexible than the other two, which would move any number that happens to be in X into register B. In all three sequences the instructions begin at address 0210.

Figure 6-12 shows two ways of moving a word from one memory location, NUMS, to another memory location, NUMD. Although the second sequence requires 4 instructions and 12 bytes of memory, as opposed to 2 and 6 for the first, it has the advantage of disturbing only the contents of register A and the destination NUMD. This would be important if the HL pair contained an address that is needed later. This points out an important problem associated with the limited number of working registers: this limitation frequently causes a considerable amount of movement in order to accomplish a small task.

6-3 INCREMENTING AND DECREMENTING INSTRUCTIONS

In high-level language programming, incrementing and decrementing are quite often needed for counting such things as loop repetitions and indexing through arrays. They are even more important when programming at the machine or assembler level, especially when using an 8-bit microprocessor that can manipulate only one byte or, perhaps, one word at a time. The 8085 instructions for performing incrementing and decrementing are defined in Fig. 6-13. There are instructions for adding 1 to the quantity in any of the seven 8-bit working registers, adding 1 to the quantity in the memory byte pointed to by the HL pair, and adding 1 to the 16-bit quantity in any register pair, and corresponding instructions for subtracting 1 from these quantities.

MOV r1, r2   (Move Register)

(r1) ← (r2)
The content of register r2 is moved to register r1.

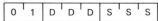

Addressing: register
Flags: none

MOV r, M   (Move from memory)

(r) ← ((H) (L))
The content of the memory location, whose address
is in registers H and L, is moved to register r.

Addressing: reg. indirect
Flags: none

MOV M, r   (Move to memory)

((H) (L)) ← (r)
The content of register r is moved to the memory
location whose address is in registers H and L.

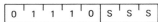

Addressing: reg. indirect
Flags: none

MVI r, data   (Move immediate)

(r) ← (byte 2)
The content of byte 2 of the instruction is moved to
register r.

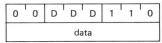

Addressing: immediate
Flags: none

MVI M, data   (Move to memory immediate)

((H) (L)) ← (byte 2)
The content of byte 2 of the instruction is moved to
the memory location whose address is in registers H
and L.

Addressing: Immed./reg.indirect
Flags: none

LDAX rp   (Load accumulator indirect)

(A) ← ((rp))
The content of the memory location, whose address
is in the register pair rp, is moved to register A. Note:
only register pairs rp = B (registers B and C) or rp = D
(registers D and E) may be specified.

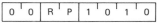

Addressing: reg. indirect
Flags: none

STAX rp   (Store accumulator indirect)

((rp)) ← (A)
The content of register A is moved to the memory
location whose address is in the register pair rp. Note:
only register pairs rp = B (registers B and C) or rp = D
(registers D and E) may be specified.

Addressing: reg. indirect
Flags: none

LDA addr   (Load accumulator direct)

(A) ← ((byte 3) (byte 2))
The content of the memory location, whose address
is specified in byte 2 and byte 3 of the instruction,
is moved to register A.

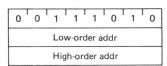

Addressing: direct
Flags: none

STA addr   (Store accummulator direct)

((byte 3) (byte 2)) ← (A)
The content of the accumulator is moved to the
memory location whose address is specified in byte
2 and byte 3 of the instruction.

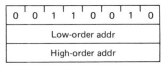

Addressing: direct
Flags: none

Figure 6-10 Byte transfer instructions. (Reprinted by permission of Intel Corporation.
Copyright 1983.)

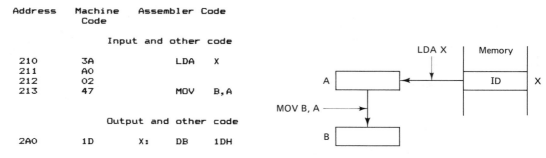

```
Address     Machine     Assembler Code
            Code

            Input and other code

   210        3A            LDA    X
   211        A0
   212        02
   213        47            MOV    B,A

            Output and other code

   2A0        1D        X:      DB     1DH
```

(a) Using direct and register addressing

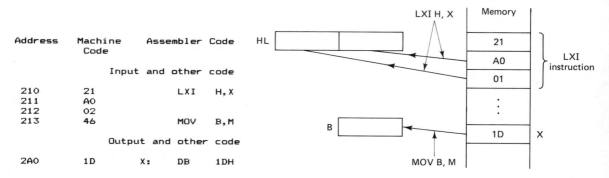

```
Address     Machine     Assembler Code
            Code

            Input and other code

   210        21            LXI    H,X
   211        A0
   212        02
   213        46            MOV    B,M

            Output and other code

   2A0        1D        X:      DB     1DH
```

(b) Using indirect addressing

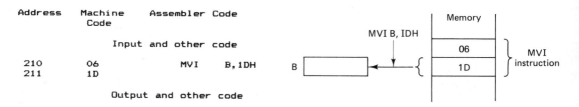

```
Address     Machine     Assembler Code
            Code

            Input and other code

   210        06            MVI    B,1DH
   211        1D

            Output and other code
```

(c) Using immediate addressing

Figure 6-11   Moving a 1-byte constant into a register.

    The INX and DCX instructions are especially important because they can be
used to increment or decrement an address in the HL pair.   Figure 6-14 shows
how 3 consecutive bytes beginning at SRC could be moved to 3 consecutive bytes
beginning at DST by using the INX instruction in conjunction with the LXI and
MOV instructions.   Examples involving the other incrementing and decrementing
instructions are given in the discussion of loops.

Address	Machine Code	Assembler Code		Remarks

Input and other code

Address	Machine Code	Assembler Code		Remarks
120	2A	LHLD	NUMS	;LOAD WORD FROM NUMS INTO HL
121	E2			
122	01			
123	22	SHLD	NUMD	;STORE HL IN NUMD
124	F6			
125	01			

Output and other code

Address	Machine Code	Assembler Code		
1E2	–	NUMS:	DS	2
1E3	–			
	.			
	.			
	.			
1F6	–	NUMD:	DS	2
1F7	–			

(a) Using word transfers

Address	Machine Code	Assembler Code		Remarks

Input and other code

Address	Machine Code	Assembler Code		Remarks
120	3A	LDA	NUMS	;LOAD FIRST BYTE INTO A
121	E2			
122	01			
123	32	STA	NUMD	;STORE BYTE IN NUMD
124	F6			
125	01			
126	3A	LDA	NUMS+1	;LOAD SECOND BYTE INTO A
127	E3			
128	01			
129	32	STA	NUMD+1	;STORE BYTE IN NUMD+1
12A	F7			
12B	01			

Output and other code

Address	Machine Code	Assembler Code		
1E2	–	NUMS:	DS	2
1E3	–			
	.			
	.			
	.			
1F6	–	NUMD:	DS	2
1F7	–			

(b) Using byte transfers

Figure 6-12   Moving a word from one memory location to another.

6-4 ARITHMETIC INSTRUCTIONS

Arithmetic operations can be performed very easily in a high-level language; all that is needed is an assignment statement. At the machine or assembler level, however, the programmer must perform every little step required to carry out a

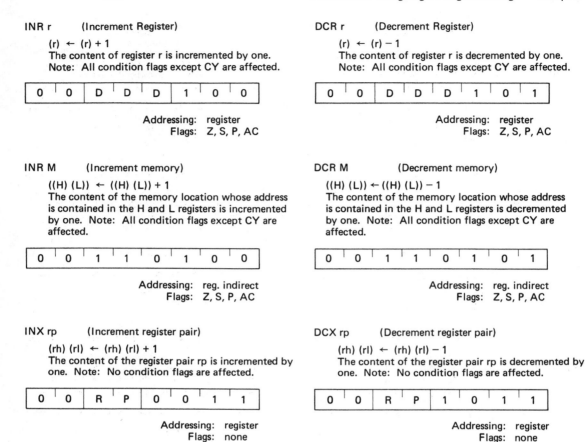

INR r   (Increment Register)

(r) ← (r) + 1
The content of register r is incremented by one.
Note: All condition flags except CY are affected.

0	0	D	D	D	1	0	0

Addressing: register
Flags: Z, S, P, AC

DCR r   (Decrement Register)

(r) ← (r) − 1
The content of register r is decremented by one.
Note: All condition flags except CY are affected.

0	0	D	D	D	1	0	1

Addressing: register
Flags: Z, S, P, AC

INR M   (Increment memory)

((H) (L)) ← ((H) (L)) + 1
The content of the memory location whose address
is contained in the H and L registers is incremented
by one. Note: All condition flags except CY are
affected.

0	0	1	1	0	1	0	0

Addressing: reg. indirect
Flags: Z, S, P, AC

DCR M   (Decrement memory)

((H) (L)) ← ((H) (L)) − 1
The content of the memory location whose address
is contained in the H and L registers is decremented
by one. Note: All condition flags except CY are
affected.

0	0	1	1	0	1	0	1

Addressing: reg. indirect
Flags: Z, S, P, AC

INX rp   (Increment register pair)

(rh) (rl) ← (rh) (rl) + 1
The content of the register pair rp is incremented by
one. Note: No condition flags are affected.

0	0	R	P	0	0	1	1

Addressing: register
Flags: none

DCX rp   (Decrement register pair)

(rh) (rl) ← (rh) (rl) − 1
The content of the register pair rp is decremented by
one. Note: No condition flags are affected.

0	0	R	P	1	0	1	1

Addressing: register
Flags: none

Figure 6-13   Incrementing and decrementing instructions.   (Reprinted by permission of Intel
Corporation.   Copyright 1983.)

calculation.   As with most other microprocessors, the 8085's instruction set enables
it to operate on numbers in either binary or BCD form.   However, no 8-bit
microprocessor has instructions for performing floating-point arithmetic operations,
and these operations must be done by lengthy sequences of assembler code.   Even
the 16-bit processors can do floating-point operations with single instructions only
if they have separate chips, called *floating-point units*.   In this section we consider
only binary and BCD operations.

6-4-1 Binary Arithmetic

Six of the 8085 instructions for operating on numbers in binary form are defined
in Fig. 6-15.   For all of these instructions, the operands are single bytes, and the
addend or subtrahend must be in the A register and is replaced by the result that
is put into the A register.   The augend or minuend may come from any working

Address	Machine Code	Assembler Code		Remarks

Input and other code

Address	Machine Code	Assembler Code		Remarks
50	21	LXI	H,SRC	;LOAD ADDR SRC INTO HL PAIR
51	80			
52	00			
53	46	MOV	B,M	;LOAD B FROM SRC
54	23	INX	H	;INCREMENT ADDR
55	4E	MOV	C,M	;LOAD C FROM SRC+1
56	23	INX	H	;INCREMENT ADDR
57	56	MOV	D,M	;LOAD D FROM SRC+2
58	21	LXI	H,DES	;LOAD ADDR DES INTO HL PAIR
59	20			
5A	01			
5B	70	MOV	M,B	;PUT (B) INTO DES
5C	23	INX	H	;INCREMENT ADDR
5D	71	MOV	M,C	;PUT (C) INTO DES+1
5E	23	INX	H	;INCREMENT ADDR
5F	72	MOV	M,D	;PUT (D) INTO DES+2

Output and other code

Address	Machine Code	Assembler Code		Remarks
80	—	SRC: DS	3	;SOURCE AREA
81	—			
82	—			
	•			
	•			
	•			
120	—	DES: DS	3	;DESTINATION AREA
121	—			
122	—			

Figure 6-14 Program segment for moving 3 bytes from one area in memory to another area in memory.

register, the memory location currently pointed to by the HL pair, or from the instruction.

Figure 6-16 gives a sequence of code that adds the numbers in NOS and NOS + 1, subtracts the sum from TOTL, adds 6 to the difference, and puts the final result in ANS. Note how the sequence is organized so that the result always ends up in the A register. A Fortran statement for performing an equivalent calculation is

$$ANS = (TOTL - (NOS(1) + NOS(2))) + 6$$

Although the segment in Fig. 6-16 can be used on either 1-byte nonnegative numbers or 2's complement numbers, the numbers are limited to 8 bits, either 0 to 255 or −128 to 127. Since only single bytes are being operated on, the arithmetic is said to be *single-precision*. To handle larger numbers that can be extended across 2 or more bytes, arithmetic instructions that accommodate carrys and borrows are needed. For this reason, the 8085 instruction set also includes the instructions defined in Fig. 6-17. In Fig. 6-18 is a sequence of code that performs the same operations as the code in Fig. 6-16, except that the operands are all 2 bytes wide. Arithmetic that works with quantities that are twice as wide as the

ADD r   (Add register)
(A) ← (A) + (r)
The content of register r is added to the content
of the accumulator. The result is placed in the
accumulator.

Addressing: register
Flags: Z, S, P, CY, AC

ADD M   (Add memory)
(A) ← (A) + ((H) (L))
The content of the memory location whose address
is contained in the H and L registers is added to the
content of the accumulator. The result is placed in
the accumulator.

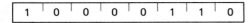

Addressing: reg. indirect
Flags: Z, S, P, CY, AC

ADI data   (Add immediate)
(A) ← (A) + (byte 2)
The content of the second byte of the instruction is
added to the content of the accumulator. The result
is placed in the accumulator.

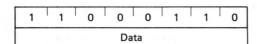

Addressing: immediate
Flags: Z, S, P, CY, AC

SUB r   (Subtract register)
(A) ← (A) − (r)
The content of register r is subtracted from the
content of the accumulator. The result is placed
in the accumulator.

Addressing: register
Flags: Z, S, P, CY, AC

SUB M   (Subtract memory)
(A) ← (A) − ((H) (L))
The content of the memory location whose address
is contained in the H and L registers is subtracted
from the content of the accumulator. The result is
placed in the accumulator.

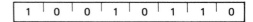

Addressing: reg. indirect
Flags: Z, S, P, CY, AC

SUI data   (Subtract immediate)
(A) ← (A) − (byte 2)
The content of the second byte of the instruction is
subtracted from the content of the accumulator. The
result is placed in the accumulator.

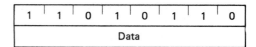

Addressing: immediate
Flags: Z, S, P, CY, AC

Figure 6-15 Binary additions and subtractions with no carry or borrow. (Reprinted by
permission of Intel Corporation.   Copyright 1983.)

processor's basic width (in this case 1 byte) is said to be *double-precision*.   In
general, working with quantities whose widths are more than the basic width is
called *multiple-precision* arithmetic.

The 8085 does have an arithmetic instruction that operates on 2-byte quantities; it is the DAD instruction defined in Fig. 6-19.   DAD can add any register
pair, including the HL pair, to the HL pair.   Among other things, it is used to
add a fixed quantity to an address in the HL pair; e.g., if the HL pair contains the
base address of a two-dimensional column-organized array and BC contains the

Address	Machine Code	Assembler Code		Remarks

Input and other code

Address	Machine Code	Assembler Code		Remarks
30	21	LXI	H,NOS	;LOAD ADDRESS NOS
				;INTO HL
31	10			
32	01			
33	7E	MOV	A,M	;LOAD (NOS) INTO A
34	23	INX	H	;INCREMENT ADDRESS
35	86	ADD	M	;ADD (NOS+1) TO A
36	47	MOV	B,A	;MOVE (A) TO B
37	3A	LDA	TOTL	;LOAD (TOTL) INTO A
38	20			
39	01			
3A	90	SUB	B	;SUB (B) FROM A
3B	C6	ADI	6	;ADD 6 TO A
3C	06			
3D	32	STA	ANS	;STORE IN ANS
3E	70			
3F	00			

Output and other code

Address	Machine Code	Assembler Code			Remarks
70	—	ANS:	DS	1	;RESULT GOES HERE
	.				
	.				
	.				
110	—	NOS:	DS	2	;NUMBERS BEING ADDED
111	—				
	.				
	.				
	.				
120	—	TOTL:	DS	1	;NUMBER SUBTRACTED FROM

Figure 6-16 Program segment demonstrating single-precision arithmetic.

length of a column, then the instruction

$$\text{DAD} \quad \text{B}$$

would change the base to the next column. As we proceed, numerous other uses for the DAD instruction will be found. Note that DAD affects only the carry flag, and would, therefore, be unsuitable for most applications involving signed numbers.

The ALU performs both addition and subtraction by carrying out an addition on two 8-bit operands. If the operation is subtraction, the 2's complement of the subtrahend is taken before this addition is executed. In either case the ALU logic views the two operands as two 8-bit positive numbers. Whenever an operand is treated in this way it is called an *unsigned integer*. Integers used in the normal way with their signs being taken into account are called *signed integers*. In double-precision addition the lower-order bytes are presented to the ALU and are added as unsigned integers. If the sum is too large, the carry flag is set. In adding the high-order bytes, the carry bit must also be added. For double-precision sub-

ADC r   (Add Register with carry)

(A) ← (A) + (r) + (CY)
The content of register r and the content of the carry
bit are added to the content of the accumulator. The
result is placed in the accumulator.

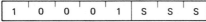

Addressing: register
Flags: Z, S, P, CY, AC

SBB r   (Subtract Register with borrow)

(A) ← (A) − (r) − (CY)
The content of register r and the content of the CY
flag are both subtracted from the accumulator. The
result is placed in the accumulator.

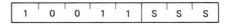

Addressing: register
Flags: Z, S, P, CY, AC

ADC M   (Add memory with carry)

(A) ← (A) + ((H) (L)) + (CY)
The content of the memory location whose address is
contained in the H and L registers and the content of
the CY flag are added to the accumulator. The result
is placed in the accumulator.

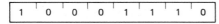

Addressing: reg. indirect
Flags: Z, S, P, CY, AC

SBB M   (Subtract memory with borrow)

(A) ← (A) − ((H) (L)) − (CY)
The content of the memory location whose address is
contained in the H and L registers and the content of
the CY flag are both subtracted from the accumulator.
The result is placed in the accumulator.

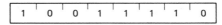

Addressing: reg. indirect
Flags: Z, S, P, CY, AC

ACI data   (Add immediate with carry)

(A) ← (A) + (byte 2) + (CY)
The content of the second byte of the instruction and
the content of the CY flag are added to the contents
of the accumulator. The result is placed in the
accumulator.

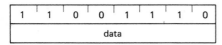

Addressing: immediate
Flags: Z, S, P, CY, AC

SBI data   (Subtract immediate with borrow)

(A) ← (A) − (byte 2) − (CY)
The contents of the second byte of the instruction and
the contents of the CY flag are both subtracted from
the accumulator. The result is placed in the accumulator.

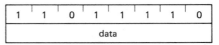

Addressing: immediate
Flags: Z, S, P, CY, AC

Figure 6-17 Binary additions and subtractions with carrys and borrows. (Reprinted by
permission of Intel Corporation.   Copyright 1983.)

traction, the 2's complement of the subtrahend is taken and then the low-order
bytes of the operands are added as unsigned integers. If the magnitude of the
subtrahend is larger than that of the minuend, the carry flag is set to indicate a
borrow. (It can be shown that this will occur if and only if the addition does *not*
result in a carry.) Then the 2 high-order bytes are subtracted and the borrow is
subtracted from the difference. These ideas can easily be extended to higher-
order multiple-precision addition and subtraction.

Address	Machine Code	Assembler Code		Remarks
		Input and other code		
30	21	LXI	H,NOS	;LOAD ADDRESS NOS INTO HL
31	10			
32	01			
33	4E	MOV	C,M	;LOAD (NOS) AND
34	23	INX	H	; (NOS+1) INTO
35	46	MOV	B,M	;BC PAIR
36	23	INX	H	
37	7E	MOV	A,M	;ADD (NOS+2)
38	81	ADD	C	;AND (NOS+3)
39	4F	MOV	C,A	;TO BC PAIR
3A	23	INX	H	
3B	7E	MOV	A,M	
3C	88	ADC	B	
3D	47	MOV	B,A	
3E	21	LXI	H,TOTL	;LOAD ADDRESS TOTL INTO HL
3F	20			
40	01			
41	7E	MOV	A,M	;SUB (BC) FROM
42	91	SUB	C	; (TOTL) AND
43	4F	MOV	C,A	; (TOTL+1) AND
44	23	INX	H	;PUT RESULT IN
45	7E	MOV	A,M	;BC PAIR
46	98	SBB	B	
47	47	MOV	B,A	
48	79	MOV	A,C	;PUT LOW ORDER DIFF
49	C6	ADI	6	;IN A AND ADD 6
4A	06			
4B	32	STA	ANS	;STORE LOW ORDER RESULT IN ANS
4C	70			
4D	00			
4E	3E	MVI	A,0	;PUT 0 IN A
4F	00			
50	88	ADC	B	;ADD CARRY
51	32	STA	ANS+1	;STORE HIGH ORDER RESULT IN ANS+1
52	71			
53	00			
		Output and other code		
70	—	ANS: DS	2	;RESULT GOES HERE
71	—			
	.			
	.			
	.			
110	—	NOS: DS	4	;NUMBER BEING ADDED
111	—			
112	—			
113	—			
	.			
	.			
	.			
120	—	TOTL: DS	2	;NUMBER SUBTRACTED FROM
121	—			

Figure 6-18 Program segment for demonstrating double-precision arithmetic.

DAD rp　　　(Add register pair to H and L)

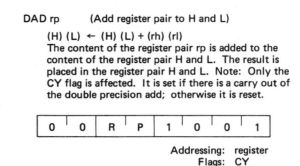

(H) (L) ← (H) (L) + (rh) (rl)
The content of the register pair rp is added to the
content of the register pair H and L. The result is
placed in the register pair H and L. Note: Only the
CY flag is affected. It is set if there is a carry out of
the double precision add; otherwise it is reset.

| 0 | 0 | R | P | 1 | 0 | 0 | 1 |

Addressing:　register
Flags:　CY

Figure 6-19　Two-byte addition. (Reprinted by permission of Intel Corporation. Copyright 1983.)

　　In the example above, the addition is accomplished by bringing the low-order byte of the augend, the contents of NOS + 2, into the accumulator and then adding to it the low-order byte of the addend, which is now in register C. The ALU will put the sum into the accumulator and the next instruction moves it to register C. Then the process is repeated using the high-order bytes, except that the ADC instruction is used instead of the ADD instruction so that the carry from the previous addition will be taken into account. If the unsigned sum resulting from the first ADD is too large to be expressed in 8 bits, the carry flag will be set. When the ADC instruction adds the high-order bytes, it will also add the contents of the carry flag. The net result is that the final answer will be the same as if two 16-bit integers had been added. The subtraction is performed similarly; the carry flag is set if a borrow is needed. The SBB instruction not only produces the high-order difference but also subtracts the borrow from this difference.

　　The 8085 has no multiply or divide instructions. These operations must be accomplished using addition and subtraction and will be considered later.

6-4-2 BCD Arithmetic

In many commercial applications of computers, it is more convenient to work with numbers in BCD (or decimal) format. Consequently, most microprocessors have features that facilitate working with this format. The 8085 accomplishes BCD arithmetic with the DAA instruction, which adjusts the sum of two digits in BCD format so that it is also in BCD format. To see how this is done, consider the following three cases:

Case 1:	3	0011	decimal 3
	+ 5	0101	decimal 5
	8	1000	decimal 8—no modification required

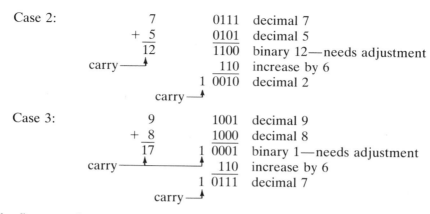

Case 2:
7   0111   decimal 7
+ 5   0101   decimal 5
─────   ─────
12   1100   binary 12—needs adjustment
carry────┘   110   increase by 6
                 1 0010   decimal 2
        carry────┘

Case 3:
9   1001   decimal 9
+ 8   1000   decimal 8
─────   ─────
17   1 0001   binary 1—needs adjustment
carry────┴────────┘   110   increase by 6
                 1 0111   decimal 7
        carry────┘

In the first case the correct answer is obtained by the addition alone, but the latter two cases had to be adjusted by adding 6 to the result. Examination of these examples leads one to suspect the rule to be:

> Add 6 to the result if it is in the range 1010 through 1111 inclusive, or if there is a carry from bit 3.

The rule is verified by noting that

$$x_{10} = \begin{cases} x_{16} & 0 \leq x_{16} \leq 9 \\ x_{16} + 6 & 9 < x_{16} \end{cases}$$

and that a carry of 2 is never required because the sum of any two decimal digits is less than 20.

To see how to extend this idea to bytes that contain two decimal digits, consider the following examples:

24   0010 0100   decimal 24
+ 37   0011 0111   decimal 37
─────   ─────────
61   0101 1011
                 110   ←add 6 to lower digit
          ─────────   because 1011 > 1001
          0110 0001

58   0101 1000   decimal 58
+ 69   0110 1001   decimal 69
─────   ─────────
127   1100 0001
                 110   ←add 6 to lower digit
          ─────────   because of carry from
          1100 0111   this digit
add 6 because ────→ 110
1100 > 1001   1 0010 0111   27 and carry 1 to next
carry ──────────────┘   byte

DAA   (Decimal Adjust Accumulator)

The eight–bit number in the accumulator is adjusted to form two four–bit Binary-Coded-Decimal digits by the following process:

1.   If the value of the least significant 4 bits of the accumulator is greater than 9 or if the AC flag is set, 6 is added to the accumulator.

2.   If the value of the most significant 4 bits of the accumulator is now greater than 9, or if the CY flag is set, 6 is added to the most significant 4 bits of the accumulator.

NOTE: All flags are affected.

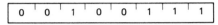

Flags: Z, S, P, CY, AC

Figure 6-20   Decimal adjust instruction for BCD additions.   (Reprinted by permission of Intel Corporation. Copyright 1983.)

The computer sets up the rule by having ordinary addition set the auxiliary carry flag if there is a carry from the low-order digit (from bit 3 to bit 4).   Then the programmer can implement the adjustment by following the addition with the DAA instruction, which adds 6 to the low-order digit if it exceeds 9 or the auxiliary carry flag is set, and adds 6 to the high-order digit if it exceeds 9 or the carry flag is set.

Address	Machine Code	Assembler Code		Remarks
		Input and other code		
50	11	LXI	D,AEND	;LOAD ADDRESS AEND INTO DE
51	10			
52	01			
53	21	LXI	H,AUG	;LOAD ADDRESS AUG INTO HL
54	00			
55	01			
56	1A	LDAX	D	;ADD LOW
57	86	ADD	M	;ORDER BYTES
58	27	DAA		;DECIMAL ADJUST
59	12	STAX	D	;STORE IN AEND
5A	23	INX	H	;INCREMENT
5B	13	INX	D	;ADDRESSES
5C	1A	LDAX	D	;ADD HIGH
5D	8E	ADC	M	;ORDER BYTES
5E	27	DAA		;DECIMAL ADJUST
5F	12	STAX	D	;STORE IN AEND+1
		Output and other code		
100	29	AUG: DB	29H,01H	
	01			
	.			
	.			
	.			
110		AEND: DS	2	
	.			
	.			
	.			

Figure 6-21   Example of four-digit BCD addition.

DAA is formally defined in Fig. 6-20.   It is presumed that for multiple-precision decimal arithmetic, a carry from the high-order digit would be used by an "add with carry" instruction in adding higher-order bytes.   In fact, multiple precision additions are the same as binary additions except that all addition instructions must be followed by a DAA instruction.

Suppose that we wish to add the BCD number 129, which is in locations 0100 and 0101, to the four-digit BCD number in locations 0110 and 0111.   The result is to be put into 0110 and 0111.   The DB directive is used to put 0129 into 0100 and 0101 and to assign the symbol AUG to 0100.   It is assumed that the contents of the other operand are not known at the time the program is assembled (they are determined by instructions within the program).   The directive DS is used to reserve the bytes at 0110 and 0111 and to associate AEND with 0110.   The desired program segment is given in Fig. 6-21.

The program first loads the least significant two digits of the addend (AEND) into the accumulator and performs a binary add with the contents of AUG.   Since AUG and AEND are in BCD format, DAA is used to adjust the result.   The BCD result is then put into AEND.   The two most significant digits from AEND + 1 and AUG + 1 are similarly added and the result is put in AEND + 1.   (To perform BCD subtraction, one could first find the 10's complement of the subtrahend and then add.   See Exercise 11.)

6-5 BRANCHING

Normally, instructions are taken from successive memory locations.   If a computer were limited to this sequential mode of operation, its efficiency and usefulness would be severely limited.   Therefore, all computers are designed to have branching instructions.   There are *unconditional branches*, which cause the program to jump out of sequence regardless of the state of the CPU, and *conditional branches*, which jump out of sequence only if a specified combination of condition flags has been set.   The conditional branches give a computer its decision-making capability. The definitions of the 8085 unconditional and conditional branch instructions are given in Fig. 6-22.   There are both an unconditional direct branch (JMP) and an unconditional indirect branch through the HL pair (PCHL).

For conditional branches, if the branch is not taken, the next instruction executed is the next instruction in sequence.   Recall that the PC points to the address in memory from which the next instruction is to be taken.   Normally, the computer simply increments the PC by the proper amount so that it will point to the next instruction in sequence.   However, if an unconditional branch is executed or the conditions in a conditional branch are met, the specified branch address is put into the PC and the next instruction is obtained from that address.

The 8085 has five condition flags, four of which can be used by conditional branch instructions.   The only flag that cannot be used as a branch condition is the auxiliary carry.   All others can be used as branch conditions, and for each flag

JMP addr   (Jump)

(PC) ← (byte 3) (byte 2)
Control is transferred to the instruction whose address is specified in byte 3 and byte 2 of the current instruction.

1	1	0	0	0	0	1	1
low-order addr							
high-order addr							

Addressing: immediate
Flags: none

PCHL   (Jump H and L indirect — move H and L to PC)

(PCH) ← (H)
(PCL) ← (L)
The content of register H is moved to the high-order eight bits of register PC. The content of register L is moved to the low-order eight bits of register PC.

1	1	1	0	1	0	0	1

Addressing: register
Flags: none

Jcondition addr   (Conditional jump)

If (CCC),
   (PC) ← (byte 3) (byte 2)
If the specified condition is true, control is transferred to the instruction whose address is specified in byte 3 and byte 2 of the current instruction; otherwise, control continues sequentially.

1	1	C	C	C	0	1	0
low-order addr							
high-order addr							

Addressing: immediate
Flags: none

CONDITION	CCC
NZ — not zero (Z = 0)	000
Z — zero (Z = 1)	001
NC — no carry (CY = 0)	010
C — carry (CY = 1)	011
PO — parity odd (P = 0)	100
PE — parity even (P = 1)	101
P — plus (S = 0)	110
M — minus (S = 1)	111

Figure 6-22   Branch instructions.   (Reprinted by permission of Intel Corporation.   Copyright 1983.)

there are two branch instructions; one will take the branch if the flag is set and the other will take the branch if the flag is clear.   The conditional branch instructions are the same except for bits 3, 4, and 5, which are used to indicate the branch condition.   The bit combination for each of the conditions is assigned according to the table included in the conditional branch definition given in Fig. 6-22.

At the assembler language level, the mnemonics are derived by adding different suffixes to the letter J.   These suffixes are also assigned according to the table in Fig. 6-22.   For example, an assembler language instruction that will branch on the zero flag being set is

JZ   BADDR

If BADDR represents memory location 0180, the machine language code is

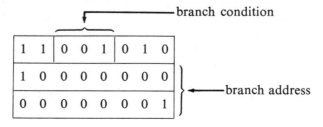

Because conditional branches are taken or not taken according to the state of the condition flags, they depend on the results produced by previous instructions. They are used primarily to

1. Branch out of sequence whenever an index or other indicator has (or has not, as the case may be) reached a specified level.
2. Take independent courses of action, depending on previous results within the program.
3. Detect an unusual or undesirable situation, such as a parity error or overflow, and branch to a program segment that will perform the special processing needed.

With regard to use 1, a conditional branch instruction is used in conjunction with a compare instruction. The 8085 compare instructions are defined in Fig. 6-23 and are essentially the same as the corresponding subtract instructions, except that the result is not stored anywhere. They are used solely to set the condition flags according to the relative values of their operands. If we wished to branch to a special routine beginning at SPR if the current contents of the accumulator are less than 8, we could use the following pair of instructions:

```
            CPI     08H
            JM      SPR
```

The compare/conditional branch instruction pair is often used to compare a count with a limit and is sometimes used in looping.

Caution. Any time a conditional branch is made depending on a previous instruction, care must be exercised to ascertain that no intervening instruction affects the flag tested by the branch. In particular, note that the transfer instructions do not affect any of the flags and could, for example, be placed between a compare instruction and its associated conditional branch with no adverse effects. However, most other instructions do affect at least one of the condition flags. In general it is poor programming practice to put instructions between the one that is intended to set or clear the flag and the conditional branch instruction that tests it, although it is sometimes unavoidable.

To demonstrate how a computer can take different actions depending on previous results, two examples are included in Fig. 6-24. The first example is analogous to the Fortran statement

```
    IF (NN .GE. 0 .AND. NN .GE. MM) GO TO 15
```

If the condition is satisfied, then the program branches to EXIT (which is assumed to correspond to the statement number 15); otherwise, it will continue at CONT.

CMP r   (Compare Register)

(A) − (r)
The content of register r is subtracted from the
accumulator. The accumulator remains unchanged.
The condition flags are set as a result of the subtraction. The Z flag is set to 1 if (A) = (r). The CY
flag is set to 1 if (A) < (r).

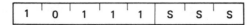

Addressing: register
Flags: Z, S, P, CY, AC

CMP M   (Compare memory)

(A) − ((H) (L))
The content of the memory location whose address
is contained in the H and L registers is subtracted
from the accumulator. The accumulator remains
unchanged. The condition flags are set as a result of
the subtraction. The Z flag is set to 1 if (A) = ((H) (L))
The CY flag is set to 1 if (A) < ((H) (L)).

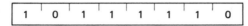

Addressing: reg. indirect
Flags: Z, S, P, CY, AC

CPI data   (Compare immediate)

(A) − (byte 2)
The content of the second byte of the instruction is
subtracted from the accumulator. The condition flags
are set by the result of the subtraction. The Z flag is
set to 1 if (A) = (byte 2). The CY flag is set to 1 if
(A) < (byte 2).

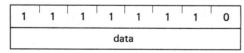

Addressing: immediate
Flags: Z, S, P, CY, AC

Figure 6-23 Compare instructions.
(Reprinted by permission of Intel
Corporation. Copyright 1983.)

The second example is analogous to

```
IF (NUM .LT. 0) THEN
        NEG=NEG+1
    ELSE IF (NUM=0) THEN
        ZER=ZER+1
    ELSE
        POS=POS+1
ENDIF
```

The location NUM is examined and NEG, ZER, or POS is incremented, depending on whether NUM is negative, zero, or positive, respectively. In any case the program continues at CONT.

With regard to the third need for conditional branching, that of accounting for unusual or undesirable results, good programming practice calls for considering every possible eventuality. Murphy's law states that if something can go wrong it will, and the programmer should provide a planned course of action for every possibility. If an action has not been planned, unintended results will occur. These results may vary from an incorrect number being logged to attempted execution of data and may produce disastrous consequences. If the microcomputer were used to control a machine tool, it could cause the production of imprecise parts or present a hazard to the operator. Unusual, but possible, occurrences are called *exceptions*.

An obvious practice, one that has not been followed in the previous examples, is to check for arithmetic exceptions. If the result of an addition, subtraction, multiplication, or division is too large for the available number of bits, there is an overflow and the programmer would probably want to include a special action to process such an event. For an unsigned addition, a typical check for an over-

Address	Machine Code	Assembler Code		Remarks
		Input and other code		
A0	3A	LDA	NN	;BRANCH TO CONT IF NN<=0
A1	E4			
A2	02			
A3	FE	CPI	0	
A4	00			
A5	FA	JM	CONT	
A6	AF			
A7	00			
A8	21	LXI	H,MM	;BRANCH TO EXIT IF MM>=0
A9	E5			
AA	02			
AB	BE	CMP	M	
AC	F2	JP	EXIT	
AD	C0			
AE	00			
AF	—	CONT:	.	
	.		.	
	.		.	
	.			
C0	—	EXIT:		
		Output and other code		
2E4	—	NN:	DB	
2E5	—	MM:	DB	

(a) IF-THEN analogy

Figure 6-24 Decision-making examples.

Address	Machine Code	Assembler Code		Remarks

Input and other code

Address	Machine Code	Label	Op	Operand	Remarks
120	3A		LDA	NUM	;LOAD NUM INTO ACCUMULATOR
121	06				
122	03				
123	FE		CPI	O	;BRANCH TO NONNEG IF >=0
124	00				
125	F2		JP	NONNEG	
126	2F				
127	01				
128	21		LXI	H,NEG	;OTHERWISE, INCREMENT NEG
129	07				
12A	03				
12B	34		INR	M	
12C	C3		JMP	CONT	;AND BRANCH TO CONT
12D	3D				
12E	01				
12F	C2	NONNEG:	JNZ	POSIT	;BRANCH TO POSIT IF >0
130	39				
131	01				
132	21		LXI	H,ZER	;OTHERWISE, INCREMENT ZER
133	08				
134	03				
135	34		INR	M	
136	C3		JMP	CONT	;AND BRANCH TO CONT
137	3D				
138	01				
139	21	POSIT:	LXI	H,POS	;INCREMENT POS
13A	09				
13B	03				
13C	34		INR	M	
13D	—	CONT:	.		
			.		
			.		

Output and other code

Address	Machine Code	Label	Op	Operand
306	—	NUM:	DS	
307	00	NEG:	DB	O
308	00	ZER:	DB	O
309	00	POS:	DB	O

(b) IF-THEN-ELSE analogy

Figure 6-24   Continued.

flow is

```
        .
        .
        .
    ADD   B
    JC    OVRF
        .
        .
        .
```

where OVRF is the beginning of the program segment designed to process the exception.

Most microprocessors include an overflow flag that is set if a signed addition or subtraction results in an overflow, but unfortunately the 8085 does not, and the following rules must be used to detect an overflow:

ADDITION—An overflow has occurred if and only if the operands have the same sign and the sum is of the opposite sign.
SUBTRACTION—An overflow has occurred if and only if the operands have opposite signs and the difference has the same sign as the subtrahend.

The implementation of these rules takes several instructions (see Exercise 12), and the programmer should carefully determine whether or not an overflow could occur for the data being considered before including this code and the code for processing the exception. Programming for an exception is not necessary if it has been found that it cannot happen, but one must make certain that it can *never* happen.

If an address is being modified by an arithmetic operation and an undetected overflow occurs (e.g., 1000 is being added to the address F12A), a subsequent branch to the computed address could cause the computer to execute the wrong instructions or attempt to execute data. Even if an overflow does not take place, the computed address may not correspond to an existing location on the computer being used. This would cause the computer to halt without giving an indication of the problem or attempting to correct it. Imagine the consequences if the computer is being used to regulate the pressure of a boiler or to control an aircraft or missile.

Larger computers are built to detect automatically the common arithmetic exceptions. If an exception occurs, a branch (caused by the hardware, not by a branch instruction) will be taken to an address which is determined by the design of the computer. A branch of this type is called a *trap* or *internal interrupt*. (Internal interrupts are distinct from external interrupts caused by I/O devices; external interrupts are discussed in Chapter 8.) The address branched to is called the *interrupt address* and the code beginning at this address is called the *interrupt routine*. An interrupt routine must be designed to identify and process all exceptions that lead to its execution. On large systems the interrupt routines are normally written by the system programmer and the ordinary user need only be concerned with the error messages generated by these routines. Because very few 8-bit microcomputers have internal interrupt capability, internal interrupts will not be discussed here.

Another common exception is division by zero. On larger computers, and even on some microcomputers, there are one or more division instructions. In most computers having division instructions, an internal interrupt will occur on a division by zero that will cause the computer to process this exception automatically. If a division instruction is not present, a program segment will need to be written to perform the division. Usually, such a segment would be preceded by a segment that would check for a zero divisor.

Some exceptions are due to unexpected events within the I/O devices. These may cause external interrupts or be detected by checking the appropriate status registers. Exceptions of this type are considered in Chapter 8.

6-6 LOOPING

It often occurs that the same instructions must be executed several times, with only minor adjustments being made between successive executions. When this is the case, memory can be conserved by using the same code over and over instead of repetitively writing the same instructions. The process of repetitively executing the same set of instructions is called *looping*.

The two basic forms of looping are shown in Fig. 6-25. Both forms involve the same four steps; only the order in which they are carried out is different. Basically, looping consists of reexecuting a set of code until a counting process fails a test, as in Fig. 6-25a, or passes a test, as in Fig. 6-25b. Each time the code is executed, some set of addresses and numbers is updated so that on the next execution the code will operate under a slightly different set of circumstances. The initialization step sets up the counting process to be used by the testing step and the address and number modifiers to be used by the modification step. The primary difference between the two forms is that "post-testing" requires the loop to be executed at least once. Under certain circumstances, the "pretesting" form may branch around the loop without executing it at all. A loop may be placed within another loop. This is referred to as *nesting*.

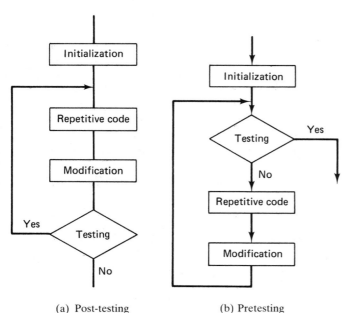

(a) Post-testing   (b) Pretesting

Figure 6-25 The two basic forms of looping.

In the example in Fig. 6-14, the transfer of a small block of data from one area of memory to another was considered.   The approach used there would require a large amount of code if a large block of data were to be moved and thus would be unreasonable.   By using a loop, any amount of data can be moved with approximately the same amount of code.

Suppose that 50 bytes of data are to be moved from the locations beginning at 0200 to the locations beginning at 0400.   The required code is given in Fig. 6-26.   The first instruction initializes the count and the next two put the initial addresses in the DE and BC register pairs.   The remainder of the instructions in the program segment is in the loop.   The first two instructions in the loop perform the necessary transfer, the next two modify the addresses involved, the next one modifies the count, and the last instruction performs the test.   If the test condition is "true," the loop is repeated; if it is "false," the program drops out of the loop. The code in the figure is analogous to the Fortran code

```
DIMENSION SRC(50), DES(50)
              .
              .
              .
DO 10 L=1,50
      DES(L)=SRC(L)
 10   CONTINUE
```

Address	Machine Code	Assembler Code		
		Input and other code		
40	2E	MVI	L,50	
41	32			
42	11	LXI	D,SRC	
43	00			Initialization
44	02			
45	01	LXI	B,DES	
46	00			
47	04			
48	1A	LOOP:	LDAX	D	Repetitive
49	02		STAX	B	code
4A	13		INX	D	
4B	03		INX	B	Modification
4C	2D		DCR	L	
4D	C2		JNZ	LOOP	Testing
4E	48			
4F	00			
		Output and other code		
200	—	SRC:	DS	50
	.			
	.			
	.			
400	—	DES:	DS	50

Figure 6-26 Large block transfer using looping.

6-7 SHIFTING AND ROTATING

All four of the 8085's shift and rotate instructions, which are defined in Fig. 6-27, actually execute 1-bit rotates, and all of them require that the operand lie in the A register. Two of them rotate only the bits in the A register, but load the carry with either the MSB of the A register (rotate left) or the LSB of the A register (rotate right). The other two treat the A register and carry flag as a 9-bit unit. By clearing the carry flag before executing rotate left through carry (RAL), a conventional left shift that inserts a 0 in the LSB of the A register is obtained. Similarly, a right shift could be performed by using a rotate right through carry (RAR). Figure 6-28 shows how the A register would be affected by each of the four rotate instructions assuming that 01101001_2 are the initial contents of the A register and the carry flag is initially set to 1.

Because a multiplication by 2 has the same effect as shifting a binary number left by 1 bit, another way of performing a left shift is to add the A register to itself. Similarly, a 16-bit quantity can be shifted left by 1 bit by putting it in the HL pair and executing a DAD H instruction.

RLC   (Rotate left)

$(A_{n+1}) \leftarrow (A_n)$; $(A_0) \leftarrow (A_7)$
$(CY) \leftarrow (A_7)$

The content of the accumulator is rotated left one position. The low order bit and the CY flag are both set to the value shifted out of the high order bit position. Only the CY flag is affected.

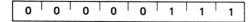

Flags: CY

RRC   (Rotate right)

$(A_n) \leftarrow (A_{n+1})$; $(A_7) \leftarrow (A_0)$
$(CY) \leftarrow (A_0)$

The content of the accumulator is rotated right one position. The high order bit and the CY flag are both set to the value shifted out of the low order bit position. Only the CY flag is affected.

Flags: CY

RAL   (Rotate left through carry)

$(A_{n+1}) \leftarrow (A_n)$; $(CY) \leftarrow (A_7)$
$(A_0) \leftarrow (CY)$

The content of the accumulator is rotated left one position through the CY flag. The low order bit is set equal to the CY flag and the CY flag is set to the value shifted out of the high order bit. Only the CY flag is affected.

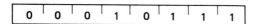

Flags: CY

RAR   (Rotate right through carry)

$(A_n) \leftarrow (A_{n+1})$; $(CY) \leftarrow (A_0)$
$(A_7) \leftarrow (CY)$

The content of the accumulator is rotated right one position through the CY flag. The high order bit is set to the CY flag and the CY flag is set to the value shifted out of the low order bit. Only the CY flag is affected.

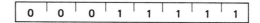

Flags: CY

Figure 6-27   Rotate instructions.   (Reprinted by permission of Intel Corporation.   Copyright 1983.)

```
Initially
(A) = 01101001
(C flag) = 1

    Instruction                        A register after operation

        RLC        (C flag) = 0           11010010
        RRC                               10110100        (C flag) = 1
        RAL        (C flag) = 0           11010011
        RAR                               10110100        (C flag) = 1
```

Figure 6-28   Examples of rotates.

To demonstrate the use of the rotate instruction and how DAD can be used to achieve a shift, let us examine how multiplication could be done on an 8085. In Chapter 2 it was seen that multiplication can be carried out by alternating the shift and add operations.   One way of programming the multiplication of two single-precision positive integers is to zero the pair of registers that is to be used to hold the product and then successively examine the bits of the multiplier, starting with the least significant bit.   If the bit is 1, the multiplicand is added to the product register pair; otherwise, no addition takes place.   Then the multiplicand is shifted one to the left and the next bit in the multiplier is tested.   This process is continued until all the multiplier bits have been examined.   The process is illustrated in Fig. 6-29.

Suppose it is known that the contents of 0140 and 0150 are positive integers and the product of their contents is desired.   Assume that QUAN is associated with location 0140 and COST with location 0150 and that the product is to appear in the HL register pair.   Figure 6-30 gives the necessary code.   The multiplication is done with a loop.   Note that the loop includes a conditional branch statement

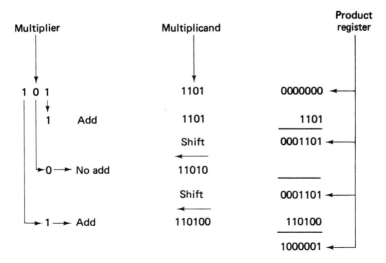

Figure 6-29   Multiplication process.

Address	Machine Code	Assembler Code		Remarks

Input and other code

Address	Machine Code	Label	Op	Operand	Remarks
60	06		MVI	B,8	;NO. OF BITS TO B
61	08				
62	21		LXI	H,QUAN	;PUT MULTIPLIER
63	40				
64	01				
65	7E		MOV	A,M	;IN A
66	21		LXI	H,COST	;PUT MULTIPLICAND
67	50				
68	01				
69	5E		MOV	E,M	;IN E
6A	21		LXI	H,0	;ZERO HL PAIR
6B	00				
6C	00				
6D	55		MOV	D,L	;AND D
6E	0F	LOOP:	RRC		;ADD DE TO HL
6F	D2		JNC	NOADD	;IF LOW-ORDER
70	73				
71	00				
72	19		DAD	D	;BIT IS 1
73	EB	NOADD:	XCHG		;SHIFT MULTIPLICAND
74	29		DAD	H	;TO THE LEFT
75	EB		XCHG		
76	05		DCR	B	;DECREMENT COUNT
77	C2		JNZ	LOOP	;AND LOOP ON NONZERO
78	6E				
79	00				

Output and other code

140	—	QUAN:	DS	1
	.			
	.			
	.			
150	—	COST:	DS	1

Figure 6-30 Single-precision multiplication of unsigned integers.

that determines whether or not the shifted multiplicand is to be added. The purpose of the RRC instruction is to put multiplier bits in the carry bit.

6-8 LOGICAL INSTRUCTIONS

All computers include in their instruction sets at least some logical instructions. The logical instructions perform the logical operations complementation, AND, OR, and exclusive OR on the bits of the operand(s) on a bit-by-bit basis. That is, complementation replaces each bit with its complement; the AND operation causes a bit in the result to be 1 only if the corresponding bits in both operands are 1; the OR causes a bit to be 1 only if the corresponding bits in either or both operands are 1; and the exclusive OR causes a bit in the result to be 1 only if exactly one of the two corresponding bits in the operands is 1. For example:

```
                         0 1 1 0 1 0 1 1
        Exclusive OR  0 1 0 1 0 0 1 0
        Result          0 0 1 1 1 0 0 1
```

The logical instructions for the 8085 are given in Fig. 6-31.

Many applications of the logical operations involve using them to selectively set, clear, change, or test bits within a byte. This is done by performing a logical operation on the byte of interest and a second byte that is called the *mask*. Such an operation is referred to as a *masking operation*. For example, if bits 2, 3, and 5 in a byte are to be set and the remaining bits are to be left unchanged, one could perform the operation

```
              10011000    Byte to be selectively set
        OR    00101100    Mask
              10111100    Result
```

Similarly, bits can be selectively changed using an exclusive OR. By setting the bits in the mask to 0 if the corresponding bits are to be cleared, and otherwise setting them to 1, an AND operation can be used to selectively clear bits.

To test a given combination of bits, we can set the corresponding bits in the mask to 1 and the remaining bits to 0. Then when the mask is ANDed with the byte to be tested, the Z flag will not be set if any of the bits being tested are 1, and will be set if all the bits being tested are 0. A branch could then be taken according to the Z flag setting.

Operations such as those defined above can be useful in a variety of situations, but they are particularly valuable in modifying bits in I/O command registers and testing bits in I/O status registers. A detailed study of I/O programming is given in Chapter 8.

Suppose that the contents of locations 0030 through 0032 are to be used as masks and that bits 2 and 3 of the contents of location 0040 are to be selectively set, bit 6 is to be cleared, and bit 5 is to be changed and then tested. The program segment is to begin in location 0010, and the symbols MASKS and CTRL are used to designate locations 0030 and 0040, respectively. Figure 6-32 gives the necessary code. MASKS, MASKS + 1, and MASKS + 2 are filled with 0C, BF, and 20, respectively. If bit 5 is set a branch is to be taken to EXIT.

As a second example, let us assume that the computer is to monitor six external relay settings and perform one of three tasks, depending on the status of these relays. Suppose that the relays are numbered 0 through 5 and that their settings are brought into bits 0 through 5, respectively, of the C register. A 0 corresponds to a relay being open and a 1 corresponds to it being closed. Which of the three tasks to be performed is determined as follows:

Task 1—If relays 0, 1, and 5 are all closed, task 1 is to be performed.

Task 2—If task 1 is not performed and if relay 2 or 3 is closed, and relay 4 is closed, task 2 is to be performed.

ANA r   (AND Register)

(A) ← (A) ∧ (r)

The content of register r is logically anded with the content of the accumulator. The result is placed in the accumulator. The CY flag is cleared.

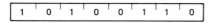

Addressing: register
Flags: Z, S, P, CY, AC

ANA M   (AND memory)

(A) ← (A) ∧ ((H) (L))

The contents of the memory location whose address is contained in the H and L registers is logically anded with the content of the accumulator. The result is placed in the accumulator. The CY flag is cleared.

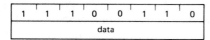

Addressing: reg. indirect
Flags: Z, S, P, CY, AC

ANI data   (AND immediate)

(A) ← (A) ∧ (byte 2)

The content of the second byte of the instruction is logically anded with the contents of the accumulator. The result is placed in the accumulator. The CY and AC flags are cleared.

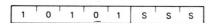

data

Addressing: immediate
Flags: Z, S, P, CY, AC

XRA r   (Exclusive OR Register)

(A) ← (A) ∀ (r)

The content of register r is exclusive-OR'd with the content of the accumulator. The result is placed in the accumulator. The CY and AC flags are cleared.

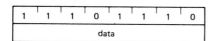

Addressing: register
Flags: Z, S, P, CY, AC

XRI data   (Exclusive OR immediate)

(A) ← (A) ∀ (byte 2)

The content of the second byte of the instruction is exclusive-OR'd with the content of the accumulator. The result is placed in the accumulator. The CY and AC flags are cleared.

data

Addressing: immediate
Flags: Z, S, P, CY, AC

ORA r   (OR Register)

(A) ← (A) ∨ (r)

The content of register r is inclusive-OR'd with the content of the accumulator. The result is placed in the accumulator. The CY and AC flags are cleared.

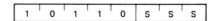

Addressing: register
Flags: Z, S, P, CY, AC

ORA M   (OR memory)

(A) ← (A) ∨ ((H) (L))

The content of the memory location whose address is contained in the H and L registers is inclusive-OR'd with the content of the accumulator. The result is placed in the accumulator. The CY and AC flags are cleared.

Addressing: reg. indirect
Flags: Z, S, P, CY, AC

ORI data   (OR immediate)

(A) ← (A) ∨ (byte 2)

The content of the second byte of the instruction is inclusive-OR'd with the content of the accumulator. The result is placed in the accumulator. The CY and AC flags are cleared.

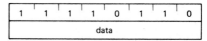

data

Addressing: immediate
Flags: Z, S, P, CY, AC

XRA M   (Exclusive OR Memory)

(A) ← (A) ∀ ((H) (L))

The content of the memory location whose address is contained in the H and L registers is exclusive-OR'd with the content of the accumulator. The result is placed in the accumulator. The CY and AC flags are cleared.

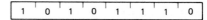

Addressing: reg. indirect
Flags: Z, S, P, CY, AC

CMA   (Complement accumulator)

(A) ← (Ā)

The contents of the accumulator are complemented (zero bits become 1, one bits become 0). No flags are affected.

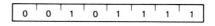

Flags: none

Figure 6-31 Definitions of logical instructions. (Reprinted by permission of Intel Corporation. Copyright 1983.)

184

Address	Machine Code	Assembler Code		Remarks
		Input and other code		
10	21	LXI	H,MASKS	;LOAD ADDR MASKS INTO HL
11	30			
12	00			
13	3A	LDA	CTRL	;LOAD (CTRL) INTO A
14	40			
15	00			
16	B6	ORA	M	;SET BITS 2 AND 3
17	23	INX	H	; INC TO MASKS+1
18	A6	ANA	M	;CLEAR BIT 6
19	23	INX	H	; INC TO MASKS+2
1A	AE	XRA	M	;CHANGE BIT 5
1B	32	STA	CTRL	;STORE IN CTRL
1C	40			
1D	00			
1E	A6	ANA	M	;TEST BIT 5
1F	C2	JNZ	EXIT	;BRANCH TO EXIT IF SET
20	2A			
21	00			
		Output and other code		
30	0C	MASKS: DB	0CH,0BFH,20H	
31	BF			
32	20			
	.			
	.			
	.			
40		CTRL: DS	1	

Figure 6-32   Program segment using masks and logical operations.

Task 3—This task is to be performed in all other cases, but not if task 1 or task 2 is performed.

Figure 6-33 shows a flowchart of the desired program and Fig. 6-34 gives the decision-making portion of the necessary code.   The first three instructions set up the required masks; then the program enters a loop.   Inside the loop the relay settings are sampled and then the instructions in 0200, 0201, and 0202 are used to determine whether or not task 1 is to be done.   If it is, the JZ instruction causes a branch to task 1; otherwise, the instructions in 0206 and 0207 test whether or not either relay 2 or relay 3 is closed.   If not, a branch is taken to task 3; otherwise, relay 4 is checked; if it is closed, a branch is taken to task 2.   If it is not closed, task 3 is performed.   All three tasks conclude with an unconditional branch that returns the program to the code that causes register C to be updated.

6-9 *CARRY FLAG, HALT, AND NO OPERATION INSTRUCTIONS*

Figure 6-35 defines four other instructions that are available on the 8085: the complement carry (CMC), the set carry (STC), the halt (HLT), and the no operation (NOP) instructions.   The first two are to complement and set the carry

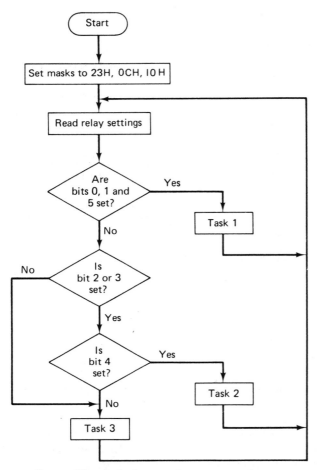

Figure 6-33 Flowchart of program needed to solve relay example.

flag. The halt instruction causes the computer to suspend execution until an external signal is relayed to the processor through one of the bus lines.

The no operation (or no op) instruction causes no machine action and is used only when one wishes to insert a label but does not want the label attached to an instruction that takes action. A no op instruction serves the same purpose as a CONTINUE instruction in Fortran and other high-level languages, as a means of providing a label for a "branch to" point that does nothing. The availability of such an instruction is very important, particularly during the development of a program, when modifications are frequently necessary. To attach the "branch to" label to an instruction that takes action as follows

```
          JZ      EXIT
           .
           .
           .
EXIT:     MOV     A,M
```

Address	Machine Code	Assembler Code		Remarks

Input and other code

```
101    06    MVI    B,23H    ;PUT MASKS
102    23
103    16    MVI    D,0CH    ;IN REGISTERS
104    0C
105    1E    MVI    E,10H    ;B, D, AND E
106    10
107          LOOP:           ;CODE FOR READING
                             ;RELAY SETTINGS INTO REGISTER C
       .
       .
       .
200    79    MOV    A,C      ;ARE BITS 0, 1
201    2F    CMA             ;AND 5 ALL
202    A0    ANA    B        ;SET?
203    CA    JZ     TK1      ;IF SO, GO TO TK1
204    00
205    03
206    79    MOV    A,C      ;IS BIT 2
207    A2    ANA    D        ;OR 3 SET?
208    CA    JZ     TK3      ;IF NOT, GO TO TK3
209    10
20A    02
20B    79    MOV    A,C      ;IS BIT
20C    A3    ANA    E        ;4 SET?
20D    C2    JNZ    TK2      ;IF SO, GO TO TK2
20E    00
20F    04
210          TK3:            ;CODE FOR TASK 3
       .
       .
       .
2FD    C3    JMP    LOOP     ;RETURN TO LOOP
2FE    07
2FF    01
300          TK1:            ;CODE FOR TASK 1
       .
       .
       .
3FD    C3    JMP    LOOP     ;RETURN TO LOOP
3FE    07
3FF    01
400          TK2:            ;CODE FOR TASK 2
       .
       .
       .
4FD    C3    JMP    LOOP     ;RETURN TO LOOP
4FE    07
4FF    01
```

Output and other code

Figure 6-34 Code for relay example.

is relatively inflexible because, in order to insert new instructions at the point labeled EXIT, the move instruction must be retyped.   If the sequence

```
        JZ      EXIT
        .
        .
        .
EXIT:   NOP
        MOV    A,M
```

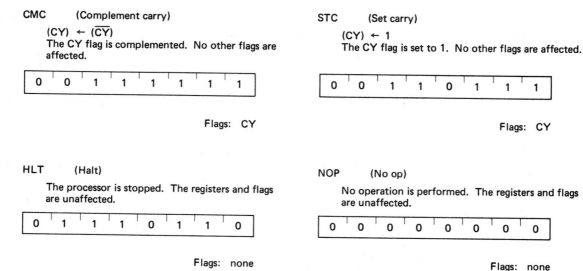

CMC   (Complement carry)

(CY) ← (C̄Ȳ)

The CY flag is complemented. No other flags are affected.

| 0 | 0 | 1 | 1 | 1 | 1 | 1 | 1 |

Flags: CY

STC   (Set carry)

(CY) ← 1

The CY flag is set to 1. No other flags are affected.

| 0 | 0 | 1 | 1 | 0 | 1 | 1 | 1 |

Flags: CY

HLT   (Halt)

The processor is stopped. The registers and flags are unaffected.

| 0 | 1 | 1 | 1 | 0 | 1 | 1 | 0 |

Flags: none

NOP   (No op)

No operation is performed. The registers and flags are unaffected.

| 0 | 0 | 0 | 0 | 0 | 0 | 0 | 0 |

Flags: none

Figure 6-35 Definitions of the CMC, STC, HLT, and NOP instructions. (Reprinted by permission of Intel Corporation. Copyright 1983.)

were used, insertions could be made without disturbing the present code. This is important during the debugging phase when message printout code may need to be temporarily included at key points (which are often "branch to" points) within a program. Finally, just as Fortran DO-loops are often terminated with CONTINUE statements, it may be desirable to put NOP instructions at the end of pretest loops, especially when loops are nested.

6-10 ASSIGNING NAMES AND CONDITIONAL ASSEMBLY DIRECTIVES

If an expression appears several times in a program, it is sometimes more convenient to give it a name and refer to it by the name. Not only does this permit a short name to replace a lengthy expression, but the name may be a meaningful abbreviation that is easy for the programmer and others to remember as they read the program. High-level languages also provide this feature, e.g., Fortran 77 includes the PARAMETER statement for assigning names to constants.

ASM-85 includes two directives for assigning names to expressions; they are the EQU and SET directives. The EQU directive has the form

        Name   EQU   Expression

where *Name* is any valid symbol (it is a character string that must be constructed using the same rules as for labels) and *Expression* is any valid expression. (Note that there is no colon following *Name*.) After an EQU directive is given, the assembler replaces all appearances of *Name* by *Expression*. If a name is assigned using EQU, it cannot be reassigned later in the same program. Except for using the SET mnemonic in place of EQU, the SET directive has the same form as the EQU directive and has the same effect on the program. The difference between the two is that a name assigned by SET can be reassigned as many times as desired.

Another reason for allowing programmers to use a name is that it provides a convenient means of changing an expression that may appear several times simply by changing the assignment. For example, assume that at several points in a program

```
            ADI       6
```

is used to add 6 to the accumulator, and the program needs to be altered so that only 4 is to be added at these points. If the program had been written with

```
            CON EQU       6
```

at its beginning and

```
            ADI       CON
```

is used everywhere in place of

```
            ADI       6
```

then the program could be changed by simply replacing the EQU directive with

```
            CON EQU       4
```

Another important feature that can be built into an assembler is one that permits the assembler to decide which source code should be assembled. This decision is based on certain factors that are known to the assembler at the time the request is encountered. The 8085 assembler language includes the directives IF, ELSE, and ENDIF for this purpose. They are inserted in a program in the form

```
    Label:   IF    Constant expression
                 .⎫
                 .⎬ Code assembled if Constant expression
                 .⎭        is true
    Label:   ELSE
                 .⎫
                 .⎬ Code assembled if Constant expression
                 .⎭        is false (optional)
    Label:   ENDIF
```

where *Label* is optional and *Constant expression* is true if bit 0 of the constant it evaluates to is 1 and false if this bit is 0. As indicated by the above form, one of two sets of code is assembled depending on the value of *Constant expression*. If the ELSE directive is not present, assembly simply continues after ENDIF.

One can immediately see the flexibility of using EQU and SET in conjunction with IF, ELSE, and ENDIF. By using EQU or SET to regulate the value of a name and then using the name in the expression in the IF directive, considerable versatility in deleting segments of the source code can be attained. The possibility of being able to delete source code selectively permits a programmer to write a general program that can be used for a variety of purposes and situations and then, for a particular situation, assemble only the needed portion of the code. System programmers rely heavily on conditional assembly when they are writing software that can be used in several different hardware and/or software configurations.

6-11 ASSEMBLY PROCESS

In an effort to clarify the structure of assembler language programs and why certain rules are necessary, this section examines the assembly process. As shown in Fig. 6-36, the input to the assembler is a source module and the output is an object module and a listing. The source module is normally a file that has been created using a text editor by typing one assembler statement per line. The object module, which consists of the machine language code and the information needed to join the module to other object modules, is also stored as a file.

A breakdown of an assembler is shown in Fig. 6-37. (It should be emphasized that the assembler discussed here is hypothetical and is simplified so that the main points are evident. The details of an actual assembler would only add clutter to this introductory discussion.) As with most assemblers, the one given here scans the source code twice and is called a *two-pass assembler*. The purpose of the first pass is to provide the assembler with the locations of the labels and that of the second pass is to generate the machine code. To locate the labels, the assembler contains a variable known as a *location counter*. As a program is being scanned, its location counter increments by amounts equal to the numbers of bytes required

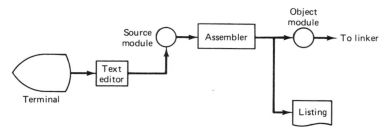

Figure 6-36   Assembler's input and output.

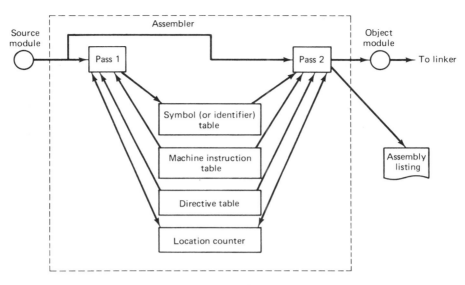

Figure 6-37 Major activity of a two-pass assembler.

by the statements. The location counter can be thought of as a pointer that dynamically indicates the relative positions, or offsets, within each segment as the assembly progresses. During the first pass the assembler uses the location counter to construct a table, called a *symbol table*, that allows the second pass to use the offsets of the labels to generate operand addresses.

The initial value of the location counter is called the *origin*. The 8085 assembler sets the origin with the ORG directive, whose format is

```
        Label:        ORG        Constant expression
```

where *Constant expression* specifies the origin, and *Label*, which is optional, permits a symbol to be assigned to the first location following the ORG directive. If the origin is not specified by an ORG directive, the origin will be assumed to be 0. The ORG directive can be used more than once, with only its first occurrence being used to set the origin. Later occurrences simply force the location counter to be set to the value specified by the operand, thereby permitting the location counter to jump forward. This could also be accomplished using the DS directive.

In writing an assembler language program, it is often convenient to refer to a location by noting its position relative to the current contents of the location counter. Therefore, a special symbol is usually designated to represent the current contents of the location counter. For the 8085 assembler, this symbol is "$". The instruction

```
        JZ        $ + 8
```

will be assembled as a branch on zero to the instruction that begins at the current contents of the location counter plus eight.   If the location counter contains 0120, the branch will be taken to location 0128.

To clarify some of these ideas, consider the example shown in Fig. 6-38.   The code in the source module is shown on the left, the symbol table that is generated by the first pass is shown at the bottom, and the machine code is shown on the right.   The steps performed by the two passes of the assembler are outlined in Fig. 6-39.   The first pass builds the symbol table.   The second pass scans the source code and converts it to machine language using the symbol table to insert the addresses as needed.

The last line in the example given in Fig. 6-38 contains the END directive. The purpose of END is to signal the assembler that the assembly is complete.   Its

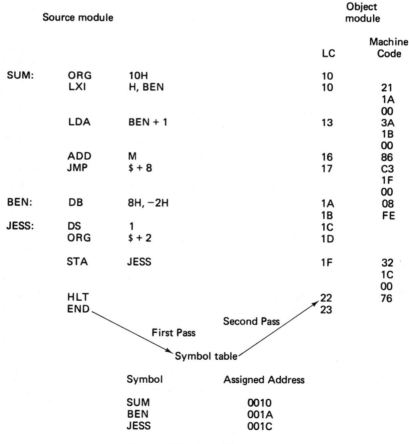

Figure 6-38   Assembly example.

Assembler language			First pass	LC	Second pass
SUM:	ORG	10H	Puts SUM in symbol table and assigns it the address 0010. Puts 0010 into LC.	10	Puts 0010 into LC
	LXI	H, BEN	Increments LC by 3.	10	Assembles op code for LXI. Finds address 1A in symbol table. Increments LC by 3.
	LDA	BEN + 1	Increments LC by 3.	13	Assembles op code for LDA. Fills in address 1A + 1 = 1B; 1A is found in symbol table. Increments LC by 3.
	ADD	M	Increments LC by 1.	16	Assembles op code for ADD M. Increments LC by 1.
	JMP	$ + 8	Increments LC by 3.	17	Assembles op code for JMP. Assembles branch address by adding 8 to LC. Increments LC by 3.
BEN:	DB	8H, −2H	Puts BEN in symbol table and assigns it to 1A. Increments LC by 2.	1A	Puts 08 in 1A and FE in 1B. Increments LC by 2.
JESS:	DS	1	Puts JESS in symbol table and assigns it address 1C. Increments LC by 1.	1C	Increments LC by 1.
	ORG	$ + 2	Increments LC by 2.	1D	Increments LC by 2.
	STA	JESS	Increments LC by 3	1F	Assembles op code for STA. Finds address 1C in symbol table. Increments LC by 3.
	HLT		Increments LC by 1.	22	Increments LC by 1.
	END		Signals end of source code.	23	Signals end of assembly.

Figure 6-39 Steps performed while assembling example in Fig. 6-38.

193

format is

$$Label:\qquad END$$

where the label is optional and there is no operand.

The major functions of the first and second passes of an assembler are flow-charted in Fig. 6-40. When a label is found in the leftmost field of a statement, it is said to be *defined*, and it is at this point that the label is associated with an offset by placing the current contents of the location counter in the symbol table along with the label's symbolic representation and other attributes. If the same label is defined twice in a source module, an error occurs.

In order to identify keywords within the assembler language, the assembler includes a table, known as the *permanent symbol table*, that contains all of the information concerning the instructions and directives that might be needed by the assembler. Among other things these tables contain the mnemonics, operation codes and associated formats, and the length information that is required for incrementing the location counter.

In addition to assembling the machine instructions, the second pass must insert the preassigned constants that occur in the data definition directives and prepare the other information that may be required to combine the output object module with other object modules. Because the operands in the instructions and directives may involve expressions, the computation of an offset may involve more than simply looking up an entry in the symbol table. The second pass is also responsible for performing these computations. When the second pass encounters the END directive, the object module and listing are output to the appropriate peripheral devices and the assembly process is terminated.

Besides the object module, the assembler outputs a listing that contains information concerning the program and its translation. Depending on the command given to invoke the assembler, this listing may consist only of a list of the errors detected during the assembly or include a complete detailed listing of the program, or something in between. A complete listing, including machine code, normally contains a listing of the program, with error messages interspersed with the code, and a cross-reference symbol table.

6-12 INSTRUCTION EXECUTION TIME

As mentioned in Chapter 5, a microprocessor must include a clock to synchronize its various activities. The clock is a pulse generator that outputs one or more pulse trains that have the same frequency but different phases. Each phase initiates different actions during the course of a clock cycle. The combination of actions taken during the execution of an instruction is called an *instruction cycle*. Because some instructions require many more actions than others, instruction cycles are subdivided into machine *cycles* and *states*. These subdivisions are usually related

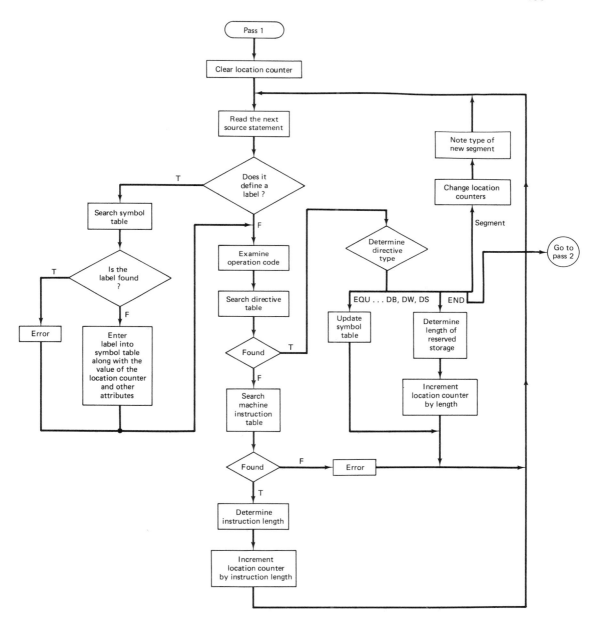

Figure 6-40 Major logic flow of an assembler.

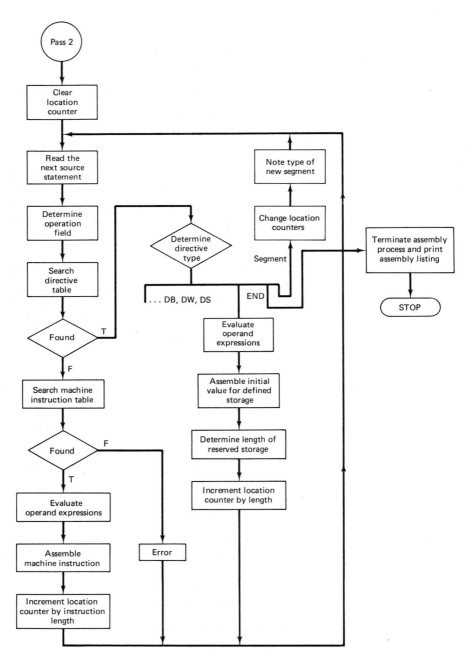

Figure 6-40 Continued.

to the number of memory or I/O accesses that are included in the instruction, and there are often two levels of subdivision.

The 8085 timing is typical. It requires a clock with a maximum pulse rate of approximately 3 MHz. Instruction cycles are divided into machine cycles, with one machine cycle for each memory or I/O access. The machine cycles are, in turn, subdivided into states. The states consist of the actions that occur during the clock cycles. The retrieval of the first byte of the instruction from memory is called the *instruction fetch*. The first machine cycle of an instruction cycle always includes the instruction fetch and is called the *fetch cycle*. The fetch cycle normally consists of four to six states, depending on what actions must be taken in addition to the instruction fetch. All other machine cycles normally consist of three states. For example, the breakdown of the timing for the instruction.

LDA   DATA

is given in Fig. 6-41.

It ordinarily takes three states (or clock cycles) to access memory. During a memory read operation, the first state is needed to send the address to memory, the second is needed by the memory to look up the requested information, and the third is used to transmit the information back to the CPU. A write operation can be broken down similarly. In either case, one of the states is used by the memory. If the memory cycle time is more than the clock cycle time, the memory needs more than one state to perform its function. Therefore, the 8085, as well as many other microprocessors, has a *wait state* during which the remainder of the system simply waits for the memory to complete its operation. If very slow memory is being accessed, more than one wait state may be required. For example, if the clock period is 300 nS and the memory access time is 700 nS, it would take five states for the CPU to get 1 byte of information from memory: the usual three states plus two wait states. The total time required would be 1500 nS.

For our purposes here, putting a byte into or taking a byte out of memory is called a memory access. Intuition is sufficient to determine the number of memory accesses made while executing an instruction. For example, the instruction

SHLD FORCE

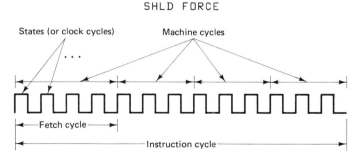

Figure 6-41   Breakdown of timing for a typical 8085 instruction.

consists of 3 bytes, 1 byte for the op code and 2 bytes for the address of FORCE. It takes three memory accesses to bring in these 3 bytes and two accesses to store the contents of the HL pair into FORCE and FORCE + 1. Memory accesses are defined more precisely and discussed in detail in Chapter 11.

Figure 6-42 summarizes the number of machine cycles and states needed for the execution of each of the 8085's instructions. The column on the right gives the number of states needed to execute the instruction, assuming that no wait states are needed, and the middle column gives the number of machine cycles. If each memory access requires a wait state and N is the number of memory accesses performed by the instruction, then, to get the number of states used, N must be added to the number in the right column. If two wait states are needed for each

Instruction		Machine Cycles	States	Instruction		Machine Cycles	States*
MOV	r1,r2	1	4	ANA	r	1	4
MOV	M,r	2	7	XRA	r	1	4
MOV	r,M	2	7	ORA	r	1	4
MVI	r	2	7	ANA	M	2	7
MVI	M	3	10	XRA	M	2	7
LXI	rp	3	10	ORA	M	2	7
XCHG		1	4	ANI		2	7
STA		4	13	XRI		2	7
LDA		4	13	ORI		2	7
STAX	B	2	7	CMA		1	4
STAX	D	2	7	JMP		3	10
LDAX	B	2	7	J(Condition)		2/3	7/10
LDAX	D	2	7	PCHL		1	6
SHLD		5	16	CALL		5	18
LHLD		5	16	C(Condition)		2/5	9/18
INX	rp	1	6	RET		3	10
DCX	rp	1	6	R(Condition)		1/3	6/12
INR	r	1	4	RLC		1	4
DCR	r	1	4	RRC		1	4
INR	M	3	10	RAL		1	4
DCR	M	3	10	RAR		1	4
ADD	r	1	4	DAD	rp	3	10
ADC	r	1	4	CMC		1	4
SUB	r	1	4	STC		1	4
SBB	r	1	4	NOP		1	4
CMP	r	1	4	HLT		1	5
ADD	M	2	7	PUSH	rp	3	12
ADC	M	2	7	PUSH	PSW	3	12
SUB	M	2	7	POP	rp	3	10
SBB	M	2	7	POP	PSW	3	10
CMP	M	2	7	SPHL		1	6
ADI		2	7	XTHL		5	16
ACI		2	7	IN		3	10
SUI		2	7	OUT		3	10
SBI		2	7	RST		3	12
CPI		2	7	EI		1	4
DAA		1	4	DI		1	4
				RIM		1	4
				SIM		1	4

* Two possible times (e.g., 7/10) indicates time depends on
   condition flag settings. First figure corresponds to no branch.

Figure 6-42   Summary of the 8085 instruction set execution times.

access, $2N$ must be added to the number in the column on the right, and so on. For example, the LXI instruction requires three memory accesses and the number of states indicated in the figure is 10. If the clock cycle time is 300 nS and the memory access time is 700 nS, it will take $10 + 3 \times 2 = 16$ states and 4800 nS to complete the LXI instruction.

It should be noted that a given microcomputer system can include memory modules of different speeds. In this case the instruction may be in a memory module that has a different speed from the module containing one of the operands. When this situation arises, the system may not need a wait state to fetch the instruction but may require wait states for getting the operand (or vice versa). If an LHLD instruction is in a 200 nS access time memory module but its operand is in 700 nS access time memory, the total number of states needed to execute the instruction, assuming a 300 nS clock cycle, is

$$16 + 3 \times 0 + 2 \times 2 = 20$$

and the total time needed is 6000 nS.

A general expression for determining the total number of states is

$$
\begin{array}{l}
\text{Basic number} \\
\text{of states} \\
\text{(in table)}
\end{array}
+
\left(
\begin{array}{l}
\text{Number of wait} \\
\text{states for} \\
\text{instruction} \\
\text{memory}
\end{array}
\times
\begin{array}{l}
\text{Number of bytes} \\
\text{in instruction}
\end{array}
\right)
$$

$$
+
\left(
\begin{array}{l}
\text{Number of wait} \\
\text{states for} \\
\text{operand} \\
\text{memory}
\end{array}
\times
\begin{array}{l}
\text{Number of} \\
\text{bytes} \\
\text{in} \\
\text{operand}
\end{array}
\right)
$$

To get the instruction execution time, the total number of states must be multiplied by the clock's period (i.e., the reciprocal of the clock's frequency).

6-13 ZILOG Z80

In Chapter 5 (see Fig. 5-9), it was seen that the Zilog Z80 is an enhanced 8085 and the major architectural differences are that the Z80 has

A dual set of PSW, A, B, C, D, E, H, and L registers
Two extra registers, IX and IY, which are used for base addressing
An overflow flag for signed arithmetic operations
Separate address and data buses

There are also significant differences in the addressing modes and instruction sets. In addition to the immediate, direct, and register indirect modes available on the

8085, the Z80 has relative addressing for its branch instructions and base addressing for most other instructions involving memory operands.

The Z80's instruction set is given in Appendix B. The more important differences from the 8085 are

- The presence of instructions (EX and EXX) for changing PSWs and register sets. They are not needed on the 8085 because there is only one set of registers.

- Data transfer, increment/decrement, arithmetic, logical, and shift/rotate instructions can use the IX and IY registers to attain base addressing.

- Branch instructions (both unconditional and conditional, but not subroutine branches and returns) permit either direct or relative addressing. For relative addressing, a 4-byte 2's complement number, which is in the second byte of the instruction, is added to the PC (which at that time points to the address of the branch instruction plus 2). For example, if the address of the branch instruction is 005A and the branch is to be taken to the address 0050, then the second byte of the instruction would be F4.

- There are block transfer instructions (LDI, LDIR, LDD, and LDDR) for moving an entire block of data (see example below) and instructions (CPI, CPIR, CPD, and CPDR) to aid in searching through an entire block of data. All of these instructions employ autoincrementing or autodecrementing.

- There is a loop instruction (DJNE) that automatically decrements the B register and causes a relative branch if the result is 0; otherwise, it continues in sequence. Presumably, before the loop is entered, the B register would be filled with the number of times the loop is to be repeated. Then each time the loop is executed, DJNE decrements B and, when 0 is reached, the loop is exited.

- There are the four 8085 rotate instructions, plus several additional shift and rotate instructions, and these instructions can address memory and registers other than the A register.

- Besides being able to selectively set, clear, and test bits using the logical instructions, the Z80 has a special set of instructions for setting, clearing, and testing individual bits.

To contrast the programming of a Z80 with that of an 8085, two examples are given in Figs. 6-43 and 6-44. The first example moves 50 bytes of data from one area in memory to another, just as did the 8085 example in Fig. 6-26. After the initialization step, the Z80 is able to perform the move with a single LDIR instruction. The second example is the Z80 counterpart to the single-precision multiply algorithm in Fig. 6-30. (Like the 8085, the Z80 has no multiply or divide instructions.) Note that, except for the relative branch instruction JR and the loop instruction DJNE, the machine language for the Z80 is identical to that of the 8085. This is due to the fact that most instructions have the same machine code

Address	Machine Code	Assembler Code		Remarks

Input and other code

Address	Machine Code	Assembler Code		Remarks
40	01	LD	BC,50	;LOAD COUNT INTO BC
41	32			
42	00			
43	11	LD	HL,SRC	;LOAD SRC INTO HL
44	00			
45	02			
46	21	LD	DE,DES	;AND DESTINATION INTO DE
47	00			
48	04			
49	ED	LDIR		;DO ENTIRE TRANSFER
4A	B0			

Output and other code

Address	Machine Code	Assembler Code		Remarks
200	—	SRC:	DS	50
	.			
	.			
	.			
400	—	DES:	DS	50

Figure 6-43 Large block transfer using LDIR instruction.

Address	Machine Code	Assembler Code		Remarks

Input and other code

Address	Machine Code	Label	Assembler Code		Remarks
60	06		LD	B,8	;NO. OF BITS TO B
61	08				
62	21		LD	HL,QUAN	;PUT MULTIPLIER IN A
63	40				
64	01				
65	7E		LD	A,(HL)	
66	21		LD	HL,COST	;PUT MULTIPLICAND IN E
67	50				
68	01				
69	5E		LD	E,(HL)	
6A	21		LD	HL,0	;ZERO D AND HL PAIR
6B	00				
6C	00				
6D	55		LD	D,L	
6E	0F	LOOP:	RRCA		;ADD DE TO HL
6F	30		JR	NC,NOADD	;IF LOW-ORDER
70	01				
71	19		ADD	HL,DE	;BIT IS 1
72	EB	NOADD:	EX	DE,HL	;SHIFT HL
73	29		ADD	HL,HL	;TO LEFT
74	EB		EX	DE,HL	
75	10		DJNZ	LOOP	;LOOP IF B NONZERO
76	F7				

Output and other code

Address	Machine Code	Label	Assembler Code		Remarks
140	—	QUAN:	DS	1	
	.				
	.				
	.				
150	—	COST:	DS	1	

Figure 6-44 Single-precision multiplication of unsigned integers.

and the register addresses are the same. For the JR and DJNE instructions the reader should verify the relative addresses appearing in the second bytes of these instructions. The parentheses around HL in the third and fifth instructions indicate register indirect addressing.

6-14 *MOTOROLA MC6809*

It is difficult to compare the architecture of the MC6809 to the 8085 or Z80, because a different philosophy was used in its design. An emphasis was placed on having a very versatile set of addressing modes. As does the Z80, the MC6809 has two registers, X and Y, that can be used for base addressing. It has two 16-bit stack pointers, as opposed to only one on the Z80 or 8085, two 8-bit accumulators that can be used as a pair to store 16-bit results, and an 8-bit page address register. It also includes an overflow flag (refer to Fig. 5-11).

In addition to the 8085 addressing modes, the MC6809 has base and relative addressing, which we have seen are available on the Z80, and page and memory indirect addressing, which are not available on the Z80. Page addressing takes only 8 bits of an operand's address from the instruction, the high-order 8 bits come from the DP (direct page) register, which, presumably, has been filled by previous instructions to point to the beginning of a frequently used block (or *page*) of data. The advantage is that the instructions referencing the page can be shorter than if a full 16-bit address were needed.

The instruction

```
LDA     N
```

loads the contents of memory location N into the A register, while

```
LDA     [N]
```

loads the contents of the address specified by the contents of location N into the A register. Also, autoincrementing and autodecrementing can be used with either one or two levels of deferral when the register indirect mode is used. The instruction

```
LDA     ,X+
```

increments the X register by 1 and then goes to the X register to get the address of the operand. The instruction

```
LDA     [,X++]
```

```
        Input and other code

                LDB         #50
                LDX         #SRC
                LDY         #DES
        LOOP    LDA         ,X+
                STA         ,Y+
                DECB
                BNE         LOOP

        Output and other code

    SRC         RMB         50
                .
                .
                .
    DES         RMB         50
```

Figure 6-45 Large block transfer using looping.

is similar except that it increments the X register by 2 and then goes to the X register to get the address of the memory location that contains the address of the operand. (The uses of indirect addressing are considered in Chapter 7.)

The MC6809 instruction set is summarized in Appendix C. The code given in Fig. 6-45 moves a block of 50 bytes from SRC to DES. It corresponds to the 8085 code and Z80 code given in Figs. 6-26 and 6-43, respectively. Note how autoincrementing is used to obviate the need of explicit increment instructions. The code for performing an 8-bit unsigned multiplication is shown in Fig. 6-46. Although the MC6809 has a multiply instruction, it has no divide instruction.

Other notable MC6809 instructions are the following instructions:

NEG—Negates its operand.

SEX—Extends the sign of the signed number in B through all of the bits in A (i.e., if B is positive, A is filled with 0's, and if B is negative, A is filled with 1's).

LEA—Loads the address of the operand (not the operand), into the specified register S, U, X, or Y.

JMP—Causes an unconditional branch to the address specified by the operand. All conditional branches use relative addressing.

```
        Input and other code

                LDA         QUAN
                LDB         COST
                MUL

        Output and other code

    QUAN        RMB         1
                .
                .
                .
    COST        RMB         1
```

Figure 6-46 Single-precision multiplication of unsigned integers.

BIBLIOGRAPHY

1. LIU, YU-CHENG, and GLENN A. GIBSON, *Microcomputer Systems: The 8086/8088 Family*, 2nd ed.   (Englewood Cliffs, N.J.: Prentice-Hall, 1984).

2. *8080/8085 Assembler Language Programming* (Santa Clara, Calif.: Intel Corporation, 1979).

3. *The MCS-80/85 Family User's Manual* (Santa Clara, Calif.: Intel Corporation, 1983).

4. UFFENBECK, JOHN, *Microcomputers and Microprocessors* (Englewood Cliffs, N.J.: Prentice-Hall, 1985).

5. WAGNER, T. J., and G. J. LIPOVSKI, *Fundamentals of Microcomputer Programming* (New York: Macmillan, 1984).

EXERCISES

1. Describe what each instruction does:
   (a) MOV   C,B   (b) MOV   A,M   (c) LDA   X
   (d) LXI   H,PRES   (e) STAX   B   (f) SHLD   TABLE

2. Given that TIME is associated with address 0120 and WGT is associated with 0094, find the machine language code for the following instructions (give your answers in hexadecimal):
   (a) LXI   D, TIME   (b) MOV   A, M
   (c) MOV B, D   (d) ADI   21H
   (e) MVI   A, 21   (f) LDAX D
   (g) XCHG   (h) INX   B
   (i) XRA   M   (j) LHLD WGT

3. Given that FLO is associated with address 0180, find the assembler language code corresponding to each of the following:
   (a) 41   (b) 7E
   (c) D6   (d) FE
       08   FF
   (e) C2   (f) 32
       80   80
       01   01

4. Write a program segment that corresponds to each of the following:
   (a) $X = X + Y - Z$
   (b) $X = Y**2 + Z*(Y+3)$
   Assume single precision.

5. Rewrite the code in the double-precision example in Fig. 6-18 for a similar triple-precision problem.

6. Write a program segment that will count the number of nonpositive integers in locations ARR through ARR + 2 and put the count in register C.

7. Write a program segment that will clear bits 0 and 1 of register D if both are set, set them if both are clear, and otherwise leave them alone.

8. Assume that AEND + 1 and AEND contain 0397_{10} and AUG + 1 and AUG contain 0285_{10}. Manually perform the operations indicated by the code shown in Fig. 6-21.

9. Rewrite the code in Fig. 6-21 given that the numbers are eight digits long and are in AEND through AEND + 3 and AUG through AUG + 3, respectively.

10. Assume that there are two 3-byte ASCII strings of capital letters beginning at ST1 and ST2, respectively. (Bit 7 of each character is set to zero so that each character fills an 8-bit byte.) Write a program segment that will put the two strings into DICT through DICT + 5 with the alphabetically lower string appearing first.

11. Assume that decimal numbers are stored in successive bytes using 4-digit 10's-complement format as follows:

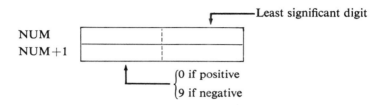

Use several 2-byte examples to verify that the following procedure for subtracting numbers in this format is valid.

1. Set C flag
2. Load A with 99H
3. Add carry
4. Subtract subtrahend from A
5. Add minuend to A
6. Decimal adjust
7. Store result
8. Repeat steps 2 through 7 for second byte

Use the above procedure to write a program that will subtract the number beginning at NUM2 from the number beginning at NUM1 and put the result in the BC pair.

12. Write a program segment that will
(a) Add OP2 to OP1, put the sum in OP2, and branch to ADDOVF if there is an overflow.
(b) Subtract OP2 from OP1, put the difference in OP2, and branch to SUBOVF if there is an overflow.

13. Write program segments that will simulate the Fortran statements given below. For simplicity, assume single precision. Let the statement number 50 be associated with the label SN50.
(a) IF (I .GT. -2) GO TO 50
(b) IF (I .EQ. J .OR. J .GT. 0) I = J + 6

14. Write a program segment that will decrement register E by 1 and branch to BEGIN if the result equals the contents of LIM.

15. Write a program segment that will test bits 2 and 4 of location TOM, branch to ERR12 if both bits are set, branch to ERR1 if bit 2 only is set, branch to ERR2 if bit 4 only is set, and continue if neither is set.

16. Assume that 10 integers are stored in the pairs of bytes beginning with WGTS such that WGTS contains the LSBs of the first integer, WGTS + 1 contains the MSBs of the first integer, and so on. Write a program segment that will add these integers and put the LSBs of the result in TOTL and the MSBs of the result in TOTL + 1. Ignore overflows. (Hint: For shorter code, use the DAD instruction.)

17. Assume the number of bytes in an array LIST is in NUM and write a program segment that will sequentially search LIST until the contents of ID are found. If the contents of ID are not in LIST, branch to NOTFND.

18. Assume the number of single-precision integers in an array LIST is in NUM and write a segment to put the elements of LIST in ascending order.

19. Rewrite the program segment in Fig. 6-30, which multiplies two single-precision positive numbers so that it uses the algorithm

$$
\begin{array}{r}
0\ 1\ 1\ 0 \\
\times\ 0\ 1\ 0\ 1 \\
\hline
0\ 0\ 0\ 0 \\
0\ 1\ 1\ 0 \\
0\ 0\ 0\ 0 \\
0\ 1\ 1\ 0 \\
\hline
0\ 0\ 1\ 1\ 1\ 1\ 0
\end{array}
$$

Note that the exchange instructions are no longer needed.

20. Write a program segment that will divide the 16-bit positive number (MSB must be 0) in the BC register pair by the 8-bit positive number in register D. The quotient is to be left in register C and the remainder in register B. If the divisor is zero, branch to ERRDZ. If the magnitude of the quotient is greater than 127_{10} branch to ERRQL. The steps for performing a division are

1. If divisor is zero branch to ERRDZ.
2. Rotate dividend left one bit.
3. Subtract divisor from high byte of dividend, if nonnegative branch to ERRQL.
4. Add divisor to high byte of dividend.
5. Set count to 7 and clear carry.
6. Rotate dividend left 1 bit.
7. Subtract divisor from high byte of dividend.
8. If the result is negative put 0 in carry and add divisor to high byte of dividend; otherwise put 1 in carry.
9. Decrement count and return to step 6 if count is nonzero.
10. Rotate low byte of dividend (quotient byte) left 1 bit.

Verify the above sequence with test data.

21. State the advantages in having an EQU directive.

22. Figures 6-38 and 6-39 illustrate the tasks performed by the two passes of an assembler. Produce similar figures for the code in
(a) Fig. 6-14   (b) Fig. 6-16

23. How many bytes are needed to store the following program segment?

```
           LXI      H,BEN
           MVI      C,8H
           ORA      A
    JAN:   LDAX     D
           ADC      M
```

How many memory accesses are needed to execute it?

24. Assume a 2-MHz clock. If the segment shown in Exercise 23 is contained in 800 nS memory and all data references are made to 1200 nS memory, determine how long it would take to fetch and execute each instruction.

25. Assuming that all memory has a 400 nS access time and that the clock frequency is 1 MHz, write a loop or a nest of loops that will take 2 min ± 0.005 S to execute.

26. The instruction set for the Zilog Z80 is summarized in Appendix B. Using the Z80 instruction set, rework the example in
   (a) Fig. 6-14   **(b)** Fig. 6-16   **(c)** Fig. 6-18
   (d) Fig. 6-21   **(e)** Fig. 6-24b   **(f)** Fig. 6-32   **(g)** Fig. 6-34

27. The instruction set for the Motorola MC6809 is summarized in Appendix C. Assume the MC6809 and rewrite the program segment indicated in
   (a) Fig. 6-14   **(b)** Fig. 6-16   **(c)** Fig. 6-18
   (d) Fig. 6-21   **(e)** Fig. 6-24b   **(f)** Fig. 6-32   **(g)** Fig. 6-34

Chapter 7

Modular Programming

Chapter 6 concentrated on individual instructions and how to put those instructions together to perform simple tasks. Although the construction of complete programs was discussed, the programs were single-module programs. Clearly, most useful programs are much more complex and must include several tasks such as those that appear in the examples of Chapter 6. The present chapter considers the formulation of complex programs from numerous small sequences, called *program modules* (or simply *modules*), each of which performs a well-defined task. Such formulation of computer code is referred to as *modular programming*.

Assembler language programs are developed by essentially the same procedure as high-level language programs, that is, by

1. Precisely stating what the program is to do.
2. Breaking the overall problem into tasks.
3. Defining exactly what each task must do and how it is to communicate with the other tasks.
4. Putting the tasks into assembler language modules and connecting the modules together to form the program.
5. Debugging and testing the program.
6. Documenting the program.

This chapter is concerned primarily with step 4. This step is similar to that followed by a hardware designer, who first breaks the design into circuit modules, which may correspond to printed circuit (PC) boards, implements the modules, and then integrates them into the desired system.

The primary aid used in subdividing a program into modules is the *hierarchical diagram*, which is a block-oriented figure that summarizes the relationships between the modules (tasks) and submodules (subtasks). A typical hierarchical diagram is shown in Fig. 7-1. These diagrams look like, and serve the same purpose as, organizational charts for corporations. The main module corresponds to the president of the corporation, the principal submodules, A, B, and C, to the vice-presidents, and so on. A hierarchical diagram shows the chain of subordination that exists among the modules and their submodules just as an organizational chart indicates the chain of command within a corporation. It helps the programmer and others to visualize the functional structure of the program. Note that a submodule may be subordinate to more than one module just as a person can appear more than once on an organizational chart.

The reasons for breaking a program into small parts are that

1. Modules are easier to comprehend.
2. Different modules can be assigned to different programmers.
3. Debugging and testing can be done in a more orderly fashion.
4. Documentation can be more easily understood.
5. Modifications may be localized.
6. Frequently used tasks can be programmed into modules that are stored in libraries and used by several programs.

With regard to item 1, the human mind is capable of concentrating on only a limited amount of material at one time. Therefore, it is necessary for us to subdivide our

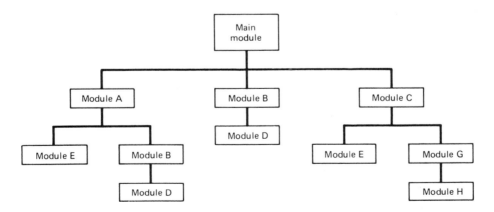

Figure 7-1   Typical hierarchical diagram.

thinking no matter what kind of problem we are confronted with. Modular programming is a natural extension of this phenomenon to programming.

When designing the modules of a program one must be concerned with how and under what circumstances the modules are entered and exited, the *control coupling*, and how information is communicated between the modules, the *data coupling*. The coupling between two modules depends on several factors, including whether they are assembled together or separately and the organization of the data. In general, the task selection and module design should be such that control coupling is kept simple and data coupling is minimized.

Most assembler languages are designed to aid the modularization process in three ways. One is to allow data to be structured so that they can be readily accessed by the various modules, another is to provide for subroutines, and the third is to permit sections of code, known as *macros*, to be inserted by the appearance of single statements, each of which contains a name and a set of arguments. The first section of this chapter discusses the way modules that are assembled separately are linked together and how programs are prepared for execution. Sections 7-2 and 7-3 examine stacks and subroutines and how they are implemented on the 8085, and Sections 7-4 and 7-5 consider subroutine linkage for the Z80 and MC6809, respectively. The next section considers macros, and the last section discusses an example that is more extensive than those presented in the first part of the chapter.

7-1 LINKING AND LOADING

The general process for creating and executing a program is illustrated in Fig. 7-2. The process for a particular system may not correspond exactly to the one diagrammed in the figure, but the general concepts are the same. In the 8085 software the linker is divided into two parts, one being called the linker and the other the locator, and the loading is done by the operating system. The arrows indicate that corrections may be made after any one of the major stages.

In constructing a program, some program modules may be put in the same source module and assembled together; others may be in different source modules and assembled separately. In any event, the resulting object modules, some of which may be grouped into libraries, must be linked together to form a load module before the program can be executed. In addition to outputting the load module, normally the linker prints a *memory map* that indicates where the linked object modules will be loaded into memory. After the load module has been created, it is loaded into the memory of the computer by the loader and execution begins. Although the *I/O* can be performed by modules within the program, normally the *I/O* is done by *I/O* drivers that are part of the operating system. All that appears in the user's program are references to the *I/O* drivers that cause the operating system to execute them. For controller applications for which the program is to

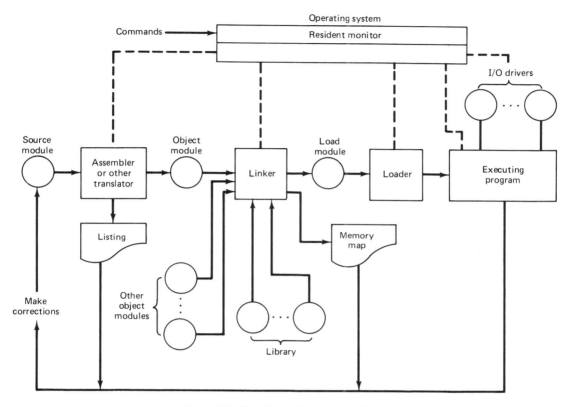

Figure 7-2   Creation and execution of a program.

be put into a machine without an operating system, the *I/O* must be done by the program itself.

Regardless of the system, the linker/loader combination must make all of the address assignments needed to allow the program to work properly.   More specifically, this combination must

1. Find the object modules to be linked.
2. Construct the load module by assigning the positions of all of the object modules being linked.
3. Fill in all addresses that could not be determined by the assembler.
4. Load the program for execution.

The object modules to be linked are determined by naming them in the command to the linker and by the operating system searching through libraries.   The format of a linker command depends on the system, but it typically contains a command word followed by a list of object modules and libraries.

Because several modules may be used to produce a program, each object module needs a name so that the system can uniquely identify it. This name may be completely different from the object file name that the programmer uses to identify the file containing the module. To assign these names, every source module must have as its first statement a NAME directive, which for ASM-85 is of the form

```
Label       NAME        Module name
```

where *Label* is optional but, if present, is associated with the first instruction or directive in the program. Also, every module must end with a directive of the form

```
Label       END        Expression
```

where, once again, *Label* is optional. If *Label* is present, it is associated with the end of the module. *Expression* must point to the first instruction in the program, and one and only one module, the main module to which the loader branches when the program begins execution, must have an *Expression* in its END directive.

Most assemblers are capable of breaking an object module into parts, called *segments*. For ASM-85 there can be an absolute segment, a code segment, a stack segment, and a data segment. Except for the stack segment, each segment has its own location counter, and the absolute, code, and data segments are formed as the assembly progresses by switching between these location counters using the ASEG, DSEG and CSEG directives. An ASEG directive causes a change from the current location counter to the absolute segment's location counter. Similarly, DSEG and CSEG result in switches to the data and code segment location counters. The assembly begins in the absolute segment. (To see how segment switching fits into the assembly process, refer back to Fig. 6-40.) The absolute segment is for code and data that must be put at particular memory locations.

The stack segment is not involved in the assembly process, since a stack is simply a special area in memory. It can, however, be given a length by using a directive of the form

```
Label       STKLN      Constant Expression
```

where *Label* is optional but, if present, is associated with the beginning, or *bottom* or *base*, of the stack. *Constant expression* designates the number of bytes being reserved for the stack. If no STKLN directive is given, the length of the module's stack segment will be zero.

Until now it has been assumed that all labels in a source module are assigned to locations within that module. The assignment is formed by placing the label in exactly one label field, and when this is done the label is said to be *defined*. If a label appears as an operand but is not defined within the module, or is defined more than once in the module, an assembler error will occur.

On the other hand, if a module is to be linked with other modules, then it is possible for it to refer to labels in these other modules. For a given module, the labels defined within it are said to be *internal* to the module, and those referred to in the module but not defined in it are said to be *external* to the module. In order to avoid an "undefined label" error, the assembler must be informed of the external labels in advance by including them in external directives of the form

EXTRN   *External label,..., External label*

which are normally placed at the beginning of the module's source code. All labels must be defined exactly once in the modules being joined by the linker. When the linker combines several object modules, it examines the symbol tables for the external labels listed in EXTRN directives and matches them with labels that are defined in other modules. If there are unpaired or multiply defined symbols, a linker error will occur.

Many linkers, including the one for the 8085, also require that each module give permission before its internal labels can be used as external labels by other modules. This is done with directives of the form

PUBLIC   *Internal label,..., Internal label*

For those systems that require PUBLIC directives, only those labels included in the PUBLIC directives can be used to satisfy external references. The labels included in the PUBLIC directives in a module are said to be *global*, and those not appearing are said to be *local* to the module.

Figure 7-3 shows the EXTRN and PUBLIC directives in three typical modules and how the matching is done by the linker. Source module 1 allows other modules access to the *global* labels VAR1 and LAB1, but not to the *local* label VAR3. It references VAR2 and LAB2, which are not defined internally and must be declared global in one of the other modules. Source module 2 permits access to VAR2, but not VAR3, and references VAR1. Source module 3 permits access to LAB2, but not LAB3, and references LAB1 and VAR2. Note that local labels such as VAR3 can appear in more than one module without an error occurring because the linker cares about only those labels that have been declared global. Also, a label such as LAB2 can be local in one module (module 2) and made global by another (module 3). Any external references to LAB2 (such as those in module 1) will be satisfied by the LAB2 in module 3.

As described in Section 6-11 and the above discussion of segments, a source module has one location counter for each segment and all location counters are initially 0, although ORG directives can be used to reset them to other values. The labels are assigned addresses according to their location counters during the

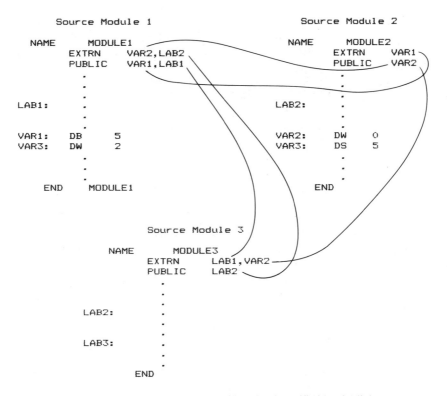

Figure 7-3 Illustration of the matching that is verified by the linker.

first pass of the assembly and the operands containing these labels are filled in during the second pass.   As a result, all modules are assembled, and their operand addresses are assigned as if the segment is going to be started at memory address 0000.   For example, if the location counter is 0030 at the time the label VAR is encountered, then

$$LXI \quad H,VAR$$

will be assembled with 0030 being put into the second and third bytes of the instruction.

Clearly, only one segment can begin at 0000, and the linker must decide how to reassign the various segments and modules to the available memory space, i.e., how to arrange the object modules and their segments as it constructs a load module. Together the assembler and linker must provide the loader with the necessary information to fill in the proper operand addresses as it loads a program for execution.

There are a variety of ways of constructing object and load modules, and Fig. 7-4 gives a representative structure for each.   Basically, an object module must contain two sets of information: (1) the *external symbol table* and (2) an intermediate form of machine language code called *binary-symbolic code*. The external symbol table contains all of the external symbols that are referenced by the module and an indicator showing whether or not they are defined within the module. Binary-symbolic code differs from machine language code in that (1) a flag is associated with each symbol reference and (2) the undefined external symbol addresses have not been inserted. Because a linker stacks several object modules together to form a load module and each object module is created without the assembler knowing the origins of the other object modules, the object modules must be such that the linker and/or loader can modify all address references. This implies that all such references must somehow be noted in the binary-symbolic code.

An operand that is adjusted after assembly is always associated with a label and the operand and label are said to be *relocatable*. Sometimes operands refer to specific memory locations that are not changed by the loader or linker; for example

```
LXI     H,60H
MOV     A,M
```

would load A from the location whose address is 0060. These operands, which are said to be *absolute*, do not have labels and do not need to be flagged in the binary-symbolic code.

A load module also consists of two basic sets of information: (1) a *load map* (or *linkage symbol table*) and (2) a slightly altered version of the binary-symbolic code called *binary-relocatable code*. The principal functions of the linker are to make the required changes in the binary-symbolic code and to digest the information in the external symbol tables of the object modules it is operating on and produce a load map. The load map designates where each object module is within the load module. Although the differences between the binary-symbolic code and the binary-relocatable code vary from system to system, one simple procedure would be to have the linker assume an origin and fill in all addresses, both for internal

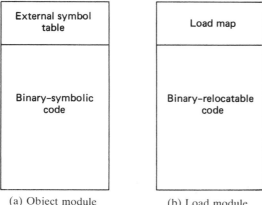

External symbol table	Load map
Binary–symbolic code	Binary–relocatable code

(a) Object module   (b) Load module

Figure 7-4 Typical structures for object and load modules.

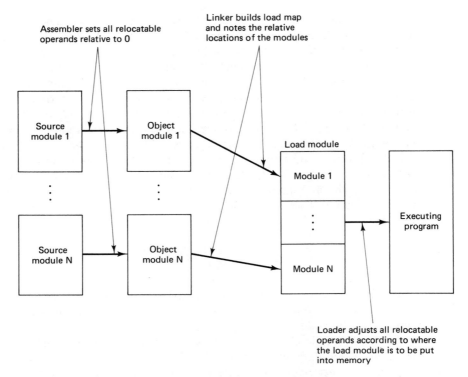

Figure 7-5 Illustration showing how the operands are changed as a program is created and loaded.

and external symbols, relative to that origin.   How object and load modules are constructed is depicted in Fig. 7-5.

7-2 STACKS

Because there are only a few registers, quite often more registers are needed than are available.   This means that the current contents of some of the registers may have to be stored in memory while a task is being performed and then restored when the task is completed.   Storing and later retrieving the BC, DE, and HL pairs could be done with the code

```
SHLD      TEMP
XCHG
SHLD      TEMP+2
MOV       L,C
MOV       H,B
SHLD      TEMP+4
```

```
  .           ⎫
  .           ⎬ perform task
  .           ⎭
LHLD        TEMP+4
MOV         B,H
MOV         C,L
LHLD        TEMP+2
XCHG
LHLD        TEMP
```

but this is cumbersome and inefficient.

In the above example, it was not important which register was stored first, second, or last; however, quite often maintaining a particular order is necessary. For example, suppose that the BC pair is to be used for holding all of the counters while nesting a set of loops. As the inner loops are entered and exited, the BC pair must be stored and retrieved, as shown in Fig. 7-6.

Both of these examples demonstrate the need for an efficient way of storing and retrieving data to and from memory in an orderly fashion. This need is satisfied by including facilities for implementing a *last-in, first-out (LIFO) stack*. Such a stack is analogous to writing messages on pieces of paper, stacking them as they are created, and then retrieving them in reverse order by taking them off the top of the stack. At any time one may place more messages on the stack, but when getting them back must always take the top one first. Figure 7-7 depicts a LIFO stack.

A stack is an area of memory that is accessed in a special way and is normally implemented by using register indirect addressing through a special register called the *stack pointer (SP)* register. The SP register is autodecremented as items are put onto the stack and autoincremented as they are taken from the stack. Putting something on the stack is called a *push* and taking it off is called a *pop*. The original contents of the SP are referred to as the *bottom of the stack* and the current contents of SP are referred to as the *top of the stack (TOS)*.

The 8085 instructions for executing pushes and pops are given in Fig. 7-8, and an illustration of an 8085's stack activity is given in Fig. 7-9. Also shown in Fig. 7-8 are the instructions for exchanging the contents of the top 2 bytes of the

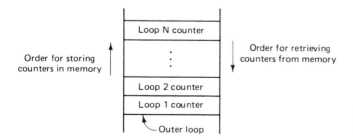

Figure 7-6 Storing and retrieving counters for nested loops.

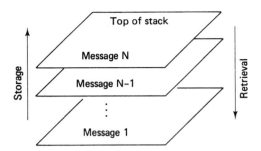

Figure 7-7 LIFO stack.

stack and the contents of the HL pair (XTHL) and for loading the SP from the HL pair (SPHL).   Setting the contents of SP could be done with the instruction

$$LXI \qquad SP,CONST$$

where CONST is either a constant or a label, or the instruction

$$SPHL$$

where HL contains what is to be put in the SP, or the instructions

```
LHLD    STPTR
SPHL
```

where the new contents of the SP are to come from the memory location STPTR. Storing the contents of SP could be done by the sequence

```
LXI     H,0
DAD     SP
SHLD    STPTR
```

The problem of storing and retrieving the register pairs can now be accomplished with the simple sequence

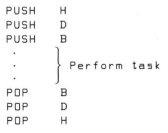

PUSH rp   (Push)

$((SP) - 1) \leftarrow (rh)$
$((SP) - 2) \leftarrow (rl)$
$(SP) \leftarrow (SP) - 2$

The content of the high-order register of register pair rp is moved to the memory location whose address is one less than the content of register SP. The content of the low-order register of register pair rp is moved to the memory location whose address is two less than the content of register SP. The content of register SP is decremented by 2. Note: Register pair rp = SP may not be specified.

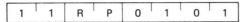

Addressing: reg. indirect
Flags: none

POP rp   (Pop)

$(rl) \leftarrow ((SP))$
$(rh) \leftarrow ((SP) + 1)$
$(SP) \leftarrow (SP) + 2$

The content of the memory location, whose address is specified by the content of register SP, is moved to the low-order register of register pair rp. The content of the memory location, whose address is one more than the content of register SP, is moved to the high-order register of register pair rp. The content of register SP is incremented by 2. Note: Register pair rp = SP may not be specified.

Addressing: reg. indirect
Flags: none

PUSH PSW   (Push processor status word)

$((SP) - 1) \leftarrow (A)$
$((SP) - 2)_0 \leftarrow (CY), ((SP) - 2)_1 \leftarrow 1$
$((SP) - 2)_2 \leftarrow (P)$, $((SP) - 2)_3 \leftarrow 0$
$((SP) - 2)_4 \leftarrow (AC), ((SP) - 2)_5 \leftarrow 0$
$((SP) - 2)_6 \leftarrow (Z)$, $((SP) - 2)_7 \leftarrow (S)$
$(SP) \leftarrow (SP) - 2$

The content of register A is moved to the memory location whose address is one less than register SP. The contents of the condition flags are assembled into a processor status word and the word is moved to the memory location whose address is two less than the content of register SP. The content of register SP is decremented by two.

Addressing: reg. indirect
Flags: none

POP PSW   (Pop processor status word)

$(CY) \leftarrow ((SP))_0$
$(P) \leftarrow ((SP))_2$
$(AC) \leftarrow ((SP))_4$
$(Z) \leftarrow ((SP))_6$
$(S) \leftarrow ((SP))_7$
$(A) \leftarrow ((SP) + 1)$
$(SP) \leftarrow (SP) + 2$

The content of the memory location whose address is specified by the content of register SP is used to restore the condition flags. The content of the memory location whose address is one more than the content of register SP is moved to register A. The content of register SP is incremented by 2.

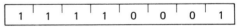

Addressing: reg. indirect
Flags: Z, S, P, CY, AC

XTHL   (Exchange stack top with H and L)

$(L) \longleftrightarrow ((SP))$
$(H) \longleftrightarrow ((SP) + 1)$

The content of the L register is exchanged with the content of the memory location whose address is specified by the content of register SP. The content of the H register is exchanged with the content of the memory location whose address is one more than the content of register SP.

Addressing: reg. indirect
Flags: none

SPHL   (Move HL to SP)

$(SP) \leftarrow (H) (L)$

The contents of registers H and L (16 bits) are moved to register SP.

Addressing: register
Flags: none

Figure 7-8 Definition of the PUSH, POP, XTHL, and SPHL instructions. (Reprinted by permission of Intel Corporation, Copyright 1983.)

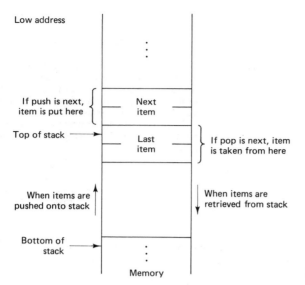

Low address

If push is next,
item is put here   Next item

Top of stack →   Last item   If pop is next, item
                                            is taken from here

When items are   When items are
pushed onto stack   retrieved from stack

Bottom of stack →

Memory

Figure 7-9   8085 stack activity.

The stack activity that occurs while this sequence is being executed is shown in Fig. 7-10.   Note that the POP operation does not destroy the information on the top of the stack; it merely places the information into the proper registers and increments the stack pointer.   If new information is pushed onto the stack, the old information lying just above the top of the stack will then be replaced.   Also note that the register contents are popped in the reverse order in which they are stored.

There are numerous uses for a stack other than temporarily storing the registers.   Some of them are associated with subroutine linkage and are discussed in the next section; others simply involve storing information that needs to be accessed repetitively while carrying out an algorithm.   As mentioned above, counters that are needed in executing nested loops are an example.   As each loop is entered, its counter could be pushed onto the stack; and during the modification and testing phases, the counter could be popped from the stack, decremented, and tested.   A nest of loops that use the C register for the counter is given in Fig 7-11.   Note that the next counter to be needed is always on the top of the stack.   Stacks are also utilized to store temporarily ASCII strings and arithmetic operands whenever the string or operand must be accessed repeatedly.

7-3 SUBROUTINES

A *subroutine* is a set of code that can be branched to and returned from in such a way that the code is as if it were inserted at the point from which it is branched to.   The branch to a subroutine is referred to as the *call*, and the corresponding branch back is known as the *return*.   The return is always made to the instruction

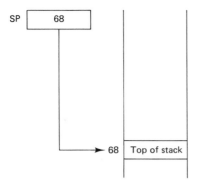

(a) Before pushing registers

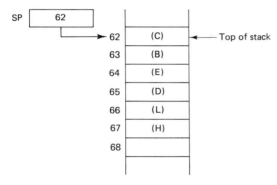

(b) After pushing registers

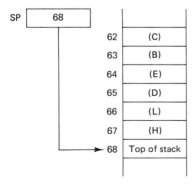

(c) After popping from stack

Figure 7-10 Temporarily storing register contents on the stack and then restoring them.

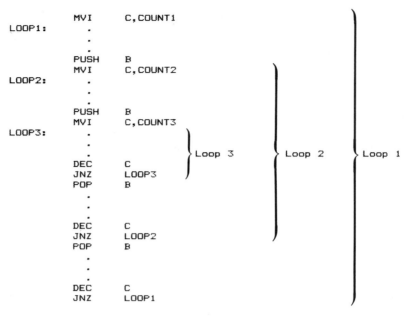

Figure 7-11   Using the stack for nesting loops.

immediately following the call regardless of where the call is located.   If, as shown in Fig. 7-12a, more than one call is made to the same subroutine, the return after each call is made to the instruction following that call.   Therefore, only one copy of the subroutine needs to be stored in memory even though it may be called several times.   When subroutines are nested, as shown in Fig. 7-12b, each return is made to the corresponding calling program, not to one higher in the hierarchy.

Subroutines provide the primary means of breaking the code in a program into modules.   Although not all modules are subroutines, most of them are, because subroutines can easily be individually designed, tested, and documented.   They can also be stored in libraries and used by a variety of programs.   In short, they offer all of the conveniences accrued to modular programming and do so in a flexible manner.   Subroutines have one major disadvantage in that extra code is needed to join them together in such a way that they can communicate with each other.   This extra code is referred to as *linkage* and is the principal subject of this section.

The following three requirements must be satisfied when calling a subroutine:

1. Unlike other branch instructions, a subroutine call must save the address of the next instruction so that the return will be able to branch back to the proper place in the calling program.
2. The registers used by the subroutine need to be stored before their contents are changed and then restored just before the subroutine is exited.

3. A subroutine must have a means of communicating or sharing data with the routine that calls it and other subroutines.

The first requirement is met by having special call and return branch instructions. These instructions for the 8085 are given in Fig. 7-13. In addition to unconditional call and return instructions, the 8085 has corresponding conditional branches. A CALL instruction not only branches to the indicated address but also pushes the return address onto the stack. The RET instruction simply pops the return address from the stack. This assumes that if the stack is accessed by the subroutine, then the stack pointer is returned to its proper value and the stack activity is not such that the return address is destroyed. Obviously, when working

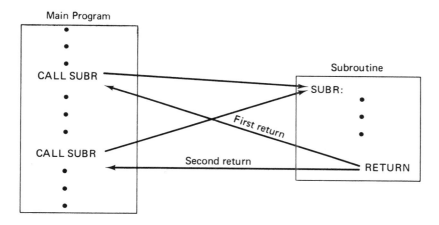

(a) Multiple calls

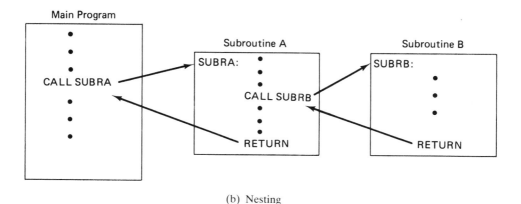

(b) Nesting

Figure 7-12 Subroutine usage.

CALL addr   (Call)

   ((SP) − 1) ← (PCH)
   ((SP) − 2) ← (PCL)
   (SP) ← (SP) − 2
   (PC) ← (byte 3) (byte 2)

The high-order eight bits of the next instruction address are moved to the memory location whose address is one less than the content of register SP. The low-order eight bits of the next instruction address are moved to the memory location whose address is two less than the content of register SP. The content of register SP is decremented by 2. Control is transferred to the instruction whose address is specified in byte 3 and byte 2 of the current instruction.

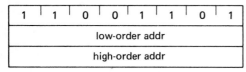

        Addressing: immediate/reg. indirect
        Flags: none

Ccondition addr   (Condition call)

   If (CCC),
     ((SP) − 1) ← (PCH)
     ((SP) − 2) ← (PCL)
     (SP) ← (SP) − 2
     (PC) ← (byte 3) (byte 2)

If the specified condition is true, the actions specified in the CALL instruction (see above) are performed; otherwise control continues sequentially.

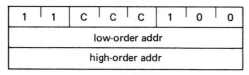

        Addressing: immediate/reg. indirect
        Flags: none

RET   (Return)

   (PCL) ← ((SP));
   (PCH) ← ((SP) + 1);
   (SP) ← (SP) + 2;

The content of the memory location whose address is specified in register SP is moved to the low-order eight bits of register PC. The content of the memory location whose address is one more than the content of register SP is moved to the high-order eight bits of register PC. The content of register SP is incremented by 2.

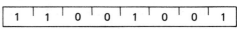

        Addressing: reg. indirect
        Flags: none

Rcondition   (Conditional return)

   If (CCC),
     (PCL) ← ((SP))
     (PCH) ← ((SP) + 1)
     (SP) ← (SP) + 2

If the specified condition is true, the actions specified in the RET instruction (see above) are performed; otherwise control continues sequentially.

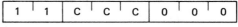

        Addressing: reg. indirect
        Flags: none

Figure 7-13   Definitions of the subroutine branch and return instructions.   (Reprinted by permission of Intel Corporation, Copyright 1983.)

with subroutines a programmer must be very careful as to how he or she manipulates the stack; otherwise, returns may be made to nonsensical locations.

   Figure 7-14 shows a typical set of subroutine calls and returns. Figure 7-15 shows the stack activity due to these calls and returns. Other stack activity that may take place while the subroutines are executing is not shown.

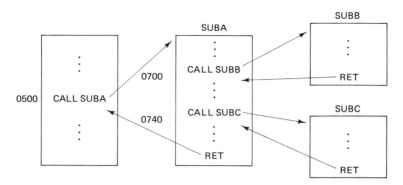

Figure 7-14 Typical set of calls and returns.

With regard to storing and restoring the register contents, this is also done by using the stack. If all of the working registers and the PSW must be stored, the sequence

PUSH   B
PUSH   D
PUSH   H
PUSH   PSW

should be placed at the beginning of the subroutine, and

POP   PSW
POP   H
POP   D
POP   B

should be placed at the end, just before the RET instruction. It is possible to have the calling program store and restore the register contents, but this has the following disadvantages:

1. The code for storing and restoring the register contents must be repeated for each call.
2. The programmer writing the calling sequence may be different from the one writing the subroutine and must know which registers are used by the subroutine.

As for passing information between a calling program and a subroutine, the first question is whether or not the subroutine always operates on the same memory locations. If it does, and all calling modules and the subroutine module are assembled together, then there is no need to pass parameters, because the assembler

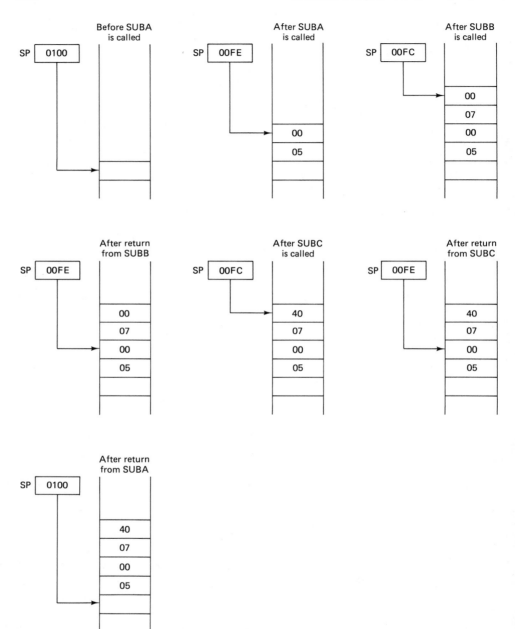

Figure 7-15   Stack activity due to calls and returns shown in Fig. 7-14.

can assign the addresses of the operands.   Even if the modules are not assembled together, by using EXTRN and PUBLIC statements the linker could be used to assign the necessary addresses.   To facilitate this situation, many assemblers and compilers accommodate the use of common areas that are freely accessible by all modules that refer to them.   In Fortran this is done by means of COMMON statements.   Many assemblers also include a means of working with common areas, but, because the ways in which common areas are defined vary considerably from one assembler to the next, common areas will not be discussed here.   In general, however, a common area is implemented by defining a purely data module that contains only statements that reserve storage areas and assign labels to these areas and then putting special statements in the code modules that refer to this data module.

The more usual case is the one in which the subroutine must operate on different memory locations each time it is entered.   Although this makes a subroutine much more flexible, it also requires the calling program to tell the subroutine what memory areas it is to be concerned with.   This is called *parameter passing* and is primarily done in one of two ways.   Either an area of memory associated with the calling program, which is referred to as a *parameter table*, is used, or the stack is used.   The parameter table or stack could contain the quantities to be operated by the subroutine, the addresses of these quantities, or a combination thereof.   For example, a subroutine that finds the sum of several elements in an array would need to be passed the address of the first element of the array, since putting the entire array in the table would waste both time and memory space. On the other hand, the number of elements to be summed could be either passed directly through the table or put in a location whose address is in the table.

If a parameter table is used, then the calling program must put the parameters or parameter addresses in the table and then store the address of the table in a place that is accessible by the subroutine, usually a register or register pair.   The subroutine would retrieve the address of the table and then retrieve and operate on the parameters.

Suppose a program is needed that must frequently add 16-digit decimal numbers.   If only a few additions are required, it may be easier simply to insert the necessary code.   If several additions are needed, it may be easier and consume less memory to use a subroutine to perform the addition.

Figure 7-16 gives a subroutine for adding two 16-digit decimal numbers and Fig. 7-17 shows a typical calling sequence.   It is assumed that each of the 16-digit numbers being added is contained in consecutive bytes in memory, with the least significant digit being in the low-order bits of the first byte, and so on, and that the result is to be similarly stored in place of the addend.   The parameters are the augend and addend, and their addresses are passed to the subroutine by putting them in a table and then putting the address of the table in the HL register pair. In the calling sequence shown, it is assumed that the numbers being added are in the 8 bytes beginning with X (= location 0140) and Y (= location 0148), respec-

Address	Machine Code	Assembler Code			Remarks
2FD	F5	DECADD:	PUSH	PSW	;STORE REGISTERS
2FE	D5		PUSH	D	;AND FLAGS
2FF	C5		PUSH	B	
300	4E		MOV	C,M	;ADDRESS OF
301	23		INX	H	;AUGEND
302	46		MOV	B,M	;TO BC PAIR
303	23		INX	H	
304	5E		MOV	E,M	;ADDRESS OF
305	23		INX	H	;ADDEND
306	56		MOV	D,M	;TO DE PAIR
307	69		MOV	L,C	;MOVE ADDRESS OF
308	60		MOV	H,B	;AUGEND TO HL
309	0E		MVI	C,8	;SET COUNT TO 8
30A	08				
30B	B7		ORA	A	;CLEAR CARRY
30C	1A	LOOP:	LDAX	D	;LOAD ADDEND
30D	8E		ADC	M	;ADD AUGEND
30E	27		DAA		;ADJUST
30F	12		STAX	D	;STORE SUM
310	23		INX	H	;POINT TO HIGHER
311	13		INX	D	;BYTES OF OPERANDS
312	0D		DCR	C	;DECREMENT COUNTER
313	C2		JNZ	LOOP	;LOOP ON NZ
314	0C				
315	03				
316	C1		POP	B	;RESTORE REGISTERS
317	D1		POP	D	;AND FLAGS
318	F1		POP	PSW	
319	C9		RET		;RETURN TO MAIN PROGRAM

Figure 7-16 Subroutine for performing 16-digit decimal addition.

tively.   The parameter address table begins with PARM (= 0220) and the entry point of the subroutine is DECADD (= location 02FD).

Except for the HL pair, the subroutine has assumed the responsibilty for saving and restoring the registers.   It is not necessary to save the HL pair because, once the parameter addresses have been retrieved, the address of the parameter table is no longer needed.   Figure 7-18 shows the contents of the stack and parameter address table just after the registers have been pushed onto the stack.   It is assumed that the stack pointer contained 0051 immediately before the registers were pushed.

If the stack is to be used, the calling program must first push the parameters or their addresses and then store the (SP) so that these contents can easily be retrieved by the subroutine.   Storing (SP) immediately after putting the parameter information on the stack is necessary because the stack may also be used by the call instruction and/or for storing the register contents.   After entering the subroutine, the pointer to the parameter information would be retrieved and the information would be taken from the stack.

In the above example, if the stack is used for passing the addresses of the augend and addend and the HL pair is used to point to the parameters on the

Address	Machine Code	Assembler Code		Remarks
	.			
	.			
	.			
124	21	LXI	H,X	;STORES PARAMETER
125	40			
126	01			
127	22	SHLD	PARM	;ADDRESSES
128	20			
129	02			
12A	21	LXI	H,Y	;IN TABLE
12B	48			
12C	01			
12D	22	SHLD	PARM+2	
12E	22			
12F	02			
130	21	LXI	H,PARM	;GETS ADDRESS OF TABLE
131	20			
132	02			
133	CD	CALL	DECADD	;SUBROUTINE BRANCH
134	FD			
135	02			
	.			
	.			
	.			
220	00	PARM: DS	4	;PARAMETER ADDRESS TABLE
	00			
	00			
	00			
	.			
	.			
	.			

Figure 7-17 Typical sequence for calling the subroutine DECADD that uses a parameter table.

stack, then the DECADD subroutine would not need to be changed. However, a calling sequence would be different. A typical calling sequence that uses the stack is given in Fig. 7-19, and the contents of the stack just after the registers are stored are shown in Fig. 7-20. Note that the stack is popped twice after the subroutine return is made so that the SP will be returned to its original value.

If the number of parameters is small and the microprocessor includes several registers, an alternative to passing the parameters through a table or the stack is to put the parameter information in the registers where the subroutine can get at it directly. This saves time, but it requires that the original contents of the registers be stored by the calling program. As indicated earlier, this may not be suitable. Most Fortran compilers are such that when a function subroutine is called, the function arguments are passed through a parameter table, but the result is passed back through a register.

Whether parameter tables or the stack passes the parameters is not important, but it is important that when working on a single project, conventions be established for providing subroutine linkage and that these conventions be consistently followed. Otherwise, confusion will result. Most Fortran compilers use parameter

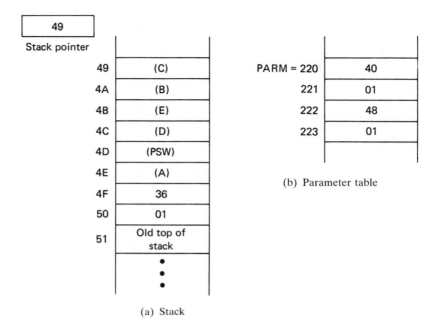

(a) Stack

(b) Parameter table

Figure 7-18 Contents of the stack and parameter address table just after the register contents have been pushed by the subroutine.

Address	Machine Code	Assembler code		Remarks
127	21	LXI	H,X	;STORE PARAMETER
128	40			
129	01			
12A	E5	PUSH	H	;ADDRESSES ON STACK
12B	21	LXI	H,Y	
12C	48			
12D	01			
12E	E5	PUSH	H	
12F	21	LXI	H,0	;PUTS STACK POINTER
130	00			
131	00			
132	39	DAD	SP	;IN HL PAIR
133	CD	CALL	DECADD	;SUBROUTINE BRANCH
134	FD			
135	02			
136	E1	POP	H	;DISCARD PARAMETER
137	E1	POP	H	;ADDRESSES
138	.			
	.			
	.			

Figure 7-19 Typical DECADD calling sequence that uses the stack for passing parameters.

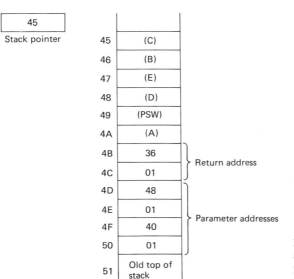

45	

Stack pointer

45	(C)
46	(B)
47	(E)
48	(D)
49	(PSW)
4A	(A)
4B	36
4C	01
4D	48
4E	01
4F	40
50	01
51	Old top of stack

Return address

Parameter addresses

Figure 7-20   Contents of the stack just after the register contents have been pushed, assuming that the stack is used for passing parameters.

tables, but languages that permit subroutines to call themselves (i.e., that permit recursive programming) use the stack.

7-4 Z80 SUBROUTINE LINKAGE

The stack for the Z80 works exactly the same way as for the 8085. The Z80 has PUSH and POP instructions for pushing and popping the IX and IY registers as well as the A/flags combination and the BC, DE, and HL pairs. The LD instruction can be used to load the SP register from memory, the IX register, the IY register, or the HL pair. The EX instruction will allow the 2 bytes at the top of the stack to be exchanged with the contents of HL, IX, or IY.

Subroutine calls and returns are also performed in the same manner as on the 8085, with the return address being pushed onto the stack by the CALL instruction and the RET instruction popping it from the stack. The Z80 also includes conditional calls and returns. Because the Z80 and 8085 are so similar, reworking the decimal addition example for the Z80 has been left to Exercise 5.

7-5 MC6809 SUBROUTINE LINKAGE

The stack and subroutine facilities of the MC6809 differ from those of the 8085 and Z80 in several respects. The MC6809 has two stack pointer registers, the system (S) and user (U) registers. Both automatically decrement by 1 before putting a byte onto the stack and automatically increment by 1 after taking a byte

from the stack.   In this regard they are similar to the SP registers on the 8085 and
Z80, but differ in that single bytes can be pushed or popped and any combination
of registers, including the PC, can be pushed or popped by one 2-byte PSH (push)
or PUL (pull) instruction.   The first byte of the instruction contains the op code
and the second indicates which registers are to be pushed or popped.   An exception
is that the S register cannot be pushed onto the S stack and the U register cannot
be pushed onto the U stack.

Figure 7-21 gives the order in which the registers are put on or taken from
the stack.   [Motorola uses CC (condition codes) as the abbreviation for the PSW.]
The instruction

$$\text{PSHS} \quad \text{CC,A,B,DP,X,Y,U,PC}$$

pushes all of the registers except S onto the S stack and

$$\text{PULS} \quad \text{CC,A,B,DP,X,Y,U,PC}$$

pops them from the S stack.   The order in which the registers are listed in the
PSH and PUL instructions is not important, because the order of the pushes and
pops is always as shown in Fig. 7-21.   The instruction

$$\text{PUSU} \quad \text{X,Y,A,B}$$

stores the X, Y, A, and B on the U stack in the order Y, X, B, and A.   The
instruction

$$\text{PULU} \quad \text{X,A,B,Y}$$

would pop them from this stack in the order A, B, X, and Y.

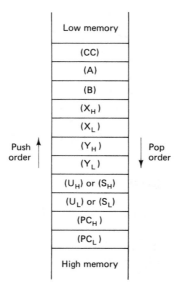

Figure 7-21   Order in which the
MC6809's registers are pushed or
popped.

The LD instruction can load either S or U using any of the addressing modes, including the immediate mode. Likewise, except for the immediate mode, the ST instruction can store the contents of S or U. Also, the LEA instruction can load S or U from a 16-bit register or a pair of bytes in memory. TFR can be used to transfer 2 bytes between S or U and the other registers. Therefore, there are many ways of storing and restoring the contents of S and U.

There are three subroutine call instructions—BSR, LBSR, and JSR. All three are unconditional and all push the return address onto the S stack (i.e., the stack pointed to by the S register). Both BSR and LBSR use relative addressing to produce the branch address by adding the current contents of the PC, which points to the instruction following the BSR or LBSR instruction, to a signed displacement that is part of the BSR or LBSR instruction. The difference between them is that for BSR the displacement is 8 bits wide and for LBSR it is 16 bits wide. The JSR instruction obtains the branch address from the last part of the instruction or register(s) or memory location(s) using the MC6809's other addressing modes.

Subroutine returns can be made in one of two ways. One would be to use the RTS instruction, which simply pops the return address from the top of the stack into the PC. The other would be to use the PULS instruction to do the same thing, except PULS could also pop other register contents. One efficient means of entering and leaving a subroutne is as follows:

```
BEGIN     PSHS     CC,A,B,DP,X,Y,U
           .
           .    }   Body of subroutine
           .
          PULS     CC,A,B,DP,X,Y,U,PC
```

The PSHS instruction would not include PC since it would be pushed by the subroutine call.

A subroutine that adds two 16-digit BCD numbers is given in Fig. 7-22a. It is written in the MC6809's assembler language and is the counterpart of the 8085 program given in Fig. 7-16. It assumes that the parameter addresses are passed through the S stack and that the U register is set to point to the position of these addresses before the call is made. A typical calling sequence that adds (MM) to the (NN) is given in Fig. 7-22b. The LEAS instruction in this sequence adds 4 to the S register so that it is restored to its original value, i.e., its value before the parameter addresses were pushed onto the S stack.

7-6 MACROS

In Figs. 7-16 and 7-17 in Section 7-3, the amount of code needed for the subroutine linkage was approximately the same as that needed to perform the addition. Therefore, unless the linkage could be shortened, the only justification for using a sub-

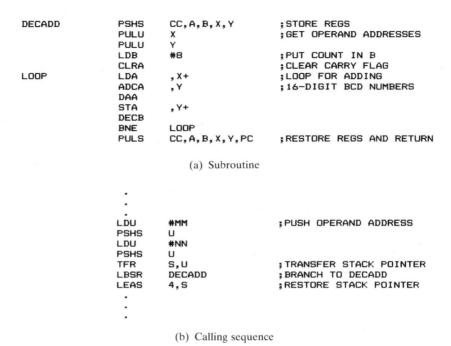

```
DECADD        PSHS    CC,A,B,X,Y        ;STORE REGS
              PULU    X                 ;GET OPERAND ADDRESSES
              PULU    Y
              LDB     #8                ;PUT COUNT IN B
              CLRA                      ;CLEAR CARRY FLAG
LOOP          LDA     ,X+               ;LOOP FOR ADDING
              ADCA    ,Y                ;16-DIGIT BCD NUMBERS
              DAA
              STA     ,Y+
              DECB
              BNE     LOOP
              PULS    CC,A,B,X,Y,PC     ;RESTORE REGS AND RETURN
```

(a) Subroutine

```
              .
              .
              .
              LDU     #MM               ;PUSH OPERAND ADDRESS
              PSHS    U
              LDU     #NN
              PSHS    U
              TFR     S,U               ;TRANSFER STACK POINTER
              LBSR    DECADD            ;BRANCH TO DECADD
              LEAS    4,S               ;RESTORE STACK POINTER
              .
              .
              .
```

(b) Calling sequence

Figure 7-22   DECADD subroutine written for the MC6809 and a typical calling sequence.

routine is for programming convenience. If there were a way of obtaining the programming convenience without using a subroutine, it would, in some cases, be more desirable. For this reason, some assemblers are designed so that a programmer need only write a set of code once and then refer to it as often as desired. Each time the code is referred to, the assembler will automatically insert the required code in the program at the point at which it is called out. A program segment used in this way is called a *macro*. Each macro is given a name, and the directive that references the macro must reference it by its name. Usually, the code in a macro is associated with its name simply by writing the code just after a specially coded line that includes the name. The association of a macro with its name is called a *macro definition*. The directives used to insert the macro at different points in the program are called *macro calls* and the insertions are called *macro expansions*.

Clearly, the ability to define, call, and expand macros is not a characteristic of a microprocessor; it is a capability of the assembler. An assembler that is capable of working with macros is called a *macro assembler*. Macro assemblers do not conserve memory or reduce the number of instructions; they simply help programmers by allowing them to write a set of repetitive code only once. Just as it is possible to store frequently used subroutines in libraries, one could store macros in libraries. Once a macro is stored in a library, a programmer need not define it in the program, but can have the assembler call it in from the library.

A macro definition includes

1. A header, which identifies the code that follows as being a macro definition
2. The prototype code to be used in expanding the macro
3. A terminating directive to mark the end of the definition

Typically, the header has the following format, which is that used by ASM-85:

```
Maco Name            MACRO            Dummy Arguments
```

where the name is the name used in a macro call (i.e., to signal an expansion of the macro) and the dummy arguments are the symbols in the definition that are to be replaced by symbols from the program when the macro is expanded. The dummy arguments are separated by commas. The terminating line is usually of the simple form

```
                        ENDM
```

The prototype code is normal code, but when the macro is called out in the program, the dummy arguments that appear in this code are replaced by corresponding symbols in the macro call. A typical macro call would have the form

```
    Label:       Macro Name         Arguments
```

where the label is optional, but if it appears, the assembler associates it with the first instruction of the expansion. The name is, of course, the name of the macro to be expanded, and the arguments are the symbols in the program that are to replace the dummy arguments. The first argument is substituted for the first dummy argument, and so on. The same macro may be called several times, and each time it is called the arguments may be different. (From this standpoint, a macro call is similar to a Fortran subroutine call.)

As an example, let us define a macro SUM that adds 1 byte in memory to another byte in memory and puts the result in a register. The macro definition is

```
        SUM      MACRO       P,Q,R
                 LXI         H,P
                 LDA         Q
                 ADD         M
                 MOV         R,A
                 ENDM
```

where P and Q represent dummy memory addresses and R is a dummy register address.   If this macro is called twice, as in

```
                    .
                    .
                    .
            SUM     X,Y,B
                    .
                    .
                    .
AD:         SUM     W1,W2,E
                    .
                    .
                    .
```

the macro expansions in the assembled program would be as follows:

```
                    .
                    .
                    .
            LXI     H,X
            LDA     Y
            ADD     M
            MOV     B,A
                    .
                    .
                    .
AD:         LXI     H,W1
            LDA     W2
            ADD     M
            MOV     E,A
                    .
                    .
                    .
```

Because macro capability is a function of the assembler, the rules for defining and using macros may vary considerably.   Some macro assemblers are quite sophisticated and include many features not indicated above.   Macros are mentioned here primarily to notify the reader of their existence and to describe the fundamentals of their use.

7-7 *AN EXAMPLE*

We shall close this chapter with a programming example that illustrates some of the programming techniques discussed previously.

The example given in Fig. 7-23 assumes that a line of characters has already been input and stored in an array LINE.   The program searches the input line for the first word and moves it into an array NAME.   This name is then used as the

```
;THIS PROGRAM EXTRACTS THE FIRST WORD FROM A LINE OF CHARACTERS
;AND STORES THAT WORD INTO ARRAY NAME.  THEN A TABLE IS SEARCHED FOR
;THE EXTRACTED WORD.  IF THE WORD IN NAME IS FOUND, THE INFORMATION
;ASSOCIATED WITH THAT WORD IS COPIED FROM TABLE INTO ARRAY INFO.
                .
                .
                .
TABLE:   DS       1600            ;TABLE TO BE SEARCHED
LINE:    DS       82              ;LINE OF CHARACTERS
NAME:    DS       8               ;ARRAY TO STORE THE EXTRACTED WORD
                                  ;FROM LINE
INFO:    DS       72              ;ARRAY TO STORE THE INFORMATION
                                  ;COPIED FROM TABLE
PARTAB:  DS       4               ;PARAMETER ADDRESS TABLE
                .
                .
                .
         LXI      H,LINE          ;SET UP PARAMETER ADDRESS TABLE TO
         SHLD     PARTAB          ;CALL SUBROUTINE EXTNAM WHICH
         LXI      H,NAME          ;COPIES THE FIRST WORD FROM LINE
         SHLD     PARTAB+2        ;TO NAME
         LXI      H,PARTAB        ;HL POINTS TO THE PARAMETER
                                  ;ADDRESS TABLE
         CALL     EXTNAM          ;CALL EXTNAM TO FIND THE FIRST WORD
         LXI      H,INFO          ;THE FOLLOWING LOOP (LOOP1)
         MVI      C,70            ;INITIALIZES ARRAY INFO WITH BLANKS
         MVI      A,' '           ;LOAD A BLANK CHARACTER INTO A
LOOP1:   MOV      M,A
         INX      H
         DCR      C
         JNZ      LOOP1
         LXI      H,TABLE         ;THE FOLLOWING NESTED LOOPS (LOOP2
                                  ;AND LOOP3) SEARCH TABLE FOR THE
                                  ;GIVEN NAME
                                  ;USE HL AS POINTER TO TABLE
         MVI      B,20            ;LOAD THE NUMBER OF ENTRIES INTO
                                  ;B AND USE IT AS COUNTER FOR THE
LOOP2:   PUSH     H               ;OUTER LOOP
         MVI      C,8             ;LOAD SIZE OF NAME INTO C AND USE
                                  ;IT AS COUNTER FOR THE INNER LOOP
         LXI      D,NAME          ;USE DE AS POINTER TO NAME
LOOP3:   LDAX     D               ;LOAD A CHARACTER FROM NAME
         CMP      M               ;AND COMPARE IT WITH ONE IN TABLE
         JNZ      OUT3
         INX      D
         INX      H
         DCR      C
         JNZ      LOOP3
         JMP      FOUND
OUT3:    POP      H               ;IF NAME IS NOT FOUND, ADJUST HL
         MVI      D,0             ;TO POINT TO THE NEXT ENTRY
         MVI      E,80            ;IN THE TABLE BY ADDING 80
         DAD      D
         DCR      B
         JNZ      LOOP2           ;IF NAME IS NOT FOUND AFTER THE
         JMP      DONE            ;ENTIRE TABLE HAS BEEN SEARCHED,
                                  ;GO TO DONE WITH INFO BEING
                                  ;FILLED WITH BLANKS
FOUND:   POP      H               ;IF NAME IS FOUND, THE FOLLOWING
         MVI      D,0             ;LOOP (LOOP4) MOVES 70 CHARACTERS
         MVI      E,10            ;FROM TABLE TO INFO
         DAD      D               ;ADD 10 INTO HL
         MVI      C,70
         LXI      D,INFO          ;DE POINTS TO INFO
```

Figure 7-23 An example of string manipulations.

```
LOOP4:      MOV      A,M
            STAX     D
            INX      H
            INX      D
            DCR      C
            JNZ      LOOP4
DONE:       .
            .
            .
;SUBROUTINE TO EXTRACT THE FIRST WORD FROM ARRAY LINE AND STORE
;IT INTO ARRAY NAME
EXTNAM:     PUSH     PSW              ;SAVE REGISTERS
            PUSH     B
            PUSH     D
            SHLD     PADSAV           ;SAVE ADDRESS OF PARAMETER TABLE
            INX      H
            INX      H
            MOV      E,M              ;LOAD ADDRESS OF NAME INTO DE
            INX      H
            MOV      D,M
            MVI      C,8
            MVI      A,' '
LOOP5:      STAX     D                ;INITIALIZE NAME WITH BLANKS
            INX      D
            DCR      C
            JNZ      LOOP5            ;THE FOLLOWING LOOP (LOOP6) SEARCH
                                      ;FOR THE FIRST NON-BLANK CHARACTER
            LHLD     PADSAV           ;LOAD ADDRESS OF PARAMETER TABLE
            MOV      E,M              ; INTO HL
            INX      H                ;LOAD ADDRESS OF LINE INTO DE
            MOV      D,M
            XCHG                      ;HL POINTS TO LINE
LOOP6:      CMP      M                ;SKIP OVER BLANKS UNTIL THE FIRST
            JNZ      OUT6             ;NON-BLANK CHARACTER IS FOUND
            INX      H
            JMP      LOOP6
OUT6:       XCHG                      ;DE HAS THE ADDRESS OF THE
            INX      H                ;FIRST NON-BLANK CHARACTER
            MOV      C,M              ;LOAD THE ADDRESS OF NAME INTO HL
            INX      H
            MOV      B,M
            MOV      H,B
            MOV      L,C              ;THE FOLLOWING LOOP (LOOP7) COPIES
            MVI      C,8              ;A WORD UP TO 8 CHARACTERS TO NAME
LOOP7:      LDAX     D                ;THE WORD IS TERMINATED
            CPI      ' '              ;WITH A BLANK
            JZ       OUT7
            MOV      M,A
            INX      D
            INX      H
            DCR      C
            JNZ      LOOP7
OUT7:       POP      D                ;RESTORE REGISTERS
            POP      B
            POP      PSW
            RET
PADSAV:     DW       1                ;SAVE AREA FOR ADDRESS OF
            .                         ;PARAMETER TABLE
            .
            .
```

Figure 7-23   Continued.

key to search a table and the information associated with this name is copied into an array INFO. Presumably, an output routine can be called to print out this information. Both arrays LINE and INFO have reserved two additional bytes so that a carriage return and line feed can be appended to the information bytes.

The code for extracting the name from the input line is implemented in a subroutine EXTNAM. This subroutine assumes that HL points to a parameter address table consisting of the addresses of LINE and NAME. The subroutine first initializes NAME with blank characters and, if the extracted name has less than eight characters, the name will be stored as left justified with trailing blanks. Then, beginning with the first nonblank character, a substring of LINE of up to eight characters is moved to NAME. The substring may be terminated by a blank or after the first eight characters have been moved.

After returning from subroutine EXTNAM, the main program searches the array TABLE, which contains 20 entries. It is assumed that each entry has 80 bytes. The first 8 bytes represent a name, and bytes 11 through 80 hold the information that is related to the name. The search continues until the first 8 bytes of an entry are matched by the string stored in NAME, or all 20 entries have been checked. If the name is found, its associated information is copied from TABLE to INFO; otherwise, INFO is filled with blanks.

BIBLIOGRAPHY

1. LIU, YU-CHENG, and GLENN A. GIBSON, *Microcomputer Systems: The 8086/8088 Family*, 2nd ed. (Englewood Cliffs, N.J.: Prentice-Hall, 1986).

2. *8080/8085 Assembler Language Programming* (Santa Clara, Calif.: Intel Corporation, 1979).

3. *The MCS-80/85 Family Users' Manual* (Santa Clara, Calif.: Intel Corporation, 1983).

4. UFFENBECK, JOHN, *Microcomputers and Microprocessors* (Englewood Cliffs, N.J.: Prentice-Hall, 1985).

5. WAGNER, T. J., and G. J. LIPOVSKI, *Fundamentals of Microcomputer Programming* (New York: Macmillan, 1984)

EXERCISES

1. Assume that A1, A2, A3, and A4 are defined in module A; B1, B2, B3, B4, and B5 are defined in module B; C1, C2, and C3 are defined in module C; and that

   Module A refers to B1, B2, B5, and C2

   Module B refers to A1, A3, A4, C1, and C2

   Module C refers to A3, B2, and B5

   Using Fig. 7-3 as a model, give the necessary EXTRN and PUBLIC statements for linking these modules together. Also indicate which labels can be local.

2. Consider a main program called M and three subroutines called A, B, and C. Suppose that the only stack usage is due to the CALL and RET instructions and the stack pointer initially points to 0100. The order in which the CALLs and RETs are made are M calls A, A calls B, B calls C, C returns to B, B returns to A, A calls C, C returns to A, and A returns to M. If the CALL in M is made from location 200, the respective CALLs in A are made from 300 and 350, and the CALL in B is made from 400, what will the contents of the stack and stack pointer be before and after each CALL and RET instruction?

3. Write an 8085 subroutine DIVIDE that will divide DEND by the contents of DVR, where DEND and DVR are global labels defined in the calling program. The operands are to be 8-bit unsigned quantities and the division is to be done by subtracting the divisor from the dividend until a negative result occurs. The quotient and remainder are to be put in the B and C registers, respectively. Also give a calling sequence. Assume that DIVIDE and the calling program are assembled separately and give the necessary EXTRN and PUBLIC statements.

4. Rewrite the subroutine in Exercise 3 using Z80 code.

5. Rewrite the code in Figs. 7-16 and 7-17 for the Z80.

6. Write an 8085 subroutine ABSOL that will take the absolute value of an 8-bit binary number.
   (a) Assume that the number is in the A register and its absolute value is to be put in the A register.
   (b) Assume that the number is pointed to by the HL pair and the absolute value is to be put in the A register.
   (c) Assume that the address of the number is pointed to by the HL pair and the absolute value is to be put in the address pointed to by (HL) plus 2.
   Also give corresponding calling sequences that use ABSOL to take the absolute value of (NUM). For part (c), first assume a parameter table is used and then assume the stack is used.

7. Rework Exercise 6 for an MC6809.

8. Write an 8085 subroutine SORT that will put the first N single-precision numbers in an array into ascending order. Use a parameter table to pass the addresses of the array and N and write a calling sequence that will sort the array beginning at ARRAY and sort the number of elements indicated by NUM.

9. Rewrite the solution to Exercise 8 assuming an MC6809 and that the stack is to be used for passing the parameter addresses.

10. Write a macro ABS that will take the absolute value indicated by the first argument and put the result in the second argument. Give a corresponding macro call that will put the absolute value of XX into ABSXX. Also give the expansion resulting from this call.

11. Define a macro ADDM that can perform memory to memory 16-bit addition.

12. Define a macro SHIFTR that can perform a multiple-bit right shift operation. The operand to be shifted can be in a register or memory location.

13. Assume that the array LINE stores a string of 72 characters. Write a program sequence to replace each "_" with a blank.

14. Assume that the array LINE stores a string of 72 characters. Write a program sequence to find the number of times A appears in the string and store that count into FREQA.

Chapter 8

Input/Output Programming

The transfer of data between the computer and its peripheral devices is called *input/output*. This is the only way to supply the microcomputer with data to be processed and to obtain the results of its calculations. Most microcomputer systems require different I/O routines, depending on the I/O instruction set, peripheral devices, bus structure, and speed requirements of the particular system. It is therefore important that users understand the various I/O programming techniques so that they can design I/O routines suitable for their specific applications. This chapter will cover the most commonly used I/O programming techniques, and each major topic will be accompanied by an example. Because different I/O programming methods are associated with different supporting hardware, some of the details in these examples may vary, depending on the bus structure and the interfaces provided in the particular system. The hardware aspects of the system bus and interfaces are discussed in Chapters 9 and 10. As in the preceding chapters, the examples are based on the Intel 8085 instruction set.

There are three basic techniques for the transfer of data between a microcomputer and its I/O devices:

1. Programmed I/O
2. Interrupt I/O
3. Direct memory access (DMA)

The first two cases, which are most likely to be found in simple applications, use a CPU register as a buffer to transfer 1 byte at a time. In the third case, data transfer bypasses the microprocessor and takes place directly between the memory and I/O devices.   Extra hardware, a DMA controller, is required to support this type of high-speed data transfer.

To support I/O programming, the microprocessor has a set of instructions, called *I/O instructions*, which are used for the following purposes:

1. To output a byte of data from the microprocessor to a peripheral device. For example, to send an ASCII character from the accumulator to a terminal.
2. To send a control command to a peripheral device.   For example, by sending a special command word to a terminal interface, it can be enabled to generate an interrupt whenever data are ready to be transferred to the microprocessor.
3. To input a byte of data from a peripheral device to the accumulator.   An example is the input of an ASCII character from a terminal.
4. To examine the status of a peripheral device so that the processor can make a data transfer decision.   For example, the status of a terminal can be checked to determine whether or not a data byte is ready to be transferred to the microprocessor.

The Intel 8085 has the following two I/O instructions:

1. IN port—An 8-bit data byte is read from the input device at the specified port (up to 256 input ports can be addressed) into the accumulator.
2. OUT port—The contents of the accumulator are sent to the output device at the specified port (up to 256 output ports can be addressed).

These instructions are defined in Fig. 8-1.   Some microprocessors such as the Motorola MC6809 do not have special I/O instructions.   Such microprocessors do not have separate I/O and memory spaces; part of the memory space is reserved for I/O addresses, and memory reference instructions are also used for I/O data transfer.   This scheme is referred to as *memory-mapped I/O*.

8-1 PROGRAMMED I/O

Among the three I/O programming techniques, *programmed I/O* is the most straightforward and requires the least amount of logic support; it is performed entirely under the processor's control.   Generally, an interface contains a number of registers that participate in I/O transfers.   Typically, a single I/O transfer will involve two registers: a status register and a buffer register.   A status register contains the current status of the I/O device and of the data being transferred. There may be two status registers, one for input and one for output.   An input or receiver buffer register receives the data from the device and temporarily holds them until the computer is ready to accept them, and an output or transmitter

IN port   (Input)

(A) ← (data)
The data placed on the eight bit bi-directional data
bus by the specified port is moved to register A.

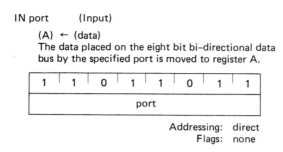

Addressing: direct
Flags: none

OUT port   (Output)

(data) ← (A)
The content of register A is placed on the eight bit
bi-directional data bus for transmission to the
specified port.

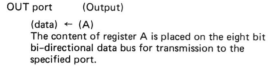

Addressing: direct
Flags: none

Figure 8-1   Definitions of the IN and
OUT instructions. (Reprinted by
permission of Intel Corporation,
Copyright 1983.)

buffer register receives the data from the processor and holds them until the I/O
device is ready to accept them.

For programmed I/O, before a data transfer is performed, the status of the
peripheral device is first brought into the processor from the status register by an
input instruction. The program then checks the status and decides on the next
action. If the device is ready for a data transfer, a byte of data is transferred from
or to the appropriate data buffer register by an input or output instruction. If the
device is not ready, the program performs a loop that checks the status repeatedly.
Once a data transfer has been completed, some bookkeeping work usually needs
to be done before the next data transfer. For example, the program must move
the data from the accumulator to memory, increment the data byte counter, adjust
the buffer pointer so that it points to the next memory location, and so on. Figure
8-2 is a flowchart of a typical programmed I/O routine.

Two examples of I/O routines using programmed I/O transfer are considered
below. In these examples, RVST, TRST, RVBUF, and TRBUF represent the
addresses of the receiver status register, transmitter status register, receiver buffer
register, and transmitter buffer register for the console terminal. Assume that
these addresses are 16, 17, 18, and 19, respectively, and that the EQU directive
is used to assign the symbols to the addresses. It is also assumed that bit 1 of
RVST is set when a character is available in the receiver buffer register, and bit 0
of TRST is set when the transmitter is ready for the next character to be loaded.

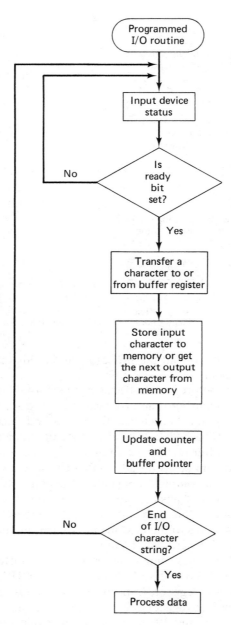

Figure 8-2 Flowchart of a typical programmed I/O routine.

The first example, shown in Fig. 8-3, inputs a string of characters from the console and terminates its operation when a carriage return (CRTN), which is 0D in hexadecimal, is detected as an input character.   If 80 characters have been read before a carriage return is encountered, an error message indicating an overflow is printed.   The two exits DONE and OVFL correspond to the CRTN detected and overflow conditions, respectively.

The next example is shown in Fig. 8-4 and is a typical output routine that allows a user to output a string of characters to the console from a buffer area. The operation terminates when a carriage return is detected in the text string.   If a carriage return does not occur in the first 80 characters in the buffer, an error routine is entered to print out a message.   Note that to print another character

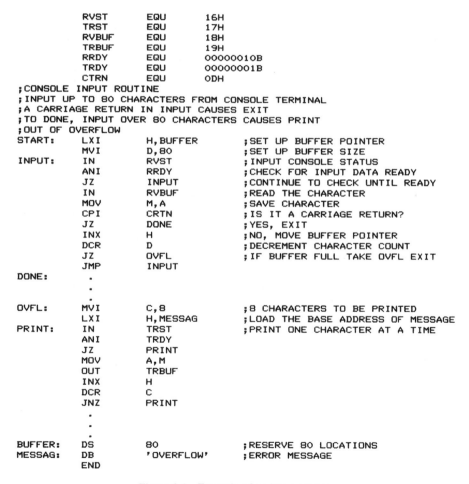

```
            RVST      EQU      16H
            TRST      EQU      17H
            RVBUF     EQU      18H
            TRBUF     EQU      19H
            RRDY      EQU      00000010B
            TRDY      EQU      00000001B
            CTRN      EQU      0DH
;CONSOLE INPUT ROUTINE
;INPUT UP TO 80 CHARACTERS FROM CONSOLE TERMINAL
;A CARRIAGE RETURN IN INPUT CAUSES EXIT
;TO DONE, INPUT OVER 80 CHARACTERS CAUSES PRINT
;OUT OF OVERFLOW
START:      LXI       H,BUFFER      ;SET UP BUFFER POINTER
            MVI       D,80          ;SET UP BUFFER SIZE
INPUT:      IN        RVST          ;INPUT CONSOLE STATUS
            ANI       RRDY          ;CHECK FOR INPUT DATA READY
            JZ        INPUT         ;CONTINUE TO CHECK UNTIL READY
            IN        RVBUF         ;READ THE CHARACTER
            MOV       M,A           ;SAVE CHARACTER
            CPI       CRTN          ;IS IT A CARRIAGE RETURN?
            JZ        DONE          ;YES, EXIT
            INX       H             ;NO, MOVE BUFFER POINTER
            DCR       D             ;DECREMENT CHARACTER COUNT
            JZ        OVFL          ;IF BUFFER FULL TAKE OVFL EXIT
            JMP       INPUT
DONE:       .
            .
            .
OVFL:       MVI       C,8           ;8 CHARACTERS TO BE PRINTED
            LXI       H,MESSAG      ;LOAD THE BASE ADDRESS OF MESSAGE
PRINT:      IN        TRST          ;PRINT ONE CHARACTER AT A TIME
            ANI       TRDY
            JZ        PRINT
            MOV       A,M
            OUT       TRBUF
            INX       H
            DCR       C
            JNZ       PRINT
            .
            .
            .
BUFFER:     DS        80            ;RESERVE 80 LOCATIONS
MESSAG:     DB        'OVERFLOW'    ;ERROR MESSAGE
            END
```

Figure 8-3   Example of an input routine.

```
                    TRST      EQU       17H
                    TRBUF     EQU       19H
                    TRDY      EQU       00000001B
                    CRTN      EQU       0DH
         START:     LXI       H,MSGBUF          ;GET BASE ADDRESS OF MESSAGE BUFFER
                    MVI       C,80              ;MAXIMUM NO. OF BYTES ALLOWED
         PRINT:     IN        TRST              ;INPUT CONSOLE STATUS
                    ANI       TRDY              ;TEST FOR TRANSMITTER READY
                    JZ        PRINT             ;CONTINUE TO CHECK STATUS UNTIL READY
                    MOV       A,M               ;LOAD CHARACTER
                    CPI       CRTN              ;IS IT A CARRIAGE RETURN?
                    JZ        EXIT              ;YES, EXIT
                    OUT       TRBUF             ;OUTPUT CHARACTER
                    DCR       C                 ;DECREMENT BYTE COUNT
                    JZ        ERROR
                    INX       H                 ;INCREMENT BUFFER POINTER
                    JMP       PRINT
         EXIT:      .
                    .
                    .
         ERROR:     .                           ;OUTPUT CARRIAGE RETURN LINE
                    .                           ;FEED AND ERROR MESSAGE
                    .
         MSGBUF:    .                           ;MSGBUF IS THE BASE ADDRESS OF
                    .                           ;THE STRING OF CHARACTERS
                    .                           ;TO BE OUTPUT TO THE CONSOLE
                    .
                    .
                    END
```

Figure 8-4 Example of an output routine.

string starting from the next line, a carriage return and a line feed (0A in hexadecimal) must be output first.   In addition, several null characters (00 in hexadecimal) may need to be inserted before printing the first element of the character string so that the carriage has enough time to move to the left margin.

8-2 INTERRUPT I/O

Simplicity is the major advantage of a programmed I/O transfer; it does not require complicated hardware to implement the interface.   However, in a programmed I/O routine, a microprocessor is idle while waiting to input or output a byte of data; it must mark time because the time when the next character is ready for input or output is unpredictable.   For example, if the input device is a terminal keyboard, most of the microprocessor time is wasted waiting for the operator to strike the next key.   Similarly, when outputting a character string to a terminal, most of the time is spent waiting for the character to be transmitted and displayed. As shown in Fig. 8-5, for a terminal with a speed of 10 characters per second, less than 0.1 percent of the CPU time is actually utilized.

It is clear that the execution time of such a routine using programmed I/O is primarily made up of the time spent in waiting for the device to accept or transmit information.   However, while the microprocessor is waiting, it could be doing something meaningful, such as processing the data already in the memory.   In other words, the microprocessor can be time-shared by two independent routines, a background routine for computation and a foreground routine for data transfer. This overlapping of computation and control of I/O devices can be accomplished via *interrupt* facilities.

Figure 8-6 illustrates the control transfer between two routines when interrupts are used. Most of the time, the microprocessor is executing the main routine. Whenever a byte of data is ready for transfer, the I/O device sends an interrupt request signal. If the request is recognized by the microprocessor, it waits until the current instruction is completed and then leaves the main routine temporarily to service the device. This action is called an *external interrupt* since it is initiated by an external device. The routine that is executed during an interrupt is referred to as an *interrupt service routine*. Once the microprocessor has completed the data transfer, it returns to the main routine where the interrupt occurred. Therefore, the microprocessor can utilize all the waiting time and still perform a data transfer when data are ready.

Because the interrupted routine is to be continued later, its status must be

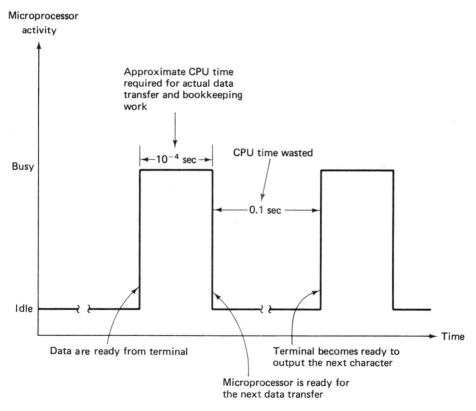

Figure 8-5 Microprocessor activity chart for programmed I/O transfer.

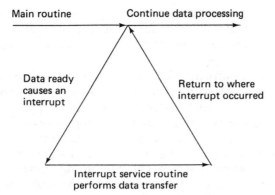

Figure 8-6 Typical interrupt sequence.

saved.   The most important information concerning the CPU status consists of the contents of the program counter (i.e., return address) and the condition flags in the PSW.   For the 8085, the instruction PUSH PSW is used to save the PSW.   In addition to the program status, the registers to be used by the service routine should also be stored before they are modified, and then restored before returning to the routine that was interrupted.   Return to the interrupted routine is accomplished by a "return from interrupt" instruction.   The 8085 uses the same RET instruction as is used by a subroutine to execute a return.

   Note that, unlike a subroutine that is initiated by a call instruction, an external interrupt may occur at random points in the interrupted program.   Therefore, the PSW and the registers that are used *must* be saved.   (This is not always required in a subroutine call.)   As an example, consider the following instruction sequence:

```
               LXI      H,ARY
               XRA      A
               STA      SUM
     LOOP:     LDA      SUM
               ADD      M
               STA      SUM
               INX      H
               LDA      COUNT
               DCR      A
               STA      COUNT
               JNZ      LOOP
                .
                .
                .
```

and assume that an interrupt occurs between

```
               LDA      COUNT
```

and

```
              JNZ         LOOP
```

If the PSW is not saved, after the return from the interrupt service routine, the JNZ instruction will test the Z flag, which is set according to the service routine, not according to the DCR instruction.

The 8085 provides five pins to input interrupt requests. These five interrupt request pins are denoted TRAP, RST 5.5, RST 6.5, RST 7.5, and INTR. Figure 8-7 shows how the 8085 responds to pending interrupt requests upon the completion of the current instruction. Associated with the latter four request pins are a set of bits, called *mask flags*. By selectively setting and/or clearing these flags, certain combinations of these requests can be caused to be ignored. Therefore, the RST and INTR interrupts are said to be *maskable*. A TRAP request will always be recognized and, therefore, it is *nonmaskable*. For the remaining four types, a request will be ignored if the CPU's interrupt enable flag (INTE) is not set to 1. Furthermore, RST 5.5, RST 6.5, and RST 7.5 can be individually masked by setting their corresponding mask bits. It is also seen from Fig. 8-7 that if simultaneous requests occur, TRAP has the highest priority, followed by RST 7.5, RST 6.5, and RST 5.5, and INTR has the lowest priority.

The interrupt enable flag can be set by the EI instruction and cleared by the DI instruction. Both instructions are defined in Fig. 8-8. The EI instruction enables the 8085 to recognize and respond to an INTR request and also to RST requests, provided that their masks are cleared. On the other hand, the DI instruction causes the 8085 to ignore all maskable interrupt requests, including the RST types.

The INTR interrupt will be discussed first. When the 8085 recognizes an INTR request from an external device, the following actions occur:

1. The instruction currently being executed is completed.
2. The INTE flag is reset to zero. This disables further maskable interrupts until an EI instruction is executed.
3. The processor returns an interrupt acknowledge signal, $\overline{\text{INTA}}$, and inputs an instruction from the interrupting device that receives the $\overline{\text{INTA}}$ signal.

The instruction mentioned in action 3 does not appear anywhere in memory and, because it is a function of the interrupting device's interface design, the programmer has no control over it. The program counter is not incremented while this instruction is executed. Since the return address must be saved during an interrupt, this instruction supplied by the interrupting device can only be a 1-byte restart (RST) instruction, or in a more sophisticated system, a CALL instruction.

The RST instruction is also defined in Fig. 8-8. The restart instruction has the form RST N, where N represents an integer in the range from 0 to 7. It will

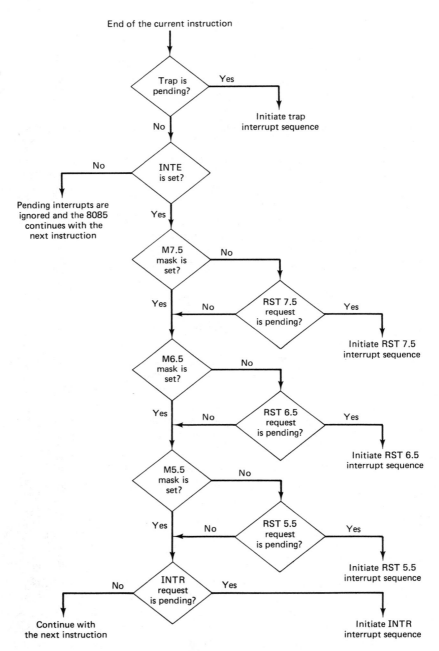

Figure 8-7   Processing of pending interrupt requests.

EI   (Enable interrupts)
The interrupt system is enabled **following the execution of the next instruction. Interrupts are not recognized during the EI instruction.**

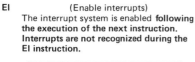

Flags: none

NOTE: Placing an EI instruction on the bus in response to $\overline{\text{INTA}}$ during an INA cycle is prohibited. (8085)

DI   (Disable interrupts)
The interrupt system is disabled **immediately following the execution of the DI instruction. Interrupts are not recognized during the DI instruction.**

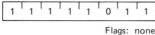

Flags: none

NOTE: Placing a DI instruction on the bus in response to $\overline{\text{INTA}}$ during an INA cycle is prohibited. (8085)

RST n   (Restart)
$((SP) - 1) \leftarrow (PCH)$
$((SP) - 2) \leftarrow (PCL)$
$(SP) \leftarrow (SP) - 2$
$(PC) \leftarrow 8 * (NNN)$
The high-order eight bits of the next instruction address are moved to the memory location whose address is one less than the content of register SP. The low-order eight bits of the next instruction address are moved to the memory location whose address is two less than the content of register SP. The content of register SP is decremented by two. Control is transferred to the instruction whose address is eight times the content of NNN.

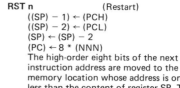

Addressing: reg. indirect
Flags: none

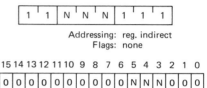

Program Counter After Restart

Figure 8-8 Definitions of the EI, DI, and RST instructions. (Reprinted by permission of Intel Corporation, Copyright 1983.)

push the contents of the program counter onto the stack and transfer control to the instruction whose address is eight times N. Then the service routine for the interrupting device will be started via a sequence of instructions occupying memory locations 8 * N to 8 * N + 7. The number 8 * N specifies an address to which the program jumps to find the appropriate service routine and is referred to as an *interrupt vector*. The 8085 uses 3 bits for interrupt vectors; this provides eight different addresses for the service routines. In order to execute a service routine with more than 8 bytes, an unconditional branch instruction is normally stored in the location pointed to by the interrupt vector. This instruction initiates an interrupt service routine located elsewhere in the memory. Figure 8-9 illustrates the use of the RST instruction. Note that because a reset will force the 8085 to branch to location 0, RST 0 should not be used by any interrupting devices.

The RST 5.5, RST 6.5, and RST 7.5 interrupts are similar to the INTR type in that they cause the CPU to clear the INTE flag and then execute a restart instruction. However, this instruction is generated internally, instead of being fetched from the interrupting device. The starting addresses corresponding to the RST 5.5, RST 6.5, and RST 7.5 interrupts are 002C, 0034, and 003C, respectively. The RST interrupts are also subject to being enabled by the EI instruction and being disabled by the DI instruction. In addition, each of the three RST interrupts can be individually masked by setting its mask flag to 1. The instructions to

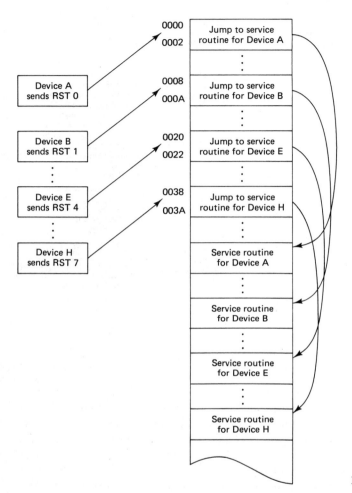

Figure 8-9 Use of the RST instruction.

examine and modify the RST mask flags are the RIM (read interrupt mask) and SIM (set interrupt mask), respectively, which are defined in Fig. 8-10.

The RIM instruction loads the current settings of the RST 5.5, RST 6.5, and RST 7.5 masks into the accumulator. Also loaded into the accumulator are the state of the interrupt enable flag, pending requests from the RST 5.5, RST 6.5 and RST 7.5 pins, and the input from the serial-in line. This instruction allows the user to determine which maskable interrupts are disabled and which RST interrupt requests have been received but not yet serviced. Figure 8-11 shows the contents of the accumulator after RIM instruction has been executed.

The SIM instruction selectively sets the masks for the RST interrupt requests according to the contents of the accumulator. Before the SIM instruction is executed, a control byte that specifies which mask bits are to be set must be stored into the accumulator. Figure 8-12 shows the format of the control byte. To change

RIM (Read Interrupt Masks) (8085 only)

The RIM instruction loads data into the accumulator relating to interrupts and the serial input. This data contains the following information.

· Current interrupt mask status for the RST 5.5, 6.5, and 7.5 hardware interrupts (1 = mask disabled)

· Current interrupt enable flag status (1 = interrupts enabled) except immediately following a TRAP interrupt. (See below)

· Hardware interrupts pending (i.e., signal received but not yet serviced), on the RST 5.5, 6.5, and 7.5 lines.

· Serial input data.

Immediately following a TRAP interrupt, the RIM instruction must be executed as a part of the service routine if you need to retrieve current interrupt status later. Bit 3 of the accumulator is (in this special case only) loaded with the interrupt enable (IE) flag status that existed prior to the TRAP interrupt. Following an RST 5.5, 6.5, 7.5, or INTR interrupt, the interrupt flag flip-flop reflects the current interrupt enable status. Bit 6 of the accumulator (I7.5) is loaded with the status of the RST 7.5 flip-flop, which is always set (edge-triggered) by an input on the RST 7.5 input line, even when that interrupt has been previously masked. (See SIM instruction).

Opcode:

7							0
0	0	1	0	0	0	0	0

Flags: none

SIM (Set Interrupt Masks) (8085 only)

The execution of the SIM instruction uses the contents of the accumulator (which must be previously loaded) to perform the following functions:

· Program the interrupt mask for the RST 5.5, 6.5, and 7.5 hardware interrupts.

· Reset the edge-triggered RST 7.5 input latch.

· Load the SOD output latch.

To program the interrupt masks, first set accumulator bit 3 to 1 and set to 1 any bits 0, 1, and 2, which disable interrupts RST 5.5, 6.5, and 7.5, respectively. Then do a SIM instruction. If accumulator bit 3 is 0 when the SIM instruction is executed, the interrupt mask register will not change. If accumulator bit 4 is 1 when the SIM instruction is executed, the RST 7.5 latch is then reset. RST 7.5 is distinguished by the fact that its latch is always set by a rising edge on the RST 7.5 input pin, even if the jump to service routine in inhibited by masking. This latch remains high until cleared by a RESET IN, by a SIM Instruction with accumulator bit 4 high, or by an internal processor acknowledge to an RST 7.5 interrupt subsequent to the removal of the mask (by a SIM instruction). The RESET IN signal always sets all three RST mask bits.

If accumulator bit 6 is at the 1 level when the SIM instruction is executed, the state of accumulator bit 7 is loaded into the SOD latch and thus becomes available for interface to an external device. The SOD latch is unaffected by the SIM instruction if bit 6 is 0. SOD is always reset by the RESET IN signal.

Opcode:

7							0
0	0	1	1	0	0	0	0

Flags: none

Figure 8-10 The RIM and SIM instructions. (Reprinted by permission of Intel Corporation, Copyright 1983.)

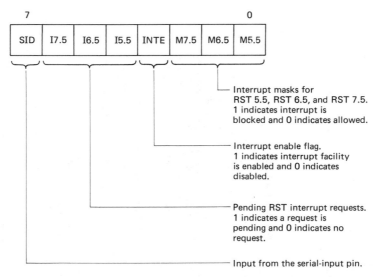

Figure 8-11 Accumulator contents after the RIM instruction.

the RST 5.5, RST 6.5, and RST 7.5 mask bits, bit 3 must be 1. As seen in the figure, the SIM instruction can also be used to clear the RST 7.5 request flag or to specify the output for the serial output line provided that bit 6 is 1. As an example, to disable RST 5.5 and RST 7.5 requests and to enable RST 6.5 requests can be accomplished by the following three instructions:

```
MVI     A,0DH
SIM
EI
```

The third type of interrupt provided by the 8085 is TRAP, which is non-maskable and has the highest priority among external interrupts. Normally, this interrupt is reserved for events that must be responded to immediately, such as power failure. When a trap is recognized, the CPU saves the return address, clears the INTE flag and then branches to 24H.

Figure 8-13 flowcharts the major steps involved in a typical I/O interrupt routine, and Fig. 8-14 shows the corresponding code. In the example, the device is assumed to send the instruction RST 1 to the 8085 during an INTR interrupt; this causes the instruction stored at location 8 to be executed. The instruction at location 8 is a branch to the beginning of a service routine. After the program status and the registers have been stored on the stack, a byte of data is transferred from the interrupting device to the memory via the accumulator. Before its return to the interrupted routine, the registers and program status are restored. The original contents of BUFPT and COUNTR are set by the main program before the input is initiated. BUFPT, which is referred to as the *buffer pointer,* is used to hold the address where the next byte of data is to be stored, and COUNTR is a counter that indicates the number of characters that remain to be input. After a character has been input, the buffer pointer and counter are updated by the service routine. If the last character has been transferred, the service routine sets a software flag that stores a 1 in the location represented by FLAG. By examining FLAG, the main program can determine the status of the I/O transfer. The parameters BUFPT, COUNTR, and FLAG may reside in the main program, the service routine, or a common area, but their addresses must be known to both.

It is important to note that the parameter linkage cannot be accomplished as it is with subroutines. The reason is that the time at which the service routine is entered is controlled by external events. Therefore, it is not possible for the main program to set up the parameter linkage at the appropriate time. The easiest solution is to assemble both the main routine and the service routine as a single programming module so that symbolic addresses are accessible to both routines. If the service routine is assembled as a separate module, BUFPT, COUNTR, and FLAG must be declared global symbols. The linker replaces these symbols by their actual locations and the external references to these symbols are resolved. A third possibility is to put the parameters in the service routine and have the service routine occupy a fixed area in memory. Then the main routine would refer to the parameters using absolute addresses. Finally, either a relocatable or absolute common area could be maintained to pass I/O data and information.

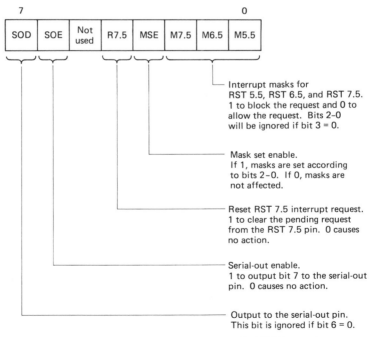

Figure 8-12 Accumulator contents before the SIM instruction.

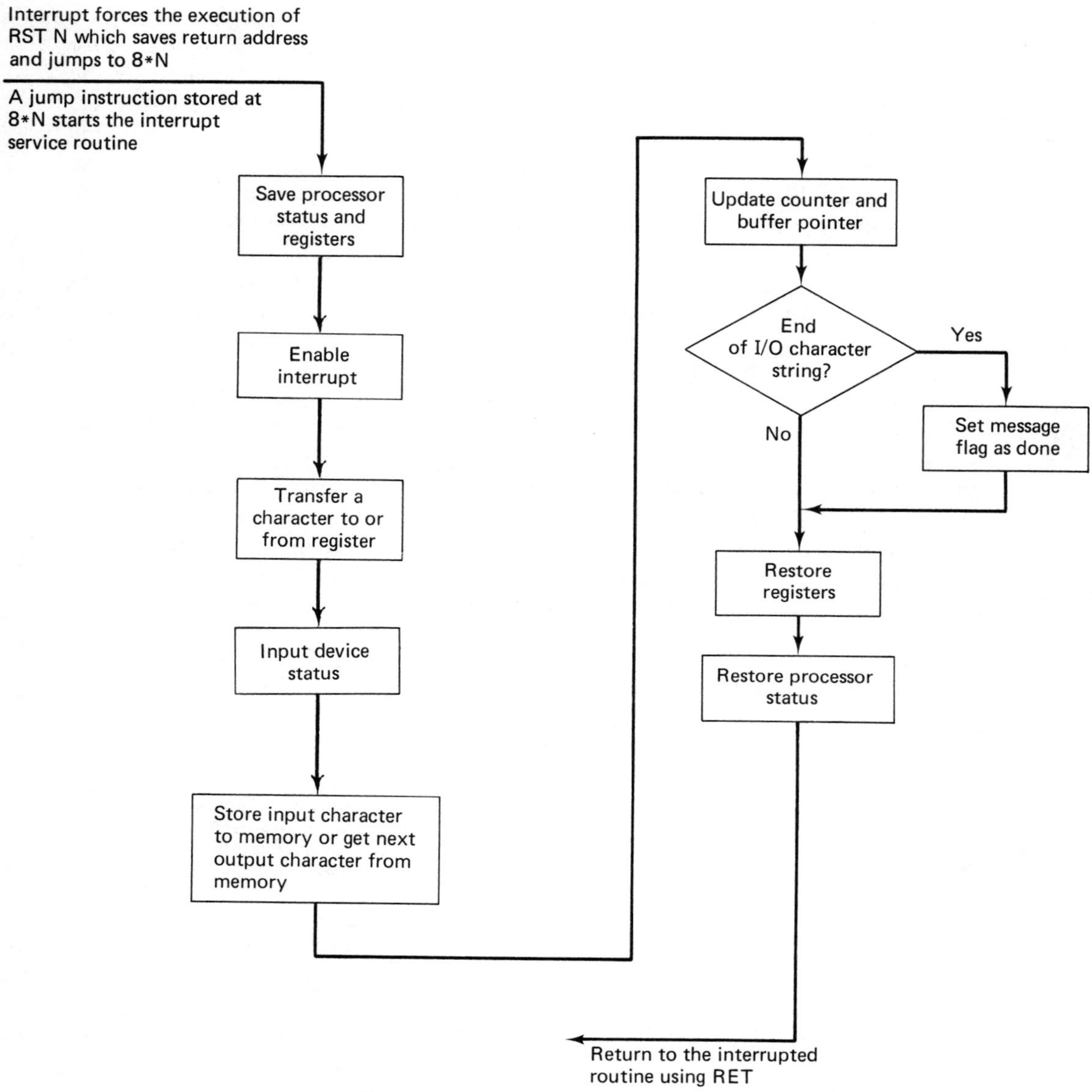

Interrupt forces the execution of
RST N which saves return address
and jumps to 8*N

A jump instruction stored at
8*N starts the interrupt
service routine

Figure 8-13   Flowchart of an interrupt-driven I/O routine.

```
            ORG      8                   ;STARTING ADDRESS FOR INTERRUPT
            JMP      INT1                ;JUMP TO INTERRUPT SERVICE ROUTINE
             .
             .
             .
INT1:       PUSH     PSW                 ;SAVE PROGRAM STATUS
            PUSH     B                   ;SAVE REGISTERS
            PUSH     D
            PUSH     H
            EI                           ;SERVICE ROUTINE CAN BE INTERRUPTED
            IN       PORT                ;INPUT DATA FROM INTERRUPTING DEVICE
            LHLD     BUFPT               ;LOAD BUFFER POINTER
            MOV      M,A                 ;STORE DATA INTO BUFFER AREA
            INX      H                   ;UPDATE BUFFER POINTER
            SHLD     BUFPT               ;SAVE BUFFER POINTER
            LDA      COUNTR              ;LOAD BYTE COUNT
            DCR      A                   ;DECREMENT BYTE COUNT
            JZ       FULL                ;BUFFER IS FULL
            STA      COUNTR
            JMP      RETURN
FULL:       MVI      A,1
            STA      FLAG                ;SET BUFFER FULL FLAG
RETURN:     POP      H                   ;RESTORE REGISTERS
            POP      D
            POP      B
            POP      PSW                 ;RESTORE PROGRAM STATUS
            RET
```

Figure 8-14   Typical interrupt routine.

8-3 POLLING

For an 8085-based system, sometimes it might be necessary for several devices to share one interrupt vector. (Usually, they are low-speed devices.) This is because the 8085 is limited to 12 interrupt vectors, 8 for INTR requests, 3 for RST requests, and 1 for the TRAP request. In such a system, an interrupt generated by any device that shares a common interrupt vector will cause a branch to the same service routine. Therefore, which device has generated the interrupt must be determined before it can be serviced; this process is called *polling*. Depending on the hardware, polling is done either by checking a special interrupt request register to see which bit has been set to 1 or by checking the interrupt bit in each device's status register.

An *interrupt request register* is a register that is accessible as an I/O port. Interrupt request lines from several devices may be connected to it and, if a device requests an interrupt, the logic associated with the interrupt request register sets the device's corresponding bit in the register to 1. Once the interrupt is acknowledged, the processor reads the interrupt request register into the accumulator. The position of the nonzero bit can be determined by rotating the contents of the accumulator to the right through the carry bit and then checking the carry bit.

A flowchart of this process is shown in Fig. 8-15, and Fig. 8-16 gives a typical polling routine. In order to enter the service routine corresponding to the interrupting device, a branch table is included in the polling routine. Each word in

Interrupt causes a branch to
the polling routine

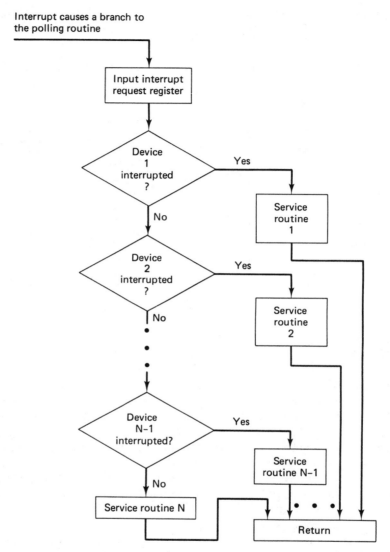

Figure 8-15 Flowchart for polling procedure using an interrupt request register.

the branch table contains the beginning address of a service routine, and the HL register pair is initialized to point to the first word of the table. In determining which device has generated the interrupt, if the carry is not set, the contents of HL are incremented by 2 so that it will point to the next word in the branch table. Once the interrupting device is identified, the entry point of the corresponding service routine is loaded into the DE pair using the pointer in the HL pair. The two instructions XCHG and PCHL are needed to transfer the beginning address from the DE pair into the PC. This causes a jump to the service routine for that device. Through this procedure, the service routine for device N may be made to be completely different from the service routine for device M, even though the two devices are associated with the same interrupt vector.

The polling routine concludes by restoring the working registers from the stack and enabling the interrupts. Immediately after the EI instruction, an RET instruction will return control to the original program. If another interrupt has occurred on one of the other request lines, it will cause an immediate interrupt and a return to the polling routine. Thus each of the interrupts will eventually be serviced even if they occur while the system is executing the polling routine. The

```
START:    PUSH     PSW
          PUSH     B
          PUSH     D
          PUSH     H
          IN       PORT        ;INPUT STATUS FROM
                               ;INTERRUPT REQUEST REGISTER
          LXI      H,TABLE     ;REGISTERS H AND L POINT
                               ;TO BRANCH TABLE
POLL:     RRC                  ;SHIFT 1ST BIT INTO CARRY
          JC       ADDR
          INX      H           ;POINT TO NEXT ADDRESS
          INX      H           ; IN BRANCH TABLE
          JMP      POLL
ADDR:     MOV      E,M         ;DEVICE CAUSING INTERRUPT IS FOUND
          INX      H           ;GET THE ADDRESS OF SERVICE
                               ;ROUTINE FOR THIS DEVICE
          MOV      D,M
          XCHG
          PCHL                 ;JUMP TO SERVICE ROUTINE
SER1:     IN       DEV1        ;INPUT DATA FROM DEVICE 1
          LHLD     BUFPT1      ;GET BUFFER POINTER FOR DEVICE 1
          MOV      M,A         ;STORE DATA IN MEMORY
          INX      H           ;UPDATE BUFFER POINTER
          SHLD     BUFPT1      ;SAVE BUFFER POINTER
          JMP      FINISH
SER2:     .
          .
          .
SER8:     IN       DEV8
          LHLD     BUFPT8
          MOV      M,A
          INX      H
          SHLD     BUFPT8
FINISH:   POP      H
          POP      D
          POP      B
          POP      PSW
          EI
          RET
TABLE:    DW       SER1        ;BRANCH TABLE, EACH
          DW       SER2        ;ENTRY IS A TWO-BYTE
          DW       SER3        ;ADDRESS OF A SERVICE
          DW       SER4        ;ROUTINE FOR A DEVICE
          DW       SER5
          DW       SER6
          DW       SER7
          DW       SER8
```

Figure 8-16 Typical polling routine using an interrupt request register.

```
START:      PUSH    PSW
            PUSH    B
            PUSH    D
            PUSH    H
POLL1:      IN      STATS1          ;POLL DEVICE 1
            ANI     INTR            ;CHECK INTERRUPT REQUEST BIT
            JNZ     SER1            ;YES, SERVICE DEVICE 1
POLL2:      IN      STATS2          ;POLL DEVICE 2
            ANI     INTR
            JNZ     SER2
POLL3:      .
            .
            .
POLLN:      IN      STATSN          ;POLL DEVICE N
            ANI     INTR            ;CHECK INTERRUPT REQUEST BIT
            JNZ     SERN            ;YES, SERVICE DEVICE N
POLLQ:      IN      STATSQ          ;POLL DEVICE Q
            .
            .
            .
SER1:       IN      DEV1            ;INPUT DATA FROM DEVICE 1
            .
            .
            .
            JMP     FINISH
SER2:       .
            .
            .
SERN:       IN      DEVN            ;INPUT DATA FROM DEVICE N
            .
            .
            .
            JMP     FINISH
            .
            .
            .
FINISH:     POP     H
            POP     D
            POP     B
            POP     PSW
            EI
            RET
```

Figure 8-17 Typical polling routine that examines each status register.

example assumes that no more than 1 bit in the interrupt request register is set. With the addition of necessary instructions to clear the request bit and to check the remaining bits in the interrupt request register before returning to the main routine, this polling routine could be made to handle simultaneous requests.

Examining the status register for each device becomes necessary if an interrupt request register is not available or there are more than eight devices using the same interrupt vector.   Figure 8-17 illustrates this polling procedure.

8-4 PRIORITY INTERRUPT SYSTEMS

The basic interrupt system described in Section 8-2 assumed that each of the eight devices connected to the INTR pin was of equal importance.   Sometimes this is not true.   For example, a system may include high-speed devices that retain information for only a short time and therefore require immediate attention.   If this is the case, it is desirable to establish a priority by allowing the service routine for one device to be interrupted by an interrupt request from a higher-priority device. A lower-priority device would be serviced by a routine that would reenable the interrupt system at its beginning.   The service routine for a high-priority device in such a system is similar to the polling routine example in that the interrupt facility is not enabled until processing has been completed.   In addition, if there are more than one interrupt request pending, the one with the highest priority will be recognized and serviced before the others.

The solution is to add priority management logic that includes a mask register that is treated as an I/O port to the system.   The priority management logic determines which interrupting device has the highest priority and compares it with the mask to decide if an interrupt request and the interrupt vector corresponding to the request with the highest priority are to be sent to the microprocessor.   Its logic implementation is discussed in Section 9.6.   The mask, which can be modified under program control, will allow or disallow an interrupt from a device, depending on its relative importance.   All requests with a priority equal to or less than this mask will be blocked from generating an interrupt to the CPU.   To allow interrupts with a higher priority within an interrupt, a service routine such as the one shown in Fig. 8-14 should be modified as follows:

```
    INT1:       .                   ;PUSH PSW AND WORKING REGISTERS
                .
                .
                .

                IN      MASKPT      ;SAVE THE PREVIOUS PRIORITY MASK
                STA     MASKSV
                MVI     A,MASK      ;SET NEW PRIORITY MASK TO IGNORE
                OUT     MASKPT      ;REQUEST WITH A LOWER PRIORITY
                EI                  ;ALLOW INTERRUPT WITH A HIGHER
                .                   ;PRIORITY
                .                   ;INPUT DATA, STORE IT IN
                .                   ;BUFFER AREA AND ADJUST BUFFER
                .                   ;POINTER
                .
    RETURN:     LDA     MASKSV      ;RESTORE THE PREVIOUS PRIORITY
                OUT     MASKPT      ;MASK
                .                   ;RESTORE WORKING REGISTERS
                .                   ;AND PSW
                .
                .
                RET
    MASKSV:     DS      1
```

The EI instruction and priority mask will allow interrupts from devices with a higher priority and block unwanted interrupts with a lower priority.   The priority mask is different in each of the service routines, and it can be modified simply by replacing the contents of the mask register whose I/O port address is MASKPT. The IN and STA instructions save the old interrupt mask in memory location MASKSV. The MVI and OUT instructions then move the mask associated with the current routine to MASKPT. These four instructions change the priority level determined by the contents of MASKPT. After the service is completed, the LDA and OUT instructions restore MASKPT to its old value.

The priority interrupt management logic may also be used to allow several devices to share a common interrupt vector and eliminate the need for individual polling. While the polling scheme requires minimal hardware, it is very slow because, in order to determine which device caused the interrupt, many instructions must be executed before servicing an interrupt. A priority interrupt system has a register to indicate which interrupting device has the highest priority. By examining this register, the microprocessor can immediately branch to the corresponding service routine through a branch table and polling can be eliminated.

8-5 DIRECT MEMORY ACCESS

If the data transfer rate to or from an I/O device is relatively low, the data transfer can be performed using either programmed or interrupt I/O. But some devices, such as disk units and analog to digital (A/D) converters, may operate at data rates that are too high to be handled by programmed or interrupt I/O. For example, a disk unit may require data to be transferred at a rate exceeding 200,000 bytes per second. This means that no more than 5 μS are available to transfer each byte to or from memory. Such a transfer rate cannot be achieved by programmed or interrupt I/O. This is because for each byte transfer, several instructions would be required to transfer the byte between the accumulator and the device, between the accumulator and memory, and update the buffer pointer and byte counter.

By transferring data directly between the memory and the device, the data transfer rate can be substantially increased. Because the microprocessor is bypassed, this I/O scheme is called *direct memory access (DMA)*. Once a DMA operation is initiated by the microprocessor, a DMA module controls the actual transfer of a block of data between memory and the external device without further intervention of the microprocessor being required. Physically, the DMA controller is a separate module that is connected to the system bus and may be a part of an I/O interface. The DMA facility can steal a memory cycle from the running program and transfer a byte of data directly from or to the memory. After the entire block of data has been transferred, an interrupt is sent to the CPU either by the DMA module or the interface. For any given bus cycle, the device that initiates the read and write commands is called the *master* and the device responding to these commands is called the *slave*. Only the CPU and DMA controllers can be masters.

Because a DMA controller is capable of performing the actual data transfer, a typical DMA controller must contain the following registers:

CONTROL REGISTER—The control register stores the command issued by the CPU. These commands include enabling the DMA, specifying the type of transfer (read or write), and specifying the interrupt condition (enable or disable).

STATUS REGISTER—The status of the DMA controller can be examined by the CPU to determine whether or not the controller is busy, the transfer operation is completed, or certain errors have occurred. Sometimes both the control and status registers are combined into a single register.

BYTE COUNTER—This register is loaded with the number of bytes to be transferred prior to the DMA operation. The contents of this register are decremented by one after each transfer. The transfer process stops when the counter becomes zero.

BUFFER POINTER REGISTER—This register contains the current address of the memory location to be accessed and is incremented by one after each byte transfer. It is loaded with the beginning address of the block before the block transfer is initiated.

In order for a DMA controller to gain the control of the bus, the 8085 has hold request (HOLD) and hold acknowledge (HLDA) pins. Whenever the CPU receives a request from the HOLD pin, it will enter the hold state after the current bus cycle is completed. During the hold state, the 8085 returns a 1 on the HLDA pin. This informs the DMA controller that it may use the bus for data transfer. After a data transfer, the DMA controller drops the hold request and the CPU regains control of the bus and resumes its normal operation. Figure 8-18 illustrates the actions that will occur during each single output DMA transfer. It should be emphasized that these actions are performed automatically by hardware.

To initiate a block transfer using DMA, the CPU needs to

1. Output the number of bytes to be transferred to the controller's byte count register.
2. Output the starting address of the buffer area to the buffer pointer.
3. Output a command to specify the transfer direction (input or output) and to start the DMA transfer.

The design of a DMA controller is rather complex. Fortunately, LSI DMA controllers are available that can greatly simplify the implementation of block transfers. In order to illustrate how to program a DMA controller, let us consider the Intel 8237 programmable DMA controller. This controller has four channels, so that up to four devices can be serviced by a single 8237. A block diagram of the 8237 is given in Fig. 8-19. Each channel contains a mode register, current

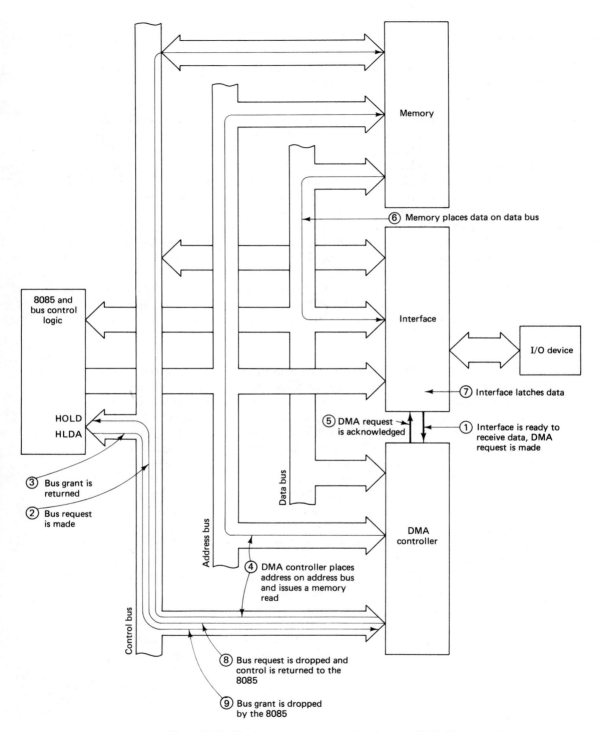

Figure 8-18 Single datum output transfer during a DMA block transfer.

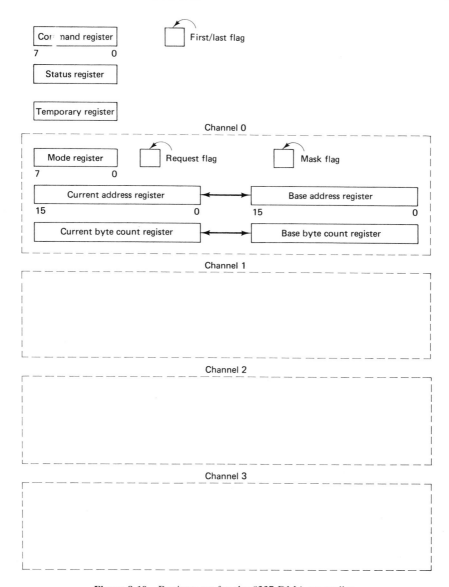

Figure 8-19   Register set for the 8237 DMA controller.

address register, base address register, current byte count register, base byte count register, request flag, and mask flag. A block transfer is completed when the current byte count changes from 0 to -1. Therefore, the actual number of bytes to be transferred will be one more than the number programmed in the current byte count register. The base address register and the base byte count register are primarily used for the autoinitialization mode. Whenever a current register is written into, the same value is also stored into its corresponding base register. Under this mode, the current address and byte count registers are restored back to their original values from the two base registers whenever the previous block transfer is completed.

The transfer mode for each channel is specified by its mode register. When a mode register is being written, the least significant 2 bits specify which channel mode register is to be written into. Figure 8-20 gives the format of the mode register. Bits 7 and 6 determine how to control the bus during the block transfer. The four possible modes are

SINGLE TRANSFER MODE (01)—After each transfer the controller will release the bus to the processor for at least one bus cycle.

BLOCK TRANSFER MODE (10)—The DMA request from the device (DREQ) needs only be active until the DMA acknowledge (DACK) of the channel becomes

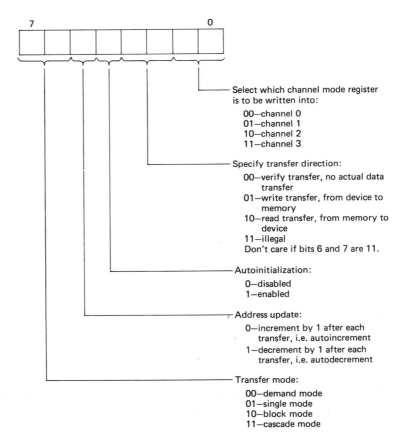

Figure 8-20   Format of the mode register.

active, after which the bus is not released until the entire block of data has been transferred.

DEMAND TRANSFER MODE (00)—This mode is similar to the block mode except that the DMA request is tested after each transfer. If it is inactive, transfers are suspended until it once again becomes active, at which time the block transfer continues from the point at which it was suspended. This allows the interface to stop the transfer in the event that its device cannot keep up.

CASCADE MODE (11)—In this mode, 8237s may be cascaded so that more than four channels can be included in the system.

The 8237 also has a temporary register, command register, and status register, all 8 bits wide. The temporary register is used only for memory-to-memory block transfers. In addition to block transfers between I/O or mass storage devices and memory, the 8237 can supervise memory-to-memory transfers. Such transfers are conducted by bringing bytes from the source memory area into the temporary register in the 8237 and then outputting them to the destination memory area. Therefore, two bus cycles are required for each memory-to-memory transfer. The channel 0 current address register is used for source addressing. The channel 1 current address and current byte count registers provide the destination addressing and counting. The destination address must increment or decrement as usual, but by setting the proper bit in the control register the source address may be held constant. This allows the same data byte to be transferred into the entire destination array.

The format of the command register is given in Fig. 8-21. A memory-to-memory transfer is enabled by setting bit 0 to 1, in which case bit 1 = 1 indicates that the source address is to be held constant. Bit 2 is used for enabling (0) or disabling (1) the controller and bit 3 specifies the type of timing. If the speed characteristics of the system permit, then bit 3 can be set to 1 to indicate compressed timing. With compressed timing only two clock cycles are needed to perform most transfers. Bit 4 determines whether the priority is fixed or rotating. Normally, channel 0 has the highest priority and channel 3 the lowest; however, if bit 4 is 1, the priority will rotate after each transfer, e.g., if the priority before a transfer is 2–3–0–1, then after the transfer it will be 3–0–1–2. By rotating the priority the controller can prevent one channel from dominating the bus. The 8237 permits the program to specify the length of the I/O write and memory write signals when normal timing is being used. A 1 in bit 5 indicates that these signals are to be extended over two clock cycles. The program can also specify whether the DREQ and DACK pins are to be active high or active low by setting or clearing bits 6 (DREQ) and 7 (DACK), respectively. Bit 6 = 1 indicates that DREQ is active low and bit 7 = 1 indicates that DACK is active high. How these bits should be set depends on the characteristics of the associated interfaces.

The format of the status register is such that the lower 4 bits indicate the states of the terminal counts of the four channels and the upper 4 bits show the current presence or absence of DMA requests. For the lower 4 bits a 1 in bit n

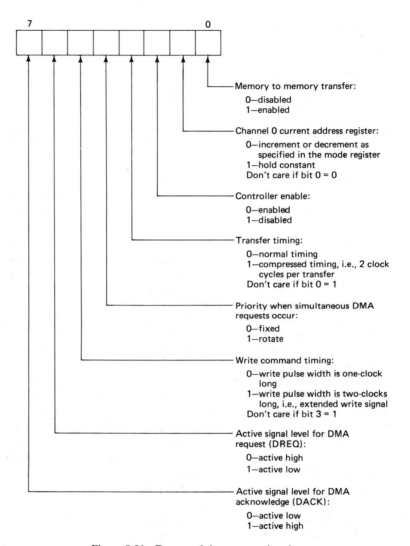

Figure 8-21 Format of the command register.

indicates that the terminal count for channel n has been reached or an external signal (EOP) to terminate the transfer has been received. For the upper four bits a 1 in bit $n + 4$ signals the presence of a request on channel n.

Each channel also has associated with it a request flag and a mask flag. A DMA request can be programmed as well as input through the DREQ pin. Setting the request flag for a channel has the same effect as the DREQ pin becoming active. When set to 1, the mask flag disables the channel so that DMA requests (either hardware or software) are not recognized. The request and mask flags are programmed using commands in which bit 2 determines the setting of the flag and bits 1 and 0 give the channel number of the flag.   The remaining bits are unused. There is also a command for adjusting all four of the mask flags at once.   For this command, bit n being set or cleared causes the mask bit for channel n to be set or cleared.

Besides the commands for setting the flags, there are a master clear command and a clear first/last flip-flop command.   A master clear command has the same effect as a RESET signal.   The first/last flip-flop is for loading the 16-bit address and count registers.   Because an 8237 can be sent only 1 byte at a time, these registers must be loaded using two outputs.   Assuming that the first/last flip-flop is initially 0, the first byte output to one of these registers is put in the low-order byte and the flip-flop is set to 1.   When the second byte is sent, the flip-flop being 1 directs it to the high-order byte of the register. Then the flip-flop is reset to 0. The purpose of the clear first/last flip-flop command is to initialize this flip-flop before outputting to the address and count registers.   Neither of the two commands discussed in this paragraph involves the transfer of data over the data bus.   They are automatically executed by the controller when a write is made to the appropriate address.

The 8237 can be programmed by accessing the block of 16 consecutive I/O ports assigned to it.   The beginning address of this block must be divisible by 16. Assuming that DMAADR represents the lowest address of the block, all valid commands are as given in Fig. 8-22.

To illustrate how to program the 8237, Fig. 8-23 shows the instructions that initiate a block transfer of 500 bytes from the input device, which is connected to channel 0, to memory beginning at BUFFER.   This program sequence assumes that the 8237 has already been initialized.   Otherwise, an instruction sequence such as

```
MVI     A,10010000B
OUT     DMAADR+8
```

might be needed.   This particular sequence specifies the signal levels, type of priority, and timing to be used and disables memory-to-memory transfer.

After the block transfer has been initiated, the CPU can perform some other tasks.   Before using the input data, the user may check the status of channel 0 by

```
BUSY:   IN      DMAADR+8
        ANI     1
        JZ      BUSY
```

to make certain the input is complete.   Alternatively, the 8237 can be connected in such a way that an interrupt is generated upon the completion of the block transfer.   In this case, the interrupt service routine is called a *completion routine*.

```
Assume that DMAADR represents the lowest I/O port assigned to the 8237.

         Command                                    Action
--------------------------------------------------------------------------------
Write/read    DMAADR             Write to/read from channel 0 current
                                 address register.

Write/read    DMAADR+1           Write to/read from channel 0 current
                                 byte count register.

Write/read    DMAADR+2           Write to/read from channel 1 current
                                 address register.

Write/read    DMAADR+3           Write to/read from channel 1 current
                                 byte count register.

Write/read    DMAADR+4           Write to/read from channel 2 current
                                 address register.

Write/read    DMAADR+5           Write to/read from channel 2 current
                                 byte count register.

Write/read    DMAADR+6           Write to/read from channel 3 current
                                 address register.

Write/read    DMAADR+7           Write to/read from channel 3 current
                                 byte count register.

Read          DMAADR+8           Read from the status register.

Write         DMAADR+8           Write to the command register.

Write         DMAADR+9           Write to a request flag.

Write         DMAADR+10          Write to a mask flag.

Write         DMAADR+11          Write to a mode register.

Write         DMAADR+12          Clear the first/last flip-flop.

Read          DMAADR+13          Read from the temporary register.

Write         DMAADR+13          Master clear (reset).

Write         DMAADR+14          Clear all mask flags.

Write         DMAADR+15          Write to all mask flags.
```

Figure 8-22   Summary of commands for the 8237.

8-6 DOUBLE AND TRIPLE BUFFERS

Often the input data are not directly transferred to the working area to be processed immediately but are temporarily stored in a different memory area first.   This preassigned space is called a *buffer area*.   Once the buffer is full, the data will be processed by the main routine.   Output may be done in a similar way.   Results generated by a processing routine may be stored in a buffer area and then transferred from there to the output device.

```
OUT     DMAADR+12       ;CLEAR FIRST/LAST FLIP-FLOP
LXI     B,BUFFER        ;LOAD THE STARTING MEMORY ADDRESS TO
MOV     A,C             ;CURRENT ADDRESS REGISTER OF CHANNEL 0
OUT     DMAADR          ;WITH THE LEAST SIGNIFICANT BYTE
MOV     A,B             ;FOLLOWED BY THE MOST SIGNIFICANT BYTE
OUT     DMAADR
LXI     B,499           ;LOAD NO. OF BYTES TO BE
MOV     A,C             ;TRANSFERRED MINUS 1 TO CURRENT
OUT     DMAADR+1        ;BYTE COUNT REGISTER OF CHANNEL 0
MOV     A,B
OUT     DMAADR+1
MVI     A,01000100B     ;SET MODE REGISTER OF CHANNEL 0
OUT     DMAADR+11       ;TO 01000100 TO SELECT SINGLE MODE,
                        ;ADDRESS INCREMENT, WRITE TRANSFER
                        ;AND TO DISABLE AUTOINITIALIZATION
MVI     A,0             ;CLEAR MASK FLAG OF CHANNEL 0
OUT     DMAADR+10       ;TO START DMA
  .
  .
  .
```

Figure 8-23   An example of programming the 8237.

In order to overlap data processing with data collecting, two buffers are required, and instead of moving the data, it is faster to change a pair of pointers. Whenever one buffer is full, the microprocessor can process the data in it while the other buffer is collecting input. For a real-time application, it is necessary that the processing of the data in one buffer be finished before the other one is full. When the other one is full, the roles of the two buffers are switched. This can be done by modifying the buffer pointers in the I/O service routine and the processing routine. The flowchart in Fig. 8-24 shows how to implement the *double-buffering* scheme. Although this figure assumes that interrupt I/O is being used, DMA could similarly be used. To make certain that no input data will be missing, for each block of data the processing time must be less than the time required for inputting the data.

Similarly, the overlapping of inputting, processing, and outputting can be achieved by using three buffers of the same size. In *triple buffering* the roles of the buffers are rotated as follows:

Stage 1—Buffer 1 for input, buffer 2 for processing, and buffer 3 for output

Stage 2—Buffer 1 for processing, buffer 2 for output, and buffer 3 for input

Stage 3—Buffer 1 for output, buffer 2 for input, and buffer 3 for processing

Repeat stages 1 to 3 until the task is completed.

8-7 KEYBOARD MONITOR DESIGN

Most microprocessor-based systems use a system console that has a keyboard with a CRT display or printer for the user-machine communication. For an interactive system, a user frequently needs to enter commands through a keyboard to instruct

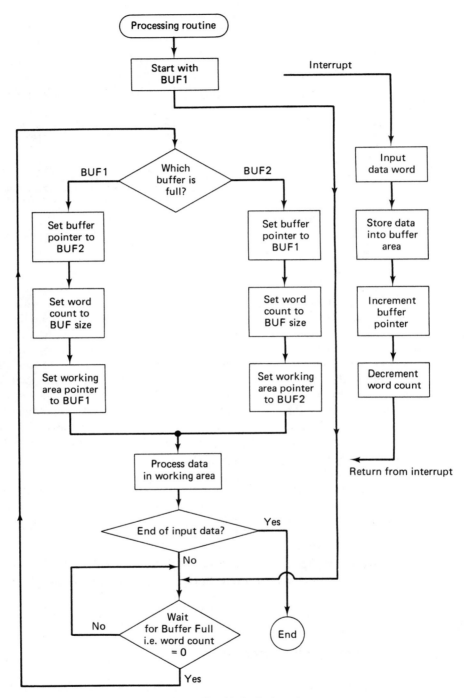

Figure 8-24 Double-buffering scheme.

272

the system to do various tasks and to request information on the current system status. A program called a *keyboard monitor* provides the system with the intelligence to input, interpret, and execute predefined commands. Even for low-cost systems, it is desirable to do program development with a keyboard monitor that can enter programs, examine and modify memory locations and registers, and dump data to a cassette tape or diskette. Another reason for examining a keyboard monitor here is that it provides a good example of I/O programming. The keyboard monitor to be described consists of routines that can execute eight commonly used commands. The syntax and functions of these commands are defined as follows:

$D—Dump a block of memory to the system console.

$DP—Dump a block of memory to a cassette tape.

$E—Examine and modify memory locations.

$ER—Examine and modify registers.

$G—Execute a program stored in memory.

$L—Load a program in binary code from a cassette tape.

$M—Move a block of data in memory.

$P—Return control to the user's program.

A key portion of the monitor is called the *command interpreter*. The command interpreter reads in a command and determines which command it is. If the command is not defined, an error message is generated. The interpreter must be able to

1. Accept ASCII character strings from the keyboard and echo them on the console.
2. Detect the beginning of a command (i.e., a $).
3. Store the command after it is terminated by a carriage return.
4. Check if the command is legal.
5. Output an error message for undefined commands.
6. Pass control to an appropriate routine to process the command.

Figure 8-25 shows the logic flow needed to implement these functions, and part of the source code is listed in Fig. 8-26.

After a legal command is recognized by the interpreter, control is then passed to an appropriate routine, which starts a dialogue with the user. For example, the memory examination routine is entered by a $E command and first prints out.

```
LOAD THE STARTING ADDRESS:
```

The user's response would be to enter an address of four hexadecimal digits. The contents of the location having this address will be printed out. At this point the

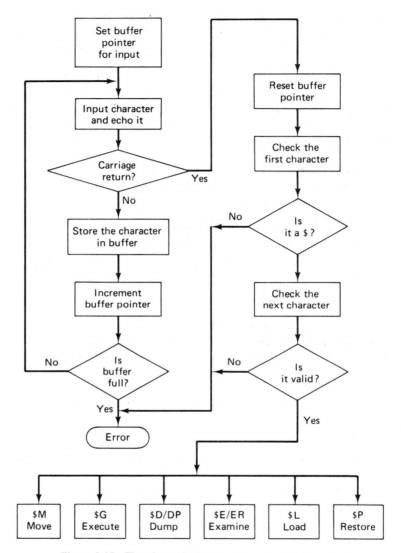

Figure 8-25 Flowchart of a keyboard command interpreter.

contents could be changed simply by typing the new contents. A control/C character terminates the examination routine and passes control back to the command interpreter. A carriage return will cause the address of the next memory location and its contents to be printed. Figure 8-27 shows the flowchart of the examine memory and examine registers commands. Note that in examining or modifying

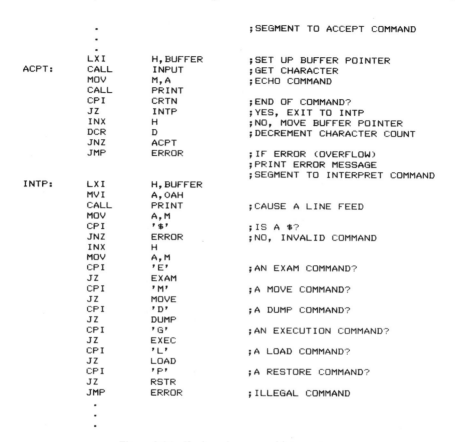

```
                 .                              ;SEGMENT TO ACCEPT COMMAND
                 .
                 .
           LXI      H,BUFFER        ;SET UP BUFFER POINTER
ACPT:      CALL     INPUT           ;GET CHARACTER
           MOV      M,A             ;ECHO COMMAND
           CALL     PRINT
           CPI      CRTN            ;END OF COMMAND?
           JZ       INTP            ;YES, EXIT TO INTP
           INX      H               ;NO, MOVE BUFFER POINTER
           DCR      D               ;DECREMENT CHARACTER COUNT
           JNZ      ACPT
           JMP      ERROR           ;IF ERROR (OVERFLOW)
                                    ;PRINT ERROR MESSAGE
                                    ;SEGMENT TO INTERPRET COMMAND
INTP:      LXI      H,BUFFER
           MVI      A,0AH
           CALL     PRINT           ;CAUSE A LINE FEED
           MOV      A,M
           CPI      '$'             ;IS A $?
           JNZ      ERROR           ;NO, INVALID COMMAND
           INX      H
           MOV      A,M
           CPI      'E'             ;AN EXAM COMMAND?
           JZ       EXAM
           CPI      'M'             ;A MOVE COMMAND?
           JZ       MOVE
           CPI      'D'             ;A DUMP COMMAND?
           JZ       DUMP
           CPI      'G'             ;AN EXECUTION COMMAND?
           JZ       EXEC
           CPI      'L'             ;A LOAD COMMAND?
           JZ       LOAD
           CPI      'P'             ;A RESTORE COMMAND?
           JZ       RSTR
           JMP      ERROR           ;ILLEGAL COMMAND
                 .
                 .
                 .
```

Figure 8-26   Keyboard command interpreter.

a register, the contents to be displayed or modified are from the memory location where that register is saved. Before returning control to the user's program, all registers are restored from their saved area.

A principal application of a keyboard monitor is in debugging assembler and machine language programs. By putting special instructions that branch to the monitor at important points in the program, called *breakpoints*, the program can be suspended and registers and memory contents can be examined at these points. Assuming the above monitor commands and an 8085 program, by putting a JMP instruction that branches to the monitor at address 8N and RST N instructions at the breakpoints the monitor could be entered from each breakpoint. The debug-

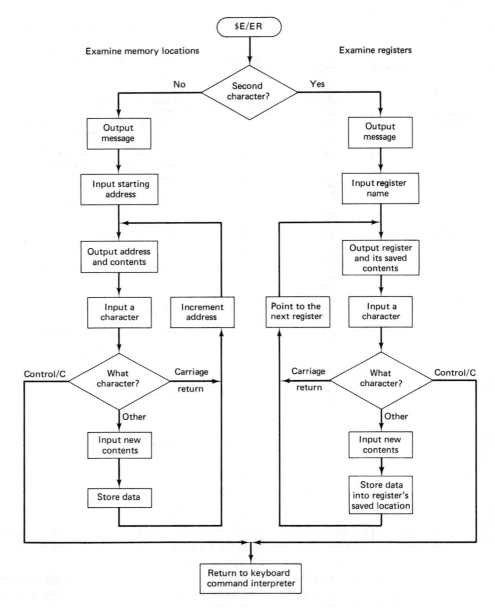

Figure 8-27 Routine to examine and modify memory locations and registers.

ging process would consist of

1. Inserting the RST instructions at the breakpoints.
2. Loading the program using $L.
3. Executing the program using $G.
4. Examining the register and memory contents and perhaps making changes whenever the monitor is entered.
5. Restarting the program at the point it was exited (i.e., the point of the last breakpoint) using $P.

Instructions, such as RST, that cause an interrupt sequence to be initiated are called *programmed,* or *software*, interrupts.

It is important to note that the data transferred between the microprocessor and a terminal are in ASCII code.   In order to interpret a memory address and its contents, a routine must be called that converts a numerical input in ASCII to its binary equivalent.   This conversion routine is required by all eight of the command-processing routines.   The conversion is relatively easy if the number is represented by hexadecimal digits because binary numbers may be formed from hexadecimal digits simply by placing the binary expansions of the digits side by side. An algorithm for converting ASCII-coded hexadecimal to binary is shown in Fig. 8-28.   Similarly, a numerical output must be converted to ASCII before it is sent to the terminal.

8-8 BCD TO BINARY CONVERSION

In the preceding section, the conversion between ASCII-coded hexadecimal and binary was discussed.   However, for most applications, decimal numbers are much more commonly used to input data and output results during the execution of user programs.   Although some microprocessors have special instructions to perform BCD arithmetic, BCD calculations are generally slower than their binary counterparts.   This is partly because an 8-bit microprocessor can operate on only two digits at a time.   If an operand has several digits, a single arithmetic operation requires many steps.   As discussed in Section 6-4-2, the 8085 has a special instruction DAA that must follow each ADD to convert the 8-bit binary result to two valid decimal digits.   In addition to being time consuming, it takes more memory space to store data in BCD form than in binary form.   Therefore, although I/O is normally done in decimal, internal calculations are often performed in binary. This means that the data must be converted from decimal to binary, processed, and then converted back to decimal for output.   Whether or not the calculations are sufficiently complicated to warrant the conversion depends on the application.

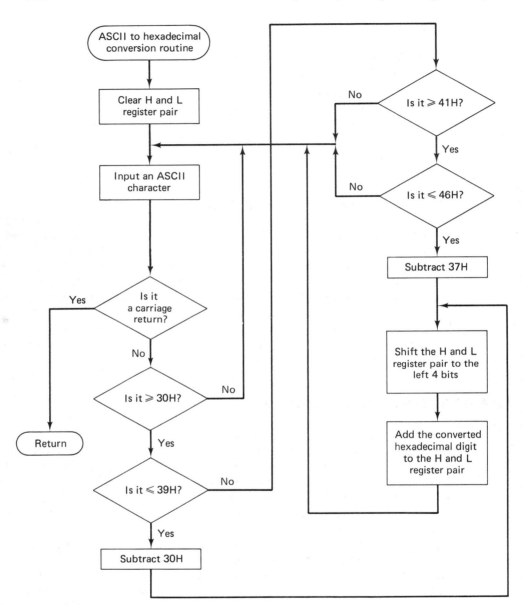

Figure 8-28 Conversion of an ASCII-coded hexadecimal number to its binary equivalent.

If an ASCII terminal is used to input data and to output results, the whole process from input to output is outlined as follows:

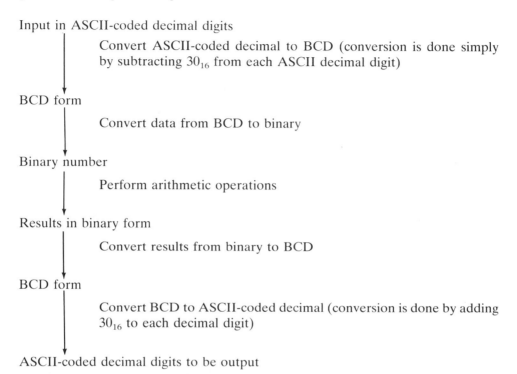

Input in ASCII-coded decimal digits

Convert ASCII-coded decimal to BCD (conversion is done simply by subtracting 30_{16} from each ASCII decimal digit)

BCD form

Convert data from BCD to binary

Binary number

Perform arithmetic operations

Results in binary form

Convert results from binary to BCD

BCD form

Convert BCD to ASCII-coded decimal (conversion is done by adding 30_{16} to each decimal digit)

ASCII-coded decimal digits to be output

Conversion between BCD and binary is not as straightforward as the conversion between hexadecimal and binary. BCD to binary conversion is based on the relation

$$d_n d_{n-1} \ldots d_1 d_0 = (((\ldots (d_n \times 10 + d_{n-1})10 \ldots)10 + d_1)10 + d_0$$

where $d_n, \ldots, d_0$ represent the decimal digits. An easy way to multiply a partial sum by 10 is to multiply it by 2 and by 8, and then add the resulting products. (Note that multiplication by 2 requires only an addition of the operand to itself.)

A program segment to convert a signed decimal number to its binary equivalent is listed in Fig. 8-29. In this sample program, the decimal number to be converted is stored in ASCII code in the byte array DIGITS, with the most significant digit being stored in the lowest address. The number may be prefixed with + or − and is terminated by a blank character. The equivalent binary number has 2 bytes and is stored into the word variable BINNUM. Furthermore, if the magnitude of the decimal number exceeds $2^{15} - 1$, an error code CODE will be set to 1 and the result will be set to -2^{15}. To simplify the implementation, the special case of -2^{15}, which has a valid binary representation, is not considered

```
CHECK       MACRO
            MOV       A,H
            CPI       0
            JM        OVERFL
            ENDM
            .
            .
            .
            XRA       A               ;SET CODE TO 0
            STA       CODE
            LXI       D,DIGITS        ;LOAD THE ADDRESS OF THE DECIMAL
                                      ; INTEGER TO BE CONVERTED
            LDAX      D               ;LOAD ITS SIGN OR MOST SIGNIFICANT DIGIT
            CPI       '-'             ;NEGATIVE INTEGER?
            JZ        MINUS           ;IF SO, SET SIGN TO 1
            CPI       '+'             ;POSITIVE INTEGER?
            JZ        PLUS            ;IF SO, SET SIGN TO 0
UNSIGN:     DCX       D               ;UNSIGNED, SET SIGN TO 0 AND
PLUS:       MVI       A,0             ;DECREMENT POINTER BY 1
            STA       SIGN
            JMP       CONVER
MINUS:      MVI       A,1
            STA       SIGN
CONVER:     LXI       H,0             ;INITIALIZE PARTIAL SUM TO 0
AGAIN:      INX       D               ;LOAD THE CURRENT DIGIT STARTING
            LDAX      D               ;FROM THE MOST SIGNIFICANT ONE
;CONVERT AN ASCII DIGIT TO BCD. IF IT IS A BLANK, EXIT FROM THE LOOP.
;IF IT IS A INVALID DIGIT, GO TO ERROR
            CPI       ' '
            JZ        NEXT
            CPI       '0'
            JM        ERROR           ;LESS THAN 0?
            CPI       3AH
            JP        ERROR           ;GREATER THAN 9?
            SUI       30H             ;CONVERT TO BCD
            PUSH      PSW             ;SAVE THE CURRENT DIGIT
;MULTIPLY PARTIAL SUM BY 10 AND CHECK OVERFLOW
            DAD       H               ;2 X (H)(L)
            CHECK                     ;JUMP TO OVERFL IF GREATER THAN 2**15 - 1
            MOV       B,H             ;SAVE 2 X (H)(L) IN (B)(C)
            MOV       C,L
            DAD       H               ;4 X (H)(L)
            CHECK
            DAD       H               ;8 X (H)(L)
            CHECK
            DAD       B               ;10 X (H)(L)
            CHECK
;ADD THE CURRENT DIGIT TO PARTIAL SUM
            POP       PSW             ;RESTORE THE CURRENT DIGIT
            MVI       B,0
            MOV       C,A
            DAD       B
            CHECK
            JMP       AGAIN           ;REPEAT FOR THE NEXT DIGIT
;CHECK SIGN. IF PLUS, STORE RESULT. OTHERWISE, TAKE 2'S COMPLEMENT
;BEFORE STORING RESULTS.
NEXT:       LDA       SIGN
            CPI       0               ;SIGN IS PLUS
            JZ        STORE
            MOV       A,H             ;SIGN IS MINUS
            CMA                       ;TAKE 2'S COMPLEMENT OF (H)(L)
            MOV       H,A
            MOV       A,L
```

Figure 8-29   Routine to convert signed ASCII decimal digits to an equivalent binary number.

```
                CMA
                MOV       L,A
                INX       H
STORE:          SHLD      BINNUM
                JMP       DONE
;IF AN INVALID DIGIT IS DETECTED, SET CODE TO 2 AND BINNUM TO 0
ERROR:          MVI       A,2
                STA       CODE
                LXI       H,0
                SHLD      BINNUM
                JMP       DONE
;IF MAGNITUDE EXCEEDS 2**15 - 1, SET CODE TO 1 AND BINNUM TO -2**15
OVERFL:         MVI       A,1
                STA       CODE
                LXI       H,8000H
                SHLD      BINNUM
DONE:           .
                .
                .
SIGN:           DS        1                   ;TEMPORARY STORAGE FOR SIGN
CODE:           DS        1                   ;ERROR CODE
BINNUM:         DS        2
DIGITS:         DS        7
                .
                .
                .
```

Figure 8-29 Continued.

here. As seen in the figure, in order to perform double-byte addition efficiently, the HL register pair is used to store the partial sum during the conversion. To shorten the code, a macro CHECK is defined to detect an overflow. The macro checks the sign bit of the H register and branches to OVERFL if that bit is 1.

To convert a decimal string with five or more digits, additions must be performed on operands consisting of 3 or more bytes, and this is very time consuming. The conversion from binary to decimal is of similar complexity. In scientific applications, extensive arithmetic operations are involved, and consequently it is desirable to use binary numbers internally. However, for many business applications, the I/O activity outweighs the computation activity and the BCD format is used internally to avoid the conversion process.

8-9 Z80 I/O

The Z80 I/O instructions are given in Fig. 8-30. The IN A, (n) and OUT (n), A, where n is the port address, are the same as the 8085's IN and OUT instructions. For the remaining I/O instructions (which have no 8085 counterparts), the port address is indicated by the contents of the C register. Except for IN r, (C) and OUT (C), r, the remaining instructions cause the transfer to be made between the port and the memory location pointed to by the HL pair. In addition, they cause the HL pair to be autoincremented or autodecremented and the B register, which is used as a counter, to be decremented. INIR, INDR, OTIR, and OTDR permit

```
Assembler Code                               Definition

  IN    A,(n)                  Inputs datum from port n to the A register.

  IN    r,(C)                  Inputs datum from the port pointed to by the
                               (C) register to register r.

  INI                          Inputs datum from the port pointed to by the
                               (C) register to the memory location pointed
                               to by HL register pair, increments the HL pair
                               and decrements register B.

  INIR                         Same as INI except that the instruction is
                               repeated automatically until (B)=0.

  IND                          Same as INI except that the HL pair is
                               decremented.

  INDR                         Same as INIR except that the HL pair is
                               decremented.


The corresponding output instructions are:

OUT  (n),A       OUT  (C),r       OUTI       OTIR       OUTD       OTDR
```

Figure 8-30   Z80 I/O instructions.

repetitive inputting and outputting. The Z80 interrupt sequence is similar to that of the 8085 in that the current instruction is completed, the interrupt enable (I) flag is cleared, and an interrupt acknowledge is sent. The Z80 has two pins for receiving external interrupt requests, the $\overline{\text{NMI}}$ pin, which is nonmaskable, and the $\overline{\text{INT}}$ pin, which is maskable. (For a pin diagram of the Z80 refer back to Fig. 5-10.) A combination of signals on two pins (the $\overline{\text{M}}_1$ and $\overline{\text{IORQ}}$ pins) indicates an interrupt acknowledge. An interrupt request on $\overline{\text{NMI}}$ causes the next instruction to be taken from address 0066.

As with the 8085, maskable interrupts are enabled and disabled using the EI and DI instructions. How maskable interrupts are handled depends on the interrupt mode. The Z80 has three modes, 0, 1, and 2, and is put into one of these modes by executing an IM 0, IM 1, or IM 2 instruction. When in mode 0, RST instructions are returned from the I/O interface, just as they are when requests are made through the 8085's INTR pin. When in mode 1, the next instruction is always taken from 0038. For mode 2, a pointer to the address of the next instruction is determined by the concatenation of the contents of the I register, which must have been previously filled with an even number using an LD I, A instruction, and a byte sent to the CPU from the I/O interface. This pointer is the address of an interrupt vector that is automatically loaded into the PC by the interrupt sequence. The idea is that, during system initialization, all interrupt vectors are put in a table beginning at the address pointed to by the I register. Then, by accessing this table, the interrupt sequence is able to load automatically the beginning address of the proper interrupt routine into the PC. A diagram of the activity following a mode 2 interrupt is shown in Fig. 8-31. For mode 0, the RST instruction pushes

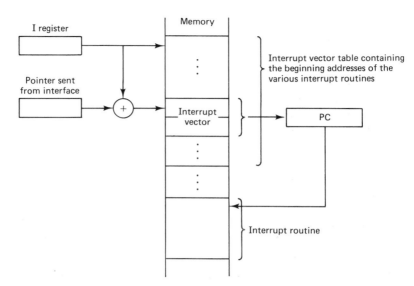

Figure 8-31   Z80 mode 2 interrupt sequence.

the PC onto the stack.   For modes 1 and 2, the PC is pushed during the interrupt sequence.

Regardless of the mode, programmed interrupts can be accomplished by inserting RST instructions in the code.   For debugging, RST instructions could be inserted at the breakpoints.

The Z80 has the RETN instruction for returning from nonmaskable interrupts and RETI for returning from maskable interrupts.   Both pop the return address from the stack and notify the I/O interface that the interrupt routine has been completed.   The difference is that RETN restores the interrupt enable flag to the value it was before the interrupt occurred, while RETI always enables interrupts.

DMA is accomplished in essentially the same way as with an 8085.   The $\overline{\text{BUSRQ}}$ and $\overline{\text{BUSAK}}$ serve the same purposes as the HOLD and HLDA pins.

8-10 MC6809 I/O

In an MC6809 system the interface registers are given memory addresses (i.e., they are memory mapped) because there is no separate I/O space.   Therefore, all of the instructions that access memory can also be used to access the interface registers, but there are no special I/O instructions.   There are obvious exceptions; for example, an STA instruction could not store a value in a register that can only be read (e.g., a data-in buffer register).

There are three interrupt pins, $\overline{\text{NMI}}$, $\overline{\text{IRQ}}$, and $\overline{\text{FIRQ}}$, and two interrupt mask flags, I and F, which are bits 4 and 6 of the CC, respectively (see Fig. 5-11). $\overline{\text{NMI}}$ is for nonmaskable interrupts and serves the same purpose as the TRAP pin on the 8085. A request on $\overline{\text{NMI}}$ causes *all* of the registers except S to be pushed onto the system stack, further interrupts to be disabled, and the PC to be filled from FFFC and FFFD. An $\overline{\text{IRQ}}$ request causes *all* of the registers except S to be pushed onto the system stack, the I mask to be set to 1 so that no further $\overline{\text{IRQ}}$ interrupts will be accepted, and the PC to be filled from FFF8 and FFF9. An $\overline{\text{FIRQ}}$ request (fast interrupt request) causes only the CC and PC to be pushed onto the system stack, both the I and F masks to be set so that no more $\overline{\text{FIRQ}}$ and $\overline{\text{IRQ}}$ interrupts will be accepted, and the PC to be filled from FFF6 and FFF7. Also the E flag in the CC, which is normally 1, is cleared to 0. The E flag is used by the interrupt return instruction (RTI) to determine which register contents are to be popped from the stack. If it is 1, all register contents except those of S are popped, and if it is 0, only the CC and PC contents are popped.

The interrupt mask bits as well as other condition flags in CC can be changed and examined with the following instructions:

ANDCC #N—This instruction logically ANDs the immediate operand into the condition code register. It is used to enable maskable interrupt facilities. For example, ANDCC #11101111 clears the I mask flag to enable the $\overline{\text{IRQ}}$ interrupt but leaves other bits unchanged.

ORCC #N—This instruction logically ORs the immediate operand into the condition code register. It is used to disable maskable interrupt facilities. For example, ORCC #01010000 sets both of the F and I mask flags to 1 to disable the $\overline{\text{IRQ}}$ and $\overline{\text{FIRQ}}$ interrupts, but other bits in CC remain unchanged.

TFR R1,R2—This instruction transfers the contents of R1 to R2. Operands R1 and R2 can be A, B, CC, or DP. The current status of interrupt mask bits can be examined by first transferring CC to A or B and then testing the contents of A or B. Of course, setting the condition code to a particular value can also be accomplished by using the TFR instruction.

Programmed interrupts are initiated by the SWI, SWI2, and SWI3 instructions. SWI pushes all registers except S, disables interrupts, and fills the PC from FFFA and FFFB. SWI is used for inserting breakpoints. SWI2 and SWI3 are the same except that they get the new PC contents from FFF4:FFF5 and FFF2:FFF3, respectively, and do not affect the I and F mask flags. These instructions are primarily for branching to frequently used routines such as a divide routine. Instructions used for this purpose are sometimes referred to as *emulation* or *trap* instructions.

Another important instruction related to interrupts is CWAI #N, where N is a mask. It causes the CC to be ANDed with N (i.e., selectively cleared according to the mask), all of the registers except S to be pushed onto the system stack, and then suspends the operation of the CPU until an interrupt request is detected. This instruction is used when processing must wait for data to be input before it can continue.

The $\overline{\text{DMAREQ}}$ and $\overline{\text{HALT}}$ pins can be used for inputting bus request and outputting bus grant signals, respectively, thus providing DMA facilities.

BIBLIOGRAPHY

1. *Introduction to Programming* (Maynard, Mass.: Digital Equipment Corporation, 1972).
2. *The MCS-80/85 Family User's Manual* (Santa Clara, Calif.: Intel Corporation, 1983).
3. *8080/8085 Assembly Language Programming Manual* (Santa Clara, Calif.: Intel Corporation, 1979).
4. PEATMAN, JOHN B., *Microcomputer-based Design* (New York: McGraw-Hill, 1977).
5. SHORT, KENNETH L., *Microprocessors and Programmed Logic* (Englewood Cliffs, N.J.: Prentice-Hall, 1981).

EXERCISES

1. Give the machine code for each of the following instructions: (a) IN 40 (b) OUT 0A5H
2. Can an I/O port be assigned address 124H? Explain your answer.
3. Write an assembler language program segment to input from the keyboard terminal and echo each input character to the CRT display. Use symbols to represent the I/O ports that are associated with the keyboard and display and the EQU directive to equate these symbols to their addresses. Assume two status registers (20 and 22) and two buffer registers (21 and 23).
4. During an interrupt, the return address must be saved before executing the service routine. How is this done for the 8085?
5. Construct a table that summarizes the 8085's interrupt facilities, and for each interrupt type indicate the condition that causes such an interrupt.
6. Assume that the current contents of PC and SP are 1234H and A500H, respectively. Determine the new contents of all affected registers and memory locations after an RST 6.5 interrupt occurs.
7. Assume that the service routine for interrupt RST 5.5 is stored beginning at location 3456H. What contents should locations 2C through 2E have?
8. Determine the maximum data transfer rate (bytes per second) if the interrupt I/O shown in Fig. 8-14 is implemented. Assume a 6 MHz clock and no wait states.
9. Assume that the polling scheme shown in Fig. 8-16 is implemented to input data from eight devices. Determine the maximum data transfer rate of the sixth device. Assume a 6 MHz clock and no wait states.
10. For a system with a memory cycle time of 800 nS, what is the maximum data transfer rate if a DMA is used?
11. Write an assembler language program segment that can read data from a keyboard and simultaneously dump data from memory to a printer. Assume that the printer sends

RST 1 during the interrupt. Further assume that RVST, RVBUF, PTST, and PTBUF represent the addresses of the keyboard status register, keyboard buffer register, printer status register, and printer buffer register, respectively.

12. Write a program segment that inputs a string of four ASCII-coded hexadecimal digits, converts it to binary, and stores the results in the HL register pair.

13. Write a program segment that converts the binary data in the HL register pair to four ASCII-coded hexadecimal digits and then outputs the character string to the system console.

14. Write a program segment using programmed I/O to input an integer consisting of four decimal digits from a keyboard, and then convert that number to its binary equivalent. The results are to be stored at memory location RESULT with the least significant byte first. Assume the addresses of the keyboard status and buffer registers to be KBST and KBUF.

15. As shown in Fig. 8-26, a routine ERROR is needed by the keyboard monitor. Write this routine and have it print out the message "COMMAND IS UNDEFINED".

16. Rewrite your answer to Exercise 13 using Z80 code.

17. Write an interrupt routine such as the one in Fig. 8-14 using Z80 code.

18. Repeat Exercise 17 using MC6809 code.

Chapter 9

System Bus and I/O Control Logic

A microcomputer consists of several modules, including a processor module, memory modules, and various I/O interfaces. These modules are connected together via the system bus. Depending on the size of the system, they may reside on separate boards or all on a single board. The heart of the processor module is the microprocessor. Even for a very simple configuration, the microprocessor must be accompanied by logic, which consists primarily of timing circuitry and bus control logic. The timing circuitry provides the necessary clock pulses for the microcomputer system, and the bus control logic interfaces the microprocessor to the system bus and generates the control signals to coordinate the bus activities during a data transfer operation or an interrupt. The role of the supporting logic is illustrated in Fig. 9-1.

This chapter will cover the major logic surrounding the microprocessor and the structure of the system bus. As with the discussion of programming in preceding chapters, the 8085 will be used as the primary example. The chapter will proceed by considering the clock and the overall timing first, followed by a discussion of the 8085's external connections (i.e., pin assignments). The third section discusses bus cycle timing. The next four sections discuss the bus control logic, which includes the interface between the microprocessor and the system bus, the generation and timing of the handshaking signals, and interrupt management. The discussion of bus control logic leads to an examination of the structure of a typical system bus, the S-100. The remainder of the chapter considers serial interrupt management and the interrupt management for the Motorola MC6809.

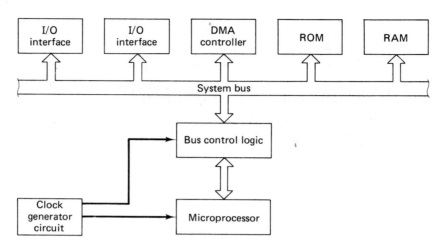

Figure 9-1   Typical microcomputer I/O architecture.

9-1 *THE PROCESSOR CYCLE AND CLOCK*

Transitions in the microprocessor's internal states and changes in the external circuitry are synchronized by the clock. The clock pulses are required to strobe signals into internal registers, flags, and flip-flops. They may also be used to generate subsequent timing signals for the control of external logic circuitry. If the clock period is too short, the machine does not have enough time to generate stable input signals for storage devices, and errors occur. On the other hand, if the clock period is too long, the machine is running at a slower rate than is necessary and time is wasted. The microprocessor might not even function properly if the clock rate is below a specified lower limit.

The 8085 operates with an internal processor clock at a maximum rate of 3 MHz. Two improved versions, 8085-2 and 8085-1, are also available, for which the maximum processor clock rates are 5 MHz and 6 MHz, respectively. At the maximum rate the duration of each state of the 8085 is 334 nS, which is the time needed to execute a micro step. As introduced in Section 6-12, the 8085 requires a certain number of machine cycles to complete each instruction. The number of machine cycles is determined by the number of memory references required in the instruction and varies from only one machine cycle for the register-to-register transfer instruction MOV r1, r2 to five machine cycles for the load HL pair instruction LHLD. Except for the first machine cycle (M_1) of each instruction, each machine cycle normally consists of three states. Because in M_1 the op code is fetched and decoded, it requires from four to six states, depending on the instruction. These possible states are T_1, T_2, T_3, T_4, T_5, and T_6, and are associated with the following major activities:

T_1—The CPU places a 16-bit memory or an 8-bit I/O port address on the address pins. This address indicates the location where the data are to be transferred to or from. A 3-bit status is output to indicate the type of machine cycle (memory read, memory write, I/O read, I/O write, op code fetch, interrupt acknowledge, etc.) along with a read or write command signal.

T_2—During this state, the 8085 drops the lower eight address signals and prepares these eight address/data pins for transferring data. It also checks the signals presented on two of the control pins (READY and HOLD, which are discussed later) to determine if it should enter a wait state (T_w) after the current state or enter a hold state after the completion of the current machine cycle. The wait and hold states provide the system with the capability of handling slow devices and DMA.

T_3—The processor inputs the 8-bit data from the address/data pins during an instruction fetch, interrupt acknowledge, operand fetch, or I/O read. If the current operation is a memory write or an I/O write, the processor places the 8-bit data on the address/data pins in T_2 and T_3.

T_4, T_5, and T_6—Only the first machine cycle of an instruction enters T_4. States T_4, T_5, and T_6 are used to decode the op code and possibly to execute the instruction.

As an example, executing the 1-byte instruction MOV r,M requires two machine cycles. The first machine cycle consists of four states in which the instruction is fetched and decoded, and the program counter is updated. The second machine cycle contains three states to fetch the operand and move it into the register r. A detailed description of the state transition sequence is given in Fig. 9-2.

The clock pulses required to operate a microprocessor are provided by a clock generator. It normally includes a crystal-based oscillator to generate timing pulses and a logic circuit to reduce the clock rate from the fundamental frequency according to the requirement of the specific microprocessor.

For the 8085, a clock generator has been integrated into the microprocessor. Therefore, only a crystal is required to provide the fundamental frequency, as shown in Fig. 9-3. If an external clock is used, X_2 can be left floating while X_1 is connected to the output of the clock driver. The maximum frequency for inputs X_1 and X_2 is 6 MHz for the 8085, 10 MHz for the 8085-2, and 12 MHz for the 8085-1. Internally, the input frequency is divided by 2 to generate the CPU clock, whose maximum frequency is 3 MHz, 5 MHz, or 6 MHz, depending on the model. Clock pulses are also required as common control signals to other devices that need to change states simultaneously (i.e., that need to be synchronized). For this purpose, the 8085 provides clock signals for other system components at the processor clock frequency through its CLK pin.

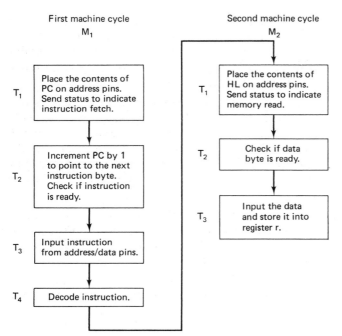

First machine cycle
M₁

Second machine cycle
M₂

T₁ — Place the contents of PC on address pins. Send status to indicate instruction fetch.

T₂ — Increment PC by 1 to point to the next instruction byte. Check if instruction is ready.

T₃ — Input instruction from address/data pins.

T₄ — Decode instruction.

T₁ — Place the contents of HL on address pins. Send status to indicate memory read.

T₂ — Check if data byte is ready.

T₃ — Input the data and store it into register r.

Figure 9-2 State transition sequence of the instruction MOV r,M.

9-2 THE 8085 PIN ASSIGNMENTS

One of the major functions of the logic that surrounds the microprocessor is to provide an interface between the microprocessor and the system bus. Therefore, in designing any microcomputer system, it is necessary to understand the function of each of the pins of the microprocessor used. As shown in Fig. 9-4, the 8085 has a total of 40 pins. Their definitions are summarized in Fig. 9-5.

The 8085 uses 16 bits to specify an address while data are transferred 8 bits at a time. During a memory reference, the address indicates a 16-bit memory location; during the execution of an I/O instruction, the upper 8 bits and lower 8 bits of the address outputs are identical and indicate an I/O port. This allows the

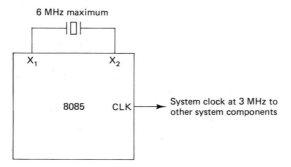

6 MHz maximum

X₁   X₂

8085   CLK → System clock at 3 MHz to other system components

Figure 9-3 Clock circuit for the 8085.

Figure 9-4 8085 pin diagram. (Reprinted by permission of Intel Corporation, Copyright 1983.)

system to have up to 64K bytes of memory and 256 I/O ports.   In order to reduce the number of pins, multiplexed data and address pins (AD_7–AD_0) are used. During a machine cycle, AD_7–AD_0 output the lower order 8 address bits in state T_1 and for the remaining part of the machine cycle the same eight pins are used to transfer data.   To indicate that AD_7–AD_0 represent valid address bits, the 8085 outputs an address latch enable (ALE) pulse.   The high to low transition of this signal can be used to latch the address into address latches so that the address will be available for the entire machine cycle.

Pin(s)	Symbol	In/Out 3-State	Description
1,2	X_1,X_2	I	X_1 and X_2 oscillator input - This clock input is internally divided by 2 to generate the processor clock. Maximum rate of X_1, X_2 depends on CPU model: 6 MHz for 8085A (3 MHz CPU clock) 10 MHz for 8085A-2 (5 MHz CPU clock) 12 MHz for 8085A-1 (6 MHz CPU clock)
3	RESET OUT	O	Reset Out - Indicates that the CPU is being reset. It can be used to reset other components in the system.
4	SOD	O	Serial Output - This output is specified by the SIM instruction.
5	SID	I	Serial Input - This input is loaded into bit 7 of the accumulator during the RIM instruction.
6	TRAP	I	Trap - Causes a non-maskable interrupt. A trap is triggered by a rising edge and the input should remain high until it is sampled.

Figure 9-5 Pin definitions for the 8085.

Pin(s)	Symbol	In/Out 3-State	Description
7-9	RST 7.5- RST 5.5	I	Restart Interrupt Requests - They are maskable restart interrupt requests. RST 7.5 is edge triggered while RST 6.5 and RST 5.5 are level triggered.
10	INTR	I	Interrupt Request - This general purpose maskable interrupt request is level triggered. When recognized, the 8085 executes an instruction provided by the interrupting device.
11	$\overline{\text{INTA}}$	O	Interrupt Acknowledge - Indicates an INTR is accepted. It can be used by the interrupting device to place an instruction on the data bus.
19-12	$AD_7\text{-}AD_0$	I/O-3	Address/Data Bus - Shared by address and data. During T_1 state of a machine cycle, it outputs the lower 8 address bits. During the remaining part of the machine cycle, it is used to input or output data.
20	V_{SS}		Ground.
28-21	$A_{15}\text{-}A_8$	O-3	Address Bus - Is used to output the upper 8 address bits.
30	ALE	O	Address Latch Enable - Outputs a pulse in T_1 of the machine cycle and is to indicate that $A_{15}\text{-}A_8$ and $AD_7\text{-}AD_0$ represent a valid address.
31	$\overline{\text{WR}}$	O-3	Write - A low indicates a memory or I/O write command.
32	$\overline{\text{RD}}$	O-3	Read - A low indicates a memory or I/O read command.
29,33,34	$S_0, S_1,$ IO/$\overline{\text{M}}$	O O-3	Machine Cycle Status - Outputs a 3-bit status to indicate the type of machine cycle as defined below.

IO/$\overline{\text{M}}$	S_1	S_0	Status
0	0	1	Memory write
0	1	0	Memory read
0	1	1	Op code fetch
1	0	1	I/O write
1	1	0	I/O read
1	1	1	Interrupt acknowledge

Figure 9-5 Continued.

Pin(s)	Symbol	In/Out 3-State	Description
			During a halt state, $S_0 = S_1 = 0$ and $IO/\overline{M}$ is in its high-impedance mode. During both hold and reset, S_0 and S_1 are undefined and $IO/\overline{M}$ is in its high-impedance mode. Normally, $IO/\overline{M}$, $\overline{RD}$, and $\overline{WR}$ are used to specify the bus operation: memory read, memory write, I/O read, or I/O write.
35	READY	I	Ready - Acknowledgment from memory or I/O device that the CPU can complete its current machine cycle.
36	$\overline{RESET\ IN}$	I	Reset - Resets the 8085 to its initial state. This signal must be 0 for at least 3 clock cycles.
37	CLK	O	Clock Out - Provides clock signals for other system components. It has the same frequency as the internal processor clock.
38	HLDA	O	Hold Acknowledge - Indicates that a HOLD request is accepted and the CPU will enter the hold state in the next clock cycle.
39	HOLD	I	Hold Request - Receives hold requests from a DMA controller.
40	V_{CC}		Power - +5 volt supply.

Figure 9-5   Continued.

The $\overline{RD}$, $\overline{WR}$, and $IO/\overline{M}$ signals indicate the type of data transfer. They can be decoded to activate memory read, memory write, I/O read, and I/O write command signals. Additional machine status is provided by status bits S_0 and S_1. A possible application of the status bits is to monitor the activity of the CPU during emulation.

The READY signal is an acknowledge from a memory or I/O interface that an input datum is available on the data bus or an output datum has been accepted. The READY signal is examined by the 8085 in state T_2. If this signal is low, the 8085 enters a wait state (T_w) until it becomes high. This allows the 8085 to communicate with slow memory and I/O devices.

The SID and SOD pins provide the capability to input or output 1 bit at a time. Input from the SID pin is loaded to bit 7 of the accumulator by the RIM instruction and, conversely, the most significant bit in the accumulator can be sent to the SOD pin by the SIM instruction. Through these two pins, the 8085 can directly communicate with a serial terminal such as a CRT or TTY under program control. This eliminates the need for a serial interface device and thus reduces the cost in a simple system.

The $\overline{\text{RESET IN}}$ pin is to initialize the 8085. A reset signal should be generated automatically when the system is turned on. In addition, a system normally has a switch that allows a user to generate manually a reset signal. For the 8085, a reset will clear the program counter and the INTE flag and will set the three RST interrupt masks, M5.5, M6.5, and M7.5, to 1. Contents of the PSW and data registers are indeterminant. Therefore, after a reset, all maskable interrupts are disabled and the 8085 begins executing at location 0. This instruction should be a branch to a read-only section of memory that stores a program for initializing the system and loading the application software or operating system. Such a program is referred to as a *bootstrap loader*. The RESET OUT pin outputs a 1 while the 8085 is in a reset. This output can be used to reset other system components.

The purposes of the hold request (HOLD), hold acknowledge (HLDA), trap (TRAP), RST interrupt requests (RST 5.5, RST 6.5, and RST 7.5), general interrupt request (INTR), and interrupt acknowledge ($\overline{\text{INTA}}$) signals are discussed in Chapter 8. The V_{CC} and V_{SS} pins are for a +5 V power supply and ground, respectively. As explained before, pins X_1 and X_2 are for the oscillator input, and the CLK pin is for the clock output.

9-3 BUS CYCLE TIMING

Each bus cycle is equivalent to a machine cycle. The timing relationships of the pin signals are different for each type of machine cycle. The 8085 has four general types of machine cycles: read, write, interrupt acknowledge, and DMA.

For a read cycle, there are three variations: memory read, I/O read, and op code fetch. The third one, which has more than three states, only occurs as the first cycle for each instruction. Figure 9-6 shows the timing of a memory read or

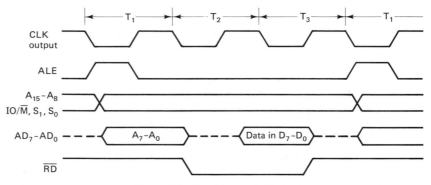

Figure 9-6 Read bus cycle timing.

I/O read cycle without a wait state. During the T_1 state, the status and address are output and they become stable by the trailing edge of the ALE signal. The upper 8 address bits remain available throughout the entire bus cycle. But in T_2 the data/address pins drop the lower 8 address bits and switch to the input mode. This prepares the 8085 to input the data in T_3. After T_3, the next machine cycle starts immediately. The only difference between memory read and I/O read cycles is the IO/$\overline{M}$ output. Although an I/O port uses only 8 bits during an I/O read cycle, a 16-bit address is sent with the upper 8 bits being identical to the lower 8 bits.

An op code fetch machine cycle consists of from four to six states. Since it basically performs a memory read operation, the timing of T_1 through T_3 is identical to a memory read cycle. In T_4 through T_6, the 8085 performs its internal operation.

A write cycle can be either a memory write or I/O write depending on the IO/$\overline{M}$ signal. As shown in Fig. 9-7, write bus cycle timing is similar to a read cycle. The major differences are that $\overline{WR}$ is activated instead of $\overline{RD}$ and that $AD_7 - AD_0$ are in the output mode to send data during T_2 and T_3. In conjunction with the IO/$\overline{M}$, the write signal causes the memory module or I/O interface to begin a write operation that puts the data on the data bus into the addressed location.

In this discussion of read and write cycle timing, it has been assumed that the memory or device is fast enough to complete a data transfer in three states. In order to tolerate low-speed devices or memory, a handshaking signal referred to as READY is sent by the device. For a read cycle, this acknowledge signal is used to indicate that the data on the data bus are stable and valid. If data are not available, READY is low, thus forcing the 8085 into a wait state (T_w), which can be repeated until a high input on the READY pin is detected. Then the microprocessor proceeds with the current bus cycle by entering T_3. During an output, this acknowledge signal is used to inform the microprocessor that the data have been received by the device. By checking this signal, the 8085 can hold the output data as long as necessary. Figure 9-8 shows the timing of a bus cycle with two wait states inserted.

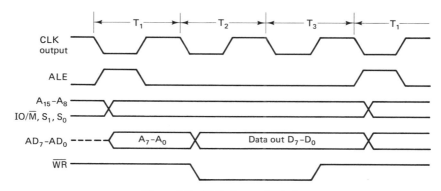

Figure 9-7   Write bus cycle timing.

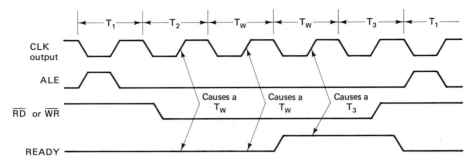

Figure 9-8 Bus cycle with wait states.

During an interrupt sequence, several machine cycles will occur depending on what instruction is provided by the interrupting device. When an INTR interrupt occurs, the first machine cycle is to input the instruction to be executed. Therefore, it has the same timing as an M_1 cycle with two exceptions: the $\overline{INTA}$ signal is sent instead of the $\overline{RD}$ command and the status indicates an interrupt acknowledge, not an instruction fetch. If the instruction is a restart instruction, two memory write machine cycles will follow to save the return address, as illustrated in Fig. 9-9. On the other hand if the instruction is a CALL, which has 3 bytes, the interrupt sequence will have five machine cycles. The first three are to input the CALL instruction (with $\overline{INTA}$ being sent instead of $\overline{RD}$) and are followed by two memory write cycles, which save the return address. For a TRAP or RST

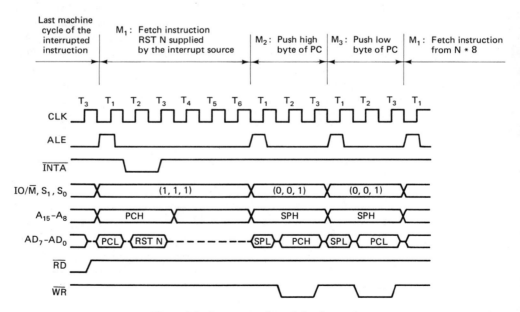

Figure 9-9 Interrupt acknowledge bus cycles.

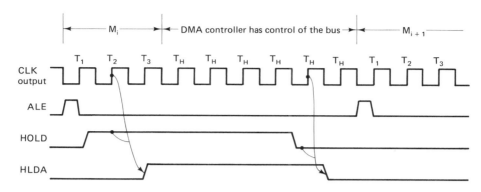

Figure 9-10   Hold request and acknowledge timing.

interrupt, an internally generated RST instruction is executed. Therefore, the first machine cycle of the interrupt sequence will be idle and no $\overline{\text{INTA}}$ is issued. The remaining two cycles are identical to that of an INTR interrupt with the supplied instruction being an RST.

It is often desirable to allow the microprocessor to operate in a configuration where more than one module can assume control of the system bus. Exchanges of bus control are essential while performing DMA transfers. During such transfers, an I/O device such as a disk controller becomes master of the bus and transfers data directly to or from memory without the processor's intervention. A bus access is defined as the period of time that a device has exclusive use of the data and address lines in the system bus.

During a DMA transfer, the DMA module sends a hold request for a bus access to the 8085's HOLD pin. The HOLD pin is tested during T_2 and T_4. If a hold request is detected, then after the current bus cycle is completed, the microprocessor returns an HLDA signal and enters the hold state (T_H). During the T_H state, all of the microprocessor's tristate outputs are put in their high-impedance state. Therefore, the bus becomes available for use by the requesting module until the hold request signal is dropped. The timing of a DMA cycle is shown in Fig. 9-10.

9-4 BUS INTERFACE

For the simplest system, the 8085 can be directly connected to memory and I/O devices. Several memory and I/O devices are available that use the same bus structure as that of the 8085; i.e., the data bus and the lower 8 address bits are multiplexed. Use of such devices allows direct connections and thus reduces the chip count of the system. To illustrate how the 8085 could be connected to devices specifically designed for the 8085, a minimum system consisting of three devices is given in Fig. 9-11.

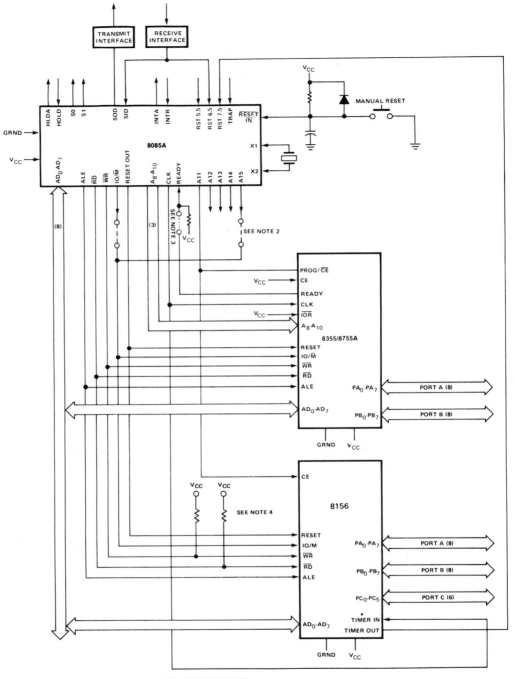

NOTE 1: TRAP, INTR, AND HOLD MUST BE GROUNDED IF THEY AREN'T USED.
NOTE 2: USE IO/M FOR STANDARD I/O MAPPING. USE A15 FOR MEMORY MAPPED I/O.
NOTE 3. CONNECTION IS NECESSARY ONLY IF ONE T$_{WAIT}$ STATE IS DESIRED.
NOTE 4: PULL-UP RESISTORS RECOMMENDED TO AVOID SPURIOUS SELECTION WHEN $\overline{RD}$ AND $\overline{WR}$ ARE
        3-STATED.

Figure 9-11 Minimum system configuration. (Reprinted by permission of Intel Corporation, Copyright 1983.)

298

The 8355 is an integrated memory and I/O device that contains 2K bytes of ROM and two parallel I/O ports. The two I/O ports are programmed through four I/O registers that are selected by AD_1 and AD_0 while $IO/\overline{M}$ is high. The 8156 consists of 256 bytes of RAM, three parallel I/O ports, and a programmable timer. In this case, AD_2, AD_1, and AD_0 (while $IO/\overline{M}$ is high) are used to select the I/O registers.

For the design given in Fig. 9-11, address bit A_{11} selects either the 8355 (A_{11} = 0) or the 8156 (A_{11} = 1). Therefore, the 2K ROM of the 8355 is accessed as memory locations 0 through 2047. On the other hand, the 256-byte RAM occupies locations 2048 to 2303. During an I/O instruction, the I/O port address is sent by the 8085 on both the upper and lower 8 address bits. Since A_{11} corresponds to the fourth I/O port address bit, the internal registers of the 8355 are accessible as I/O ports 0 to 3. For the 8156, its I/O registers occupy port addresses 8 through 15.

Serial data transfer is accomplished by the 8085 itself through the SOD and SID pins. A CRT terminal can be connected to this system through the transmitter and receiver interface. Also shown in this example is how to connect the READY input to the 8085. For a device that is fast enough, the READY pin can be connected to a pull-up resistor to eliminate the wait state. For a slow device, this pin should also be connected to the tristate ready output pin of the device (or ready logic, which generates a ready signal for the device). Another method is to include a circuit to insert a wait state(s) in each bus cycle to accommodate slow devices.

The complexity of the system bus and the required logic surrounding the microprocessor can vary widely, depending on the system requirements. Although the simple configuration discussed above consists of only two devices in addition to the microprocessor, the application of this system is very limited. First, for most memory and I/O devices, the address and data are not multiplexed. This requires a separate data bus from the address bus. Second, the data bus is not buffered, thus limiting the number of devices in the system to be very small. Third, the system lacks the capability of handling interrupts and DMA and provides only limited expansion.

A complex microcomputer system may include bus control logic, which generates the handshaking signals to ensure proper data transfer to or from the 8085. Typically, the bus control logic must be capable of performing the following functions:

1. Interfacing the microprocessor to the system bus for gating data on and off the data lines and for placing addresses on the address lines.
2. Resolving the priority of simultaneous interrupt requests and generating the interrupt signal to the microprocessor.
3. Handling exchanges of bus control between the microprocessor and DMA modules which are capable of acquiring control of the system bus.

A block diagram of the bus control logic in a typical 8085-based microcomputer is

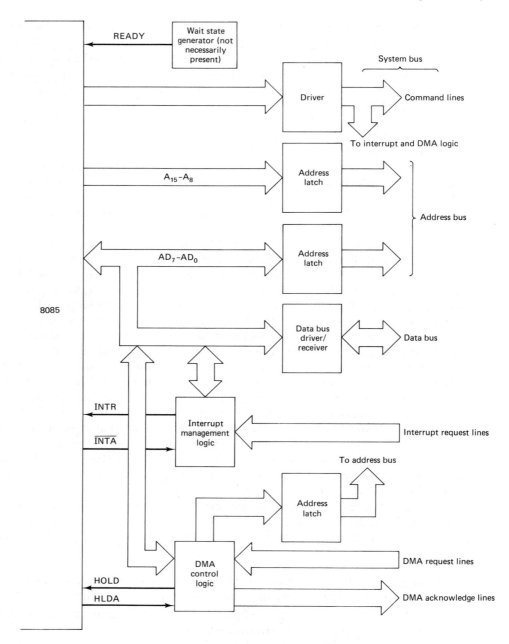

Figure 9-12   Bus interface logic.

shown in Fig. 9-12.   Each block will be further examined in the following three sections.

9-5 BUS TRANSCEIVERS AND LATCHES

Most microcomputers are constructed around a single common system bus.   Various memory and I/O device modules are connected to the common system bus, but the microprocessor's output driving capability is sufficient only for small systems in which memory size and I/O requirements are minimal and the entire system is contained on a single printed circuit (PC) board.   Thus a more typical system requires bus drivers to support memory and I/O device interfaces that are likely to be on separate boards.   On the other hand, receivers are used to increase noise immunity and to reduce input loading.

The Intel 8286 is an 8-bit bidirectional bus driver/receiver, or transceiver, specifically designed to provide additional driving capability.   As shown in Fig. 9-13, for each of the 8 bits there are two separate tristate gates: one serves as a receiver and the other as a driver.   A tristate gate has the ability to be forced into a high-impedance mode and be effectively removed from the circuit.   The 8286 is symmetric with respect to its two sets of data pins—either the pins A_7–A_0 can be the inputs and B_7–B_0 the outputs, or vice versa.   When the output enable ($\overline{OE}$) is high, the output of each gate is forced to the high-impedance state (disabled) so that data cannot flow in either direction.   When it is low, the device is selected (enabled) and the direction of the data flow is determined by the transmit (T) pin.

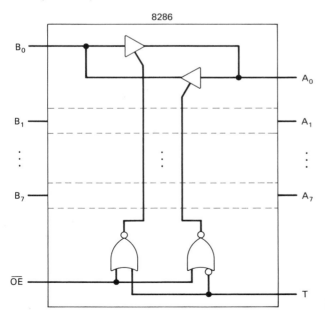

Figure 9-13 Internal logic of an 8286.

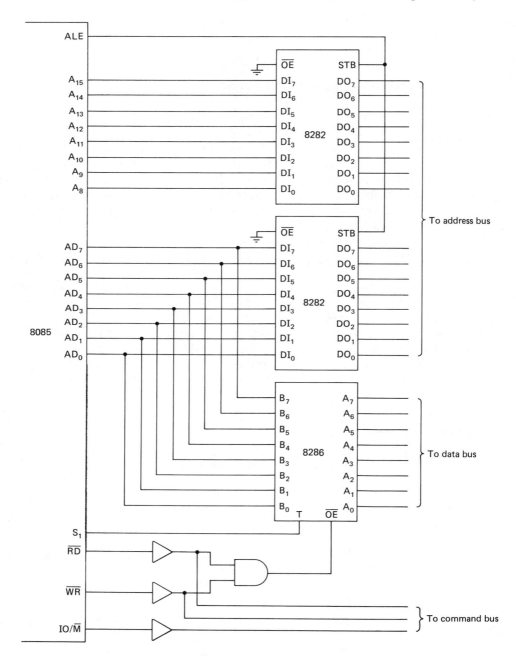

Figure 9-14 Interface between the 8085 and system address and data buses.

A high on the T control pin causes A_7-A_0 to be the inputs and a low on T results in B_7-B_0 being the inputs.

In addition to data tranceivers, the interface of the 8085 to the system bus requires address latches. This is because standard memory devices use separate data and address buses. For the 8085, the lower 8 address bits are available only during T_1 of a bus cycle. Address latches are required so that a full 16-bit address is available during the entire bus cycle. The Intel 8282 and 8212 devices are typical 8-bit latches.

An interface of the 8085 to the system data and address buses using the Intel 8286 and 8282 devices is shown in Fig. 9-14. Two 8282s are used to provide a 16-bit address. The upper one serves as a buffer for $A_{15}-A_8$. For the 8282, a trailing edge on the strobe (STB) pin latches the bits applied to the input data pins DI_7-DI_0. Therefore, STB is connected to the 8085's ALE pin and DI_7-DI_0 are connected to eight of the address pins. An active low signal on pin $\overline{OE}$ enables the latch's outputs DO_7-DO_0, and a high on this pin forces the outputs into their high-impedance state. For a system that does not include a DMA controller, this pin is grounded. Otherwise, it should be controlled by the DMA controller (discussed in Section 9-7) to let a DMA device have access to the address bus.

As can be seen in Fig. 9-14, the T control pin of the 8286 is connected to 8085's S_1 pin to specify the data flow direction. Status bit S_1 indicates whether the 8085 is in the input mode ($S_1 = 1$) or in the output mode ($S_1 = 0$), and this signal is available during the entire bus cycle. The $\overline{OE}$ pin is activated by the $\overline{RD}$ or $\overline{WR}$ command. This configuration assumes that during an INTR interrupt, the interrupt management logic places an instruction directly on the AD_7-AD_0 pins instead of the data bus. Otherwise, the $\overline{OE}$ pin should also be enabled by the $\overline{INTA}$ signal. Note that while the 8085 is in the hold state, both ports A and B of the 8286 should be in their high-impedance state.

Sometimes a system bus is designed in a way that the address and/or data signals are inverted. Both the 8282 and 8286 have companion chips that are the same as the 8282 and 8286 except that they are faster and cause an inversion between their inputs and outputs. The companion for the 8282 is the 8283 and the companion for the 8286 is the 8287.

9-6 INTERRUPT PRIORITY MANAGEMENT

The 8085 provides four maskable interrupt request pins: RST 5.5, RST 6.5, RST 7.5, and INTR. An RST interrupt always causes an internal restart instruction to be executed and therefore, an RST pin normally is not shared by more than one device. However, the INTR pin can serve several interrupting devices if the system requires it. This is because, during an INTR interrupt, the 8085 can input a restart instruction from the interrupting device. As discussed in Chapter 8, the source of the request can be identified by using the 3-bit vector in the instruction as a pointer to a branch instruction that branches to the starting address of the service

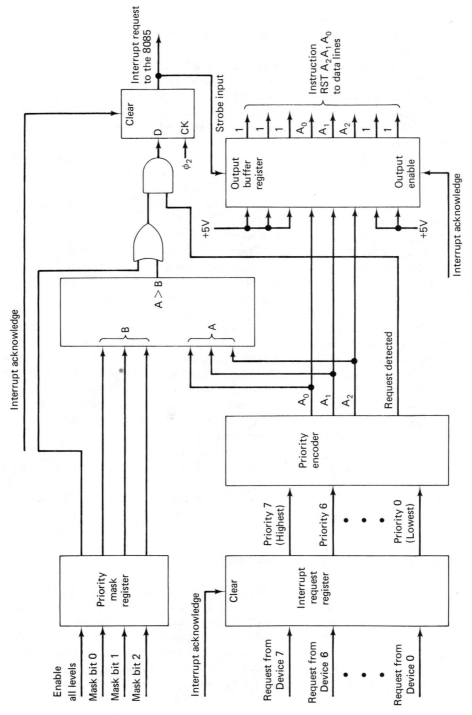

Figure 9-15 Priority-vectored interrupt management logic.

routine. Alternatively, a priority-vectored interrupt management facility could assign the interrupt vector. For the INTR interrupts such an interrupt facility is normally limited to eight levels because of the fact that only 3 bits are reserved to indicate the interrupt vector in a restart instruction. Figure 9-15 shows the major logic needed to provide an eight-level priority-vectored interrupt facility.

An I/O device may request an interrupt at any time by applying a signal to its interrupt request line. The request is then strobed into and stored in the interrupt request register. If more than 1 bit of this register is set to 1, the priority encoder determines which one has the highest priority and encodes it into a 3-bit vector $A_2A_1A_0$ that represents the priority level of the request being chosen. If no request is made, the priority encoder's request detected output line is 0, and this prohibits an interrupt request from being sent to the 8085. A request will cause a restart instruction having $A_2A_1A_0$ as its operand to be generated and stored in the output buffer register. Once the interrupt request is accepted by the 8085, the microprocessor returns the interrupt acknowledge signal, indicating that it is ready to input and execute the instruction supplied by the interrupt management logic. The contents of the output buffer are then placed on the data lines and the microprocessor begins its interrupt sequence at eight times $A_2A_1A_0$.

When interrupt nesting (interrupts within interrupts) is permitted, it is desirable to have a priority mask that can be set under program control. (See Section 8-4.) This allows the interrupt service routine to change the priority of interrupts permitted within the service routine. As shown in the top part of Fig. 9-15, the programmable mask is implemented by adding a priority mask register and a comparator to the priority-vectored interrupt management logic. The priority mask register is treated as an I/O port so that a 3-bit mask can be written into this register by an output instruction. The interrupt vector generated from the priority encoder is fed into the comparator through lines A and the mask is fed into the comparator through lines B. If an interrupt has a priority higher than the mask, the interrupt flip-flop is set; otherwise, the request is ignored. A fourth output bit from the priority mask register is needed to recognize the interrupt with the lowest priority level (level 0). If this bit is 1, it overrides the output of the comparator. Once the request is acknowledged, the interrupt request flip-flop and interrupt request register are cleared and the RST $A_2A_1A_0$ instruction is input and executed by the microprocessor.

Intel has made available a device called a programmable interrupt controller (8259A) that greatly simplifies the implementation of interrupt priority management logic. When used in an 8085-based system, this device generates a 3-byte subroutine call instruction in response to an interrupt acknowledge. This feature eliminates the restriction associated with the restart instruction that the interrupt vector address must be 0, 8, 16, . . . , or 56. This device can also be programmed to support more advanced microprocessors such as the 8086, and can support a cascade configuration in which more than one 8259A is tied together to provide up to 64 interrupt request lines. However, we limit the discussion here to a single

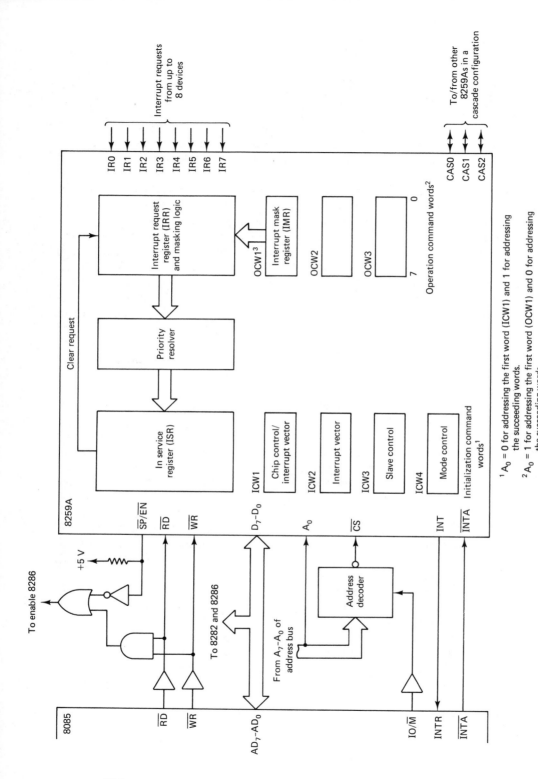

Figure 9-16 Organization of the 8259A programmable interrupt controller.

8259A in an 8085-based system.   Figure 9-16 shows the organization of the 8259A and how to connect it to an 8085.

When an interrupt request(s) has been received, it is first latched into the interrupt request register.   If the corresponding mask bit in the interrupt mask register is 1, the request is blocked.   Otherwise, it is passed on to the priority resolver, which determines which unmasked request has the highest priority, and then an interrupt request is sent to the 8085.

Assuming that the INTE flag of the 8085 is set, the CPU will enter its interrupt sequence at the completion of the current instruction.   During the interrupt sequence the 8085 sends out an $\overline{\text{INTA}}$ pulse, which causes the 8259A to set the corresponding in-service bit in ISR and clear the corresponding IRR bit and place the op code of the CALL instruction on the data bus.   Since the 8085 recognizes that a call instruction has 3 bytes, it initiates two additional $\overline{\text{INTA}}$ pulses to input the operand of the call instruction from the 8259A.

Once an ISR bit is set, it prevents any interrupt request of a lower priority from being passed to the 8085.   If the automatic end of interrupt mode is selected (i.e., AEOI bit in ICW4 is 1), the ISR bit is cleared by the third $\overline{\text{INTA}}$ pulse. Otherwise, it remains set until it is specifically cleared by sending an end of interrupt (EOI) command to the OCW2 register in the interrupt service routine.

The 8259A has seven programmable registers with each having 8 bits.   These registers are divided into two groups; one group contains the initialization command words (ICWs) and the other group contains the operation command words (OCWs). The initialization command words are normally set by an initialization routine when the microcomputer system is first brought up and remain constant throughout its operation.   By contrast, the operation command words are used to dynamically control the processing of interrupts.

The 8259A has an even address ($A_0 = 0$) and an odd address ($A_0 = 1$) associated with it and the initialization command words must be filled consecutively by using the even address for ICW1 and the odd address for the remaining ICWs.

The definitions of the bits in ICW1 are

BITS 7-5—Used only in an 8080 or 8085-based system.   As mentioned before, during an interrupt, the 8259A supplies a call instruction.   The subroutine address, i.e., the operand of the call instruction, has 2 bytes, $A_{15}-A_0$.   Bits $A_{15}-A_8$ are always taken from OCW2.   When bit 2 (ADI) of the ICW1 is 1, address bits A_7-A_5 are taken from bits 7−5 of the ICW1 and A_4-A_0 are set to N × 4, where N corresponds to the request level, IRN.   When ADI = 0, address bits A_7 and A_6 are taken from bits 7 and 6 of the ICW1 and A_5-A_0 are set to N × 8.

BIT 4—Always set to 1.   It directs the received byte to ICW1 as opposed to OCW2 or OCW3, which also use the even address (A0 = 0).

BIT 3 (LTIM)—Determines whether the edge-triggered mode (LTIM = 0) or the level-triggered mode (LTIM = 1) is to be used.   The edge-triggered mode causes the IRR bit to be cleared when the corresponding ISR bit is set.

Bɪт 2 (ADI)—Specifies the subroutine address interval.   If set to 1, the interval = 4, i.e., 4 bytes between the subroutine addresses of consecutive request levels. Otherwise interval = 8.

Bɪт 1 (SNGL)—Indicates whether or not the 8259A is cascaded with other 8259As. SNGL = 1 when only one 8259A is in the interrupt system.

Bɪт 0 (IC4)—Is set to 1 if an ICW4 is to be output to during the initialization sequence.   Otherwise, the contents of ICW4 are cleared.

ICW2 is to be initialized to store the most significant byte of the call address. ICW3 is used only for a multiple 8259A configuration.   When the SNGL bit in the ICW1 is set to 1, ICW3 will not be input by the 8259A.

ICW4 is output to only if bit 0 (IC4) of ICW1 is set to 1.   The bits in ICW4 are defined as follows:

Bɪт 7-5—Always set to 0.

Bɪт 4 (SFNM)—If set to 1, the special fully nested mode is used.   This mode is utilized in systems having more than one 8259A.

Bɪт 3 (BUF)—BUF = 1 indicates that the $\overline{SP/EN}$ is to be used as an output to disable the system's 8286 transceivers while the CPU inputs data from the 8259A.   If no transceivers are present, BUF should be set to 0 and, in systems involving only one 8259A, a 1 should be applied to the $\overline{SP/EN}$ pin.

Bɪт 2 (M/S)—This bit is ignored if BUF = 0.   For a system having only one 8259A, this bit should be 1; otherwise, it should be 1 for the master and 0 for the slaves.

Bɪт 1 (AEOI)—If AEOI = 1, then the ISR bit that caused the interrupt is cleared at the end of the third $\overline{INTA}$ pulse.

Bɪт 0 (μPM)—μPM = 0 indicates the 8259A is in an 8080- or 8085-based system. This bit being 1 implies an 8086/8088 system.

A typical program sequence for setting the contents of the ICWs, which assumes that the even address of the 8259A is 20, is

```
MVI        A,57H
OUT        20H
MVI        A,10H
OUT        21H
MVI        A,0CH
OUT        21H
```

The first two instructions cause the requests to be edge-triggered, indicate that only one 8259A is being used, and inform the 8259A that an ICW4 will be output.   The next two instructions set ICW2 to 10.   In conjunction with ICW1, it causes the eight request levels to generate calls to eight locations equally spaced at intervals of four starting at location 1040.   ICW3 is not output to because SNGL = 1; therefore, the last two instructions set ICW4 to 0C, which informs the 8259A that the special fully nested mode is not to be used, the $\overline{\text{SP}/\text{EN}}$ is used to disable transceivers, the 8259A is a master, EOI commands must be used to clear ISR bits, and the 8259A is part of an 8080- or 8085-based system.

There are three OCWs. The command word OCW1 is used for masking interrupt requests; when the mask bit corresponding to an interrupt request is 1, then the request is blocked. OCW2 and OCW3 are for controlling the mode of the 8259A and receiving EOI commands. A byte is output to OCW1 by using the odd address associated with the 8259A and bytes are output to OCW2 and OCW3 by using the even addresses. OCW2 is distinguished from OCW3 by the contents of bit 3 of the data byte. If bit 3 is 0, the byte is put in OCW2, and if it is 1, it is put in OCW3. Both OCW2 and OCW3 are distinguished from ICW1, which also uses the even address, by bit 4 of the data. If bit 4 is 0, then the byte is put in OCW2 or OCW3 according to bit 3. There is no ambiguity in ICW2, ICW3, ICW4, and OCW1 all using the odd address because the initialization words must always follow ICW1 as dictated by the initialization sequence, and an output to OCW1 cannot occur in the middle of this sequence.

Figure 9-17a shows the format of OCW2. Bits 7–5 specify an operation. If the SL bit = 1, bits 2–0 specifies the IR level to be acted on by the operation. Otherwise, the operation does not require an IR level being specified. Two types of EOI commands are available: specific EOI, which clears the IR bit as specified by bits 2–0, and nonspecific EOI, which clears the nonzero IR bit of the highest priority. The other operation is to change the priority levels associated with the request lines. Normally IR0 has the highest priority and IR7 the lowest. Priority can be rearranged in two ways. One is to assign the highest priority to the IR level specified by L2, L1, and L0. The other way is through rotation, which rotates the priorities so that after being serviced a request line receives the lowest priority. For example, assume that the current ISR contains 00100100 and IR0 has the highest priority. Then after a rotate command is sent to OCW2 and the request on IR2 is recognized, bit 2 of ISR is cleared and the new priorities are

IR3	IR4	IR5	IR6	IR7	IR0	IR1	IR2
(Highest)							(Lowest)

The command word format of OCW3 is given in Fig. 9-17b. Bits 6 and 5 are for enabling and disabling the special mask mode. If a byte is sent to OCW3 in which both ESMM and SMM are set to 1, then unmasked interrupt requests are processed as they arrive (provided that the processor's INTE flag is 1) and the priority order is ignored. By subsequently sending a byte to OCW3 in which ESMM = 1 and SMM = 0, a switch back to the priority ordering of interrupts can be made. If a byte with the ESMM bit equal to 0 is sent to OCW3, then the SMM bit will have no effect and the special mask mode will not change.

The P (polling) bit is used to place the 8259A in polling mode. This mode assumes that the CPU is not accepting interrupts (INTE = 0) and an input instruction is used to determine which interrupt device is to be serviced. When the P bit is 1 the next $\overline{\text{RD}}$ signal would cause the appropriate bit in the ISR to be set

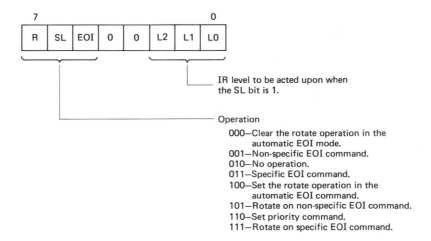

(a) OCW2

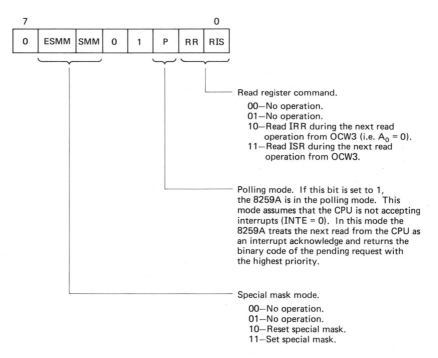

(b) OCW3

Figure 9-17   Formats of the OCW2 and OCW3.

just as if $\overline{\text{INTA}}$ signal had been received, and would return to the A register in the 8085 a byte of the form

I	—	—	—	—	W2	W1	W0

where $I = 1$ indicates that an interrupt is present and W2, W1, and W0 give the IR level of the highest-priority interrupt. For example, if $P = 1$, the priority ordering is

$$\text{IR3, IR4, IR5, IR6, IR7, IR0, IR1, IR2}$$

there are unmasked interrupts on IR4 and IR1, and the instruction

$$\text{IN} \qquad 80\text{H}$$

(where 80 is the even address of the 8259A) is executed, then

1	—	—	—	—	1	0	0

is input to the A register.

When $P = 0$, bits 1 and 0 of the OCW3 allow the programmer to examine the contents of the interrupt request register or the interrupt service register by inputting from OCW3. Note that the contents of IMR can always be read by using the odd address of the 8259A.

9-7 DMA CONTROLLER

In order for the system to include more than one device capable of performing DMA transfers, control logic is required to resolve simultaneous DMA requests. This logic is normally implemented based on an LSI device called a DMA controller. A typical example of DMA controller is the 8237. As discussed in Section 8-5, the device has four pairs of DMA request and acknowledge pins. Therefore, by adding an 8237 to the system, it can provide DMA transfers for up to 4 peripheral devices.

Figure 9-18 gives a configuration of an 8085-based system that includes an 8237. The DMA controller is connected to the system address and data buses. Bus control exchange between the 8085 and 8237 is communicated by the HOLD/ HLDA signals. Because the CPU needs to access the 8237 to initiate a block transfer and to check its status, the device can act as a slave just like other I/O devices. When $\overline{\text{CS}}$, which is connected to an address decoder, and HRQ are both low, the device becomes a slave. As a slave, it responds to I/O read ($\overline{\text{IOR}}$) and I/O write ($\overline{\text{IOW}}$) commands and accepts address bits A_3–A_0 to select the internal register to be accessed.

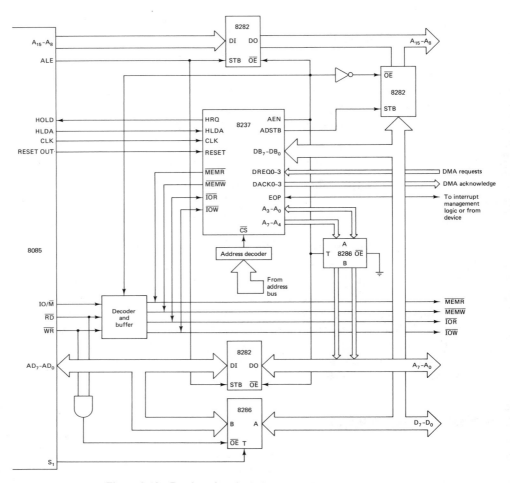

Figure 9-18 Bus interface including an 8237 DMA controller.

During a DMA transfer, the 8237 becomes the bus master. For each DMA transfer cycle, the 8237 activates the $\overline{IOR}$ and $\overline{MEMW}$ simultaneously, for an I/O-to-memory operation, or $\overline{IOW}$ and $\overline{MEMR}$ for a memory-to-I/O operation. Therefore, the $\overline{IOR}$ and $\overline{IOW}$ are bidirectional pins, and $\overline{MEMR}$ and $\overline{MEMW}$ are output pins. Because these signals do not match with the $\overline{RD}$, $\overline{WR}$, and $IO/\overline{M}$ signals output by the 8085, decoding logic such as that shown in Fig. 9-19 is needed to perform the translation between the two sets of signals. During a DMA cycle, the output of this decoder is disabled by the AEN signal in order to let the 8237 issue bus commands. Of course, the memory and I/O interfaces in the system must be designed so that they respond to $\overline{MEMR}$, $\overline{MEMW}$, $\overline{IOR}$, and $\overline{IOW}$ instead of $\overline{RD}$, $\overline{WR}$, and $IO/\overline{M}$.

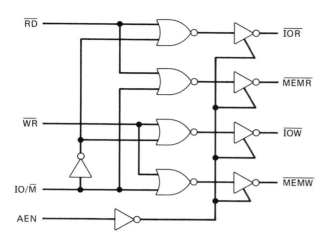

Figure 9-19   Command decoder.

As a bus master during a DMA transfer cycle, the 8237 must supply a 16-bit memory address. It puts the low-order byte of the address on pins A_7–A_0 and sets AEN to 1 during the entire bus cycle. The upper address byte is sent out via pins DB_7–DB_0 along with a pulse on the address strobe (ADSTB) pin at the beginning of the DMA cycle. As shown in Fig. 9-18, the ADSTB signal should be used to strobe the upper 8 address bits into an 8282 latch connected to the A_{15}–A_8 address lines. The AEN signal is used to disable the 8085 from the command bus and to disable the outputs of the two address latches, which are connected to the 8085. An active AEN signal also enables the 8282 address latch and the 8286 transceiver connected to the controller. This allows the address generated by the 8237 to be placed on the address bus. During a DMA cycle, the 8085 is also logically disconnected from the data bus because both $\overline{WR}$ and $\overline{RD}$ signals are high.

The $\overline{EOP}$ pin may be connected to the interrupt management logic. In such a configuration, at the end of a block transfer, an interrupt request will be sent to the 8085. When connected to a peripheral device, this pin allows an external signal to terminate a DMA operation.

9-8   SYSTEM BUS STRUCTURE

As discussed earlier in this chapter, for reasons of simplicity, flexibility, and low cost, most microcomputers are constructed around a single system bus. If the modules are on separate PC boards with the same number of edge pins, which is usually the case, the bus construction is such that any module can be physically plugged into any edge connector on the bus. Physically, a system bus is a group of bidirectional lines that connect the edge connectors together. A system bus is normally implemented either by multiconductor flexible cables or by heavy conducting strips etched on a backpanel. A major advantage of using flexible cables is that modules may be placed anywhere within a reasonable range to accommodate various spacing and heat-dissipation requirements. In addition, it is very easy to expand the system by adding cable and edge connectors. The second method is particularly suitable for low-cost mass production. However, a back plane requires that all modules in the system must reside in the same chassis.

Although the implementation is straightforward, the number of lines included in a system bus and the exact definitions of the lines have not been standardized. Various companies design their microcomputer systems using buses with different line assignments or even different numbers of bus lines. This prevents the system components, such as memory modules and interfaces for commonly used peripherals that are designed for one system, from being directly plugged into another system.

Among the various buses being used, a popular one for the early personal microcomputer products, is the *S-100 bus*, which consists of 100 lines. Many manufacturers based their designs on the S-100 bus, but only some of the 100 lines are used in a standard way; the remainder are either not used or are assigned to special control functions associated with the individual product. The 100 lines included in the S-100 bus are more than adequate for microprocessor-based systems. A special committee of the Institute of Electrical and Electronics Engineers (IEEE) proposed a definition for 93 out of 100 lines. These 93 lines are defined according to their function, position (pin number), polarity, and timing. The other 7 lines may be assigned for individual applications or for future expansion. Even with 93 lines, the bus provides many features that may not all be required for most systems. The defined lines can be grouped as follows:

DATA—Sixteen bidirectional data lines are allocated to support a 16-bit microprocessor or DMA device. An 8-bit device can use the least significant 8 bits for output and the other 8 bits for input.

ADDRESS—Sixteen lines are dedicated to providing a standard memory space of 64K bytes. However, eight more lines are reserved to specify 8 extended address bits. This extension feature allows the system to address up to 16 megabytes.

INTERRUPT—Eight bus lines are reserved for vectored interrupts to provide eight levels of request priority.

STATUS—Eight status signals are specified. They consist of instruction fetch, memory read, memory write, input, output, interrupt acknowledge, halt acknowledge, and request for a 16-bit data transfer.

CONTROL SIGNALS—A total of 11 lines is reserved to carry handshaking and control signals. These signals are used for data transfer during any bus cycle, indication of the beginning of a bus cycle, request of maskable and non-maskable interrupts, and so on.

DMA CONTROL—In order to include a DMA module or other processor modules in the system, eight lines are assigned for bus control exchange. These signals primarily allow a DMA module to gain control of data, address, status, and handshaking lines.

MISCELLANEOUS CONTROL—Nine lines are reserved for various purposes, such as clock, memory inhibit, master reset, power failure, and so on.

POWER and GROUND—Nine lines are used to provide the various power supply voltages and grounds.

9-9 *THE DAISY-CHAIN PRIORITY STRUCTURE*

Section 9-6 discussed a parallel scheme to resolve simultaneous interrupt requests based on their priorities. Although the highest priority is determined with a minimal delay, the system bus must have several interrupt request lines, one for each priority level. In addition, the number of interrupting devices allowed for such a system is restricted by the number of interrupt request lines. There is another commonly used scheme to determine the priority which is serial in nature. A single interrupt request line actually passes through each device and forms a serial priority structure called a *daisy chain*. The priority is determined by the physical location of each device. The one located closest to the processor has the highest priority.

In a daisy-chain priority structure, each interface module contains a network that is inserted into the daisy-chain. As shown in Fig. 9-20, each of these networks has two inputs, one of which is the interrupt request from the device and the other is the output of the next-higher-priority network in the chain. For the highest-priority module, the second input is the interrupt acknowledge signal from the processor.

If there is at least one device requesting service, an interrupt request is sent to the processor. The interrupt acknowledge from the processor propagates through each priority network until it encounters the one whose interrupt input is 1. The inverted interrupt input is ANDed with the interrupt acknowledge line, and therefore the interrupt acknowledge signal is blocked from propagating to the next lower device. Since both the interrupt and interrupt acknowledge signals are 1 at this point, the AND of the two signals will cause a 1 to be sent to the device's interrupt control logic, which will place an interrupt vector on the data bus. Devices with a lower priority (i.e., farther down the daisy chain) will not see the interrupt acknowledge even if they have also requested an interrupt. However, once the interrupt request from the higher-priority device has been serviced (or, more specifically, interrupts have been reenabled by an EI instruction), the interrupt request from the lower-priority device will be recognized.

There are two advantages to the daisy-chain priority structure. First, only one interrupt request line is needed in the system bus, provided that each individual request has an open collector output. Second, a new module with any desired priority can be added into the system simply by inserting the module into the proper

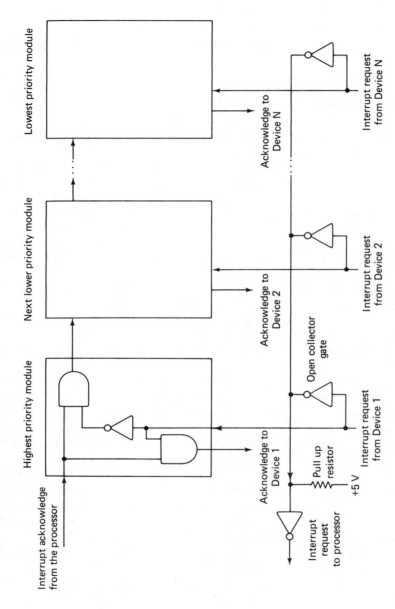

Figure 9-20 Daisy-chain structure.

physical position. The number of devices that can be included in the system is limited only by the number of interrupt vectors. Obviously, the priority associated with each device is not programmable. Another drawback is that priority masking cannot be implemented with daisy-chaining alone. An interrupt structure with a combination of both daisy-chaining and parallel interrupt priority management logic is commonly used by minicomputers.

9-10 MC6809 HARDWARE INTERRUPT ENHANCEMENTS

Because during an interrupt sequence the MC6809 does not input a vector from the interrupt device, the source of the request is not identified. Without adding hardware support, this type of interrupt structure can support more than one device only through a polling scheme such as the one described in Chapter 8. However, a vectored interrupt can be added to an MC6809-based system with the logic shown in Fig. 9-21. The interrupt request issued by a device is sent to a priority encoder that determines which request has the highest priority. It then encodes the request into an 8-bit vector 000XXX00 and signals the processor via the $\overline{IRQ}$ line. This vector is then stored in an addressable register and can be read and cleared by the processor. More than eight priority levels can be handled by this arrangement if the upper 3 bits of the vector register are also used.

The initialization portion of the service routine will first input the vector and place it in the index register. Then a branch instruction uses a branch table and the indexed addressing mode to branch to the service routine associated with the

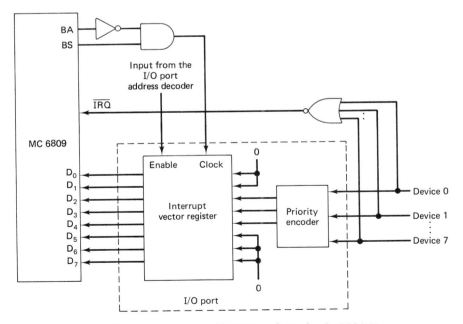

Figure 9-21 Priority-vectored interrupt scheme for the MC6809.

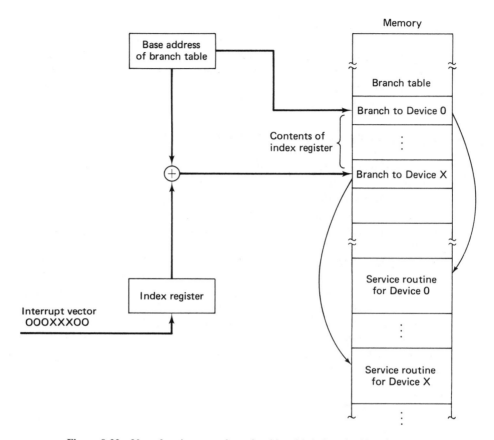

Figure 9-22   Use of an interrupt branch table with indexed addressing mode.

interrupting device.   For example, the instruction

```
JMP         BRTABL,X
```

where X indicates the indexed addressing mode, will branch to the address that
results from adding BRTABL to the contents of the index register.   As a result,
different points in the branch table will be entered, depending on the vector
000XXX00, which is unique to each device.   A branch instruction that leads to
the desired service routine is stored in each entry in the branch table.   The entire
process is illustrated in Fig. 9-22.   Because a branch instruction is 3 bytes long,
the lower 2 bits of a vector must be zero in order to reserve 4 bytes between
consecutive entry points.

Also, Motorola has made available the MC6828 LSI device to support priority-
vectored interrupts for the MC6800 microprocessor family.   This device, called
the priority interrupt controller (PIC), provides eight interrupt request inputs and

can be expanded to more interrupt requests by cascading PICs.   The PIC generates a modified address to a ROM, which is connected to the PIC and, in response to an interrupt request, the microprocessor branches to the corresponding service routine.   The device also allows the user to program a mask level.   Any interrupt requests with priorities lower than this mask level will be ignored.

Reset of an MC6809 is controlled by the RESET pin.   A request on this line causes the processor to execute the routine whose address is stored at FFFE and FFFF.   Unlike an interrupt, the machine state is not saved.

BIBLIOGRAPHY

1. *The MCS-80/85 Family User's Manual* (Santa Clara, Calif.: Intel Corporation, 1983).
2. *Microsystem Components Handbook, Vol. I* (Santa Clara, Calif.: Intel Corporation, 1985).
3. SHORT, KENNETH L., *Microprocessors and Programmed Logic* (Englewood Cliffs, N.J.: Prentice-Hall, 1981).
4. LIU, YU-CHENG, and GLENN A. GIBSON, *Microcomputer Systems: The 8086/8088 Family— Architecture, Programming, and Design,* 2nd ed.   (Englewood Cliffs, N.J.: Prentice-Hall, 1986).
5. *Motorola Microprocessors Data Manual* (Phoenix, Ariz.: Motorola, Inc., 1981).
6. LEVENTHAL, LANCE A., *6809 Assembly Language Programming* (Berkeley, Calif.: Osborne/McGraw-Hill, 1981).
7. ELMQUIST, KELLS A., HOWARD FULLMER, DAVID B. GUSTAVSON, and GEORGE MORROW, "Standard Specification for S-100 Bus Interface Devices," *Computer,* 12, no. 7 (July 1979), 28–52.

EXERCISES

1. Draw a timing diagram for an I/O read bus cycle with one wait state.   In the timing diagram also specify the outputs for the $IO/\overline{M}$, S_1 and S_0 pins.
2. Referring to Fig. 8-16, determine the total execution time for the first six instructions in the routine.   Assume a 6 MHz clock with no wait states.
3. Referring to Fig. 8-16, determine the total number of bus cycles that will occur during the execution of the first six instructions in the routine.   How many of them are memory reference cycles and how many are I/O cycles?
4. Design a priority-vectored interrupt system using a daisy-chain structure for the INTR pin of the 8085.   Assume that the system includes seven interrupting devices, DEV1, . . . , DEV7, which, during the interrupt sequence, place the respective instructions RST 1, . . . , RST 7 on the data bus.
5. Could a daisy-chain structure be used to provide a priority-vectored interrupt capability for the $\overline{IRQ}$ pin of the MC6809 or an RST interrupt pin of the 8085?   Why?

6. Show the interrupt management logic needed to support the polling scheme that uses an interrupt request register (see Section 8-3). Assume that RST 1 is to be issued during an interrupt sequence.

7. Referring to Sec. 9-3, which control or handshaking signals are used to ensure proper data transfer during an I/O write bus cycle? During a memory read bus cycle?

8. Write an initialization sequence for an 8259A, which has an even address of 40H, that will cause the

1. Request to be level-triggered.
2. Subroutine address interval to equal 4.
3. Operands of inserted Calls to start at 0580H.
4. AEOI mode to be used to clear interrupt requests.
5. IMR to be cleared.

9. Write an instruction sequence that will cause the priority of an 8259A, whose even address is 40H, to be IR4, IR5, IR6, IR7, IR0, IR1, IR2, IR3

10. Give an instruction sequence that will cause the requests on IR2, IR5, and IR6 of an 8259A, whose even address is 40H, to be masked.

11. In Section 9-10, a scheme was presented to provide vectored-interrupt capability for an MC6809-based system. For this scheme, show the necessary MC6809 instructions to implement the initialization portion of the interrupt service routine and to set up the branch table. (See Appendix C.)

12. Another method to provide vectored-interrupt capability for an MC6809-based system involves address modification. During the last step of the maskable interrupt sequence, the MC6809 sends out the addresses FFF8 and FFF9, and inputs the service routine pointer from these two locations. With external logic, parts of the addresses FFF8 and FFF9 can be modified to point to different locations, depending on the interrupting device selected. Show the logic necessary to implement this scheme.

Chapter 10

Input/Output Interfaces

An I/O interface serves as a buffer between the system bus and the peripheral device. This is necessary because the protocol used on the system bus is quite different from that adopted by a particular peripheral. The interface is designed to accept and send signals that are compatible with the bus control logic and timing. By using an I/O interface, a peripheral can be designed independently from the bus structure on which it is to be used. To connect the same peripheral to two different bus structures, only the interface must be redesigned.

An I/O interface must be able to

1. Interpret the address and memory or I/O select signal to determine whether or not it is being referenced and, if so, determine which of its registers is being accessed.
2. Determine whether an input or output is being conducted and accept output data or control information from the bus or place input data or status information on the bus.
3. Input data from or output data to the associated I/O device and convert the data from parallel to the format acceptable to the I/O device, or vice versa.
4. Send a ready signal when data have been accepted from or placed on the data bus, thus informing the processor that a transfer has been completed.
5. Send interrupt requests and, if there is no interrupt priority management in the bus control logic, receive interrupt acknowledgments and, perhaps, send a restart instruction or interrupt pointer.

This chapter covers the design of the interfaces that are most commonly included in microcomputer systems. Various LSI devices that support interface design will be examined as well. The first section discusses the important features of interfaces in general. The next two sections consider serial interfaces and parallel interfaces, respectively. The remaining three sections introduce typical I/O devices such as timers, keyboard/display controllers, and diskette controllers.

10-1 A TYPICAL INTERFACE

A typical I/O interface includes the major logic shown in Fig. 10-1. Data registers serve as temporary storage for the data being transferred. Two data registers, one for input and the other for output, may be needed if the peripheral is capable of both input and output. Although each can be assigned to a different I/O address (i.e., I/O port), a single I/O address can be used to represent both registers because one is read only while the other is write only. The *control register*, which is write only, is used to receive the various commands and other information sent to the peripheral device. In conjunction with the control register, the associated logic regulates the flow of data between the peripheral and the system bus. The *status register*, which is read only, stores the current status of the device (e.g., input data ready, output data register empty, errors detected, etc.) Sometimes the control register and the status register share the same I/O address and are referred to as the *control/status register*.

During an input operation, a data byte is received from the peripheral and stored in the input data register by the control logic. A data ready status is then reported in the status register, which can be examined by the processor. This data byte may then be read to the processor under programmed I/O, as described in Section 8-1. Also, if the interrupt enable bit in the control register is set, the ready data causes an interrupt request. This allows the processor to input data under interrupt I/O, as described in Section 8-2. Output is performed by a similar but reversed sequence. The processor waits until the output data register is empty. This can be detected either by checking the status register or by recognizing an interrupt. A data byte is then sent and stored in the output data register from the CPU. This data byte is transmitted to the peripheral by the control logic whenever the peripheral is ready to accept it.

The implementation of the interface logic requires many logic gates, flip-flops, registers, and so on. However, several standard LSI interface devices have been made available by different companies. An interface design is therefore significantly simplified by using an LSI interface device as the heart and adding the necessary surrounding logic. The surrounding logic consists of two parts: the interface to the system bus and the interface to the peripheral. The first part is independent of the peripheral and will be examined in the remainder of this section.

Although the pins of an interface device vary from one device to the next, the following pins are common to most interface devices:

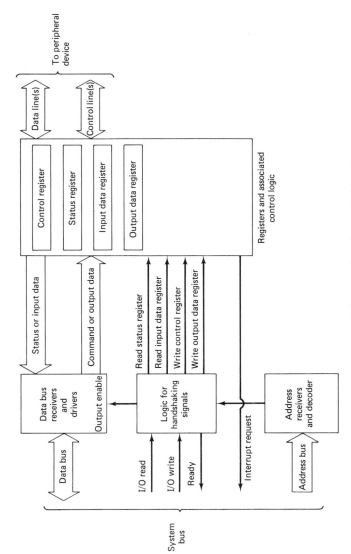

Figure 10-1 Layout of the major logic in a typical interface.

DATA PINS—They are bidirectional tristate pins to provide input or output.

$\overline{\text{RD}}$ (READ) PIN—An active signal on this pin indicates that the CPU is reading data or status from the device. An $\overline{\text{RD}}$ signal enables the data pins for output.

$\overline{\text{WR}}$ (WRITE) PIN—An active signal on this pin indicates that the CPU is writing data or a command to the device. The $\overline{\text{WR}}$ signal causes the device to input data from its data pins.

$\overline{\text{CS}}$ (CHIP SELECT) PIN—A low on this pin selects the device. If the device is not selected, reading or writing cannot be performed and the data pins will be in their high-impedance state.

REGISTER SELECT PINS—These pins are used during a read or write operation to select an internal register to read from or write to.

Some devices may also include an interrupt request pin that may be identified as a ready status pin and/or a reset pin to reset the device to an initial state.

Figure 10-2 illustrates the major logic of an interface using an LSI device. A typical interface device includes tristate data pins so that they can be connected

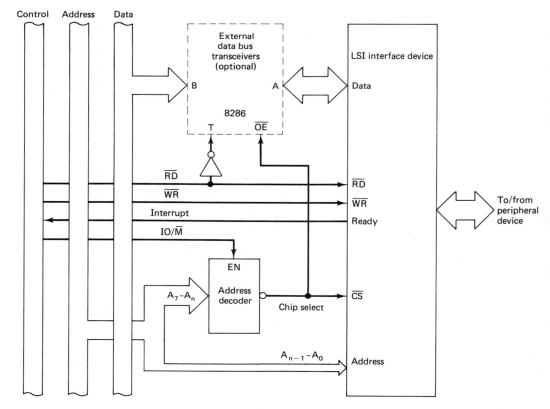

Figure 10-2   Typical I/O interface using an LSI interface device.

directly to the data bus. This configuration is applicable for small single-board systems. For multiboard systems, external transceivers are typically inserted as a data bus interface to reduce the bus loading. The data transceivers are enabled when the chip select signal becomes active. If they are enabled, they act as drivers during a read operation and receivers during a write operation.

The address bus interface requires address decoding logic. Because there are many I/O interface modules connected to the system bus, and each data, status, or control register on an interface module has a different address, a decoder is required to determine which register is addressed by the current I/O instruction.

As shown in Fig. 10-2, the upper part of the address, bits A_7–A_n, are fed into an address decoder that determines if the interface device is referenced. The decoder is enabled only when $IO/\overline{M} = 1$, indicating that A_7–A_0 represent an I/O address. The low-order address bits can be directly sent to the address pins of the device for selecting an internal register during a read or write operation. This technique requires that the interface device be assigned a consecutive block of I/O ports. In addition, the lowest address of the assigned block must be divisible by 2^n, where n is the number of address pins. For example, if there are two registers A and B that can be read from and two registers C and D that can be written into, then the read and write signals and bit 0 of the address bus could be used to specify the register as follows:

Write	Read	Address bit 0	Register being accessed
0	1	0	A
0	1	1	B
1	0	0	C
1	0	1	D

Therefore, registers A and C are referenced with an even address, and registers B and D must have the next odd address.

An address decoder can be easily implemented with an AND gate, as shown in Fig. 10-3a. In this example, the internal registers of the device are to be accessed as I/O ports from C4 through C7. The disadvantage of this approach is that the wiring must be modified if the port addresses assigned to the device are to be changed due to a system modification. A more flexible approach is to use a comparator, as illustrated in Fig. 10-3b. The received address bits are fed directly into the comparator, which includes jumpers or switches that designate the bit pattern to be matched. By removing or installing jumpers or by changing switch positions, a port address can be easily modified.

A third method, which is frequently used when several interface devices reside on the same PC board, is given in Fig. 10-3c. This method provides chip select signals for several devices with a binary decoder. The most significant 3 address bits along with $IO/\overline{M}$ are used to enable the decoder. If it is enabled, one and only one $\overline{CS}$ signal will be activated according to address bits A_4, A_3, and A_2.

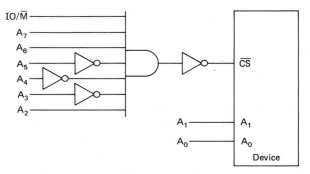

(a) Address decoding using an AND gale

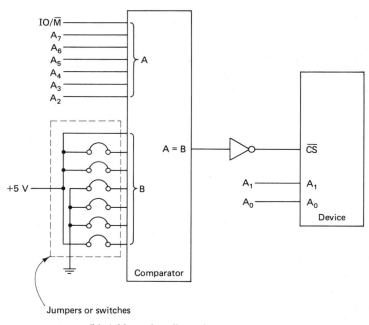

(b) Address decoding using a comparator

Figure 10-3 Typical methods for decoding an address.

As discussed in Section 9-3, proper data transfer between the processor module and an I/O interface relies on the handshaking signals $\overline{RD}$, $\overline{WR}$, IO/$\overline{M}$, and ready. The CPU issues an $\overline{RD}$ or $\overline{WR}$ command along with IO/$\overline{M}$, and unless the CPU board has ready generator logic, the interface must respond with a ready, indicating that the data have successfully been placed on or gated from the data bus. The logic given in Fig. 10-4 illustrates how this is accomplished. A ready signal is generated whenever an $\overline{RD}$ or $\overline{WR}$ command is received. A delay circuit can be inserted to force the CPU into one or more wait states, depending on the

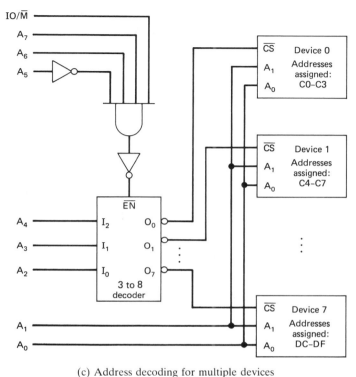

(c) Address decoding for multiple devices

Figure 10-3   Continued

speed of the device.   In order to have more than one I/O device in the system, the ready line is connected to the system bus through a tristate driver whose output is enabled by the chip select logic.   As pointed out in Section 9-3, once the processor module receives the ready response, it clears the read or write signal and drops the address and/or data signals.   This causes the interface logic to deactivate the ready signal and, if necessary, to disable the data bus drivers.   Thus the bus cycle is completed.

One other alternative in interface design is to treat I/O ports as memory locations.   This scheme is referred to as *memory-mapped I/O* and requires the interface to respond to memory read and memory write commands.   Therefore, the address decoder given in Fig. 10-2 must be modified, as illustrated in Fig. 10-5.

The major advantage of memory-mapped I/O is that the device registers can be accessed and manipulated by any instruction or addressing mode that references memory operands, thus providing programming flexibility and reducing coding. For example, consider the instruction sequence that polls eight status registers and branches to DONE if bit 0 of any one of them is set to 1.   If I/O ports A0 through

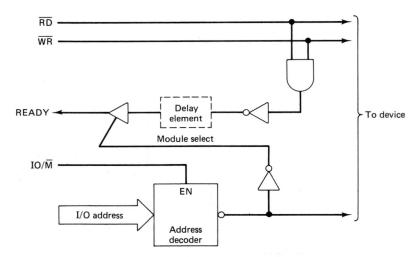

Figure 10-4 Ready signal generator.

A7 are assigned to the eight status registers with a regular I/O interface, this sequence will be implemented as follows:

```
AGAIN:      IN      0A0H
            ANI     1
            JNZ     DONE
            IN      0A1H
            ANI     1
            JNZ     DONE
             .
             .
             .
            IN      0A7H
            ANI     1
```

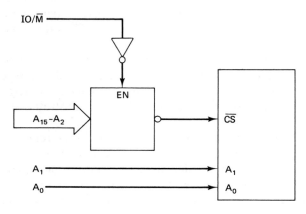

Figure 10-5 Memory-mapped I/O.

```
                                JNZ         DONE
                                JMP         AGAIN
               DONE:            ·
                                ·
                                ·
```

On the other hand, if a memory-mapped I/O interface is used with the assumption that port addresses are FFA0 through FFA7, the polling sequence can be shortened as follows:

```
        LOOP:       LXI         D,0FFA0H
                    MVI         C,8
        AGAIN:      LDAX        D
                    ANI         1
                    JNZ         DONE
                    INX         D
                    DCR         C
                    JNZ         AGAIN
                    JMP         LOOP
        DONE:       ·
                    ·
                    ·
```

Because the same address may not be assigned to both memory and an I/O device, memory-mapped I/O causes the maximum number of available memory locations to be reduced.

10-2 SERIAL INTERFACES

Serial data transmission is a common, low-cost, simple method for transmitting data between a computer and low-speed devices. Data transmitted serially, i.e., one bit at a time, may require only a single conductor pair or communication channel. Normally, the data transfer rate is specified in *baud rate*, which is the number of unit-time intervals per second. In this discussion, the signal in each interval is either logic 1 or logic 0; therefore, the baud rate corresponds to the data transfer rate in bits per second.

Because data are transferred in parallel on the system bus, a serial interface must be capable of performing serial-to-parallel conversion during input and parallel-to-serial conversion during output. When separate lines are used for sending and receiving data, data can be transferred in both directions simultaneously and the system is said to be *full duplex*. For a *half duplex* system, a single line is used for both transfer directions and therefore data can only be transferred in one direction at a time.

There are two basic types of serial communication. There are *asynchronous serial communication*, in which special bit patterns separate the characters, and *synchronous serial communication*, which allows characters to be sent back to back but must include special "sync" characters at the beginning of each message and special "idle" characters in the data stream to fill up time when no information is being sent.   An asynchronous transmission may include dead time of arbitrary lengths between the characters, while in a synchronous transmission the characters must be precisely spaced even though some of the characters may contain no information.   Although both types may waste time sending useless bits, the maximum information rate of a synchronous line is higher than that of an asynchronous line with the same bit rate because the asynchronous transmission must include extra bits with each character.   On the other hand, the clocks at the opposing ends of an asynchronous transmission line do not need to have exactly the same frequency (as long as they are within permissible limits) because the special patterns allow for resynchronization at the beginning of each character.   For a synchronous transmission the activity must be coordinated by a single clock since it is the clock that determines the position of each bit.   This means that the clock timing must be transmitted as well as the data.

10-2-1 *Asynchronous Serial Transmission*

Asynchronous serial data transmission is typically used for transmitting data between a computer and ASCII terminals.   Normally, the data transfer rate ranges from 110 baud up to 9600 baud.   A character transmitted in the asynchronous serial mode consists of the following four parts:

1. A start bit
2. Five to 8 data bits
3. An optional even- or odd-parity bit
4. One, $1\frac{1}{2}$, or 2 stop bits

The timing for an 11-bit format, consisting of a start bit, 8 data bits and 2 stop bits, transmitted at 1200 baud, is illustrated in Fig. 10-6.   At the end of each character, the signal always goes to the logical 1 state for the stop bit.   It remains 1 until the start of the next character, which begins with a start bit of logical 0. The logical 1 and logical 0 states are also called *mark* and *space*, respectively.   The 1 to 0 transition preceding the start bit allows the receiver to recognize the arrival of the incoming character; consequently, a gap of arbitrary length is tolerable between successive characters.

Asynchronous serial transmission offers the major advantage that no common clock line is required and the connection between the device and system can be reduced to one pair of signal lines.   Instead of a common clock, there are two independent clocks, one on the interface and one in the device.   The frequencies of these two clocks are much higher than the baud rate, typically 16 times as high.

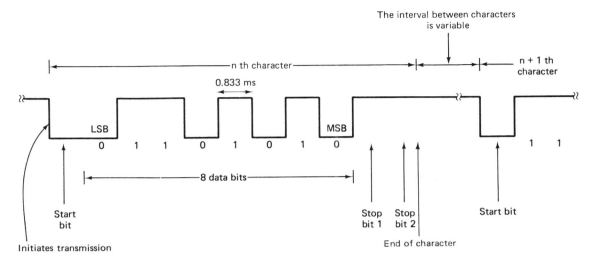

Figure 10-6 Typical 11-bit data format for asynchronous serial transmission.

By using the start bit, the clock on the receiver end can be resynchronized at the beginning of each character, thereby compensating for a minor frequency deviation between the two clocks.

To connect an asynchronous serial input device to a computer, the interface must be capable of performing the following major functions:

1. Recognition of the start and stop bits
2. Serial-to-parallel conversion of the data bits in the incoming character
3. Detection of errors

For an asynchronous serial output the interface must convert data from parallel to serial and insert the parity, start, and stop bits. These functions are normally provided by a single standard LSI device, called a *Universal Asynchronous Receiver and Transmitter (UART)*. The UART contains the necessary logic for both receiving and transmitting asynchronous serial data. In addition, a UART is constructed so that the number of data bits, the number of stop bits, whether or not there is a parity bit, and the type of parity (even or odd) may be set under program control. A block diagram of a UART is shown in Fig. 10-7.

During an input operation, the UART first waits for a 1 to 0 transition from the serial input signal line. Once it is detected, the input line is sampled at the end of the eight receiver clock (R_c) pulses. As shown in Fig. 10-8, the exact sampling point varies from $7\frac{1}{2}$ to $8\frac{1}{2}$ R_c clock periods from the transition. Because the frequency of R_c is 16 times the baud rate, this places the sampling point close to the center of the start bit of the incoming character. After a valid start bit has been recognized, the serial data line is sampled every 16 pulses and shifted into a

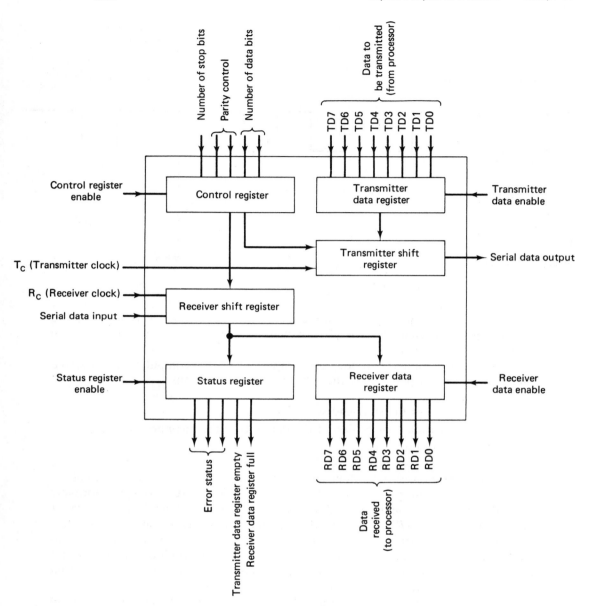

Figure 10-7 Block diagram of a UART.

serial-to-parallel shift register. The first sampled bit corresponds to the least significant data bit. A separate receiver data register is necessary because once a character has been received, the shift register must be made available for the next incoming character. The character stored in the receiver data register must be input by the processor before the next character is assembled; otherwise, an *overrun*

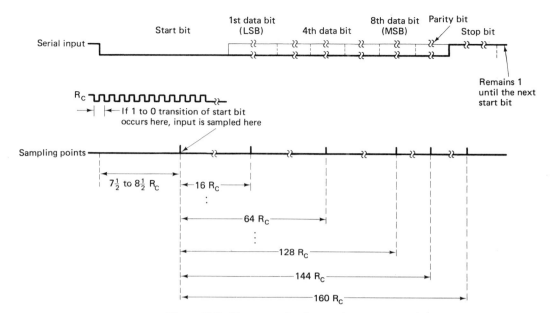

Figure 10-8 Data reception in asynchronous transmission.

error bit is set in the status register.   The allowable time for the processor to input this character depends on the baud rate and total number of bits in each character.

The parity bit and stop bit(s) are sampled exactly as data bits except the stop bit(s) is not shifted into the shift register.   If even parity is used, the parity bit is set so that the total number of 1's in the data and parity bits is even.   For odd parity the total number is odd.   If the received parity bit does not match the one internally generated by the data bits, a parity error is indicated in the status register. The stop bit(s) is used for detecting another type of error, called a *framing error*. This error is caused by the fact that the receiver clock may not run at a frequency of exactly 16 times the baud rate.   As a result, the offset of the sampling point from the center of a data bit accumulates while the data bits are being received. If the difference between the clock frequency and 16 times the baud rate is within tolerance, the character will be received correctly and R_c will be synchronized by the start bit of the next character.   However, if the frequency of R_c is off by more than the allowable amount, the sampling point will not be within the proper bit frame, and erroneous data bits will be received.   This type of error may be detected by checking the sampled stop bit(s); if it is 0 instead of 1, a framing error occurs.

During an output operation, a character is first sent to the transmitter data register.   After the previous character has been transmitted, a start bit is transmitted followed by a data bit after every 16 transmitter clock (T_c) pulses.   An internally generated parity bit (if parity is desired) and a stop bit(s) are transmitted after the last data bit.   Note that R_c and T_c may come from the same clock if input and output data have the same baud rate.

The serial input and serial output of the UART are TTL signals, which are suitable for transmission only over a short distance. Therefore, a device is needed to convert the signal from the TTL type to a type that is more suitable for transmission. Two signal standards have been established for transmitting data over an extended distance: the *EIA RS-232-C* and the *20-milliampere current loop* standards. The RS-232-C standard is the latest version of the interface standard adopted by the Electrical Industry Association. According to this standard, a received signal with a voltage level greater than 3 V is interpreted as a logical 0 and a voltage level less than -3 V is interpreted as a logical 1. The RS-232-C standard also specifies that the transmitter driver must output a signal from -5 to -15 V for a logical 1 and 5 to 15 V for a logical 0. This allows at least 2 V of noise margin.

The other principal standard for serial communication is based on current levels instead of voltage levels; a current flow indicates a logical 1 and absence of current indicates a logical 0. Historically, this standard has been used with mechanical teleprinters. To drive the solenoids associated with the printer, the interface is designed to provide a current source of 20 mA. Consequently, this standard is referred to as the 20-mA current loop standard. For most computer/terminal interfaces based on this standard, the terminal is the passive device and the interface is the active device that provides the current source for both the transmitter and receiver.

Figure 10-9 depicts the design of both RS-232-C and 20-mA loop conversion logic. The conversion between RS-232-C and TTL requires only an RS-232-C line driver and receiver pair, such as the Motorola MC1488 and MC1489A devices. The line driver converts the TTL serial output of the UART to the RS-232-C signal and the receiver converts the RS-232-C serial input from the terminal to a TTL signal. The conversion between 20-mA loop and TTL signals can be performed using optical couplers. The input signal turns on the LED, which is coupled to a phototransistor that generates the desired current signals.

10-2-2 Synchronous Serial Transmission

For asynchronous transmission, at least 2 bits, a start bit and a stop bit, are required in each character for resynchronization. This reduces the overall character transfer rate significantly, particularly for the case in which a large number of characters are to be transmitted as a packet. As an example, suppose that a communication link can transmit data at 9600 baud. The maximum data transfer rate in the asynchronous mode with a character format consisting of 8 information bits, 1 start bit, and 1 stop bit would be $9600/(8 + 1 + 1) = 960$ characters per second. If the start and stop bits are not transmitted with each character, the maximum data transfer rate could reach $9600/8 = 1200$ characters per second. This leads to the other principal type of serial data transmission, which is called *synchronous transmission*. In the synchronous transmission mode, data are transmitted with no gaps between characters. Individual characters are defined by time rather than the start and stop bits. The first bit of one character immediately follows the last bit of the previous character. In order to indicate to the receiver the beginning of an information bit stream, every transmission begins with at least one special *syn-*

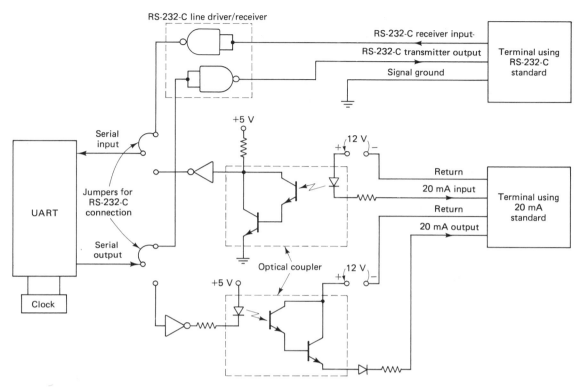

Figure 10-9   An interface between a UART and a terminal.

chronizing (*sync*) *character*.   The sync characters are deleted from the data stream by the receiver after synchronization is achieved.   For data reception, once the sync character(s) is detected, the interface converts every 8 serial input bits into one character and sends it to the processor.   For data transmission, the interface serially sends out the sync character(s) followed by the bit stream that is generated by the characters sent to the interface from the processor.

Because there are no start and stop bits attached to each character, a common clock must be used by both the receiver and transmitter to ensure proper data retrieval.   Otherwise, if the data bit stream were long, the receiver clock would drift out of synchronization.   This means that a clock line must be added to the communication link or the receiver clock signal must be retrieved from the transmitted data signal.

10-2-3 8251A Programmable Communication Interface

Because serial data transmission has been adopted by a large variety of peripherals, many microprocessor manufacturers have designed their own asynchronous serial interface devices that perform the same fundamental functions as the UART.

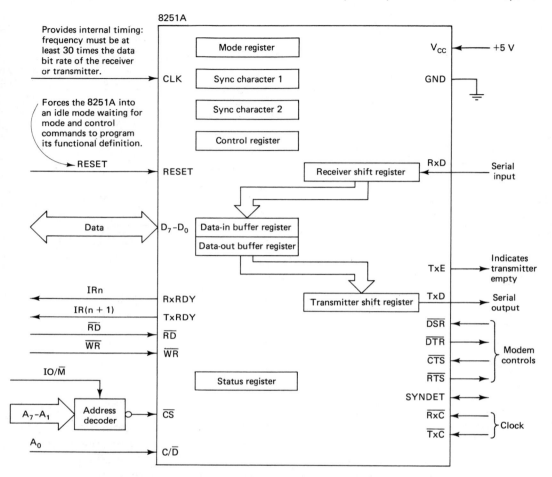

Figure 10-10   8251A Programmable Communication Interface.

Some of these devices include additional features that reduce the required surrounding logic when they are used with a particular microprocessor family.   One example is Intel's 8251A Programmable Communication Interface (PCI), which is an LSI device designed for both asynchronous and synchronous serial communication.   A block diagram and pin configuration are shown in Fig. 10-10.

The data-in buffer and data-out buffer registers share the same port address. For input, the serial bit stream arriving on the RxD pin is shifted into the receiver shift register and then the data bits are transferred to the data-in buffer register, where they can be input by the CPU.   Conversely, on output the data bits put in the data-out buffer register by the CPU are transferred to the transmitter shift register and, along with the necessary synchronization bits, are shifted out through the TxD pin.   Among other things the contents of the mode register, which are initialized by the executing program, determine whether the 8251A is in asynchronous mode or synchronous mode and the format of the characters being received and transmitted. The control register, which is also set by the program, controls the operation of the interface, and the status register makes certain information available to the executing program. Clearly, the sync character registers are for storing the sync characters needed for synchronous communication.

Even though all seven of the registers on the left side of Fig. 10-10 can be accessed by the processor, the 8251A is associated with only two port addresses. The $C/\overline{D}$ (command/data) pin is connected to the address line A_0, and A_0 differentiates the two port addresses. The 8251A internally interprets the $C/\overline{D}$, $\overline{RD}$, and $\overline{WR}$ signals as follows:

$C/\overline{D}(=A_0)$	$\overline{RD}$	$\overline{WR}$	
0	0	1	Data input from the data-in buffer
0	1	0	Data output to the data-out buffer
1	0	1	Status register is put on data bus
1	1	0	Data is put in mode, control, or sync character register

where 1 means that the pin is high and 0 means that it is low. All other combinations cause the three-state D_7–D_0 pins to go into their high-impedance state.

Whether the mode, control, or sync character register is selected depends on the accessing sequence. A flowchart of the sequencing is given in Fig. 10-11. After a hardware reset or a command is given with its reset bit set to 1, the next output with $A_0 = 1$ (i.e., with $C/\overline{D} = 1$, $\overline{RD} = 1$, and $\overline{WR} = 0$) is directed to the mode register. The formats of the mode register for both the asynchronous and synchronous cases are defined in Fig. 10-12. If the two LSBs of the mode are zero, then the interface is put in its synchronous mode and the MSB determines the number of sync characters. In the synchronous mode, the next 1 or 2 bytes output with $A_0 = 1$ become the sync characters. If the two LSBs of the mode are not both 0, then the 8251A enters its asynchronous mode. In either case, all subsequent bytes prior to another reset go to the control register if $A_0 = 1$ and the data-out buffer register if $A_0 = 0$.

In the synchronous mode the baud rates of the transmitter and receiver, which are the shift rates of the shift registers, are the same as the frequencies of the signals applied to $\overline{TxC}$ and $\overline{RxC}$, respectively, but in the asynchronous mode the three remaining possible combinations for the two LSBs in the mode register dictate the baud rate factor. The relationship between the frequencies of the $\overline{TxC}$ and $\overline{RxC}$ clock inputs and the baud rates of the transmitter and receiver is

$$\text{Clock frequency} = \text{Baud rate factor} \times \text{Baud rate}$$

If 10 is in the LSBs of the mode register and the transmitter and receiver baud rates are to be 300 and 1200, respectively, then the frequency applied to $\overline{TxC}$ should be 4800 Hz and the frequency at $\overline{RxC}$ should be 19.2 kHz.

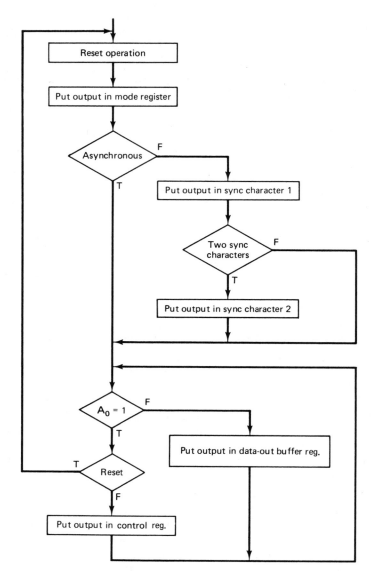

Figure 10-11   Flowchart of the disposition of output.

In both the asynchronous and synchronous modes, bits 2 and 3 indicate the number of data bits in each character, bit 4 indicates whether or not there is to be a parity bit, and bit 5 specifies the type of parity (odd or even). For the asynchronous mode the two MSBs indicate the number of stop bits, but for the synchronous mode bit 6 determines whether the SYNDET pin is to be used as an

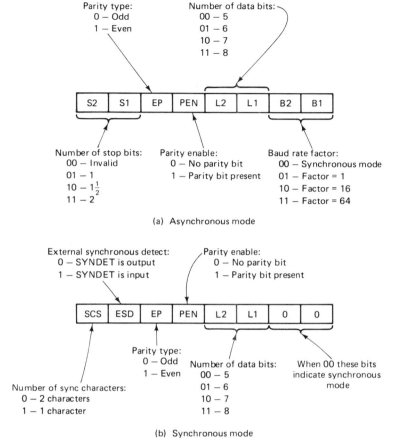

Figure 10-12   Format of the mode register.

input or as an output and, as mentioned above, bit 7 indicates the number of sync characters.

If the SYNDET pin is used as an output it becomes active when a bit-for-bit match has been found between the incoming bit stream and the sync character(s). If the search for sync characters is conducted by an external device, then SYNDET can be used to input a signal, indicating that a match has been found by the external device. The pin also has a meaning during asynchronous operation, but in this case it can only be an output. This output is called the break detect signal and goes high whenever a character consisting of all 0s is received.

Four control pins are designated to facilitate interfacing to modems. The word *modem* is an abbreviation of *modulator-demodulator*. For example, a modem may modulate digital signals being transmitted into voice tones and demodulate voice tones being received into digital signals, thus permitting the transmission of

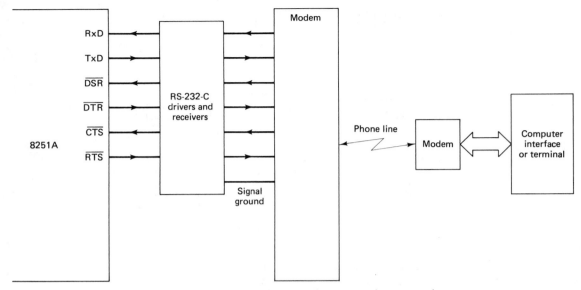

Figure 10-13 Asynchronous modem connection.

digital information over telephone lines. The so-called intelligent modems are capable of accepting commands to dial numbers, detect busy signals, answer incoming calls, and perform internal tests. With a modem, a computer can communicate with another computer or access on-line data base services that provide financial information, news, electronic mail, computer shopping, and the like.

Figure 10-13 illustrates the use of an 8251A for interfacing to a modem. The $\overline{\text{DSR}}$ and $\overline{\text{CTS}}$ signals are for sending status from the modem to the 8251A. They can be used to indicate that the modem's power is on and that the modem is ready to transmit. The $\overline{\text{DTR}}$ and $\overline{\text{RTS}}$ are output control signals from the 8251A to the modem. They are normally used for modem control such as data terminal ready and request to send. To satisfy the RS-232-C standard, drivers and receivers are needed to convert the TTL-compatible signals to the proper voltage levels (see Fig. 10-9) between the 8251A and modem.

The control register, whose format is given in Fig. 10-14, is write only and controls the actual operation of the 8251A. Outputting a command to this register causes the device to perform a specified function such as outputting a $\overline{\text{DTR}}$ and/or $\overline{\text{RTS}}$ signal, enabling the transmitter and/or receiver, resetting the device, and so on.

A program sequence that initializes the mode register and gives a command to enable the transmitter and begin an asynchronous transmission of 7-bit characters followed by an even-parity bit and 2 stop bits is

```
MVI        A,11111010B
OUT        51H
MVI        A,00110011B
OUT        51H
```

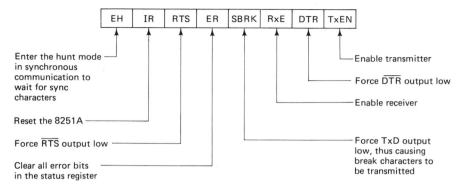

In all cases, a 1 will cause the indicated action

Figure 10-14   Format of the control register.

This sequence assumes that the mode and control registers are at address 51H and the clock frequencies are to be 16 times the corresponding baud rates.   The sequence

```
MVI        A,00111000B
OUT        51H
MVI        A,16H
OUT        51H
OUT        51H
MVI        A,10010100B
OUT        51H
```

would cause the same 8251A to be put in synchronous mode and to begin searching for two successive ASCII sync characters.   As before, the characters are to consist of 7 data bits and an even-parity bit, but there will, of course, be no stop bits.

The format of the status register is given in Fig. 10-15.   Bits 1, 2, 6, and 7 reflect the signals on the RxRDY, TxE, SYNDET, and $\overline{\text{DSR}}$ pins.   TxRDY indicates that the data-out buffer is empty.   Unlike the TxRDY pin, this bit is not affected by the $\overline{\text{CTS}}$ input pin or the TxEN control bit.   RxRDY indicates that a character has been received and is ready to be input to the processor.   Either the TxRDY and RxRDY bits can be used for programmed I/O or the signals on the corresponding pins can be connected to interrupt request lines to provide for interrupt I/O.   The TxRDY bit is automatically cleared when a character is made available for transmitting and the RxRDY bit is automatically cleared when the character that set it is input by the processor.   Bit 2 indicates that the transmitter shift register is waiting to be sent a character from the data-out buffer register.   During synchronous transmissions, while this bit is set, the transmitter will take its data from the sync character registers until data are put in the data-out buffer register.   Bits 3, 4, and 5 indicate parity, overrun, and framing errors, respectively.   When an error is detected, the bit having the corresponding error type will be set to 1.

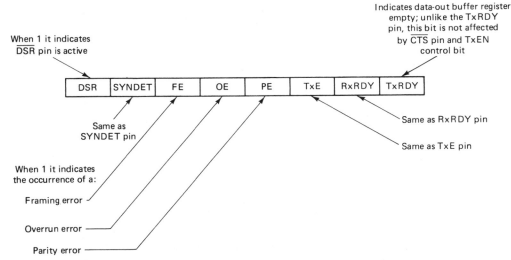

Figure 10-15 Format of the status register.

Figure 10-16 gives a typical program sequence that uses programmed I/O to input 80 characters from the 8251A, whose data buffer register's address is 50, and put them in the memory buffer beginning at LINE. The inner loop continually tests the RxRDY bit until it is set by a character being put in the data-in buffer register. Then the newly arrived character is moved to the buffer and the error bits are checked. If the present character arrived before the previous character

```
            MVI     A,00110111B  ;ENABLE TRANSMITTER AND RECEIVER
            OUT     51H          ;AND CLEAR ERROR BITS
            LXI     D,LINE       ;USE DE AS POINTER TO LINE BUFFER
            MVI     C,80         ;USE C AS COUNTER
BEGIN:      IN      51H          ;WAIT FOR INPUT
            ANI     02H
            JZ      BEGIN
            IN      50H          ;INPUT NEXT CHARACTER AND
            STAX    D            ;PUT IT IN LINE BUFFER
            INX     D
            MOV     B,A          ;SAVE THE CURRENT CHARACTER
            IN      51H          ;CHECK ERROR
            ANI     00111000B    ;BITS AND
            JNZ     ERROR        ;IF NO ERROR, CONTINUE
            MOV     A,B          ;IF THE CURRENT CHARACTER IS
            XRI     0DH          ;CR, TERMINATE INPUTTING
            JZ      DONE
            DCR     C            ;OR IF 80 CHARACTERS HAVE
            JNZ     BEGIN        ;BEEN INPUT, TERMINATE INPUTTING
            JMP     DONE
ERROR:      CALL    ERROUT       ;ERROR IS DETECTED, CALL ERROUT
DONE:         .
              .
              .
```

Figure 10-16 Inputting a line of characters through an 8251A.

was input or a parity or framing error occurred during transmission, then the input ceases and a call is made to an error routine that would presumably examine the individual error bits, print an appropriate message, and clear the error bits.

Because inputting a character automatically resets the RxRDY bit, unless another character is received before the inner loop is reentered the inner loop must cycle until the RxRDY bit is reset to 1 by the next incoming character. If the incoming characters have fewer than 8 bits, the unused MSBs in the data buffer register are always zeroed. Also, the parity bit is not passed to the processor and checks for parity errors can only be made by examining the parity error bit in the status register. On output, if a character is less than 8 bits long, the unneeded MSBs in the data-out buffer register are ignored.

10-3 PARALLEL INTERFACES

In a serial I/O transmission, only 1 bit is transmitted at a time on a single pair of data lines. Although it requires a minimum number of lines, it is too slow to handle peripherals such as high-speed printers or A/D and D/A converters. Such devices require parallel I/O interfaces in which all bits in the word are transmitted at the same time, 1 bit per line. For parallel transmission, proper data transfer between the device and its interface is accomplished by handshaking signals instead of synchronization bits or characters.

A few microprocessor manufacturers have made available LSI devices to facilitate parallel interface design. Intel's Programmable Peripheral Interface is a typical parallel interface device.

10-3-1 8255A Programmable Peripheral Interface

The Intel 8255A Programmable Peripheral Interface (PPI) is a general-purpose I/O component to interface peripherals to the system bus. As illustrated in Fig. 10-17, the device has a control register and three 8-bit ports, A, B, and C. These ports are divided into two groups of 12 bits. Each group can be individually programmed for an operation mode. The control register and three port registers are selected by pins A_1 and A_0. Therefore, the lowest port address assigned to an 8255A must be divisible by 4. A summary of the 8255A's addressing is

```
A₁  A₀  RD  WR  CS    Transfer Description
 0   0   0   1   0    Port A to data bus
 0   1   0   1   0    Port B to data bus
 1   0   0   1   0    Port C to data bus
 0   0   1   0   0    Data bus to port A
 0   1   1   0   0    Data bus to port B
 1   0   1   0   0    Data bus to port C
```

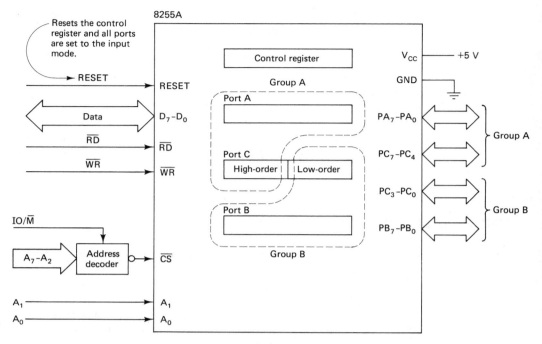

Figure 10-17 Block diagram of the 8255A.

1	1	1	0	0	Data bus to control register if $D_7 = 1$; if $D_7 = 0$, input from the data bus is treated as a Set/Reset instruction
x	x	x	x	1	D_7-D_0 go to high-impedance state
1	1	0	1	0	Illegal combination
x	x	1	1	0	D_7-D_0 go to high-impedance state

where 0 is low and 1 is high.

Because the bits in port C are sometimes used as control bits, the 8255A is designed so that they can be output to individually using a Set/Reset instruction. When the 8255A receives a byte that is directed to its control register, it examines the data bit 7. If this bit is 1, the data are transferred to the control register, but if it is 0, the data are treated as a Set/Reset instruction and are used to set or clear the port C bit specified by the instruction. Bits 3–1 give the bit number of the bit to be changed and bit 0 indicates whether it is to be set or cleared. The remaining bits are unused.

The contents of the control register specify which modes groups A and B are in, as shown in Fig. 10-18. Group A can be operated in one of three modes, mode

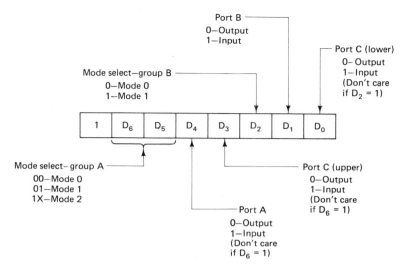

Figure 10-18 Format of the 8255A's control register.

0, mode 1, and mode 2, while group B can only be in mode 0 or 1.   These modes are

MODE 0—This mode is called the basic input/output mode.   If a group is in mode 0, it is divided into two sets.   For group A these sets are port A and the upper 4 bits of port C, and for group B they are port B and the lower 4 bits of port C.   Each set may be used for inputting or outputting, but not both.   For example, if the address decoder enables the 8255A when $A_7-A_2 = 001110$, then the following instructions

```
MVI      A,91H
OUT      3BH
```

initialize the 8255A to have port A as input, port B as output, PC_3-PC_0 as input, and PC_7-PC_4 as output.

MODE 1—This mode is called the strobed input/output mode.   When a group is in this mode, its 8-bit port (A or B) is used either for input or for output, and three pins from port C are used for handshaking signals.   Figure 10-19 shows input and output configurations in mode 1 along with their corresponding control words.   If group A is programmed as mode 1 for input, the three handshaking signals are

PC_4 $\overline{STB_A}$ A 0 applied to this pin causes PA_7-PA_0 to be latched, or "strobed," into port A.   This signal is typically used by the

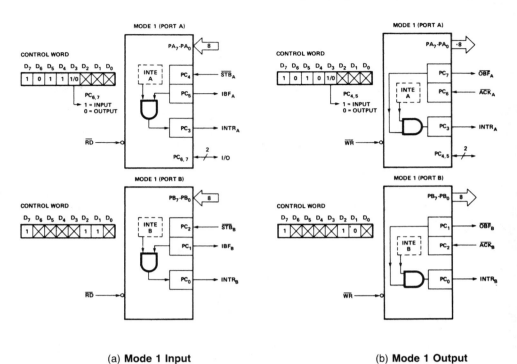

(a) **Mode 1 Input**   (b) **Mode 1 Output**

Figure 10-19   Mode 1 input and output configurations.   (Reprinted by permission of Intel Corporation, Copyright 1985.)

		peripheral to inform the 8255A that the input data byte is ready.
PC$_5$	IBF$_A$	Indicates that the input buffer is full. It is 1 when port A contains data that have not yet been input to the CPU. When a 0 is on this pin the device can send a new byte to the interface.
PC$_3$	INTR$_A$	It is used as an interrupt request. This output becomes 1 when $\overline{STB}_A$ is low, IBF$_A$ is high, and the INTE A flag is set to 1. The INTR$_A$ signal is cleared automatically when the CPU inputs from the 8255A. The interrupt enable flag, INTE A, is controlled by bit set/reset of PC$_4$.

Pins PC$_6$ and PC$_7$ can be programmed as output to provide control signals or as input to read status from the peripheral.

The handshaking signals used for output are

PC$_7$	$\overline{OBF}_A$	Indicates that the output buffer is full. It outputs a 0 to the device when port A is outputting new data to be taken by the device.

PC_6	$\overline{ACK}_A$	Device puts a 0 on this pin when it accepts data from port A.
PC_3	$INTR_A$	It serves the same purpose as in input, but the interrupt enable flag is controlled by bit set/reset of PC_6. In addition, $INTR_A$ is cleared by a write to the 8255A.

Pins PC_4 and PC_5 serve the same purpose as described above for PC_6 and PC_7. If group B is in mode 1, port B is input to or output from according to bit D_1 of the control register ($D_1 = 1$ indicates input). For input, PC_2 and PC_1 are denoted $\overline{STB}_B$ and IBF_B, respectively, and serve the same purposes for group B as $\overline{STB}_A$ and IBF_A do for group A. Similarly, for output PC_1 and PC_2 are denoted $\overline{OBF}_B$ and $\overline{ACK}_B$. PC_0 becomes $INTR_B$ and its use is analogous to that of $INTR_A$. The interrupt enable for group B is controlled by set/clear of PC_2 for both input and output.

MODE 2—This mode, which is called the strobed bidirectional bus input/output mode, applies only to group A. In mode 2, port A is used for both input and output, and five of the port C pins are used for handshaking. The pin configuration is shown in Fig. 10-20. These five handshaking signals are $\overline{OBF}_A$ (output buffer full), $\overline{ACK}_A$ (acknowledge for output data), $INTR_A$ (interrupt request), $\overline{STB}_A$ (input data ready), and IBF_A (input buffer full). They have the same meanings as in mode 1, with $INTR_A$ being shared by both input and output.

While group A is in mode 2, group B may be in either mode 0 or mode 1. However, if group B is in mode 0, only PC_2–PC_0 can be used for input or output because group A has borrowed PC_3 to use as an interrupt request line. Normally, if group A is in mode 2, PC_2–PC_0 would be connected to

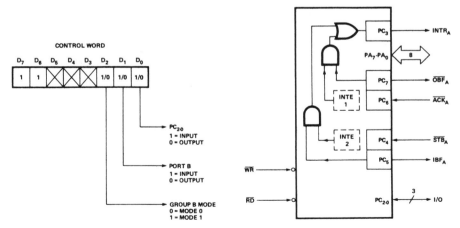

Figure 10-20 Mode 2 configuration. (Reprinted by permission of Intel Corporation, Copyright 1985.)

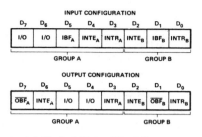

(a) **Mode 1 Status Word Format**

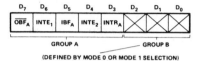

(b) **Mode 2 Status Word Format**

Figure 10-21 Format of the 8255A's status. (Reprinted by permission of Intel Corporation, Copyright 1985.)

control and status pins on the device attached to the port A lines. Port B may also be used for this purpose.

In mode 1 or 2, the status of the handshaking signals can be obtained by reading from port C. Figure 10-21 defines the status word formats for both modes.

10-3-2 A/D and D/A Example

Figure 10-22 shows how an 8255A could be connected to an A/D and D/A subsystem. Since during an A/D conversion the analog voltage must remain unchanged, a sample-and-hold circuit is needed to keep the analog signal constant while the conversion is being performed. Group A is configured as an input in mode 1. A conversion is initiated by a signal from the 8255A's PC_7 pin, which prompts the converter to output a busy signal. The busy line is connected to both a sample-and-hold control pin (S/H) and a negative edge-triggered one-shot. While the busy signal is high, the sample-and-hold circuit maintains a constant output, and when the busy signal goes down at the end of the conversion, the one-shot is triggered. The output from the one-shot is complemented and applied to the $\overline{STB}_A$ (PC_4) input on the 8255A. This causes the digitized sample to be strobed into port A. For the D/A portion of the subsystem, port B is configured as an output port in mode 0, which is directly connected to the binary input of the D/A converter. No handshaking is used.

Given that port A, port B, port C, and the control register have addresses

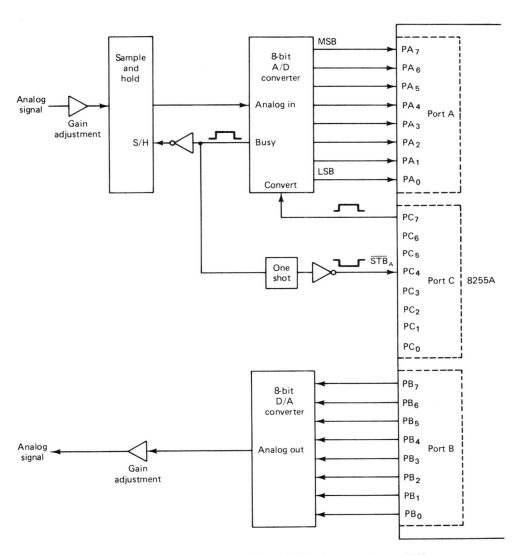

Figure 10-22 Interfacing an A/D and D/A subsystem using an 8255A.

F8, F9, FA, and FB, respectively, the sequence

```
MVI        A,10110000B
OUT        0FBH
```

would cause port A to be put in mode 1, port B to be put in mode 0, and PC_7 to be an output.   The sequence

```
MVI        A,00001111B
OUT        0FBH
MVI        A,00001110B
OUT        0FBH
```

would output a pulse to the convert pin of the A/D converter.   Note that the
address associated with the Set/Reset instruction is the same as the address of the
control register.   The first two instructions cause PC_7 to be set and the last two
cause it to be cleared.   A sequence for providing a programmed I/O input of the
converted data is

```
AGAIN:     IN         0FAH
           ANI        00100000B
           JZ         AGAIN
           IN         0F8H
```

For outputting a byte from register A to the D/A converter, only the instruction

```
OUT        0F9H
```

is needed.   As soon as the byte arrives at port B its bits are immediately applied
to the input pins of the D/A converter, which, in turn, immediately converts it to
an analog signal.
    In this example, it has been assumed that the sampling rate is provided by
the program and that the gains of the input and output analog amplifiers are
manually adjusted.   The sampling rate can be adjusted by including a delay loop
between two conversions, such as

```
           LDA        N
           MOV        C,A
LOOP:      NOP
           DCR        C
           JNZ        LOOP
```

    Frequently, programmable clocks and gain control devices are associated with
A/D and D/A subsystems so that the timing of the sampling and D/A outputs are
more precisely controlled and the gains can be dynamically changed.   Also, a
DMA controller is often used in conjunction with an A/D and D/A subsystem so
that high-speed input and output can be attained.
    Only 8-bit A/D and D/A converters are included in the design shown in Fig.
10-22.   This limits the resolution to only 1 part in 256.   If the voltage range of
the input or output were -10 V to $+10$ V, the resolution would be

$$\frac{20}{256} = 0.078 \text{ V}$$

For higher resolutions, 10-, 12-, or 14-bit converters are required. To accommodate the greater number of bits, a combination of ports A and B could be used (see Exercise 16).

10-4 PROGRAMMABLE TIMERS AND EVENT COUNTERS

Quite often a device is needed to mark intervals of time for both the processor and external devices, count external events and make the count available to the processor, and provide external timing that can be programmed from the processor. Such a device is called a *programmable interval timer/event counter*, and some of its uses are as follows:

1. Interrupt a time-sharing operating system at evenly spaced intervals so that it can switch programs.
2. Output precisely timed signals with programmed periods to an I/O device (e.g., an A/D converter).
3. Serve as a programmable baud rate generator.
4. Measure time delays between external events.
5. Count the number of times an event occurs in an external experiment and provide a means of inputting the count to the computer.
6. Cause the processor to be interrupted after a programmed number of external events have occurred.

A typical interval timer/event counter has an initial count register and a counter. The counter itself is not directly available to the processor, but must be initialized from the initial count register and can be read only by first transferring its contents to the counter out register. The counter operates by starting at an initial value and counting backward to 0. A counter may have two control pins, CLK and GATE, and one output pin, OUT. The CLK input determines the count rate, GATE is for enabling and disabling the CLK input and perhaps other purposes, and the OUT output becomes active when the count reaches 0 or, possibly, when a GATE signal is received. OUT may be connected to an interrupt request line in the system bus so that an interrupt will occur when the count reaches 0, or to an I/O device which uses it to initiate specific I/O activity.

The operation is basically to enter a count in the initial count register, transfer the count to the counter, and cause the counter to count backward as pulses are applied to the CLK input. The current contents of the counter can be input at any time without disturbing the count by transferring them to the counter out register and then reading them. By buffering the count through the counter out register, it does not have to be input to the processor immediately. The zero count indication would normally be applied to both the OUT pin and one of the bits in the status register. Thus either programmed I/O or interrupt I/O could be used to detect the zero count.

Among other things the control register includes the mode of operation. The mode determines exactly what happens when the count becomes 0 and/or a signal is applied to the gate input. Some possible actions are the following:

1. The GATE input is used for enabling and disabling the CLK input.
2. The GATE input may cause the counter to be reinitialized.
3. The GATE input may stop the count and force OUT high.
4. The count will give an OUT signal and stop when it reaches 0.
5. The count will give an OUT signal and automatically be reinitialized from the Initial Count Register when the count reaches 0.

The modes could be defined by combinations of these possibilities.

As an example, consider the application of an interval timer to a time-sharing operating system. In this case a clock would be connected to the CLK input and OUT to an interrupt request line, possibly to a nonmaskable line. The GATE input would not be needed. When the system is brought up the initial count register would be filled with

$$\text{Initial count} = \text{Clock frequency} \times T$$

where T is the length of each time slice in seconds, and the mode would be set so that each time the count reaches 0 the contents of the initial count register would be transferred to the counter and OUT would become active. Since OUT is used as an interrupt request, an interrupt routine for switching programs would be entered at the end of each period of T seconds.

A diagram of Intel's 8254 interval timer/event counter is given in Fig. 10-23. The 8254 consists of three identical counting circuits, each of which has CLK and GATE inputs and an OUT output. Each can be viewed as containing a Control and Status Register pair, a Counter Register (CR) for receiving the initial count, a Counter Element (CE) that performs the counting but is not directly accessible from the processor, and an Output Latch (OL) for latching the contents of the CE so that they can be read. The CR, CE, and OL are treated as pairs of 8-bit registers. (Physically, the registers are not exactly as depicted, but to the programmer the figure is conceptually accurate.)

The registers can be accessed according to the following table:

$\overline{CS}$	$\overline{RD}$	$\overline{WR}$	A_1	A_0	Transfer
0	1	0	0	0	To counter 0 CR
0	1	0	0	1	To counter 1 CR
0	1	0	1	0	To counter 2 CR
0	1	0	1	1	To a control register or indicates a command
0	0	1	0	0	From counter 0 OL or status register
0	0	1	0	1	From counter 1 OL or status register
0	0	1	1	0	From counter 2 OL or status register

8254

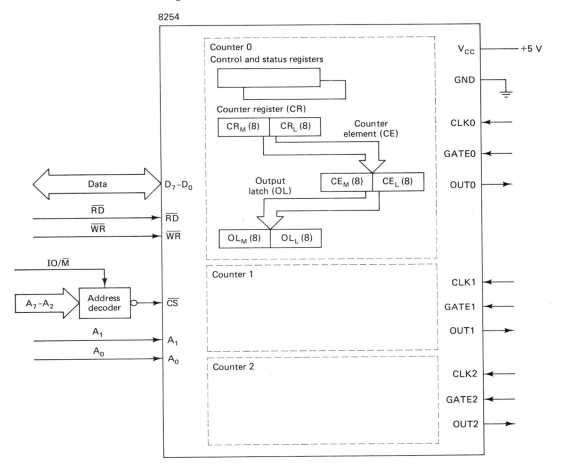

Figure 10-23 Block diagram of the 8254.

where 0 means low and 1 means high.   All other combinations result in the data pins being put into their high-impedance state.   When $A_1 = A_0 = 1$, whether a control register is being written into or a command is being given depends on the MSBs of the byte being output.   For the last three combinations, whether an OL or status register is read is determined by a previous command.

    There are two types of commands, the counter latch command, which causes the CE in the counter specified by the two MSBs of the command to be latched into the corresponding OL, and the read back command, which may cause a combination of the CEs to be latched or "prepare" a combination of status registers to be read.   To prepare a status register means to cause it to be read the next time a read operation inputs from the counter.   When the two MSBs are 00, 01, or 10, a counter latch command is indicated, but if they are 11, a read back is to be performed.   In a latch command bits 5 and 4 must be 0 and the remaining bits are unused. The read back command has the format

1	1	$\overline{\text{COUNT}}$	$\overline{\text{STAT}}$	CNT2	CNT1	CNT0	0

If the $\overline{\text{COUNT}}$ bit is 0, then the CEs for all the counters whose CNT bits are 1 are latched. If CNT0 = CNT2 = 1 but CNT1 = 0, then the CEs in counters 0 and 2 are latched but the CE in counter 1 is not latched. Similarly, $\overline{\text{STAT}}$ = 0 causes the counters' status registers to be prepared for input. CEs can be latched and status registers can be prepared in the same command.

The formats of the control and status registers are given in Fig. 10-24. If the two MSBs of an output are both 1, they indicate that the output is to be a read back command; otherwise, they specify a counter. If they specify a counter and bits 4 and 5 are both 0, then a latch command is indicated and it is directed to the control register of the counter specified by the top 2 bits, but if they are not both 0, then they indicate the type of the input from OL or output to CR. The combination 01 indicates that the Read/Write operations are from/to the OL_L/CR_L, 10 indicates that they are from/to the OL_M/CR_M, and 11 indicates that these operations are to occur in pairs, with the first byte coming from/going to OL_L/CR_L and the second from/to OL_M/CR_M. A 1-byte write to CR will cause the other byte to be zeroed. Bits 1, 2, and 3 determine the mode and bit 0 specifies the format of the count.

Given that N is the initial count, the modes are:

MODE 0 (INTERRUPT ON TERMINAL COUNT)—GATE = 1 enables counting and

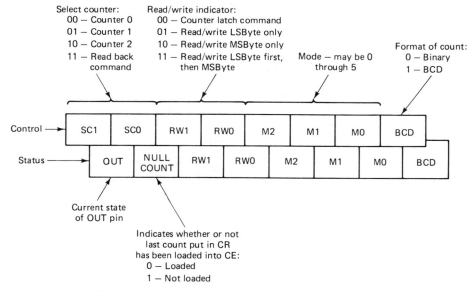

Figure 10-24 Control and status registers for 8254 counters.

GATE $= 0$ disables counting, and GATE has no effect on OUT. The contents of CR are transferred to CE on the first CLK pulse after CR is written into by the processor, regardless of the signal on the GATE pin. The pulse that loads CE is not included in the count. OUT goes low when there is an output to the control register and remains low until the count goes to 0. Mode 0 is primarily for event counting.

MODE 1 (HARDWARE RETRIGGERABLE ONE-SHOT)—After CR has been loaded with N, a 0 to 1 transition on GATE will cause CE to be loaded, a 1 to 0 transition at OUT, and the count to begin. When the count reaches 0 OUT will go high, thus producing a negative-going OUT pulse N clock periods long.

MODE 2 (PERIODIC INTERVAL TIMER)—After loading CR with N, a transfer is made from CR to CE on the next clock pulse. OUT goes from 1 to 0 when the count becomes 1 and remains low for one CLK pulse; then it returns to 1 and CE is reloaded from CR, thus giving a negative pulse at OUT after every N clock cycles. GATE $= 1$ enables the count and GATE $= 0$ disables the count. A 0 to 1 transition on GATE also causes the count to be reinitialized on the next clock pulse. This mode is used to provide a programmable periodic interval timer.

MODE 3 (SQUARE-WAVE GENERATOR)—It is similar to mode 2 except that OUT goes low when half the initial count is reached and remains low until the count becomes 0. Hence the duty cycle is changed. As before, GATE enables and disables the count and a 0 to 1 transition on GATE reinitializes the count. This mode may be used for baud rate generation.

MODE 4 (SOFTWARE-TRIGGERED STROBE)—It is similar to mode 0 except that OUT is high while the counting is taking place and produces a one-clock-period negative pulse when the count reaches 0.

MODE 5 (HARDWARE-TRIGGERED STROBE—RETRIGGERABLE)—After CR is loaded, a 0 to 1 transition on GATE will cause a transfer from CR to CE during the next CLK pulse. OUT will be high during the counting but will go low for one CLK period when the count becomes 0. GATE can reinitialize counting at any time.

For all modes, if the initial count is 0, it will be interpreted as 2^{16} or 10^4, depending on the format of the count. The above descriptions were only to provide an overall idea of the operation of the 8254 in the various modes. For a detailed description of the modes, the reader should look in Reference 2.

Figure 10-25 shows how an 8254 could be used to provide a programmable sample rate generator for an A/D subsystem. By using all three of the 8254's counters, not only can the program set the sample rate, but it can also determine the period over which the samples are taken. Suppose that counter 0 is put in mode 2, counter 1 in mode 1, and counter 2 in mode 3 and that L, M, and N are their initial counts. If F is the frequency of the clock, then the frequency applied to CLK1 will be F/N. This will result in OUT1 producing a pulse having a period of MN/F. Therefore, pulses will occur at OUT0 at a frequency of F/L for a period

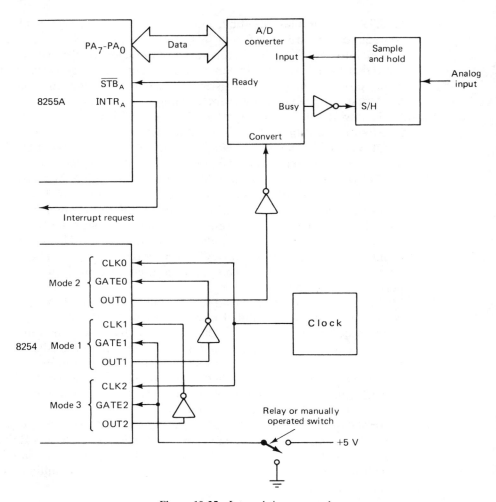

Figure 10-25 Interval timer example.

of MN/F seconds.   By applying OUT0 to the Convert input of the A/D converter, F/L samples per second will be taken for MN/F seconds beginning after the three counters have been initialized and the relay or manually operated switch has been closed.   After each converted sample has been transmitted to port A of the 8255A, an interrupt request is made through the INTR_A and an interrupt routine is used to input the sample.   An initialization sequence for the system is given in Fig. 10-26.   The sequence assumes that the addresses associated with the 8254 are 70 through 73; LCNT, MCNT, and NCNT contain L, M, and N; and L and N are less than 256.   It sets the counters to their modes and puts the initial counts in the CRs.   The initial counts L and N are to be in binary and M is to be in BCD.

```
MVI    A,00010100B   ;OUTPUT COUNTER 0
OUT    73H           ;CONTROL - MODE 2
LDA    LCNT          ;OUTPUT COUNTER 0
OUT    70H           ; INITIAL COUNT - BINARY
MVI    A,01110011B   ;OUTPUT COUNTER 1
OUT    73H           ;CONTROL - MODE 1
LDA    MCNT          ;OUTPUT COUNTER 1
OUT    71H           ; INITIAL COUNT - BCD
LDA    MCNT+1
OUT    71H
MVI    A,10010110B   ;OUTPUT COUNTER 2
OUT    73H           ;CONTROL - MODE 3
LDA    NCNT          ;OUTPUT COUNTER 2
OUT    72H           ; INITIAL COUNT - BINARY
 .
 .
 .
```

Figure 10-26   Initialization of counters for the A/D example.

10-5 KEYBOARD AND DISPLAY

For low-cost small systems, especially single-board microcomputers and micro-processor-based instruments, the front panel (or *console*) is often implemented by using simple keyboard and display units as input and output devices.   Through a keyboard, data, memory addresses, and machine code can be entered in the hex-adecimal form.   In addition to the numeric keys, a keyboard may include functional keys to enter monitor and control commands.   For output, memory addresses and data can be displayed on light-emitting diode (LED) display devices.

10-5-1 Keyboard Design

Unlike a terminal, a mechanical contact keyboard, for which the key switches are organized in a matrix form, does not include any electronics.   Figure 10-27 illus-trates how a 64-key keyboard can be interfaced to a microcomputer through two parallel I/O ports such as those provided by an 8255A.   When a key is depressed, the corresponding row and column are shorted to form a path.   By detecting the row and column positions of the contact closure, the code word representing the depressed key is determined.   This process is called keyboard scanning and is accomplished as follows.   The output port sends a 0 to row 0 and 1's to all seven of the other rows.   The column lines are then read and checked.   If a 0 is not found in row 0, then the process is repeated for row 1, then for row 2, and so on. When a 0 is found, a depressed key is detected whose row position is known from the combination that was output and column position is known from the input. By combining the row and column positions of the 0, a unique word that indicates the position of the depressed key can be found.

Two major problems are associated with keyboards; they are contact bounce and striking keys at about the same time.   When a key is depressed or released, the contact may bounce between its open and close positions several times before

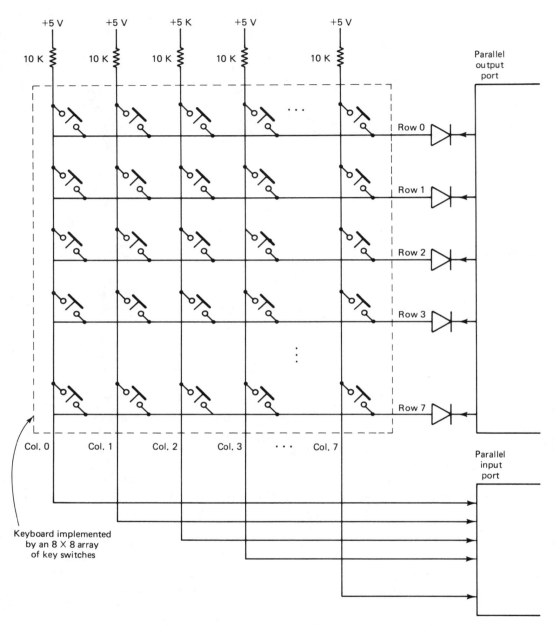

Figure 10-27   Organization of a mechanical keyboard.

it settles to a close or open position. The duration of the bouncing varies and is normally less than 10 mS. Contact closures due to bouncing must be discarded to prevent false key detection and this operation is called *debouncing*. Debouncing can be accomplished through either hardware or software, but the software approach requires too much processor time for most applications. Multiple key closings are most easily handled by scanning the entire array and inputting the closures in the order they are detected.

10-5-2 Display Design

Various types of devices are available for numeric and alphanumeric displays. Seven-segment LED displays such as the one shown in Fig. 10-28 are typically used for hexadecimal digit display. A digit in seven-segment code is fed to the input pins of a through g and DP. The input can be represented by active low or active high signals, depending on whether the display unit is of a common anode or a common cathode type. An individual segment is lit when the corresponding LED is forward biased.

Figure 10-29 shows the segments to light for each hexadecimal digit. Also shown in the figure are the seven-segment codes for which the least significant bit of each code enables segment a of the display, the next bit enables segment b, and so on.

Figure 10-30 shows a multiple-digit display that is configured from eight seven-segment display units. In order to reduce the device count by eliminating external data latches from the display units, they can be connected to two 8-bit parallel output ports and operated in a multiplexed mode. All display units share the common segment lines and only one unit is selected at a time through the digit

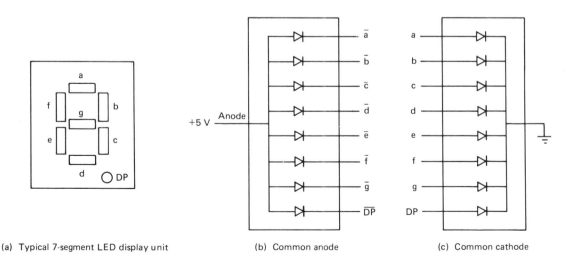

(a) Typical 7-segment LED display unit   (b) Common anode   (c) Common cathode

Figure 10-28   Seven-segment LED display unit.

Hexadecimal Digit	Segments	Seven-Segment Code
0	a,b,c,d,e,f	3F
1	b,c	06
2	a,b,d,e,g	5B
3	a,b,c,d,g	4F
4	b,c,f,g	66
5	a,c,d,f,g	6D
6	a,c,d,e,f,g	7D
7	a,b,c	07
8	a,b,c,d,e,f,g	7F
9	a,b,c,d,f,g	6F
A	a,b,c,e,f,g	77
b	c,d,e,f,g	7C
C	a,d,e,f	39
d	b,c,d,e,g	5E
E	a,d,e,f,g	79
F	a,e,f,g	71

Figure 10-29   Seven-segment code equivalent for hexadecimal digits.

select lines.   Each display is driven for 1 mS and after rotating through all eight units, the first one is returned to and the sequence is repeated.   Thus, the displays are repeatedly refreshed to give the illusion of a continuously lit multiple-digit display.

Since a typical average current through each turned-on segment could be as high as 20 mA and more than one segment may be lit per digit, the resulting current exceeds the driving capability of a regular TTL gate.   Therefore, digit drivers and segment drivers are needed.   A low on the base of a digit driver transistor turns the transistor on and effectively connects that display unit to +5 V.   A low on the base of a segment driver transistor turns on the transistor, thus letting current flow through the segment.   In addition, since the voltage drop across a forward-biased segment diode is constant, a resistor in series with each segment is required to limit the current, thus protecting the display and drivers.   The resistance of these resistors depends on the desired display brightness.

Another type of hexadecimal digit display is the Texas Instruments (TI) TIL311 shown in Fig. 10-31, which uses a matrix-dot array of 20 LEDs.   It inputs a 4-bit binary number and internally decodes the digit input to light the LEDs corresponding to the equivalent hexadecimal digit.   Since it has built-in latches and constant current drivers, the input is TTL compatible, thus eliminating a need for external drivers and current-limiting resistors.   Also, the input latch holds data for constant display and refresh is no longer required.

10-5-3 Keyboard/Display Controller

Although interfacing a keyboard and multiple-digit display to parallel I/O ports is simple from a hardware standpoint, while inputting and outputting the processor would be tied up by keyboard scanning and display refreshing routines.   The Intel 8279 keyboard/display controller is an LSI device designed to release the processor from performing the time-consuming scan and refresh operations.

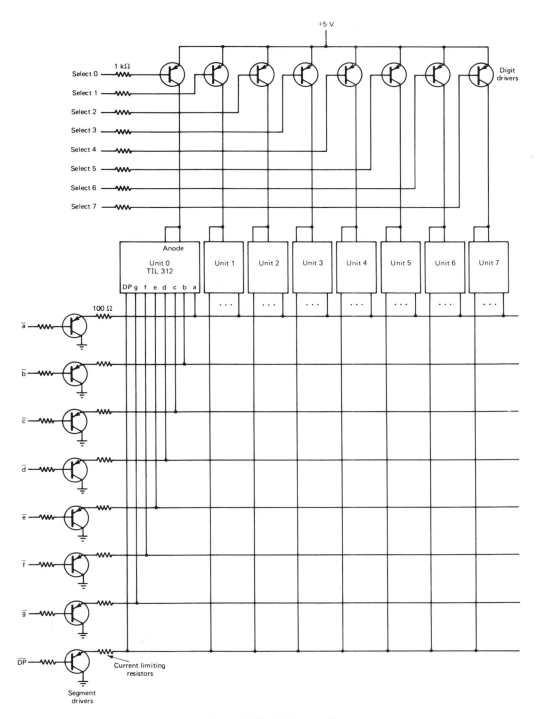

Figure 10-30 Eight-digit display.

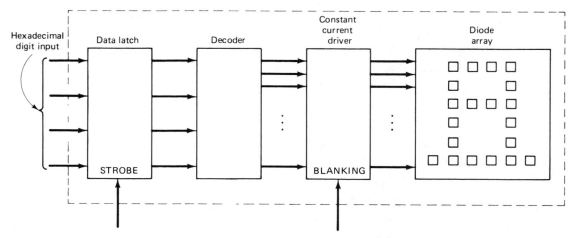

Figure 10-31 TI TIL311 matrix-dot hexadecimal display.

Figure 10-32 shows the general structure of the 8279 and its interface to the bus. The control and status registers share the odd address and the data buffer register uses the even address. The addressing is according to the following table:

$\overline{CS}$	$\overline{RD}$	$\overline{WR}$	A_0	Transfer Description
0	1	0	0	Data bus to data buffer register
0	1	0	1	Data bus to control register
0	0	1	0	Data buffer register to data bus
0	0	1	1	Status register to data bus

where 1 means high and 0 means low.

For keyboard control, the 8279 constantly scans each row of the keyboard by sending out row addresses on SL_2–SL_0 and inputting signals on the return lines RL_7–RL_0, which represent the column addresses. Note that the SL_3–SL_0 lines are used for both keyboard scanning and display refreshing and will accommodate up to 16 display units. When a depressed key is detected, the key is automatically debounced by waiting 10 mS to check if the same key remains depressed. If a depressed key is detected, an 8-bit code word corresponding to the key position is assembled by combining the encoded column position, row position, shift status, and control status as shown below.

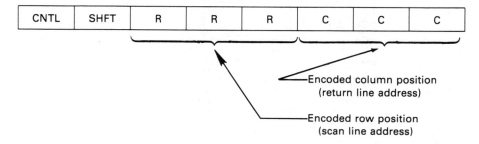

The SHFT and CNTL pins are used primarily to support typewriter-like keyboards that have shift and control keys. The key position is then entered into the 8×8 first-in/first-out (FIFO) sensor memory, and the IRQ (interrupt request) line is activated if the sensor memory was previously empty.

The control and timing registers are physically a collection of flags and registers that are accessed by commands that are sent to the 8279's odd address. The three MSBs of a command determine its type, and the meaning of the remaining 5 bits depends on the type. Although there are eight types, only three of them are considered here. (For the other types as well as other detailed information about the 8279, see Reference 2.) The formats of the three commands of interest to us are:

KEYBOARD DISPLAY MODE SET—Specifies the input and display modes and is used to initialize the 8279. Its format is

```
0  0  0  D  D  K  K  K
            ‾‾‾  ‾‾‾‾‾
             ↑     └──Control bits to set input mode:

                      000   Encoded keyboard scan mode with 2-key
                            lockout
                      001   Decoded keyboard scan mode with 2-key
                            lockout
                      010   Encoded keyboard scan mode with N-key
                            rollover
                      011   Decoded keyboard scan mode with N-key
                            rollover
                      100   Encoded sensor matrix scan mode
                      101   Decoded sensor matrix scan mode
                      110   Strobed input with encoded display scan
                      111   Strobed input with decoded display scan

                     ─Control bits to set display mode:

                      00    Left entry, 8 8-bit displays
                      01    Left entry, 16 8-bit displays
                      10    Right entry, 8 8-bit displays
                      11    Right entry, 16 8-bit displays
```

READ FIFO SENSOR MEMORY—Specifies that a read from the data buffer register will input a byte from the FIFO memory and, if the 8279 is in the sensor mode, it indicates which row is to be read. This command is required before inputting data from the FIFO memory. Its format is

```
0  1  0  I  X  A  A  A
                  ‾‾‾‾‾
                    └──Row address to be read in a sensor mode

                 ─Don't care

              ─Autoincrement bit; if I = 1, the next input is
               from the next byte in the FIFO
```

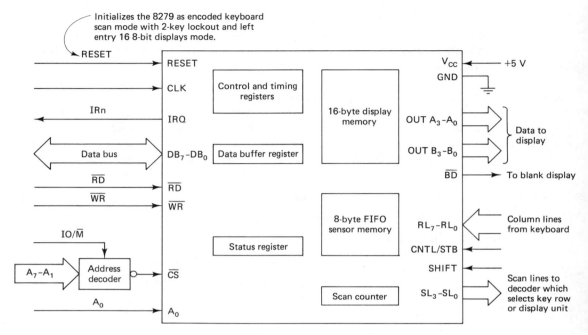

Figure 10-32 Block diagram of the Intel 8279.

Note that if the input mode is a keyboard scan mode, a read is always from the byte which first entered the FIFO, hence the I and AAA bits are ignored.

WRITE TO DISPLAY MEMORY—Indicates that a write to the data buffer register will put data in the display memory. This command must be given before the CPU can send the characters to be displayed to the 8279. Its format is

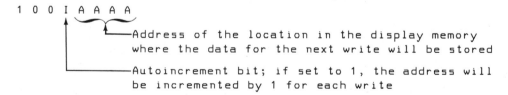

```
1 0 0 I A A A A
```
Address of the location in the display memory where the data for the next write will be stored

Autoincrement bit; if set to 1, the address will be incremented by 1 for each write

The 8279 provides two options for handling the situation in which more than one key is depressed at about the same time. With the two-key lockout option, if another key is depressed while the first key is being debounced, the key that is released last will be entered into the FIFO. If the second key is depressed within two scan cycles after the first is debounced and the first key remains depressed after the second one is released, then the first depressed key is recognized. Otherwise, both are ignored. The N-key rollover option treats each key depression independently. If more than one is depressed, after they are depressed they are all entered in the order they were sensed.

In addition, the 8279 has a sensor matrix mode under which signals on the return lines are stored into the FIFO at the row corresponding to the scan address. Unlike a keyboard scan mode, the SHFT and CNTL status and the scan address are not entered. This mode keeps an image of the status of the sensor matrix and is useful when information from several devices is input by polling each device through the scan lines.

The status of the FIFO is kept in the status register. Bits 0, 1, and 2 of this register give the number of data bytes currently in FIFO memory and bit 3 = 1 indicates that this memory is full. Bits 4 and 5 indicate underflows, which occur when an attempt is made to read from an empty FIFO memory, and overflows, which occur when an input to a full FIFO memory is attempted. In both cases a 1 signifies the presence of the error. A 1 in bit 6 reflects a closure when the 8279 is in its sensor matrix mode and a multiple closure when it is in special error mode. Bit 7 shows whether or not the display is available.

For display control, the 8279 provides a 16-byte display memory and refresh logic. Each address in the display memory corresponds to a display unit, with address 0 representing the leftmost display unit. Once the CPU loads the characters to be displayed into this memory, the 8279 needs no further instructions and the processor is released from refreshing the display units. The output is accomplished by the 8279 repeatedly sending out characters over the lines OUT A_3–A_0 and OUT B_3–B_0 and unit select addresses over SL_3–SL_0. Although the display memory can be directly addressed, the processor may sequentially enter data to the display memory either from the left or from the right. For the autoincrement left entry, after each write to the display the address is incremented by 1, so that the next character appears in the next display unit to the right. The autoincrement right entry allows characters to be displayed in the form used by many electronic calculators. It causes the display to be shifted left one character and stores the next character from the right.

Figure 10-33 illustrates one way in which a 64-key keyboard and an eight-digit seven-segment display can be connected to an 8279. Both the keyboard and display are scanned and refreshed under the control of the select signals SL_2–SL_0. The SL_3 pin is not connected because there are only eight display units. Both 3 to 8 decoders have active low outputs. One decoder selects one row of keys while the other decoder enables one of the eight digit drivers.

To demonstrate how to program an 8279, let us assume that the device is connected to a keyboard and multiple-digit display as shown in Fig. 10-33. The 8279's addresses are E8 and E9, and the interrupt request pin IRQ is not used. First, the device must be initialized by sending a mode set command to the control register. The following instructions set the keyboard/display controller to its encoded keyboard scan mode, with two-key lockout, and its left entry eight 8-bit displays mode:

```
MVI        A,0
OUT        0E9H
```

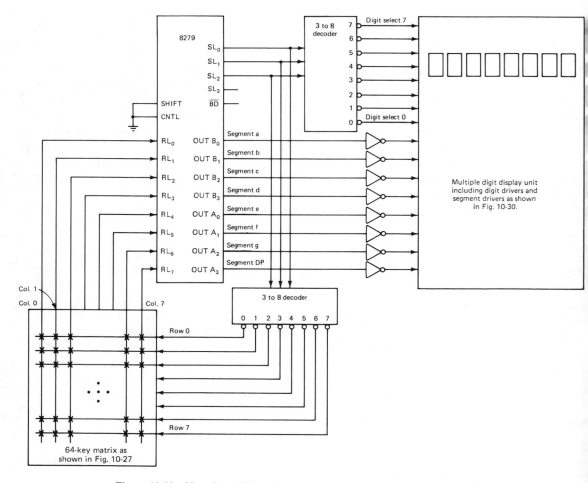

Figure 10-33   Use of an 8279 to interface a keyboard and a multiple-digit display.

Then characters generated by the depressed keys can be read through the FIFO memory. A program segment that uses programmed I/O to input eight keywords and store them in an 8-byte array KEYS with the first byte at the highest address is

```
           LXI      D,KEYS+7
           MVI      C,8
           MVI      A,01000000B
           OUT      0E9H
LOOP:      IN       0E9H
           ANI      0FH
           JZ       LOOP
           IN       0E8H
```

```
;TABLE DEFINES THE 7-SEGMENT CODE FOR EACH HEXADECIMAL DIGIT
TABLE:     DB        3FH,06H,5BH,4FH,66H,6DH,7DH,07H,7FH,6FH,77H
           DB        7CH,39H,5EH,79H,71H
DIGITS:    DS        8               ;STORE DIGITS TO BE DISPLAYED
           .
           .
           .
           MVI       A,10010000B     ;OUTPUT COMMMAND FOR
           OUT       0E9H            ;WRITING TO DISPLAY RAM
           MVI       C,8             ;USE C AS COUNTER
           MVI       B,0
           LXI       D,DIGITS+7      ;USE DE AS POINTER, INITIALLY
                                     ;POINTS TO THE LAST DIGIT
LOOP:      PUSH      B               ;SAVE C
           LXI       H,TABLE
           LDAX      D               ;LOAD THE NEXT DIGIT
           MOV       C,A             ;MOVE IT TO C
           DAD       B               ;ADD BC TO HL
                                     ;TO PERFORM CODE CONVERSION
           MOV       A,M             ;A HAS THE EQUIVALENT 7-SEGMENT CODE
           OUT       0E8H
           DCX       D               ;POINT TO THE NEXT DIGIT
           POP       B               ;RESTORE C
           DCR       C               ;DECREMENT COUNTER
           JNZ       LOOP            ;REPEAT THE LOOP FOR 8 TIMES
           .
           .
           .
```

Figure 10-34   A sample program for displaying a hexadecimal number using seven-segment display units.

```
           STAX      D
           DCX       D
           DCR       C
           JNZ       LOOP
```

The first two instructions set up DE and C as a pointer and counter, the next three instructions cause the input from the even address to come from the FIFO, the three instructions beginning at LOOP force the processor to idle until an input is ready, and the following two instructions transfer the input data to KEYS. The last three instructions cause the sequence to repeat until eight characters have been read.

To display digits, the CPU must first give a write display memory command and then output a seven-segment code to the display memory. As an example, Fig. 10-34 shows an instruction sequence to display eight hexadecimal digits. In the example, it is assumed that the eight digits are stored in the array DIGITS, one digit per byte with the least significant digit being stored at the lowest address.

10-6 DISKETTE CONTROLLERS

The primary means of storing large quantities of data are magnetic tape and disk units, although magnetic bubble memory (MBM) is currently having some impact in this area. Magnetic tapes and disks have two major advantages over MBMs:

portability between systems and capacity. Magnetic tapes tend to cost less per byte of stored information and be the most durable, but disks have much lower access times. Tapes and disks come in many sizes and shapes and the designs of the equipment for reading from and writing onto them vary correspondingly. It is not possible to give a reasonable presentation of the numerous types of tape and disk units in the space available here; therefore, we will concentrate on what is by far the most popular mass storage units in microcomputer systems, the *diskette*, or *floppy disk*, units.

The physical construction and overall data storage format of a diskette are shown in Fig. 10-35. The diskette is a Mylar disk that is coated with a magnetic substance. It has a spindle hole in the center and at least one index hole that is slightly offset from the center. The purpose of the index hole(s) is to give the diskette drive a reference point(s) while the drive is storing or retrieving data. The diskette is sealed in a square jacket that also has a spindle hole and index

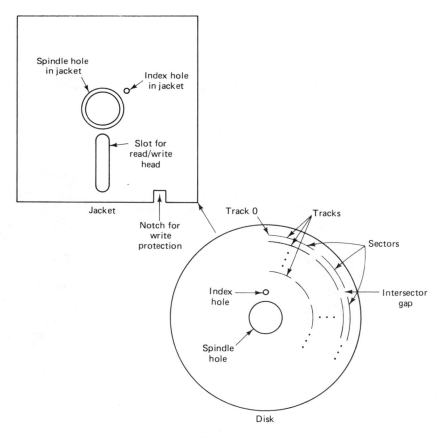

Figure 10-35 Construction of a diskette.

hole. In addition, the jacket has a slot so that the drive's read/write head can contact the diskette's surface, and a write protect notch.

The data are bit serially stored (ie., as a succession of bits) in concentric circles called *tracks* and are grouped into arcs known as *sectors*. Some diskette drives have only one read/write head and can only store and retrieve data from one surface of the diskette, while others have two read/write heads and can utilize both surfaces. If both surfaces can be accessed, then the pairs of tracks that are the same distance from the center of the diskette are referred to as *cylinders*.

There are two standard sizes for diskettes, ones with 8-in. jackets and ones with 5.25-in. jackets. Some have only one index hole and are said to be *soft sectored*, while others have an index hole for each sector and are said to be *hard sectored*. Each sector on a soft-sectored diskette must start with formatting information that marks the beginning of the sector and only the first sector of a track is marked by an index hole. For a hard-sectored diskette the beginnings of all sectors are marked by index holes.

The tracks (and cylinders) are numbered, with the outermost track being given the number 0. The sectors are also numbered and on a soft-sectored diskette, the first sector after the index hole is assigned the number 1. When a diskette is inserted in a drive, the spindle passes through the spindle hole and the diskette is clamped to the spindle and is continuously rotated within its jacket at 360 rpm. The read/write head moves in and out so that it can be positioned over any desired track. Once positioned, the rotational motion causes the sectors within the selected track to pass under the head, thus permitting the individual sectors to be accessed. When a read or write is to be performed, the head is lowered, or *loaded*, onto the surface of the diskette through the slot in the jacket, and is then positioned over the desired track. For a soft-sectored diskette, the drive waits until the index hole is encountered and then begins to read the sector formatting information. Upon finding the needed sector the drive may begin its read or write operation. In the case of a hard-sectored disk the sector is found by means of the index holes.

The time needed to access a sector is subdivided into

LOAD TIME—For bringing the head in contact with the diskette.
POSITION TIME—For positioning the head over the track.
ROTATIONAL TIME—For rotating the diskette until it is over the desired sector.

Typical average load, position, and rotational times are 16, 225, and 80 mS, respectively. Once a sector is found the average information transfer rate in bytes per second is approximately

$$\text{Bytes per sector} \times \text{Sectors per track} \times \text{Speed in rpm}/60$$

(This includes the time wasted in traversing gaps in the data.)

In order to make our discussion more specific, let us now limit it to a single type of diskette, the IBM 3740-compatible, soft-sectored, 8-in. diskette. These diskettes contain 77 tracks and either 15 sectors (single density) or 26 sectors (double density), although our examples will permit from 8 to 26 sectors. Normally, only 75 of the tracks are used, thus allowing for two bad tracks. The good tracks are numbered 0 through 74.

The track and sector format of these diskettes is illustrated in Fig. 10-36. There is a gap between each of the sectors, and the index hole indicator must become active during the gap between the last sector and first sector of each track. Each sector contains an identification field and a data field, both of which begin with a sync field. There is a gap between the two fields that gives the head time to be turned on or off, depending on whether the previous or following data field was or is to be accessed. The identification field contains an address mark followed by the cylinder (or track) number, head number, sector number, number of data bytes in the sector, and 2 error-detection bytes. The data field consists of an address mark followed by the data bytes and 2 error-detection bytes.

The address mark in the identification field of the first sector is usually different from those in the other sectors and the address marks in the identification fields are different from those in the data fields. Also, the address marks for the data field differ, depending on whether the field contains useful information or is occupied by filler bytes.

There are two principal methods for generating the error-detection bytes. One is to obtain a *checksum* by summing all of the bytes in the field that occur before the checksum (and ignoring any overflow). The other is to consider the bits in the field as coefficients of one big binary polynomial and let the error-detection bytes be the remainder, called *cyclic redundancy check* (*CRC*), that results from dividing this polynomial by a fixed polynomial of degree 16. It is the latter method that is assumed in Fig. 10-36.

The bit pattern of the serially stored information is shown in Fig. 10-37. The information is grouped into cells, each of which is divided into four intervals, with the first interval containing a clock pulse. The third interval is for indicating a

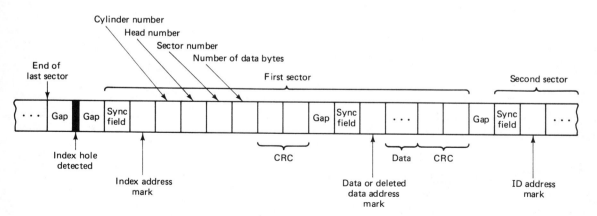

Figure 10-36 Track and sector format for a soft-sectored diskette.

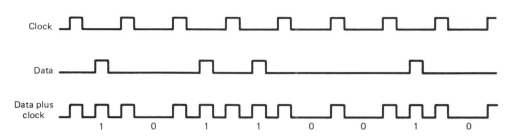

Figure 10-37 Bit pattern of stored data.

data bit and will contain a pulse if the data bit is 1.   A representative value for the cell period for a 360 rpm drive is 4 μS.

Figure 10-38 shows how a typical diskette controller would appear in a diskette subsystem.   Because the information is serially stored on the diskette, the inputs from and outputs to the diskette drive are bit streams.   Therefore, the input bytes are received by a shift register before they are transferred to the data buffer register, and the output bytes are put in a shift register so that they can be shifted out in serial form.   The output electronics must be such that the pulses from the write clock input are interspersed with the data bits to produce the format given in Fig. 10-37.

Because most disk controllers are designed to service more than one drive, some of the pins on the controller must be reserved for drive selection lines.   Other control outputs to the drive should include a step pulse line for stepping through the tracks, a step direction signal, and a head load signal.   There should be control inputs for inputting signals indicating when the head is positioned at track 0, a fault or error has occurred, or the diskette is write protected, and a pulse each time the index hole is sensed.

For reading data from the disk the data must be separated from the clock pulses.   This is done by using a phase-locked-loop circuit to provide a data window signal.   (A phase-locked loop constantly tracks the frequency of the read data input signal and locks an oscillator to that frequency.)   The controller outputs the VCO signal to turn the phase-locked loop on and off.   The phase-locked loop operates in either single-density mode (FM) or double-density mode (MFM), depending on the MFM signal (1 for MFM mode and 0 for FM mode.)   For writing data there should be a write enable and low-current lines in addition to the output data line.   The low-current line is needed because less current is used when writing to the inner tracks, those tracks with numbers greater than 43.

If a diskette having 26 sectors and 128 data bytes per sector is rotated at 360 rpm, the average transfer rate is approximately

$$26 \times 128 \times 360/60 = 19,968 \text{ bytes/second}$$

which gives an average period of about 50 μs.   Taking into account the gaps, the actual period for transferring a byte is normally 32 μS (or 4 μS per bit).   Although

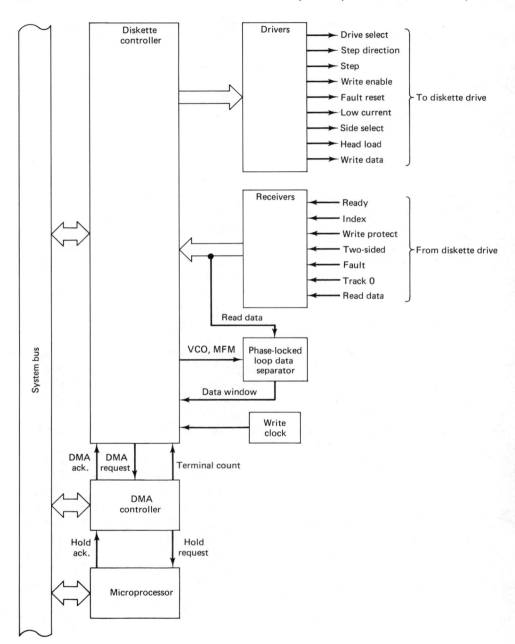

Figure 10-38 Diskette subsystem.

it would be possible to perform transfers at this rate without a DMA controller, it is much more efficient to use one.   Consequently, disk controllers normally have DMA request, DMA acknowledge, and terminal count pins.   Another reason for using a DMA controller with a disk controller is that disk transfers always involve blocks of data, not single bytes.

As an example of a diskette controller let us consider the Intel 8272, whose organization is diagrammed in Fig. 10-39.   It has two registers that can be addressed

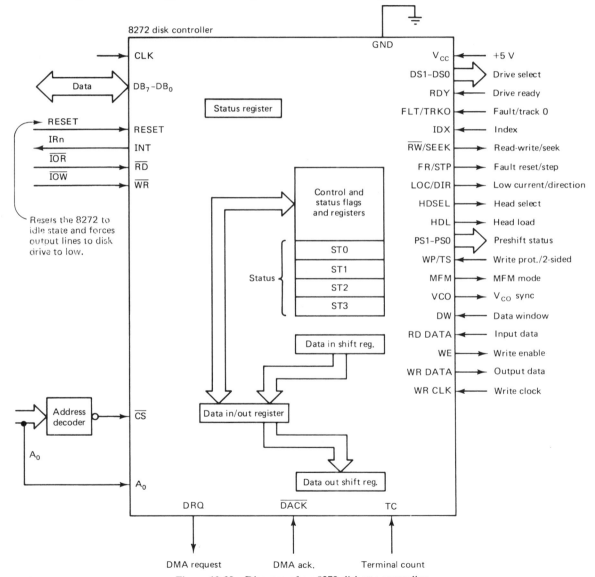

Figure 10-39   Diagram of an 8272 diskette controller.

by the processor, a status register that is read when $A_0 = 0$ and a data in/out register that is accessed when $A_0 = 1$. The format of the status register is given in Fig. 10-40. There are several other control, status, and parameter registers and flags that can be addressed via the data in/out register. Whether these registers and flags are being accessed or data I/O is being performed with the diskette drive depends on the sequencing.

Operations executed by the controller are divided into a command phase, an execution phase, and a result phase. During the command phase bytes are sent to the control registers and flags via the data in/out register. Then the requested operation is performed during the execution phase and, upon completion of the operation, the result phase is entered and status information is read by the processor. The outputs during the command phase and inputs during the result phase are performed using single-byte transfers, even though any data transfer that takes place in the execution phase is normally supervised by a DMA controller.

The possible 8272 commands are

READ DATA—Reads data from a data field on a diskette.

WRITE DATA—Writes data to a data field on a diskette.

READ DELETED DATA—Reads data from a field marked as being deleted.

WRITE DELETED DATA—Writes a deleted data address mark and puts filler characters in the data field.

READ A TRACK—Reads an entire track of data fields.

READ ID—Reads the identification field.

FORMAT A TRACK—Writes the formatting information to a track using program supplied formatting parameters.

SCAN EQUAL
SCAN LOW OR EQUAL   } Scans the data for specified condition and makes an
SCAN HIGH OR EQUAL   } interrupt request when the condition is satisfied.

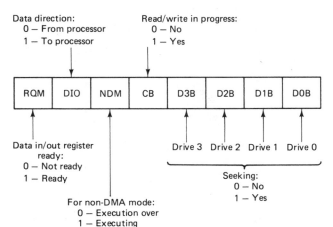

Figure 10-40   Format of the 8272's status register.

RECALIBRATE—Causes the head to be retracted to track 0.

SENSE INTERRUPT STATUS—Reads status information from ST0 after interrupts caused by ready line changes and seek operations.

SPECIFY—Sets the step rate, head unload time, head load time, and DMA mode.

SENSE DRIVE STATUS—Inputs the drive status from ST3.

SEEK—Positions head over a specified track.

The sequence needed to complete four of these commands is given in Fig. 10-41 as an example.   The read data command includes all three phases, the seek command includes only the command and execution phases, the sense drive status command includes only the command and result phases, and the specify command consists only of the command phase.   In all cases, the commands must be performed in their entirety (including the result phase, if applicable) or they will be considered incomplete.   If an invalid command is given, the 8272 will return the status byte ST0 in response to the next input from the data in/out register.

Several of the commands require that some of the status bytes ST0, ST1, ST2, and ST3 be read during their result phases.   These registers contain bits for indicating such things as CRC errors, overrun errors, drive selected, end of seek, whether or not the diskette is two-sided, and so on.

As an example, consider an 8272 whose even address is 2A.   The 8272 could be initialized to a step rate of 6 mS per track, a head unload time of 48 mS, a head load time of 16 mS, and the DMA mode by the specify command sequence

```
          CHECK      2AH,80H
          MVI        A,03H
          OUT        2BH
          CHECK      2AH,80H
          MVI        A,63H
          OUT        2BH
          CHECK      2AH,80H
          MVI        A,10H
          OUT        2BH
```

where the macro CHECK is defined as follows:

```
          CHECK      MACRO      PORT,STAT
                     LOCAL      AGAIN
          AGAIN:     IN         PORT
                     ANI        0C0H
                     XRI        STAT
                     JNZ        AGAIN
                     ENDM
```

The second line causes the label AGAIN to become AGAIN0, AGAIN1, AGAIN2, . . . , with successive calls.   The reason the CHECK macro is needed before each output is that the two MSBs of the status register must be 10 before each command

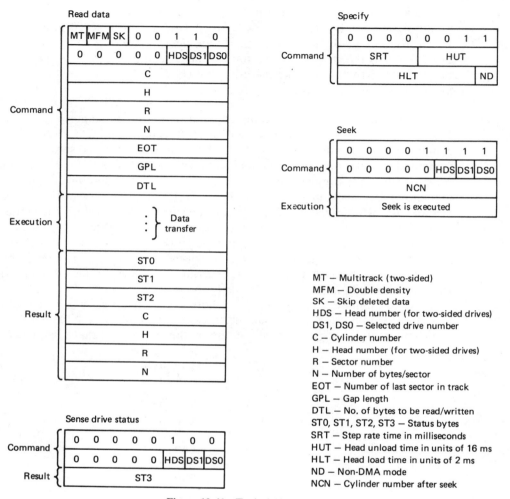

Figure 10-41   Typical 8272 commands.

byte is written into the 8272. Also during the result phase, these 2 bits must be 11 before each byte is read from the 8272's data register.

The seek command sequence

```
CHECK    2AH,80H
MVI      A,0FH
OUT      2BH
CHECK    2AH,80H
MVI      A,02H
OUT      2BH
CHECK    2AH,80H
MVI      A,30
OUT      2BH
```

would cause the head on drive 1 to be moved to cylinder 30 and head 0 to be selected.   Figure 10-42 gives the sequence needed to read data from a diskette. It is assumed that the associated DMA has been initialized before the read data routine is called so that DMA transfer may begin as soon as the read operation is performed.   The status and result bytes would be input only after the execution phase and the read is known to be complete (e.g., after an interrupt on completion has occurred).

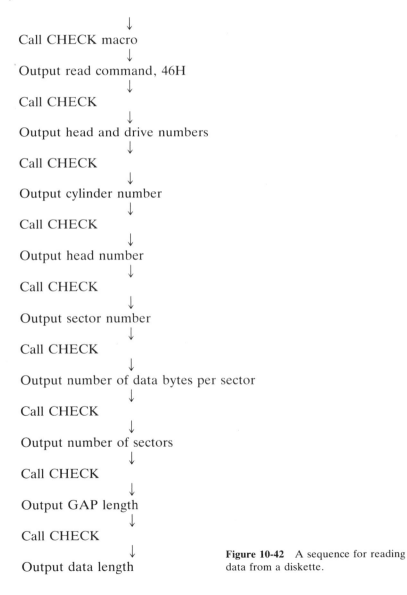

Call CHECK macro

Output read command, 46H

Call CHECK

Output head and drive numbers

Call CHECK

Output cylinder number

Call CHECK

Output head number

Call CHECK

Output sector number

Call CHECK

Output number of data bytes per sector

Call CHECK

Output number of sectors

Call CHECK

Output GAP length

Call CHECK

Output data length

Figure 10-42   A sequence for reading data from a diskette.

BIBLIOGRAPHY

1. *The MCS-80/85 Family User's Manual* (Santa Clara, Calif.: Intel Corporation, 1983).
2. *Microsystem Components Handbook, Vol. II* (Santa Clara, Calif.: Intel Corporation, 1985).
3. LIU, YU-CHENG, and GLENN A. GIBSON, *Microcomputer Systems: The 8086/8088 Family—Architecture, Programming, and Design*, 2nd ed. (Englewood Cliffs, N.J.: Prentice-Hall, 1986).
4. SHORT, KENNETH L., *Microprocessors and Programmed Logic* (Englewood Cliffs, N.J.: Prentice-Hall, 1981).
5. STONE, HAROLD S., *Microcomputer Interfacing* (Reading, Mass.: Addison-Wesley, 1982).

EXERCISES

1. Implement the address decoding logic shown in Fig. 10-3b by using 4-bit comparators.
2. Redesign the circuit in Fig. 10-3c by replacing the AND gate with another 3 to 8 decoder and explain any advantage from using this implementation.
3. Assume that the mode register of an 8251A contains 01011010 and the baud rate for data transmission is to be 1200 baud.
   (a) Determine the frequency of the RxC and TxC clocks.
   (b) Determine the pulse widths of each data bit on the RxD and TxD pins.
   (c) Determine the maximum number of characters that can be transferred per second.
4. Assume that the UART shown in Fig. 10-7 is used to interface an input terminal to a system bus. Also assume that the receiver data register is assigned to port 04. Draw a logic diagram showing how the receiver register full and receiver data enable pins are to be connected and how to generate an interrupt request.
5. In order to justify the use of the receiver data register in a serial interface, compare the amount of time that the processor would have to read a character before an overrun error occurs with and without a receive data register. For the comparison, assume that data are transmitted in asynchronous mode at 4800 baud with an 11-bit data format.
6. Could the UART be used as an interface device for synchronous data transmission? Why?
7. Based on the word format and data recapture scheme discussed in Section 10-2-1, determine the permissible frequency range of the receiver clock for which no framing errors will occur if the data transfer rate is 9600 baud, there are 8 bits per character, and no parity bit.
8. A message of 1000 bytes is to be transmitted over a communication link at 9600 baud. Determine the minimum amount of time required to transmit the message in asynchronous mode. Assume that the data format consists of 1 start bit, 1 stop bit, and no parity bit. What is the required amount of time if the data transmission is in synchronous mode with two SYNC characters?
9. Assume the 7-bit ASCII code, even parity, and 2 stop bits and sketch the timing diagram of the letter A as it is transmitted over an asynchronous serial communication link.

10. Given that the sequence shown below is output with $A_0 = 1$ following a reset, describe the action taken as each output is received by the 8251A.

$$00010100$$
$$00010110$$
$$00010110$$
$$00110011$$

$\left.\begin{array}{l} \cdot \\ \cdot \\ \cdot \end{array}\right\}$ Output with $A_0 = 0$

$$01000000$$

(See the flowchart in Fig. 10-11.)

11. Write a program sequence that will initialize an 8251A so that it will transmit and receive asynchronous characters containing 7 information bits, 1 stop bit, and no parity bit. The baud rate factor is to be 16. The even address associated with the 8251A is to be FA. Extend the sequence so that the following message will be sent:

TERMINAL IS READY TO ACCEPT INPUT

12. Extend the program sequence in Exercise 11 so that it will use programmed I/O to input a line of characters (with line size = 80) and echo each character while it is received.

13. Assume that the address decoding logic enables an 8255A when $A_7 - A_2 = 011101$. Write an instruction sequence to initialize the 8255A for a basic I/O mode and then execute the following steps:

Step 1: Input from port A.

Step 2: If PA_2 is 1, set PC_0 to 1 and go to step 1; otherwise, go to step 3.

Step 3: Check PA_4. If $PA_4 = 1$, set PC_1 to 1 and go to step 1; otherwise, stop.

14. Design an 8-digit display using an 8255A as the interface and TIL 311 display units (see Fig. 10-31). First show the connections between the 8255A and the display. Then give a flowchart for a display routine.

15. Draw a flowchart of a keyboard scanning routine. Assume that the interface is implemented by using an 8255A as shown in Fig. 10-27.

16. By also using port B as a mode 1 input, modify the design in Fig. 10-22 so that a 12-bit A/D converter can be serviced. Give a program sequence for inputting a sample and storing it in the word whose location is represented by SAMPLE.

17. Describe how an 8254 could be used to count the pulses input to it for a period of time that is controlled by a second input. At the end of the overall counting time an interrupt request is to be made on an IR2 line, and after every 20 of the pulses has been counted an interrupt request is to be made on an IR3 line. Also write a program sequence for initializing the 8254.

18. Suppose that an 8254 is connected to a 100 KHz clock. Write an instruction sequence that will initialize the 8254 as a programmable clock generator with a frequency = 1, 2, 3, . . . , or 10 KHz. Assume that location FREQ specifies the frequency in KHz and the accuracy of this programmable clock generator is to be within $\pm$ 5 μS.

19. Write a program segment that will read a depressed key and display that digit on the left-most display unit. The port addresses of the 8279 are to be F4 and F5.

20. Write a program sequence that will use the sense drive status command of an 8272 to put a 1 in location FLAG2 if drive 2 is write-protected.

21. Give a set of instructions that will loop until one of the drives in an 8272-based diskette subsystem is not busy and will then branch to ROUTn, where n is the number of the drive that is first found to be idle.

22. Draw a flowchart of the complete sequence needed to output a block of data to an 8272-based diskette subsystem that includes an 8237 DMA controller. The flowchart should take into account the initialization steps for both the diskette and DMA controllers, as well as the steps to execute the phases of the write data command.

Chapter 11

Solid State Memory Subsystems

Main memory, which is usually referred to simply as memory, is directly accessible to the CPU and stores the current program being executed. For microcomputer systems, semiconductor memory devices are used as basic building blocks to implement main memory. Each memory device contains an array of memory cells to store information. In addition, necessary over-head electronics are built into the device so that most memory devices provide TTL-compatible input data, output data, and control signals, and require only a +5 V supply. As technologies improve, semiconductor memory devices of higher density, lower cost, and increased speed become available in a variety of sizes.

According to the accessing scheme, solid state memory can be divided into two categories: random-access memory and serial (or sequential) memory. For random-access memory, stored information can be accessed by specifying the addresses in a random fashion. The time required to read the contents from a location is independent of its address. Contrarily, data can only be read out of a sequential memory in the same order in which they were originally written. Because the access time varies, depending on the location in which the data are stored, sequential memories are not used as main memory. Typically, they are used for buffer memory in terminals and other peripherals and for mass storage. Examples of large-scale solid state serial memory devices are magnetic bubble memories and charge-coupled devices. Magnetic tapes and disks are also often referred to as serial memories, although they are usually referred to as mass storage devices.

Random-access semiconductor memory is further classified into two categories: read/write (RAM) and read-only (ROM). In each category, the memory device can be implemented by either bipolar or MOS technologies. Bipolar ROMs have typically been used for control memories in microprogrammed CPUs. Because of the high cost, high power dissipation, and low bit density, bipolar RAMs are only used when high speed is required (such as in cache memory).

This chapter will first discuss the design of read/write memory modules using both static and dynamic RAMs. Because static RAMs are easier to use, our discussion will begin with an examination of the structure and timing of a typical static RAM device. This will be followed by a design example of a 16K-byte memory module. Dynamic RAM, nonvolatile memory, and ROM modules will be considered in Sections 11-5 through 11-7. Section 11-8 will present an overview of serial memories and the last two sections will introduce magnetic bubble memories and charge-coupled devices.

11-1 MEMORY SYSTEM CONFIGURATION

In a microcomputer system, the actual size of the main memory may vary over a wide range, depending on the application. However, the maximum size of the memory is limited by the number of addressing bits and the data length of the microprocessor used. As indicated in preceding chapters, 8-bit microprocessors are usually limited to 64K bytes. In order to provide the flexibility of configuring different memory capacities based on requirements, the memory is organized in a modular form as shown in Fig. 11-1. Each module provides a storage segment of M bytes, where M is a power of 2. If memory modules of 16K bytes each are used, memory can be configured in sizes that are multiples of 16K, and a memory of 64K would consist of four modules.

A module normally contains several memory chips and its own control and

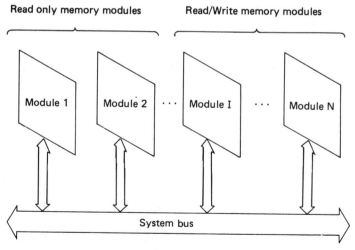

Figure 11-1 Modular memory system configuration.

bus interface logic.   Each module is assigned to an address range, which is specified by its interface logic.   During a memory reference, the address is sent to all memory modules and only the one that contains that address is activated.   Data are then read from or written into the selected memory module.   Because each memory module has its own control and bus interface logic, it is easy to include different types of memory in the system.   For instance, in the block diagram of Fig. 11-1, the first several memory modules are constructed of ROMs where permanent programs and/or data could be stored.   The remaining memory is read/write memory.   It is also possible to include in a single system memory modules of different speeds, thus allowing the cost/speed requirements to be optimized.

11-2 STATIC RAM DEVICES

In semiconductor memory, the medium of storage is provided by memory cells; each cell stores 1 bit of information.   For static memory devices, a cell is commonly implemented using six MOS transistors, as shown in Fig. 11-2.   Information is stored according to the states of transistors Q_1 and Q_2.   This cross-coupled transistor pair is such that when one transistor is on, the other is off, and vice versa. A 1 is assigned to the state that exists when Q_2 is on and Q_1 is off, and a 0 is assigned to the opposite state (Q_2 off and Q_1 on).   The transistors Q_3 and Q_4 serve as resistors and Q_5 and Q_6 act as enable gates.   During a write operation, first the cell is selected by raising the voltage level on the select line.   When this is done, transistors Q_5 and Q_6 act as short circuits, so that the Read/Write 1 line is applied to the gate of Q_2 and the Read/Write 0 line is applied to the gate of Q_1.   To write a 1 into the cell, a 1 is placed on Read/Write 1 and a 0 is placed on Read/Write 0; this causes Q_2 to be turned on and Q_1 to be turned off.   On the other hand, if

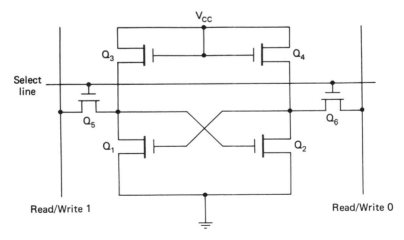

Figure 11-2   Six-transistor static RAM cell.

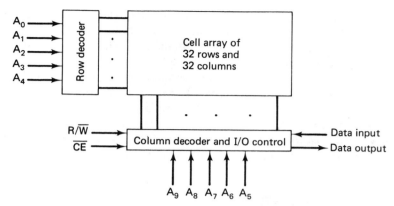

Figure 11-3 Block diagram of a typical 1K × 1 static RAM.

a 0 is to be written into the cell, a 1 is placed on Read/Write 0 and a 0 is placed on Read/Write 1. In either case, once they are set the states of Q_1 and Q_2 will remain unchanged until the next write operation. The cell can be read simply by applying a voltage to the select line. When this is done, the state of Q_1 is applied to the Read/Write 0 line and the state of Q_2 is applied to the Read/Write 1.

The number of memory cells and their arrangement in a static memory device vary considerably. A 256 × 4 RAM contains 256 locations, each having 4 bits, while a 4K × 1 configuration provides 4K locations, each containing only 1 bit. The general organization of a static RAM can be described using the block diagram of Fig. 11-3, which illustrates a 1K × 1 RAM. The memory cells are organized in a matrix of 32 rows and 32 columns. Address bits A_9 through A_0 are divided into row and column addresses and together specify one of the 1024 cells. Row address inputs (A_4–A_0) are decoded to select one of the 32 rows of storage cells. Column address inputs (A_9–A_5) not only select the column, but also enable the corresponding I/O circuits consisting of drivers and sense amplifiers. These circuits permit a stored bit to be output during a read operation and to be changed during a write operation. The read/write ($R/\overline{W}$) control input specifies the type of operation, high for read and low for write. The chip enable input ($\overline{CE}$) is used to select the appropriate set of memory chips on a memory module that contains more words than a single set of chips provides. If the chip is enabled, a read or write operation will proceed as specified by the $R/\overline{W}$ control input. Otherwise, the read/write signal will not be recognized and the output is forced into a high-impedance state. This allows the data outputs of several memory chips to be directly tied together so that 2K × 1, 4K × 1, and so on, memories can be constructed from 1K × 1 chips. When this is done, the bit being output not only depends on the signals on the address lines, but also depends on which chip receives the chip enable signal. This is explained in more detail in Section 11-4.

Because all the input and output pins are TTL-compatible, no interface between the MOS and TTL signal levels is necessary. Most static RAMs require only a single voltage source of +5 V.

As with most other digital devices, it is easy to connect semiconductor memory devices together because they have built-in supporting electronics. However, the timing constraints of the input signals are critical and the timing requirements vary from one device to another. To ensure proper operation, the control logic in a memory module must provide address inputs and control signals that satisfy the timing parameters as specified by the manufacturer of the memory devices being used. The input timing during a memory read operation is different from the input timing during a memory write operation. Both cases will be examined in the next section.

11-3 STATIC MEMORY DEVICE TIMING

The most important timing parameter to be considered in selecting a memory device is the *access time*. This is defined as the time delay between a stable input and a valid data output. Because the access time specifies how fast a data word can be read out of the memory device, it is commonly used to indicate the speed of the device. The maximum time delay from an address input to a data output is longer than the delay between a chip enable and a data output, and consequently the former timing figure is normally considered to be the access time. The access time for commonly used MOS RAMs varies from 35 nS to 400 nS.

For a read operation, once the output data are valid, the address input cannot be changed immediately to start another read operation. This is because the device needs a certain amount of time, called *read recovery time*, to complete its internal operations before the next memory operation. The sum of the access time and read recovery time is the *memory read cycle time*. This is the time needed between the start of a read operation and the start of the next memory cycle. The memory write cycle time can be similarly defined and may be different from the read cycle time. Figure 11-4a illustrates the timing of a memory read cycle. The address is applied at point A, which is the beginning of the read cycle, and must be held stable during the entire cycle. In order to reduce the access time, the chip enable input should be applied before point B. The data output becomes valid after point C and remains valid as long as the address and chip enable inputs hold. The R/$\overline{\text{W}}$ control input is not shown in the timing chart for the read cycle, but should remain high throughout the entire cycle.

A typical write cycle is shown in Fig. 11-4b. In addition to the address and chip enable inputs, an active-low write pulse on the R/$\overline{\text{W}}$ line and the data to be stored must be applied during the write cycle. The timing of data input is less restrictive and can be satisfied simply by holding the data input stable during the entire cycle. However, the application of the write pulse has two critical timing parameters: the address setup time and the write pulse width. The *address setup time* is the time required for the address to stabilize and is the time that must elapse before the write pulse can be applied. In Fig. 11-4b the address setup time is the time interval between points A and B. The *write pulse width* defines the amount

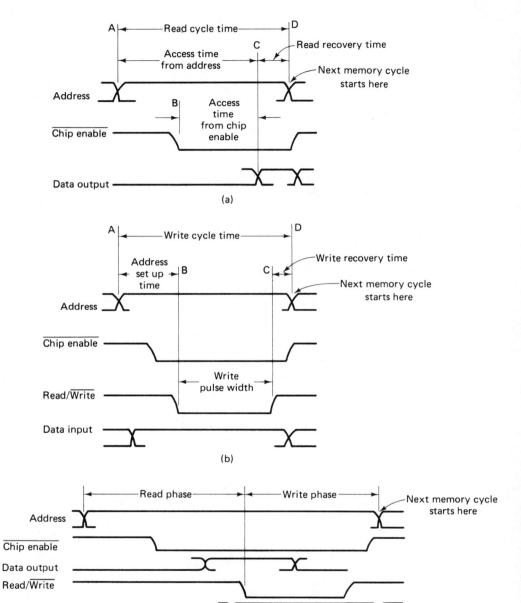

Figure 11-4 Typical timing for memory reference cycles: (a) a read cycle; (b) a write cycle; (c) a read-modify-write cycle.

of time that the write input must remain active low. The *write cycle time* is the time interval between points A and D and is the sum of address setup time, write pulse width, and write recovery time. Both the read and write recovery times may be zero for some memory devices.

In addition to read and write cycles, there is a special memory cycle called *read-modify-write*, which is often mentioned in memory design literature. Consider the execution of a machine instruction whose destination operand is also one of the source operands (e.g., increment or decrement an operand in memory by 1). During the execution of such an instruction, the contents of a memory location are read out and processed by the CPU and then the results are stored back into the same memory location. Obviously, this can be achieved using two separate memory reference cycles, a read cycle followed by a write cycle with the address unchanged. However, it is possible to reduce the total memory reference time, which is the sum of the read cycle and write cycle times, by combining them into a single read-modify-write cycle. Except for dynamic RAM with one transistor cells, semiconductor memory has nondestructive readout (i.e., the contents of a memory location remain unchanged when it is read). Therefore, as shown in Fig. 11-4c, only the write recovery time following the read operation and the address setup time for the write operation will be saved. This is a relatively small time savings; consequently, read-modify-write cycles will not be considered in the design examples given in the succeeding sections.

It is important to note that the access time and cycle time discussed in this section are the minimum timing requirements for the memory devices themselves. The access time and cycle time for the memory system as a whole are considerably longer because of the delays resulting from the system bus logic and memory interface logic.

11-4 RAM MEMORY MODULE DESIGN

A memory module is constructed using many memory chips of the same type as basic building blocks. The logic to control these memory chips and the interface to the system bus can be implemented using standard logic devices. Because static RAMs are easy to use and require less control logic, memory module design that employs static RAMs will be discussed first. The additional control logic required when dynamic RAMs are used will be discussed in Section 11-5.

A typical memory module can be divided into three functional units: the memory chip array, the control logic, and the bus interface. The block diagram in Fig. 11-5 illustrates the interrelationship among the three functional units.

The memory chip array consists of several identical RAM chips and provides the storage medium. The memory chips are organized in an array consisting of several rows and columns. To provide the desired word length, a row has more than one memory chip, each chip contributing part of the data word. The number of memory locations on each chip and the number of chips in a column determine

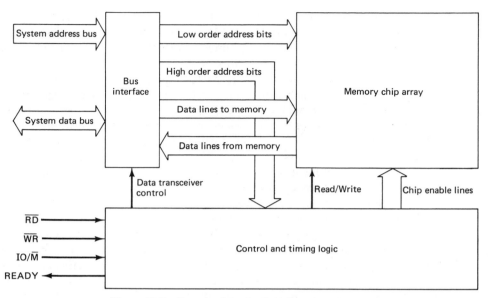

Figure 11-5 Organization of a RAM memory module.

the capacity of the module in words. The table in Fig. 11-6 illustrates the total number of memory chips required to implement the given memory modules. Also shown is the number of chips needed in each row and column. A large variety of RAM chip capacities is available, and only a few with representative capacities are included in the table. The ratio of the memory word length to the number of cells contained in each location on a chip gives the number of chips in each row, and the ratio of the memory capacity in words to the number of locations on each chip gives the number of chips in each column. For instance, a 4K × 8 memory module requires a total of 32 1K × 1 RAMs. These chips are arranged in four rows of eight chips each. To provide the same memory capacity, only 8 1K × 4 RAMs are needed, with only two chips in each row.

      The control logic receives a read or write command and then sends the appropriate chip enable and read/write signals to the memory chip array. The high-order address bits are fed to the control logic and are decoded to determine if the memory module is selected. If so, the row that contains that address is enabled and all others remain disabled. To indicate to the processor that data are ready after a memory read cycle, a handshaking signal is normally applied to an acknowledge line in the system control bus.

      The bus interface logic regulates the direction of data and address flows during memory references. Data are gated from the system bus and sent to the memory chip array during a memory write. For a memory read, data flow is in the opposite direction. The memory module is a slave module, and commands are initiated by the processor or a DMA module. The memory receives its address from the bus, and the high-order bits of the received address are routed to the control logic to

Memory size	Type of RAM	No. of chips in each column	No. of chips in each row	No. of chips in the module
4K × 8	1K × 1	4	8	32
	4K × 1	1	8	8
	256 × 4	16	2	32
	1K × 4	4	2	8
16K × 8	1K × 4	16	2	32
	4K × 1	4	8	32
	8K × 1	2	8	16
	16K × 1	1	8	8
32K × 8	4K × 1	8	8	64
	8K × 1	4	8	32
	16K × 1	2	8	16
64K × 8	16K × 1	4	8	32
	64K × 1	1	8	8
1M × 8	256K × 1	4	8	32
	1M × 1	1	8	8

Figure 11-6   Memory size versus number of memory chips in a module.

enable a row, while the low-order bits are sent to each memory chip to select a particular word from the chips in the enabled row.

To illustrate the structure of a chip array, let us consider the implementation of a 16K × 8 static RAM memory module. The decision as to which type of memory device should be used in a design is normally based on the density, power consumption, and cost of the memory device and the speed requirement of the system. In our example, Intel's 2147H 4K × 1 static RAM device, whose block diagram is shown in Fig. 11-7, is used. For this device, the $\overline{CS}$ (chip select) and $\overline{WE}$ (write enable) inputs and DI (data-in) and DO (data-out) pins have the following relationships:

```
CS  WE    Function          DI and DO
H   X    Not selected   DO pin is in its
                        high-impedance state
L   H    Read           Data bit is output on
                        the DO pin
L   L    Write          Data bit is input from
                        the DI pin
```

When the device is not selected (i.e., $\overline{CS}$ is high), it will go into a standby state, which permits it to operate at reduced power.

To provide a storage capacity of 16K words of 8 bits each, the memory chip array consists of 32 chips organized in four rows and eight columns, as shown in

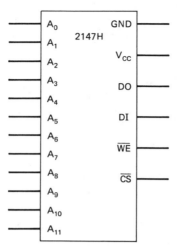

Figure 11-7 A pin diagram of 4K × 1 static RAM.

Fig. 11-8.   Because a 4K × 1 RAM has 12 bits for address input, the lower 12 address lines ($A_{11}-A_0$) from the bus interface are connected to each chip in the array. A row provides a storage segment of 4K words, with each chip in the row contributing 1 bit.   A row is selected by feeding 2 more address bits from the bus interface into the memory control logic and using them to generate the proper one of four row enable signals.   If this module has been assigned to starting memory address 0, the rows correspond to memory locations 0 to 4095, 4096 to 8191, 8192 to 12287, and 12288 to 16383.   When the module is selected, only one row is enabled, so that in each column all four data outputs are tied together to contribute just 1 data output bit.   Each data input bit is fed into all four elements in its corresponding column, and the read/write control is connected to every element in the array.   The data output and data input lines are connected to bus interface logic, and the read/write signal is generated by the control logic.

The control logic, which primarily consists of the decoding circuit and logic to generate the enable signal for the data transceivers and the write enable ($\overline{WE}$) signal, is shown in Fig. 11-9.   Under the assumption that the system has 16 address bits, the most significant 2 bits determine which module is selected.   The B input to the comparator can be set to any one of the four combinations, so that the starting address of the storage segment provided by the memory module can be assigned to any 16K boundary in the 64K memory addressing space.   An output of 1 from the comparator indicates that the module has been selected and enables one row of memory chips according to address bits A_{13} and A_{12}.

The operation of the chip array is controlled by the $\overline{WE}$ signal, which is activated by the $\overline{WR}$ command.   In case that the timing of $\overline{WR}$ is not compatible with the $\overline{WE}$ signal for the memory device used, the $\overline{WE}$ signal generator can be implemented by cascading two monostable multivibrators.   By properly selecting the external capacitors and resistors connected to the two multivibrators, the required address setup time and write pulse width can be achieved.

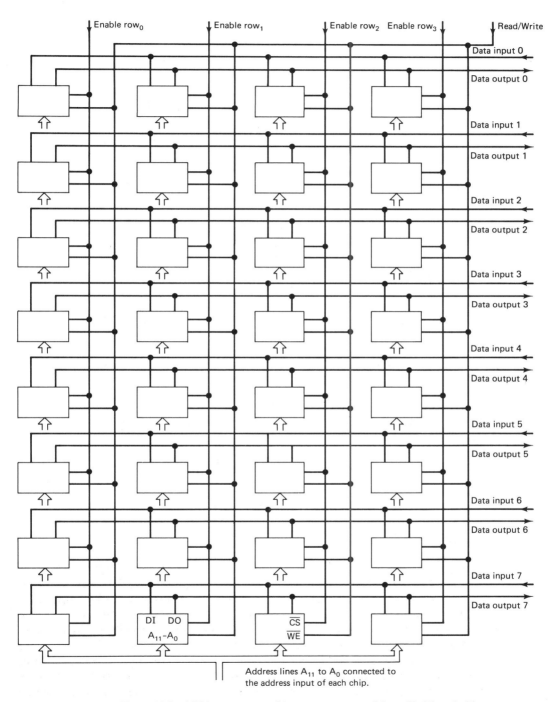

Figure 11-8   16K-byte memory chip array constructed from 32 4K × 1 chips.

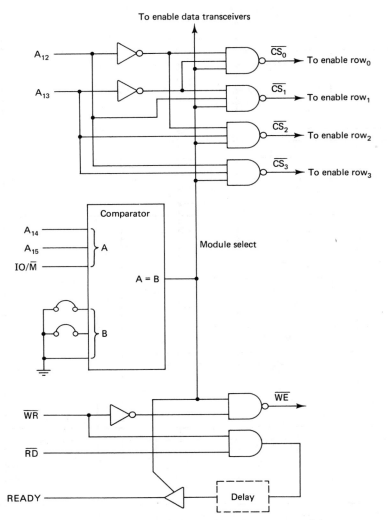

Figure 11-9   Control logic for a 16K × 8 memory module.

For slow memory it is desirable to generate an acknowledge signal indicating when data are ready during a read cycle or when data have been received during a write cycle.   The control logic shown in Fig. 11-9 also provides this feature.

The design of the address and data bus interface is shown in Fig. 11-10.   The data transceivers (8216s) provide the interface between the bidirectional system data bus and separate data-in and data-out bus emerging from the chip array.   The chip select ($\overline{CS}$) input enables the 8216 while the data-in enable ($\overline{DIEN}$) input specifies whether the device functions as a receiver or as a transmitter.   When $\overline{CS}$ is low, data flow from DI to DB when $\overline{DIEN}$ is low and from DB to DO when

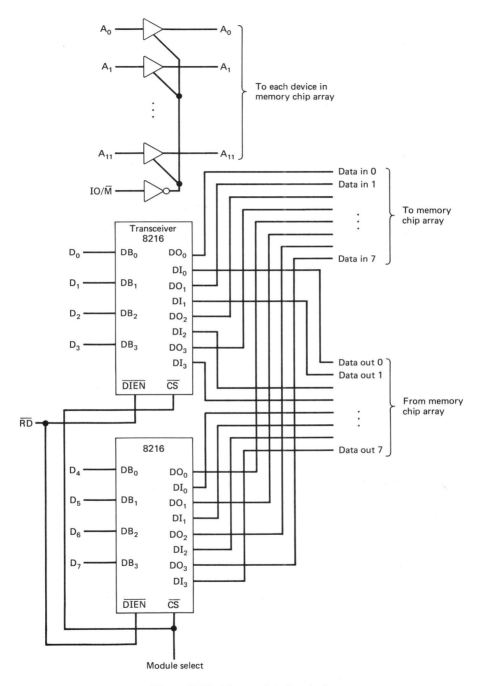

Figure 11-10 Memory interface logic.

$\overline{\text{DIEN}}$ is high. If the memory device has bidirectional data pin(s), each pair of DI and DO pins of the 8216s should be tied together. The least significant 12 address bits are fed to each memory device in the chip array. This requires that these address lines be buffered to reduce the bus loading.

As pointed out in the preceding section, the address sent to the memory chips must be held unchanged during an entire memory cycle. Similarly, it is desirable that the data input be stable during a memory write cycle. Therefore, if the CPU and its associated system bus logic do not hold address and data information long enough for the memory module to complete its operation, high-speed latches must be included in the interface to serve as a memory address register (MAR) and a memory data register (MDR). With the MAR and MDR, the memory module can hold the address and data as long as is necessary during a memory cycle.

Because of the supporting circuits, the memory access time and memory cycle time are considerably longer than that associated with the memory device itself. The memory access time for the system can be measured from the time the CPU places a stable address on the address bus until the stable data arrive at the CPU. It is determined by the following factors:

1. The propagation delay associated with transferring data and addresses on the system bus
2. The delay due to the address bus and data bus interface on the memory module
3. The access time of the memory devices being used
4. The delay due to the system bus control logic on the processor module

Faster system access times and cycle times can be achieved by using Schottky devices to implement the interface and control logic on the memory module.

11-5 DYNAMIC RAM AND REFRESH

There are several reasons why dynamic RAMs are attractive to memory designers, especially when the memory is large. Three of the main reasons follow:

1. *High density*—For static RAM, a typical cell requires six MOS transistors. The structure of a dynamic cell is much simpler and can be implemented with three, or even one, MOS transistor. As a result, more memory cells can be put into a single chip and the number of memory chips needed to implement a memory module is reduced. A common size for a dynamic RAM chip is $64K \times 1$; $1M \times 1$ devices are also available.
2. *Low power consumption*—The power consumption per bit of dynamic RAM is considerably lower than that of static RAM. The power dissipation is less than 0.005 mW per bit for dynamic RAM and typically 0.09 mW per bit for

static RAM. This feature reduces the system power requirements and lowers the cost. In addition, the power consumption of dynamic RAM is extremely low in standby mode; this makes it very attractive in the design of nonvolatile memory.

3. *Economy*—Dynamic RAM is less expensive per bit than static RAM. However, dynamic RAM requires more supporting circuitry, and therefore there is little or no economic advantage when building a small memory system.

Just like static RAMs, the memory on a dynamic memory chip is organized in a matrix formed by rows and columns of memory cells. The simplest type of dynamic RAM cell contains only one transistor and one capacitor, as shown in Fig. 11-11. Whether a 1 or 0 is contained in a cell is determined by whether or not there is a charge on the capacitor. During a read operation, one of the row select lines is brought high by decoding the row address (low-order address bits). The activated row select line turns on the switch transistor Q for all cells in the selected row. This causes the refresh amplifier associated with each column to sense the voltage level on the corresponding capacitor and interpret it as a 0 or a 1. The column address (high-order address bits) enables one cell in the selected row for the output. During this process, the capacitors in an entire row are disturbed. In order to retain the stored information, the same row of cells is rewritten by the refresh amplifiers. A write operation is done similarly except that the data input is stored in the selected cell while the other cells in the same row are simply refreshed.

As a result of the storage discharge through pn-junction leakage current, dynamic memory cells must be repeatedly read and restored; this process is called

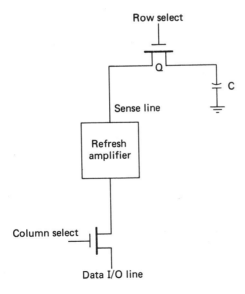

Figure 11-11 Typical one-transistor dynamic RAM cell.

memory refresh. The storage discharge rate increases as the operating temperature rises, and the necessary time interval between refreshes ranges from 1 mS to 100 mS. When operating at 70°C, a typical refresh time interval is 2 mS. Although in a read or write a row of cells is refreshed, the randomness of memory references cannot guarantee that every word in a memory module is refreshed within the 2-mS time limit. A systematic way of accomplishing a memory refresh is through memory refresh cycles.

In a *memory refresh cycle*, a row address is sent to the memory chips, and a read operation is performed to refresh the selected row of cells. However, a refresh cycle differs from a regular memory read cycle in the following respects:

1. The address input to the memory chips does not come from the address bus. Instead, the row address is supplied by a binary counter called the *refresh address counter*. This counter is incremented by 1 for each memory refresh cycle so that it sequences through all the row addresses. The column address is not involved and is held fixed during the refresh cycle.

2. During a memory refresh cycle, all memory chips are enabled so that memory refresh is performed on every chip in the memory module simultaneously. This reduces the number of memory refresh cycles. In a regular read cycle, at most one row of memory chips is enabled.

3. In addition to the chip enable control input, a dynamic RAM may have a data output enable control. These two control inputs are combined internally so that the data output is forced to its high-impedance mode unless both control inputs are activated. During a memory refresh cycle, the data output enable control is deactivated. This is necessary because all the chips in the same column are selected and their data outputs are tied together. On the other hand, during a regular memory read cycle, only one row of chips is selected; consequently, the data output enable signal to each row is activated.

Consider a memory module of 16K bytes implemented by 4K × 1 dynamic RAMs. The memory chip array consists of four rows and eight columns. Each chip has 64 rows and 64 columns of memory cells and thus requires 6 bits for the row address and 6 bits for the column address. The block diagram in Fig. 11-12 shows the logic needed to generate the memory refresh address, the chip enable, and the data output enable signals during a memory refresh cycle. The memory refresh cycle signal, which indicates that a memory refresh is in progress, can be generated by a refresh cycle timing generator on the memory module, an external DMA device, or even the CPU. If the current cycle is a refresh cycle, the 2 to 1 multiplexer selects the row address from the refresh address counter. Otherwise, the row address comes from the address receiver, as discussed in Section 11-4. Assuming that every cell in the chip array must be refreshed within a 2-mS time interval, a refresh cycle is required for every $2 \times 10^{-3} \div 64 = 31.25$ μS. At the end of each refresh cycle (i.e., the 1 to 0 transition of the refresh signal), the binary counter is incremented by 1 so that it points to the next row to be refreshed.

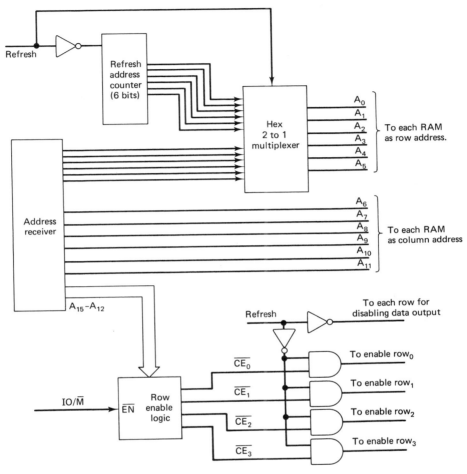

Figure 11-12   Block diagram of a memory refresh address generator.

During a refresh cycle, all chips on the module are enabled for performing a read operation by activating the row enable signals, and the data output of each chip is disabled by deactivating the data output enable signal.

In addition to requiring refresh logic, there is another disadvantage in using dynamic RAMs. During a refresh cycle, the memory module cannot initiate a read or write cycle until the refresh cycle has been completed. As a result, a read or write request will take up to twice as long to complete if a refresh is in progress. Assuming a cycle time of 400 nS (for all memory cycles—refresh, read or write),

$$\frac{64 \times 400 \times 10^{-9}}{2 \times 10^{-3}} \times 100\% = 1.28\%$$

of the memory time is spent on refresh.

For dynamic RAM devices, because of their high bit density, the row address and column address share the same set of pins, thus reducing the device's pin count. Some manufacturers have produced single ICs that include the refresh support logic and other logic needed in controlling the row/column address pins. Toward this end, Intel has made available its 8203 dynamic RAM controller, which is specifically designed to support its 64K $\times$ 1 (2164) and 16K $\times$ 1 (2117, 2118) dynamic RAM devices. The block diagrams for the 2164 and 8203 are shown in Fig. 11-13. (The 8203 can be put in one of two modes according to its 16K/$\overline{64K}$ pin; only the assignments for the 64K mode are shown.) The 2164 has four 128 $\times$ 128 cell arrays but only eight address pins, A_7–A_0. This means that the row address and the column address must share the same pins and be received one after the other. The row address is strobed by a negative-going pulse on the $\overline{RAS}$ pin and, with $\overline{RAS}$ still low, the column address is strobed by a negative-going pulse on the $\overline{CAS}$ pin. The most significant row and column address bits specify one of the four cell arrays. During a memory refresh cycle, the address input A_7 is not used and all four cell arrays perform their refreshes simultaneously. This allows the entire device to be refreshed in 128 cycles.

The timing diagrams for the read, write, and refresh-only cycles are shown in Fig. 11-14. For a read cycle, $\overline{WE}$ must be inactive before the $\overline{CAS}$ pulse is applied and remain inactive until the $\overline{CAS}$ pulse is over. After the column address is strobed, $\overline{RAS}$ is raised and with $\overline{RAS}$ high and $\overline{CAS}$ low the data bit is made available on DOUT. For a write cycle the DIN signal should be applied by the time $\overline{CAS}$ goes low, but after the $\overline{WE}$ pin goes low. The write is performed through the DIN pin while $\overline{RAS}$, $\overline{CAS}$, and $\overline{WE}$ are all low. The DOUT pin is held at its high-impedance state throughout the write cycle. For the refresh-only cycle only the row address is strobed and the $\overline{CAS}$ pin is held inactive. The DOUT pin is kept in its high-impedance state.

The 8203 is designed to output signals whose timing meets the 2164 requirements. The $\overline{OUT_7}$–$\overline{OUT_0}$ lines provide the properly sequenced row and column addresses, $\overline{RAS_1}$–$\overline{RAS_0}$ provide the row address strobes for up to two banks of 2164s, and $\overline{CAS}$ and $\overline{WE}$ supply the column address strobe and write enable signals for all of the 2164s in the module. (Note that the addresses output by the 8203 are inverted. This does not cause a problem, but it does mean that all 0's on the address lines will access the cells having row and column addresses that are all 1's.)

The bank select input B0 determines the $\overline{RAS}$ pin to be activated. AL_7–AL_0 are used to generate the row address and AH_7–AH_0 the column address. Normally, the refresh cycle timing is generated inside the 8203, but the REFRQ pin allows the refresh cycles to be initiated by an external source. The module selection is made through the $\overline{PCS}$ pin. It is called the protected chip select pin because once it becomes active the memory cycle cannot be aborted, even if it immediately returns to its inactive state. The $\overline{RD}$ and $\overline{WR}$ inputs specify whether a memory read or write is to be conducted.

The $\overline{XACK}$ output is a strobe indicating that data are available during a read cycle or that the data have been written during a write cycle. It can be used to

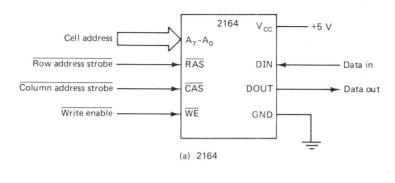

(a) 2164

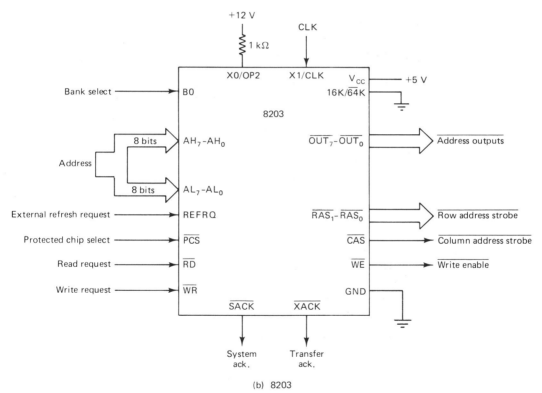

(b) 8203

Figure 11-13 Pin assignments for the 2164 dynamic RAM and its associated 8203 controller.

strobe data into data output latches and to send the ready signal to the processor. The $\overline{SACK}$ output signals the beginning of a memory access cycle and if a refresh cycle is taking place when a memory request is made, the $\overline{SACK}$ signal is delayed until the read or write cycle begins.   If the memory device access time is known to be sufficiently low to guarantee that a read or write will be completed during

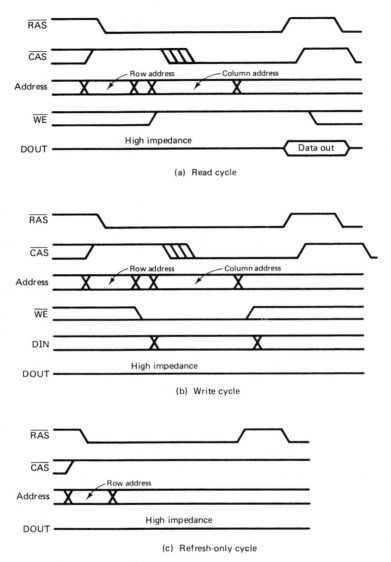

(a) Read cycle

(b) Write cycle

(c) Refresh-only cycle

Figure 11-14 Timing diagrams for the 2164.

the T_3 cycle, the $\overline{\text{SACK}}$ output may be used as the ready signal instead of the $\overline{\text{XACK}}$ output, thus saving wait states that might occur if $\overline{\text{XACK}}$ is used.

Either an oscillator must be connected across X0 and X1 or, if OP2 is connected to $+12\text{V}$, an external clock signal must be applied to CLK. This signal may come from a bus clock line or a clock included in the memory module. Only $+5$ V is needed for the main power supply, but if the OP2 input is used, a

+ 12V voltage is required.   (REFRQ is actually a dual-purpose pin that can be used for advanced reads, but this feature as well as the read-modify-write cycle will not be considered here.)

Figure 11-15 illustrates how an 8203 and eight 2164s could be used to construct a 64K-byte memory module.   In this example, a 16-bit address bus is assumed. For a system with more than 16 address lines, the IO/$\overline{\text{M}}$ signal that is used to enable the 8203, address receiver, and data latch and transceiver should be replaced with the complement of the module select signal.   The module select signal is supposed to be high when IO/$\overline{\text{M}}$ is low and the address bits higher than A_{15} match with the assigned memory range.

Another way of reducing the number of chips needed in the support circuitry for dynamic RAM is to put a set of refresh logic on each memory device, thus permitting the device to refresh itself.   Such a device is called an integrated RAM and, except for memory accesses sometimes being held up by refresh cycles, the device appears to the user to be a static RAM.   An example of this approach is the Intel 2186/7 which is an 8K $\times$ 8 integrated RAM.   The 2186/7 has pin assignments that are essentially the same as for Intel's static RAM devices.   In particular, it has $\overline{\text{OE}}$, $\overline{\text{WE}}$, and $\overline{\text{CE}}$ pins that serve the same purposes.

11-6 *A NONVOLATILE SEMICONDUCTOR MEMORY SYSTEM*

One major disadvantage of using MOS RAMs to construct main memory is that the stored information may be lost as a result of even very short power failures. The solution is to provide a backup power supply to support the system if the main supply fails.   Because of the cost, normally only part of the memory system is protected from power failure.   During a power failure, the status and vital data within the program being executed can be stored in the nonvolatile memory modules; then by restoring this information, the program can continue after the main power is restored.

Some MOS RAMs consume much less power while they are just maintaining information than when they are performing read/write operations.   To reduce the drain on the backup power supply during a power failure, the memory module can be forced into a standby mode in which all memory chips are disabled and the stored data are simply retained.   Because of this feature, batteries become a practical way to provide backup power for MOS memory over reasonable lengths of time.

Figure 11-16 shows a power supply with a battery backup.   During normal operation, the power is supplied by a power supply that converts an ac line voltage into a regulated dc voltage that is maintained at V_{CC}.   The output of the battery is lower than the normal V_{CC}, and consequently diode D1 is forward-biased and diode D2 is cut off.   If the main power fails, the capacitor discharges until its voltage is lower than the output of the battery.   At this time, D2 is forward-biased and the battery supplies the power to the memory.   Once the main supply is

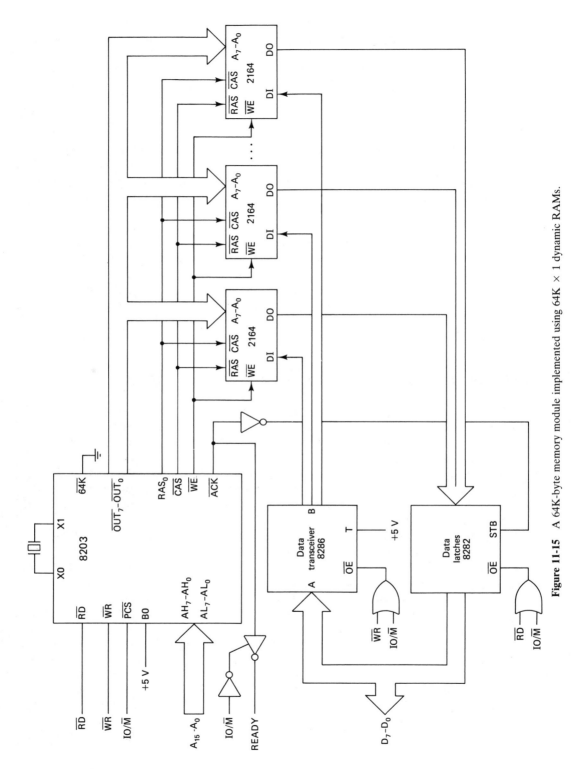

Figure 11-15 A 64K-byte memory module implemented using 64K × 1 dynamic RAMs.

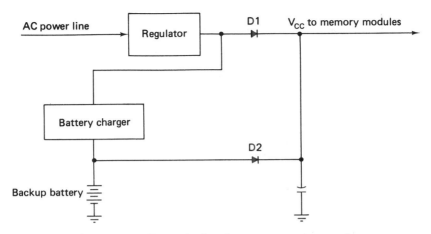

Figure 11-16 Battery backup for a memory power supply.

restored, D2 is cut off and the battery is recharged.   Another circuit that is commonly used to switch power between the main supply and the battery is one that includes a relay.   The relay is such that power comes from the main supply during normal operation and from the battery during power failure.   The relay is controlled by a power-loss-detection circuit.

The type and numbers of batteries required in the backup supply are determined by the following factors:

1. The supply current required by the memory modules
2. The battery discharge characteristics
3. The size, weight, and cost of the batteries
4. The maximum length of time memory must be supplied by backup batteries

Because a memory module consists of a memory chip array and supporting logic, the total discharge current requirement can be calculated by

$$\text{Discharge current} = \frac{N_m \times P_m + P_s}{V}$$

where N_m = number of memory chips
P_m = power dissipated by each memory chip
P_s = total power dissipated by the supporting logic
V = supply voltage

The required supply current is significantly less if the memory is forced into standby mode during a power failure.   Another way to reduce standby power is by using low-power-dissipation CMOS devices for the memory interface and control logic.

The capacity of a battery is rated in terms of ampere-hours at specific discharge currents.   However, the ampere-hour rating tends to decrease as the discharge current rating increases. The maximum protection time that can be provided by a backup power source is the ratio of the ampere-hour rating to the discharge current, provided that the discharge current is less than or equal to its rating. For example, assume that a battery has a capacity of 3.2 A-h at a 1-A discharge current and that a memory module draws 0.8 A. Then the battery can supply the power to the memory module for up to 4 h. Three such batteries in parallel will be able to provide protection for at least 12 h.

A desirable feature for a backup battery is a nearly constant output voltage during discharge. Batteries that satisfy this criterion are commercially available in both the rechargeable and nonrechargeable types. Examples of the nonrechargeable type are mercury and silver-oxide batteries, which offer large capacity, yet small size. Nickel-cadmium and lead-calcium batteries are widely used rechargeable batteries. Although they are considerably larger and heavier than most batteries, the fact that they can be recharged whenever main power is restored may be required in some applications.

11-7 ROM MODULES

In a microcomputer system, normally part of the memory is read-only memory. ROM can be used to store a variety of programs and data that are permanent in nature. One program that is commonly stored in ROM is a bootstrap loader. When the system power switch is turned on, the bootstrap loader automatically loads the monitor from a mass storage device, thus allowing the user to bring up the system without manually depositing the necessary instructions to load the monitor. If a monitor such as the one discussed in Chapter 8 is stored in ROM, a bootstrap loader is not necessary and the user can immediately begin to input commands. Because ROMs do not allow write operations, the user's program and data are stored in RAM memory.

ROM also has a wide variety of applications in digital system design. Typical examples are code conversion, character generation for display, implementation of sequential circuits, and generation of logic functions. In the latter case, ROMs may replace complex combinational logic networks, thereby obviating the need for several SSI packages. In these applications the address lines serve as inputs and the data lines serve as outputs. When an address is applied, the contents of the corresponding memory location are applied to the output data lines; therefore, by programming the ROM, any desired input/output characteristics can be achieved. By developing patterns within the ROM and sequencing through blocks of addresses, time-dependent output patterns can be obtained.

According to the ways in which information can be initially entered (i.e., in which the ROM can be programmed), read-only memories are divided into two major types: ROM and PROM. For the former type data are entered during their manufacture, and for the latter type the user may enter the data using a piece of equipment called a PROM programmer. (PROM programmers will be discussed in Chapter 12.) If the contents of a PROM can be erased and reprogrammed, it is called an EPROM.   One example is the Intel 2764 8K × 8 EPROM.   The 28-pin dual-in-line device has a transparent quartz window so that an ultraviolet light can be used to erase its contents.   Although EPROMs provide maximum flexibility during the development of a system, they are much more expensive than ROMs. For large production runs, ROMs are usually used after the system development is completed.

The memory cell configurations of ROMs and PROMs are characterized by having several bits in a word, typically 4 or 8 bits.   This feature reduces the number of devices required in a memory module and optimizes the board design.   For example, a 16K × 8 EPROM module requires only two Intel 2764s and, as shown in Fig. 11-17, the interconnections are simplified by the absence of write circuitry. The 8-bit tristate data outputs of the two chips are directly tied together in pairs, and only one device is enabled at a time by the chip select control input.

To program the Intel 2764, the V_{PP} input should be maintained at 21 V, $\overline{OE}$ should be 5 V, and $\overline{CE}$ should be grounded during the entire process.   The data to be written and their addresses are input through pins D_7 to D_0 and A_{12} to A_0 using TTL level signals.   At each address location to be programmed, a 50-msec, negative-going, TTL program pulse must be applied to the $\overline{PGM}$ input pin.

In summary, the advantages of ROM memory are that it is fast, it simplifies the module design, and it is nonvolatile.   The limitation is that it can only be used to store information that does not need to be changed.

11-8 SERIAL MEMORIES

A serial memory, as opposed to a random-access memory, is one in which the information must be accessed in a fixed order.   The access time is variable because the information is in a queue and the read or write mechanism must wait until the memory location to be accessed has its turn.   In most serial memories the information is not stationary as it is in the memories considered above, but is circulated either electrically or mechanically and is accessed through stationary read and write mechanisms.

Prior to the late 1970s serial memories consisted almost entirely of magnetic tape and disk units (and, to a lesser extent, magnetic drums) and there existed what is known as the *access gap*.   Random-access memories are fast but are relatively expensive.   Magnetic tape and disk units provided inexpensive storage but were several orders of magnitude slower.   The access gap is the large difference in average access time between the two storage concepts.   Figure 11-18 shows the approximate costs and average access times of the memory devices presently being used.   From the figure it is seen that the access gap has been filled with three different technologies:

1. Magnetic bubble memory (MBM)
2. Charge-coupled device (CCD)
3. Electron-beam addressable memory (EBAM)

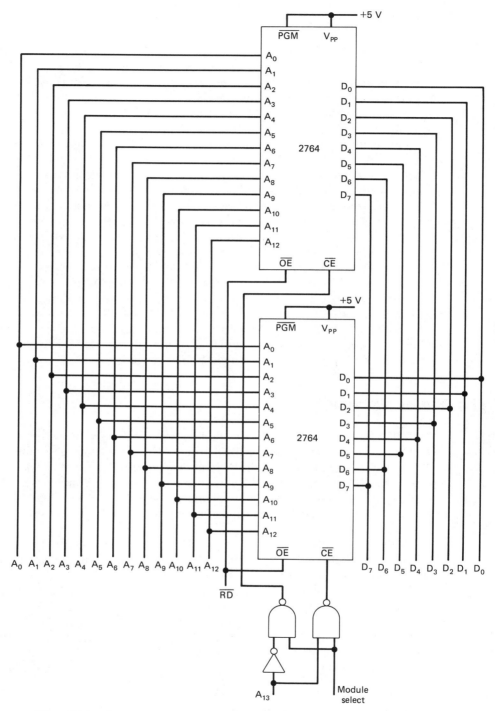

Figure 11-17 Interconnection of two 8K × 8 EPROMs to provide 16K bytes of storage.

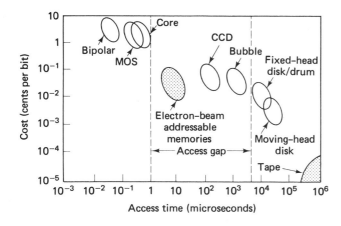

Figure 11-18 Cost versus access time for various types of memory. (Copyright © 1978 by The Institute of Electrical and Electronics Engineers. Reprinted by permission from *Computer*, 15, no. 5 [May 1978], p. 36.)

In an MBM bits are stored in small magnetic domains, called *bubbles*, and in a CCD bits are stored as packets of charge located in small areas, called *potential wells*, within a semiconductor material. In both cases the information bits are guided along fixed paths to positions where they may be changed, read, deleted, etc. (as opposed to the memories discussed above in which the information was stored in fixed positions and electronic signals were used to determine which position was to be read from or written into). An EBAM is constructed so that an electron beam is used to access the positions within the memory.

The cost of producing a memory can be broken down into two major components, the incremental cost (in cents per bit), which is associated with the memory itself, and the overhead cost, which is due to the circuitry and mechanical parts that are needed to support the memory. These two components are depicted in Fig. 11-19, which illustrates the relative cost versus capacity curves of both the MBM and EBAM memories. Semiconductor memories tend to have small overhead costs, but large per bit costs, and disk and tape units require expensive controllers and drives, but the cost of the medium is negligible. Of the three memory types that fill the access gap, EBAMs are associated with the highest overhead cost but the lowest incremental cost. Therefore, even though they are faster they cannot compete with the other memory types for capacities of less than 30 megabits (see Reference 6). Because only large EBAMs are economically feasible, they are incompatible with most 8-bit microcomputer applications and will not be discussed further.

Both MBM and CCD memories require more supporting circuitry than MOS memories. They both must have the controlling circuitry needed to electronically guide the stored information along circuitous paths. Also, CCDs must be refreshed and require extra refresh circuitry. Although MBMs are nonvolatile they tend to have defects and in order to sustain reasonable yields, they must include a certain amount of redundancy. This redundancy, along with the need for magnetic field coil drivers and sense amplifiers, forces MBMs to include a substantial amount of support circuitry.

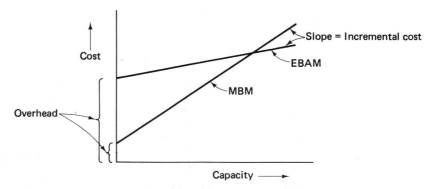

Figure 11-19   Illustration of the cost components of the MBM and EBAM memories.

In addition to production cost, there is the cost of maintaining a memory system. Because magnetic tape and disk units involve mechanical motion they are much more expensive to maintain than the other types of memory. This can be an overriding factor if cost calculations are for a long period of time. In addition, the solid state memories are more reliable and therefore reduce the downtime cost of a system.

The *average access time* of a serial memory is the average amount of time it takes to locate a block of data within the memory. Magnetic tape and disk units must wait until the needed information passes a read/write head. In the case of a moving head disk there are two time components, the time needed to position the head and the time required for the information to rotate under the head after it has been positioned. Mechanical motion is extremely slow when compared with electromagnetic activity and, therefore, tape and disk units have much slower access times than MBMs or CCDs. On the other hand, the serial nature of MBMs and CCDs prevent them from having access times that approach those of random-access memories. MBMs are slower than CCDs because it takes longer to move a magnetic bubble than a packet of charge.

A second important time-related quantity associated with serial memories is the *transfer rate*. The transfer rate is the rate in bits (or bytes) per second at which information can be transferred to or from a memory after the information has been located. The time between transfers, the reciprocal of the transfer rate, is much less than the average access time, but primarily depends on the same factors (mechanical motion or charge or bubble mobility).

Other factors important to classifying memories are volatility and portability and interchangeability of the actual storage medium. Disks and tapes can be carried from one system to another and can be interchanged, thus providing these means of storing data with an important advantage over other storage techniques. They, as well as MBM, are also nonvolatile. Because MBMs are nonvolatile, portable MBM units could be constructed; however, the cost of the storage medium (the magnetic bubble chips) and the surrounding logic that would need to accompany the portable unit would be extremely expensive when compared with the cost of a tape or disk.

11-9 MAGNETIC BUBBLE MEMORIES

There are several materials having the property that when they form a film on a substrate, the film will include randomly distributed magnetic domains whose uniaxial fields are perpendicular to the plane of the film.   By applying an external magnetic field in the direction opposite to that of one of these domains the domain can be reduced to what is called a *magnetic bubble*, or eliminated altogether.   By applying a magnetic field whose direction is in the plane of the film the magnetic bubbles can be moved within the film.   If a permalloy pattern is applied to the magnetic film, the bubbles can be forced to move along paths that are dictated by the pattern.   Finally, if a conducting network is inserted between the film and the pattern, currents in the network can be used to locally control the magnetic field so that individual bubbles can be generated, eliminated (or "annihilated," which is the current term in use), increased in size and split (replicated), or caused to transfer from one path to another.

A cross section of a magnetic bubble device is shown in Fig. 11-20.   The most widely used substrate is the nonmagnetic single crystal material gadolinium gallium garnet (GGG).   The magnetic film material is primarily chosen according to the minimum size of bubbles that can be maintained within the film, the field strength of the bubbles, and the mobility of the bubbles.   Synthetic garnet is often used for this purpose.   Bubbles in synthetic garnet films range from 1 to 10 microns in diameter and can be moved around using 100 KHz signals.   Hexagonal ferrite films can provide much smaller bubbles but the bubbles are less mobile.   A variety of amorphous metal films can be used to attain extremely small bubbles, but they tend to be unstable and are sensitive to temperature (see Reference 5).

The permalloy pattern can be based on a variety of shapes.   One of the most popular shapes is the chevron, shown in Fig. 11-21.   Also shown in this figure is the motion of a bubble relative to the pattern as the in-plane magnetic field changes direction.   The in-plane field is an externally applied rotating field that causes each

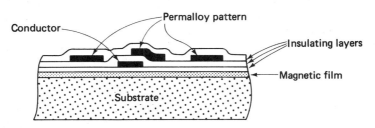

Figure 11-20   Cross section of an MBM.

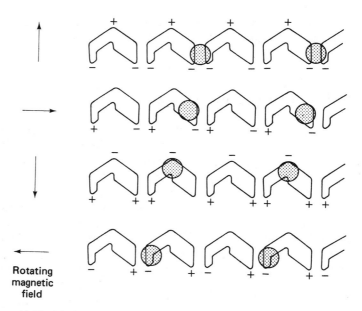

Figure 11-21 Motion of magnetic bubbles along a chevron path. (Reprinted by permission of Texas Instruments, Inc., Copyright © 1977.)

bubble within the film to be shifted one chevron position for each revolution of the field. The overall construction of an MBM unit, including its controlling circuitry, is shown in Fig. 11-22. (The paths shown in this figure are provided by the widely used T-bar shape.)

The basic interrelationships of the paths that guide the bubbles and the principal functions that must be performed within a magnetic bubble device are illustrated in Fig. 11-23. A 1 is indicated by the presence of a bubble and a 0 by its absence. Bubble-no bubble (1-0) combinations are continually rotated within the minor loops. If there are n minor loops, information is stored in or retrieved from the minor loops n bits at a time as the desired information passes under the transfer circuitry, which is part of the conductive network that has been placed just above the magnetic film. During a read operation, once a bit combination, called a *page*, has been transferred to the major loop, it is circulated within the major loop. If the page is to be passed to external circuitry and also placed back into memory, it is replicated and the copy is directed to a detector, while the original continues around the major loop and is transferred back into the minor loops at the same position from which it was taken. (Although only one detector is shown, generally two detectors are included and are operated differentially so as to reduce noise.) If the page is to be replaced by zeros, it is transferred to an annihilation path instead of being returned to the minor loops. A write into memory consists of applying signals to the generation circuitry at the proper time, circulating the

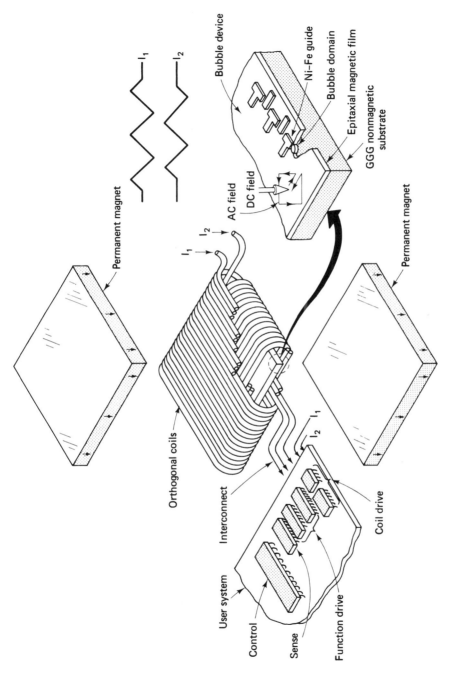

Figure 11-22 The construction of an MBM unit. (Copyright © 1978 by The Institute of Electrical and Electronics Engineers. Reprinted by permission from *Computer*, 15, no. 4 [April, 1978], p. 30.)

I_1

I_2

Permanent magnet

Bubble device

Ni-Fe guide

Bubble domain

Epitaxial magnetic film

GGG nonmagnetic substrate

AC field

DC field

I_2

I_1

Orthogonal coils

Interconnect

Permanent magnet

I_2

I_1

Coil drive

User system

Control

Sense

Function drive

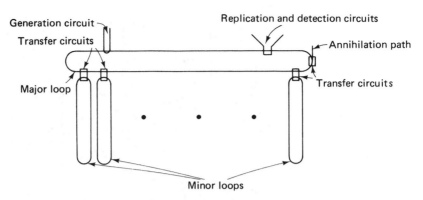

Figure 11-23 Typical path structure for an MBM.

generated bits around the major loop, and then transferring them (in parallel) into the minor loops.

The primary problem with magnetic bubble devices is the difficulty in fabricating a flawless chip. In order to obtain reasonable yields, more minor loops than are actually used are put onto a chip and defects in some of the minor loops are permitted. However, the positions of the bad loops must be known so they can be accounted for when writing into or reading from the memory. The bits being input must be interspersed with meaningless bits that are to be transferred into the defective minor loops. The bits in a page being read are not all useful and the positions of the bad bits must be known so that they can be eliminated from the output. This significantly complicates the external circuitry and is usually taken care of by including a PROM that contains the pattern of the good and bad loops and controls the insertion and deletion of the meaningless bits.

As an example, the Texas Instruments TIB0203 (or TBM0103) has 157 minor loops and allows for 13 defective loops; thus the page size is 144 bits. Each minor loop contains 641 bits so that the total capacity is

$$144 \times 641 = 92{,}304 \text{ bits}$$

It can be operated by applying a 100 KHz rotating magnetic field, and when this frequency is used the average access time is about 4 ms and the transfer rate is approximately 50 K bits/s. The TIB0203 is contained in a 14 pin dual-in-line square package that consumes about 0.6 W and measures approximately 1 in. on a side. Another Texas Instruments product is the TIB0303 MBM, which includes 252 minor loops, 224 of which are usable. Each minor loop contains 1137 bubble positions, thus providing a total capacity of 254,688 bits. It consumes about 0.9 W and if a 100 KHz rotating field is used its average access time is approximately 7.3 mS.

Figure 11-24 shows a simplified block diagram of the circuitry needed to connect a TIB0203 MBM to a system bus. The major controlling circuitry is in a Texas Instruments TMS9916 (or TMS5502) controller. The function timing, function drive, coil driver, and sense amplifier blocks could be implemented using

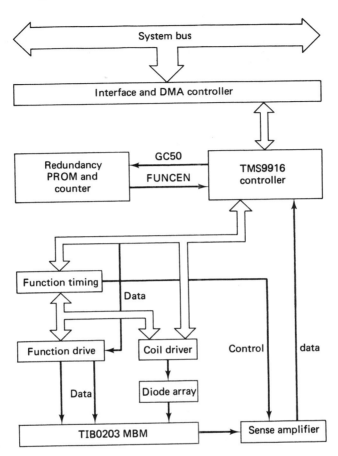

Figure 11-24 Block diagram of an MBM and its control circuitry.

SN74LS361, SN75380, SN75382, and SN75281 chips, respectively. (Texas Instruments also markets kits that include combinations of these devices and VSB53 diode arrays made by Varo Semiconductor, Inc.) The system bus interface could be designed as described in Chapter 10 and could include a DMA controller such as the one discussed in Section 9-7.

A block diagram of the TMS9916 controller is shown in Fig. 11-25a. The TMS9916 includes a shift register to convert between the serial data of the MBM and the parallel data of the system bus. The parallel data is buffered by a 20-byte first in-first out (FIFO) stack. The TMS9916 is controlled by a sequencer circuit and also includes 15 one-byte registers that contain the number of the page to be accessed, the command currently being decoded by the sequencer, the number of the page currently under the transfer circuits, etc. These registers are accessed using a 4-bit address from the system bus interface and the eight bidirectional data

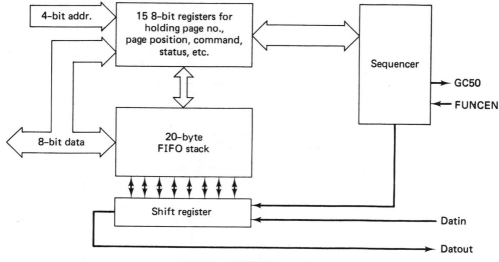

(a)   The TMS9916 controller.

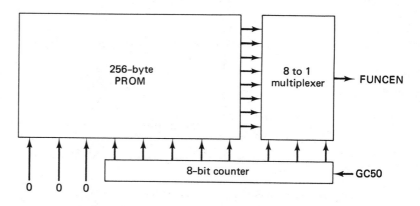

(b)   The redundancy PROM and counter.

Figure 11-25   Logic needed to control a TIB0203 MBM and its support circuitry.

lines. The sixteenth address indicates that the data are to be passed to or from the top of the FIFO stack.

The purpose of the "Redundancy PROM and Counter" block in Fig. 11-24 is to store the good-bad minor loop sequence and to transmit this sequence to the TMS9916 controller as the controller reads or writes a page of data. An expanded diagram of this block is shown in Fig. 11-25b. Because there are 157 minor loops in a TIB0203 and since

$$157 < 8 \times 20 = 160$$

only the first 20 bytes of the PROM are needed; therefore, the 3 most significant address bits are set to 0.   Before a page is read the counter is cleared.   Then the TMS9916 issues a signal from its GC50 pin each time a bit is input from the MBM and this signal is used to increment the counter.   The 5 MSBs of the counter are used to sequence through the first 20 bytes of the PROM, and the 3 LSBs of the counter are used to control an 8 to 1 multiplexer that selects which of the 8 data bits from the PROM is to be output to the FUNCEN pin of the TMS9916.   During a read operation the TMS9916 uses the FUNCEN signal to determine which 13 bits in the 157-bit input stream are to be ignored.   During a write operation it uses the FUNCEN signal to insert the necessary meaningless bits.

The permanent magnets that sandwich the memory (see Fig. 11-22) preserve the information in the memory even when the power is turned off, thereby giving bubble memory its nonvolatility.   Several memory devices could be placed in a single cavity between two permanent magnets and the entire combination could be interfaced to a computer through common control circuitry.   If this is done the primary change in the control section would be the addition of module select circuitry.   If eight MBM modules were to be included in a single unit, then 3 bits from the system bus interface could be applied to a decoder circuit that would select one of eight module enable lines.   Each enable line would be connected to a module and only that module which is enabled could be read from or written into.   The same 3 bits could also be used as the MSBs in the PROM address. Because each MBM has its own good-bad minor loop sequence, the 256-byte PROM would need to contain eight combinations of 157 bits (or 20 bytes) each.   Each 20-byte block could begin at a 32-byte boundary and the three MSBs would select the proper 20-byte block.   (A complete design is requested in Exercise 12.)

The important factors to be considered when deciding which type of memory should be selected for a given application are cost, reliability, speed, nonvolatility, capacity, and portability.   This means that MBMs are best suited for those applications that require nonvolatility, reliability, and access times less than those provided by disk units, but do not require portability or exceedingly large capacities. MBMs are commonly used in those applications in which the same information must be semipermanently stored and/or repetitively accessed (e.g., telephone messages, catalog data, automatic dialer tables, accounting tables, etc.).   Their reliability and ruggedness make them suitable for event recorders and instrument storage elements.

11-10 CCD MEMORIES

A CCD memory is formed by a string of closely spaced MOS capacitors, referred to as basic cells, with an information bit stored as a charge level in a cell.   In order to keep the charge packets separated and to move them to adjacent cells, each cell has multiple electrodes controlled by a multiphase clock.   For each cell, a voltage applied on one electrode is different from the others and therefore a *potential well*

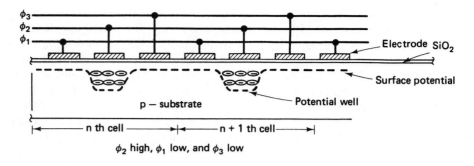

ϕ_2 high, ϕ_1 low, and ϕ_3 low

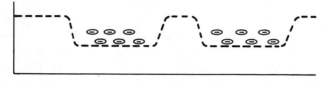

ϕ_1 low, ϕ_2 high, and ϕ_3 high

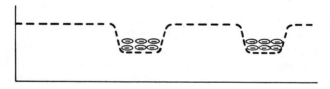

ϕ_1 low, ϕ_2 low, and ϕ_3 high

Figure 11-26   Charge transfer in a three-phase CCD.

is formed that traps the charge in the cell.   By applying a multiphase clock, a potential well can be moved from one electrode to the next, thus causing the corresponding trapped charge to move.   As a result, after a complete cycle, the information stored in a CCD memory, which can be viewed as a large shift register, is shifted by 1 bit.   Typical data shift rates are between 50 KHz and 5 MHz.

To illustrate the principles of a charge transfer operation, a three-phase CCD memory, whose cross section is shown in Fig. 11-26, will be assumed.   Each cell has three electrodes controlled by the clock phases ϕ_1, ϕ_2, and ϕ_3, respectively. Assuming that ϕ_2 is high and both ϕ_1 and ϕ_3 are low, the surface potential under the second electrode of each cell is higher than it is under the two adjacent electrodes.   Therefore, electrons cluster in the potential well and the potential gradient prevents them from moving away.   By raising the voltage of ϕ_3 and then lowering the voltage of ϕ_2, trapped electrons are moved under the third electrode of each cell.   This charge transfer mechanism is also shown in Fig. 11-26.   Similarly, the electrons can be transferred to the first and then the middle electrode of the next cell and thus a shift cycle is completed.   Information is written into the first cell through the charge injection circuitry and is read out from the last cell through the charge level detection circuitry.   A read or write can be performed between two shift cycles.   Two-phase CCD memories are commercially available that require only two electrodes per cell and result in a more compact cell size.   This is accomplished by a built-in asymmetry in the cell that allows charge transfer in one direction only.

Unlike regular shift registers, CCDs are dynamic devices because the stored charges in each cell are gradually reduced through leakage currents and transfer losses.   It is necessary to have a CCD organized as several circular shift registers with the output being fed back into the input through refresh amplifiers.   Therefore, except when the input is in a write mode, the information in a CCD is continually being circulated and refreshed.   There is a minimum clock rate, determined by the refresh timing requirements, at which the information stored in the CCD device must be circulated.   For example, a CCD memory organized as circular shift registers of 4K bits each with a maximum refresh period of 4 mS requires a minimum clock rate of 1 MHz.

The length and the number of circular registers internal to a CCD memory have direct impact on the access time and the complexity of the associated supporting logic.   To reduce the access time, a CCD memory can be organized in the form of many small circular registers.   An example is shown in the simplified block diagram of Fig. 11-27.   The device shown in this figure has 256 circular registers, each with 256 bits.   Any one of the registers can be accessed for a read or write operation by specifying the address input A_7 through A_0.   These registers are shifted simultaneously under the control of a two-phase clock.   Because any cell can be accessed within at most 256 shifts, a maximum access time of approximately 256 μS can be achieved if a 1 MHz clock is used.   However, each register must have its own refresh circuitry and the 8 to 256 decoding logic is rather complex.

Another architecture uses a smaller number of larger circular registers.   This reduces the amount of decode, refresh, and I/O circuitry required.   For example, the Texas Instruments TMS3064, a 64K bit CCD memory, is organized as 16 addressable registers, each of which contains 4K bits and is accessible through 4 address lines.   As shown in Fig. 11-28, each of the 4K-bit registers is implemented by a serial-parallel-serial (SPS) loop consisting of a 32-bit input shift register, 32 parallel shift registers of 127 bits each, and a 32-bit output shift register.   Input data are shifted into the top register at the full clock rate and, after 32 shifts, the contents of the input shift register are shifted downward into the 32 parallel shift registers.   The last bit of each of the parallel shift registers is simultaneously shifted into the bottom register.   The shift rate of the bottom register is the same as that of the input register.   Because the power dissipation is directly proportional to the shift rate and the vertical registers are operated at a much slower frequency, 1/32 of the data rate, the SPS architecture offers the advantage of very low power dissipation.   In addition, each SPS loop requires only one refresh circuit and the

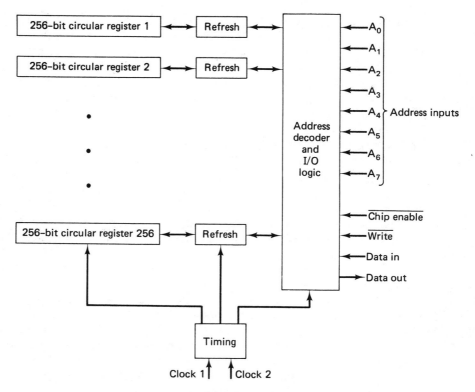

Figure 11-27   Simplified block diagram of a CCD memory.

decoder, which needs to select only one of these 16 loops, is less complex. This results in a higher bit density and lower cost per bit. However, due to the length of each loop, the TMS3064 has a long access time.

A typical application of CCD memory is to replace a fixed-head disk or drum as a fast auxiliary mass storage system. In such an application, the processor sends the CCD memory system the starting address and the number of bytes (or words) to be transferred. As pointed out in the preceding discussion on the internal organization and operation of CCDs, the cell that corresponds to the starting location of the desired data block may not currently be in the proper position to be read from or written into. A number of shifts may therefore need to be performed before starting a read or write. This quasiserial nature requires a CCD memory system to have the necessary logic to perform both address decoding and searching.

A simplified block diagram illustrating the major control logic that is needed in the design of a CCD memory system is depicted in Fig. 11-29. It is assumed that the array is made up of several CCDs and that each CCD contains several addressable loops. The address register contains the starting address of the data

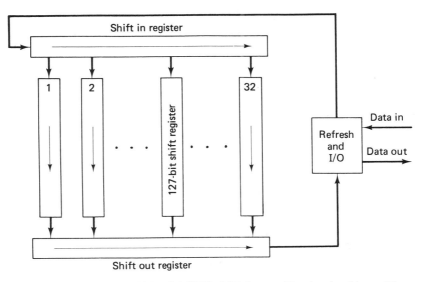

Figure 11-28 Serial-parallel-serial (SPS) CCD loop. (Reprinted, with modifications, by permission of Texas Instruments, Inc., Copyright © 1978.)

block to be accessed. The address bits are divided into three groups. The high address group is fed into the decoder to enable the appropriate CCD(s) for the forthcoming read or write operation. The middle group of address bits is routed to the address inputs of each CCD device in the chip array and selects the internal circular register containing the data block. The low address group is compared with the cell counter to determine if a read/write should begin. The cell counter keeps track of which cells in the internal circular registers (one cell per register) are currently in the read/write position. After each shift operation, this counter is incremented by the control clock. All of the registers in the CCDs are shifted repeatedly until the desired starting location is found. Then a read/write signal is activated after each shift cycle until the entire data block has been read or written.

The memory array consists of CCD chips organized either in a parallel or serial form. For a parallel configuration, eight CCDs are enabled at one time, each contributing 1 bit. Consequently, the total number of CCDs must be a multiple of 8 for a byte organization and a multiple of 16 for a 16-bit word organization. This requires only one shift cycle to read or write 1 byte (or word) of data and thus a greater data transfer rate can be achieved. For a serial configuration, each data byte is contained in the same CCD. This provides a greater flexibility in configuring various storage sizes. For example, a 160K byte storage unit can be implemented using twenty 64K bit CCDs organized in a serial form. Because data are transferred to/from the chip array bit by bit, the input data register and the output data register must be parallel-in-serial-out (PISO) and serial-in-parallel-out (SIPO), respectively. For a parallel chip array configuration, these two registers are parallel-in-parallel-out registers.

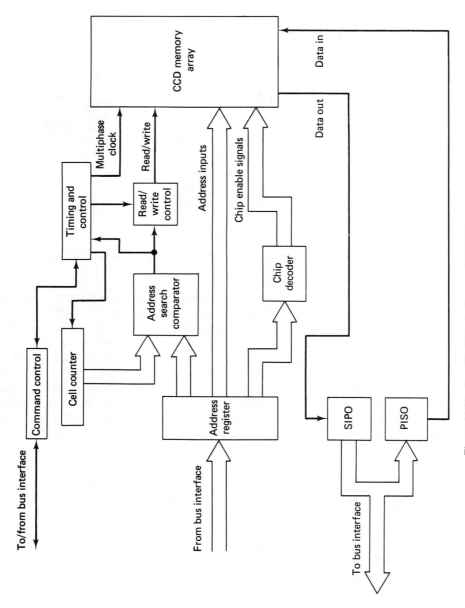

Figure 11-29 Simplified block diagram of a CCD memory system.

420

While performing any of the three functions, refreshing, searching, or transferring data, all the CCD chips in the array are shifted simultaneously.   However, the shift frequency may vary depending on which of these functions is being executed.   Most of the power dissipation of a CCD memory system is due to shift operations and is directly proportional to the clock rate.   It is therefore desirable to clock the CCDs at the minimum frequency while refreshing is being executed, and at the maximum rate while searching is being performed.   The shifting rate associated with a data read or write falls in between these two limits and is determined by the interface.   In order to achieve optimal power dissipation and access time, the timing and control logic of a sophisticated CCD memory system should provide three shifting rates.

BIBLIOGRAPHY

1. *Intel Memory Components Handbook* (Santa Clara, Calif.: Intel Corporation, 1984).
2. *M6800 Microprocessor Applications Manual* (Phoenix, Ariz.: Motorola, Inc., 1975).
3. LUECKE, GERALD, JACK P. MIZE, and WILLIAM N. CARR, *Semiconductor Memory Design and Application* (New York: McGraw-Hill, 1973).
4. BLAKESLEE, THOMAS R., *Digital Design with Standard MSI and LSI* (New York: John Wiley, 1975).
5. TOOMBS, DEAN, "An Update: CCD and Bubble Memories," *IEEE Spectrum*, 15, no. 4 (April 1978), 22–30.
6. TOOMBS, DEAN, "CCD and Bubble Memories," *IEEE Spectrum*, 15, no. 5 (May 1978), 36–39.
7. *TIB0203 Magnetic Bubble Memory and Associated Circuits* (Dallas, Tex.: Texas Instruments Inc., 1978).
8. *TMS9916 Bubble Memory Controller* (Dallas, Tex.: Texas Instruments Inc., 1978).
9. *The MOS Memory Data Book for Design Engineers* (Dallas, Tex.: Texas Instruments Inc., 1978).
10. YANG, EDWARD S., *Fundamentals of Semiconductor Devices* (New York: McGraw-Hill, 1978).

EXERCISES

1. For a 32K byte memory with a single error-detection (parity) bit for each byte, determine the configuration of the chip array in terms of the numbers of memory chips in each row, in each column, and in the entire module using 8K × 1 RAMs.   Repeat for 16K × 1 RAMs.

2. A typical 1K × 4 static RAM is shown in the following figure.   Design a 4K-byte memory chip array using this device.

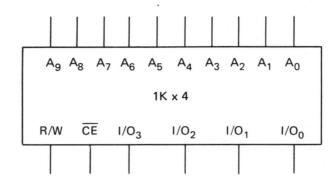

3. Construct the address decoding and row enabling logic for the chip array designed in Exercise 1 (using 8K × 1 RAMs).

4. Assume that a 16K memory module is assigned to the memory segment from 32K to 48K. Specify the B input to the comparator in the control logic diagram in Fig. 11-9.

5. Under the assumptions given in Exercise 4, determine the inputs A_{11} through A_0 and $\overline{CS}_3$ through $\overline{CS}_0$ to the memory chip array shown in Fig. 11-8 for each of the following addresses received by the module:
   (a) 0123
   (b) A135
   (c) ACFF
   (d) DF12

6. Summarize the advantages and disadvantages of dynamic RAMs as opposed to the static RAMs.

7. Construct the necessary control logic for the 16K byte ROM module in Fig. 11-17.

8. One of the major applications of ROM is to replace SSI packages in implementing complex logic functions. Consider the following Boolean function:

$$f = X_0 X_1 \overline{X}_2 X_3 X_4 X_5 X_6 X_7 \overline{X}_8 + \overline{X}_0 \overline{X}_1 X_2 \overline{X}_3 X_4 X_5 X_6 X_7$$
$$+ X_2 \overline{X}_3 \overline{X}_4 \overline{X}_5 X_6 X_7 X_8 + X_0 \overline{X}_2 X_3 X_4 X_5 X_6 \overline{X}_7 \overline{X}_8$$

How many basic logic gates (i.e., inverters, 2-input AND gates, and 2-input OR gates) will be required to implement this function? If a 512 × 8 ROM is used to implement the same function and the least significant data output bit is used as the output f, what should the contents in the ROM be? (*Hint:* Only the least significant data bit of each word is important.) Also, discuss the propagation delay associated with each approach.

9. How many Boolean functions can be implemented by a single 2K × 8 ROM and what are the restrictions on the input variables of these functions?

10. Design a two-digit decimal counter using a 256 × 8 ROM and an 8-bit register only.

11. Construct a table whose entries rank ROMs, RAMs, core memories, EBAMs, CCDs, MBMs, disk units, and tape units according to cost, speed, capacity, reliability, portability, and nonvolatility.

12. Draw a block diagram of an MBM mass storage unit that includes eight TIB0203s. Redraw the diagram assuming that contiguous pairs share common sense amplifiers. For both cases draw the module select and redundancy PROM circuitry in detail.

13. Normally the minor loop spacing results in blank positions in the major loop (i.e., only every second, third, etc., position in the major loop contains an information bit). If only every other position contains an information bit and the frequency of the rotating field is 100 KHz, what is the transfer rate?

14. Assuming that a 640K bit CCD memory system is implemented using the device shown in Fig. 11-27 operated at 1 MHz, calculate the maximum and the average access times.

15. For a serial CCD chip array, each data word is stored in the same device. However, because each CCD has many circular registers, control logic can be designed so that a data word is stored in 16 internal registers, each storing one bit of the data word. Discuss the advantages of using this data storage configuration.

Chapter 12

Development Tools

The development of a microprocessor-based digital system starts after the need and objectives of the system are clearly defined. The actual design will not begin until an initial study phase has been completed. During the study phase, different approaches and various microprocessors will be carefully evaluated according to their ability to satisfy the objectives and performance requirements and according to their cost. Normally, many of the functions to be performed by the system can be achieved either by software or hardware. A typical example of the trade-offs that can be made between software and hardware is in the interrupt handling of multiple I/O devices. Implemented in software, a polling routine does not require any supporting logic for interrupt handling, and only one request line is needed in the system bus. However, interrupts are serviced much faster with the addition of vectored interrupt management logic. Once the fundamental decisions regarding the hardware and the software have been made and the microprocessor to be used has been selected, the major hardware features such as I/O devices, memory size, and bus structure can be determined, and the design may be partitioned into software and hardware tasks. At that time, the design work that leads to constructing the system hardware and to writing the software to run the system may begin.

The major steps involved in the hardware development are:

1. The creation of a detailed logic diagram for each module in the system (e.g., control module, memory, I/O interface, and so on). Timing diagrams of the important control signals should be included.
2. The selection of the devices needed to implement the system based on their cost, speed, and power consumption.

3. The construction of each module on a test board, called a *breadboard*. In order to make it easy to debug and modify, the breadboard is built by wire wrapping or soldering.

4. The testing of the circuits by tracing signal flows and comparing them to logic diagrams and timing charts. It may take several iterations to locate and correct the design and wiring errors.

5. The assembly of the various modules into a complete system called a *prototype*. The prototype is tested for hardware errors both before and after the software has been installed.

The software development proceeds as follows:

1. If the software is complex, it is partitioned into subprograms so that several persons may work on it simultaneously. This also makes the software easy to debug and modify.

2. A detailed flowchart or pseudocode for each programming module is designed.

3. The flowchart or pseudocode is translated into code. The code is most likely assembler code or high-level language code, although for small projects it may be machine code. If the code is not in machine language, it must be converted to machine code using an assembler or compiler.

4. Each programming module is debugged; if logic errors are detected, the source code is modified, reassembled, and tested again. Several iterations may be necessary.

5. The modules are put together in a top-down manner to form the complete software package. The package is tested in steps until the whole package is debugged.

Note that the software development does not have to wait until the prototype hardware has been built. Once the system architecture has been decided upon, the software and hardware can be developed in parallel, although interaction between the two design groups will increase as the development progresses. By using software development tools such as cross-assemblers, simulators, and complete microcomputer development systems, most of the software can be fully debugged. However, the time-dependent segments, which involve I/O and interrupts, cannot be completely tested until they are installed in the prototype.

The final step in the design sequence is to integrate the prototype hardware and software. The prototype system is not error-free at this point, and extensive testing and debugging must be performed. After the system has been completely checked out, the breadboards can be replaced by printed circuit boards for mass production.

This chapter will center on the discussion of various development tools, including cross-assemblers, simulators, microcomputer development systems, emulators, and logic state analyzers. The roles of these tools in the development of software and hardware as well as in the debugging of integrated prototype systems will be considered.

12-1 CROSS-ASSEMBLERS

The functions performed by a cross-assembler are essentially the same as those performed by a self-assembler. These include the translation of mnemonic instructions into machine code, the execution of assembler directives, the detection of syntax errors, and the processing of macros. The difference between the two is that a cross-assembler is executed in a host machine rather than in the microprocessor in which the assembled program is to be run. A cross-assembler is written in a high-level language so that it can be run on a variety of host computers. In conjunction with a simulator, a designer can develop and test all but the time-dependent software before the hardware has been built. Cross-assembled programs can also be simulated for the purpose of evaluating various microprocessors and predicting the system performance during the early phase of architecture design.

As seen in the early chapters, to develop a program in machine language is a tedious process in which errors are easy to make and difficult to isolate. The need for an assembler is almost a requirement, even for simple microprocessor-based systems. For most microprocessors, cross-assemblers and simulators are available at minimal cost. Because they can run with little modification under any computer that supports the high-level language in which they are written, they serve as low-cost yet valuable tools for the development of microprocessor software. The user can create and correct the software with an on-line text editor in a time-sharing system. Cross-assemblers and simulators for widely used microprocessors, that are designed to run in personal computers, are also available.

The role and usage of a cross-assembler in the process of microprocessor software development are depicted in Fig. 12-1. The outputs produced by the cross-assembler consist of a listing, which serves as a programming aid, and a load module. The listing contains the line number, location, and machine code for each assembled instruction, as well as the source code. In addition, a cross-reference table that lists all the symbols defined in the source program along with their addresses is generated. If syntax errors are detected, the types of errors and where they occur are identified so that the source program can be easily corrected and reassembled. Once the assembler errors have been corrected, the load module may be used as input to a simulator, which simulates the execution of each instruction. Program status, register contents, and memory contents can be displayed under the control of simulator commands. Therefore, logic errors can be detected without executing the load module in the actual microprocessor. The process of correcting errors, reassembling, and testing using the simulator may need to be repeated several times.

The load module may be loaded through direct linkage (i.e., downloading)

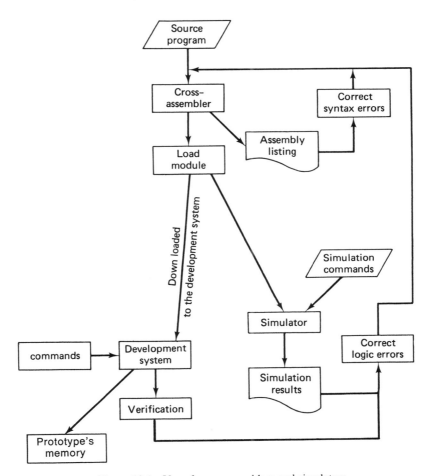

Figure 12-1 Use of cross-assemblers and simulators.

into a development system or a microcomputer so that it can be tested by the actual microprocessor. The development system permits the software to execute in an environment that is similar to the one for which it was created. Although there may be some subtle timing errors that are missed at this stage, very few errors should remain when the load module is finally installed in the prototype. After the software has been debugged using a simulator and/or a development system, it is then integrated into the prototype system by putting it into PROMs and then installing the PROMs, or by loading it through the prototype's input device.

The load module produced by the cross-assembler typically consists of ASCII-coded hexadecimal digits. In other words, the code consists of the ASCII characters for the hexadecimal digits 0 through 9 and A through F. Because the program may be quite long, the load module is segmented into several records,

```
LINE  ADDR  B1 B2 B3 B4  ERROR

  1   0000  2A 19 00          START: LHLD  OPR2      ; LOAD OPR2 TO H,L
  2   0003  EB                       XCHG           ; MOVE OPR2 TO D,E
  3   0004  2A 17 00                 LHLD  OPR1      ; LOAD OPR1 TO H,L
  4   0007  7D                       MOV   A,L       ; SAVE LOW BYTE OF OPR1 IN A
  5   0008  44                       MOV   B,H       ; SAVE HIGH BYTE OF OPR1 IN B
  6   0009  19                       DAD   D         ; ADD OPR1 AND OPR2
  7   000A  22 17 00                 SHLD  OPR1      ; STORE SUM TO OPR1
  8   000D  93                       SUB   E         ; SUBTRACT LOW BYTE
  9   000E  32 19 00                 STA   OPR2      ; STORE IT TO OPR2
 10   0011  78                       MOV   A,B       ; MOVE HIGH BYTE OF OPR2
 11   0012  9A                       SBB   D         ; SUBTRACT HIGH BYTE
 12   0013  32 1A 00                 STA   OPR2+1    ; STORE IT TO OPR2+1
 13   0016  76                       HLT
 14   0017  32 00            OPR1:   DW    032H
 15   0019  48 00            OPR2:   DW    048H
 16   001B                           END


TOTAL ASSEMBLER ERRORS =   0


                              SYMBOL TABLE

*  1

A       0007      B     0000      C    0001      D    0002
E       0003      H     0004      L    0005      M    0006
OPR1    0017      OPR2  0019      PSW  0006      SP   0006
START   0000
STOP  ---

LOAD MODULE

:1B0000002A1900EB2A17007D441922170093321900789A321A00763200480037
:00
```

Figure 12-2 Sample listing and load module produced by an 8085 cross-assembler.

428

each of which contains part of the machine code and several control fields, which
provide compatibility with the development system's loader.   An example of a
load module produced by an 8085 cross-assembler is shown in Fig. 12-2.   The
output listing is given in the same figure for comparison.   In the example, the load
module consists of two records, each having the following format:

RECORD MARK—The first character is a colon and indicates the beginning of a
    record.

RECORD LENGTH—The second and third characters are in hexadecimal and rep-
    resent the total number of bytes of machine code and data.   A record length
    of zero indicates the end of a load module.

LOAD ADDRESS—The next four-digit field represents the starting memory address
    at which the machine code and data in the record are to be loaded.

RECORD TYPE—The next two digits indicate the type of load module.

MACHINE CODE—The machine code starts after the record type field and, as in-
    dicated above, each byte of machine code or data is represented by two ASCII
    characters (0–9, A–F).

CHECKSUM—This field provides for error checking during the load process.   The
    checksum field consists of two ASCII-coded hexadecimal digits that are the
    2's complement of the sum of all bytes in the record excluding the record
    mark.   The loader will generate the checksum field and will compare it with
    the one supplied by the load module.   If they are not equal, the load process
    is terminated.

Sometimes the output of the cross-assembler is not passed to a development
system but is downloaded directly to a PROM programmer.

12-2 SIMULATORS

The simulation of a microprocessor is the process of executing a program written
in the instruction set of the given microprocessor on a different computer.   The
architecture of the microprocessor is simulated by a block of memory in the host
machine.   That is, the PC, PSW, working registers, and microprocessor's memory
are represented by memory locations, and each instruction is simulated by several
instructions in the host machine.   During the simulation, the contents of these
memory locations are the same as the register contents would be if the same program
were executed in the microprocessor being simulated.   In conjunction with a cross-
assembler, a simulator allows a user to develop and verify the program in a computer
other than the target microprocessor.

The input to the simulator comes from two sources, one of which is the cross-
assembler whose output is the load module.   The second input source is the user,
whose input consists of the simulation commands.   For an on-line system, the user
successively enters commands through a terminal and examines the displayed results

to determine the next simulation command. This interactive environment makes the simulator a valuable debugging tool.

A simulator allows the user to trace the program execution, dump memory images, and display the microprocessor's status. Typical commands for a microprocessor simulator are:

START—The PC is set to the address specified in the command. Simulation starts from that address, executing one instruction at a time.

STOP—Simulation halts at the specified address and a table showing the status of the program execution is printed out. The output consists of the total number of machine cycles elapsed during the simulation, the last instruction executed, the last address referred to, and the contents of the PC, SP, PSW, and working registers.

TRACE—This command is used to single-step through the instructions in a specified program segment. The status of program execution is printed out after the execution of each instruction.

DUMP—Three addresses, N_1, N_2, and N_3, must be specified in this command. When the instruction located at address N_1 is executed, the contents of all memory locations from N_2 and N_3 are printed out.

DISTRIBUTION—This command prompts an output listing of all instructions and the number of times each was used during the program's execution.

ADDRESS STOP—The status of the program simulation is printed out when the instruction located at the specified address is executed.

OPERAND STOP—The status of program simulation is printed out when the specified address is referenced.

PATCH—The patch command can be used to change the program being processed by the simulator. Two parameters are required in the command; the first one is the address where a change is to be made and the second is the two hexadecimal digits that are to become the new contents of the addressed byte.

DATA—This command is used in conjunction with an input instruction such as the 8085's IN B instruction. It is followed by two hexadecimal digits and loads the simulated accumulator with these digits just as device B would load its data into the accumulator of the target microprocessor.

SET ROM—This command sets up a simulated ROM in memory with the lower address and upper address specified by parameters in the command. Any attempt to write into this region will produce an error message.

To illustrate some of the features of an 8085 simulator, let us reconsider the cross-assembler output shown in Fig. 12-2. In the sample program, two operands OPR1 and OPR2 are defined by DW assembly directives to have values of 0032_{16} and 0048_{16}. The two operands are added and subtracted and the sum and difference are stored back into OPR1 and OPR2, respectively. Figure 12-3 shows the results generated by the dump and trace commands of the simulator. The command DUMP 0,0,1A displays the contents of the memory segment occupied by the sample

```
COMMAND?
DUMP 0,0,1A
                              OPR1  OPR2
PC = 0000
DUMP
0000  2A 19 00 EB 2A 17 00 76  7D 44 19 22 17 00 93 32 19
0010  00 78 9A 32 1A 00 76     32 00  48 00  76 76 76 76

PC    INST   EA   (EA)   NPC    CZSPI    A    B  C  D  E   H  L   SP     CYCLE
0016  HLT                0017   10110   EE   00 00 00 48  00 7A  0000   000113


COMMAND?
DUMP 16,0,1A
                       OPR1+OPR2   OPR1-OPR2
PC = 0016
DUMP
0000  2A 19 00 EB 2A 17 00 76  7D 44 19 22 17 00 93 32 19
0010  00 78 9A 32 1A 00 76  7A 00  EA EE  76 76 76 76

PC    INST   EA   (EA)   NPC    CZSPI    A    B  C  D  E   H  L   SP     CYCLE
0016  HLT                0017   10110   EE   00 00 00 48  00 7A  0000   000113


COMMAND?
TRAC 0,16

PC    INST          EA     (EA)   NPC    CZSPI    A    B  C  D  E   H  L   SP     CYCLE
0000  LHLD  0019    0019   48     0003   00000   00   00 00 00 48  00 48  0000   000016
0003  XCHG                        0004   00000   00   00 00 00 48  00 00  0000   000020
0004  LHLD  0017    0017   32     0007   00000   00   00 00 00 48  00 32  0000   000036
0007  MOV   A,L                   0008   00000   32   00 00 00 48  00 32  0000   000040
0008  MOV   B,H                   0009   00000   32   00 00 00 48  00 32  0000   000044
0009  DAD   D                     000A   00000   32   00 00 00 48  00 7A  0000   000054
000A  SHLD  0017    0017   7A     000E   00000   32   00 00 00 48  00 7A  0000   000070
000E  SUB   E                     000D   10100   EA   00 00 00 48  00 7A  0000   000074
000D  STA   0019    0019   EA     0011   10100   EA   00 00 00 48  00 7A  0000   000087
0011  MOV   A,B                   0012   10100   00   00 00 00 48  00 7A  0000   000091
0012  SBB   D                     0013   10110   FF   00 00 00 48  00 7A  0000   000095
0013  STA   001A    001A   FF     0016   10110   FF   00 00 00 48  00 7A  0000   000108
0016  HLT                         0017   10110   FF   00 00 00 48  00 7A  0000   000113
```

Figure 12-3 Representative outputs resulting from 8085 simulator dump and trace commands.

program after the first instruction is executed; this listing includes the initial values of the two operands. The command DUMP 16,0,1A prints out the memory image of the same area after the last instruction is executed. As shown in the figure, the two operands have been replaced by the sum 007A and the difference FFEA. The command TRAC 0,16 causes the simulator to print the contents of the registers and the PSW after each instruction has been executed. Logic errors can be located by examining the trace output. However, it is important to note that a simulation cannot detect errors which are time-dependent, such as those associated with I/O and interrupts. The CYCLE column generated by the TRAC command shows the total number of machine states that have been executed. From the last entry in this column it is seen that 113 machine states are required to complete the program segment. If this program is executed in a 5 MHz 8085 with no wait states, the actual execution time would be 113 × 200 nS = 22.6 µS.

12-3 SDK-85 SYSTEM DESIGN KIT

The Intel SDK-85 is a simple single-board microcomputer based on the 8085 microprocessor. The board contains minimal logic that is designed to provide an inexpensive tool for execution and examination of simple programs. As shown in Fig. 12-4, the major features included in an SDK-85 are

1. An 8085A CPU operated with a 6.14 MHz crystal (i.e, 3 MHz processor clock).
2. 2K-byte ROM-IO (constructed from an 8355 or 8755) to store the monitor.
3. 256-byte RAM-IO (constructed from an 8155) to store the user's program and data.
4. 38 parallel I/O lines provided by the ROM-IO and RAM-IO devices.
5. A 20 mA serial interface for teletypewriter connection. This serial interface is provided through the SID and SOD pins of the 8085 with a software generated baud rate of 110.
6. A seven-segment display configured in a four-digit address field and a 2-digit data field.
7. A 24-key keypad that consists of 8 function keys for specifying monitor commands and 16 dual-purpose keys for entering hexadecimal digits and for entering register names.

In addition, the SDK-85 provides a 45-square inch wire-wrap area which allows the user to develop prototype interfaces for his or her applications. Through the bus expansion connector, the user has direct access to all bus lines consisting of 8 data lines, 16 address lines, and 15 control lines.

The on-board 2K ROM-IO device occupies the memory address range from 0000 to 07FF. It is used to store the system monitor that can select either the

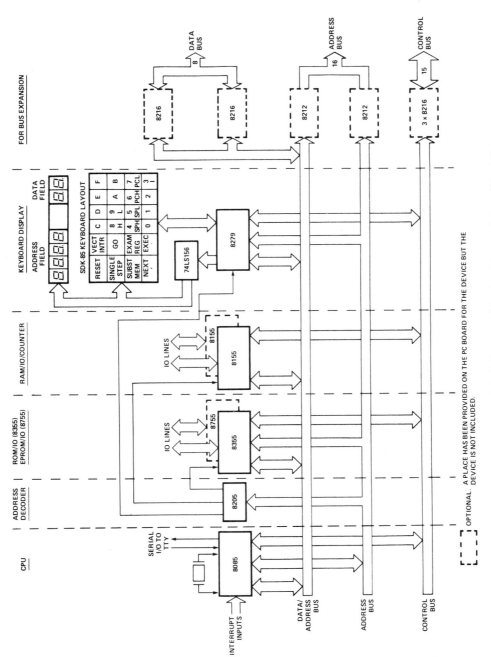

Figure 12-4 SDK-85 functional block diagram. (Reprinted by permission of Intel Corporation, Copyright 1978.)

433

keypad/display or a teletypewriter as a system input/output device. The keypad mode and teletypewriter mode are determined by the strapping connections. The range of on-board RAM is 2000 to 20FF. However, the locations from 20C2 to 20FF are reserved for storing jump instructions to various interrupt service routines and are also used by the monitor as the stack area for saving registers and for providing temporary storage. Therefore, the user's program must be loaded into the area between 2000 and 20C2. Both the ROM and RAM capacities can be extended by inserting an 8355 and 8155, respectively, into the prewired expansion area. An 8355 expands the ROM range to 0000–0FFF and an 8155 adds 256 bytes of RAM from 2800 to 28FF. Also the number of I/O lines will be increased from 38 to 76.

In the keypad/display mode, monitor commands are input through eight command keys. Among them, the NEXT (,) key is used to separate keypad entries and to increment the address field to the next consecutive memory location or register. The EXEC (.) key is used to terminate the current command. The remaining keys provide six monitor commands. In describing their formats, the following notations are used: [A] indicates that A is optional; [A]* indicates one or more optional occurrences of A; and ⟨B⟩ indicates that B is a variable. The six keypad monitor commands are summarized below.

EXAMINE REGISTER—Examines and, if needed, modifies any of the 8085's registers. It can also be used to examine/modify all of the 8085's registers.
Syntax: EXAM REG⟨reg key⟩,[[⟨new contents⟩],]*.

GO—Transfers control of the SDK-85 from the keyboard monitor to the user's program in memory. The starting execution address, (i.e., initial PC) is given by the entered address. If the starting address is not specified, the current PC is used.
Syntax: GO[⟨address⟩].

RESET—Starts the monitor and initializes the 8085. For the display/keyboard mode, the message "- 80 85" will be displayed.
Syntax: RESET

SINGLE STEP—Causes instructions in memory to be executed individually. After each instruction execution, control is returned to the monitor. Pressing the "." key terminates the single step command so that the user may display memory or register contents to verify the program's execution. To resume the single step mode, press the single step key and the "," key, but do not enter an address.
Syntax: SINGLE STEP[⟨address⟩],[,]*.

SUBSTITUTE MEMORY—Displays the contents of selected memory locations. For a location in RAM, the contents can also be modified by this command. A memory location is entered as one to four hex digits and the contents are displayed as two hex digits. This command is used to deposit user program instructions and data into RAM for execution.
Syntax: SUBST MEM⟨address⟩,[[⟨data⟩],]*.

VECTOR INTERRUPT—Causes an RST 7.5 interrupt. If the INTE flag is enabled and the RST 7.5 interrupt type is not masked, the control is passed to location 20CE through a jump instruction stored at location 3C.
Syntax: VECT INTR

In addition to the commands discussed above, the user can always stop the program's execution and return to the monitor via an RST 1 instruction. This instruction is used to set up breakpoints in the user program.

Figure 12-5 illustrates some of the SDK-85 commands. This example is based on the same program as the one in Fig. 12-2. Since for the SDK-85, the space to store the user's program starts from address 2000, the machine code assumes that an ORG 2000H statement is added to the program. In the figure, the necessary command sequence to load the program, step through the program, and examine the results is given along with the actual display caused by each command. Normally SHP and SHL should be initialized so that the stack pointer points to the user area during the execution of the user's program.

In the teletypewriter mode, the SDK-85 is still reset by the RESET key. However, other commands may be input via a terminal. There are six monitor commands: Display Memory, Examine/Modify Register, Go, Insert Instructions, Move Memory, and Substitute Memory. The Insert Instructions command is used to deposit multiple bytes into RAM. The Move Memory command and Display Memory command allow the user to move blocks of data in memory and to display multiple memory locations, respectively. Other commands have the same meanings as they do in the keypad mode.

12-4 MICROCOMPUTER DEVELOPMENT SYSTEMS

A complete microcomputer system that is used to test both the software and hardware of other microcomputer-based systems is called a *microcomputer development system*. Such a system provides hardware and software support from initial program development to debugging the prototype system.

In addition to the processor module, other major hardware components of a development system include

LARGE MEMORY—A development system is run under the control of a rather sophisticated monitor that occupies a considerable amount of memory. To support the system software and to provide the user with enough storage for program development, the main memory of a typical development system ranges from 32K to 640K bytes.

DISKETTE UNIT—To eliminate the need to key in a program each time it is run, a mass storage device is a necessity. Just as a disk unit is a required part of a large computer system, a diskette unit is a standard mass storage device in a development system. Diskettes are used to store system programs, user

Command	Display	New Contents	Comments
RESET	– 80 85		Reset the SDK-85
SUBST MEM 2000,	2000 **.	2A	Deposit machine code into memory
,	2001 **.	19	starting at location 2000H
,	2002 **.	20	LHLD OPR2
,	2003 **.	Eb	XCHG
,	2004 **.	2A	
,	2005 **.	17	
,	2006 **.	20	LHLD OPR1
,	2007 **.	7d	MOV A,L
,	2008 **.	44	MOV B,H
,	2009 **.	19	DAD D
,	200A **.	22	
,	200b **.	17	
,	200C **.	20	SHLD OPR1
,	200d **.	93	SUB E
,	200E **.	32	
,	200F **.	19	
,	2010 **.	20	STA OPR2
,	2011 **.	78	MOV A,B
,	2012 **.	9A	SBB D
,	2013 **.	32	
,	2014 **.	1A	
,	2015 **.	20	STA OPR2+1
,	2016 **.	CF	RST 1
,	2017 **.	32	
,	2018 **.	00	OPR1 = 0032
,	2019 **.	48	
,	201A **.	00	OPR2 = 0048
.	–		Terminate substitute memory command
EXAM REG SPH	SPH **.	20	Initialize SP to 20C2
,	SPL **.	C2	
.	–		Terminate examine register command
SINGLE STEP 2000,	2003.Eb		Starting at 2000H, step through the program
,	2004.2A		After each instruction
,	2007.7d		execution, the address and
,	2008.44		the first byte of the next
,	2009.19		instruction are displayed
,	200A.22		Execute DAD D
.	–		Terminate single step mode
EXAM REG H,	H 00		HL has 007A
,	L 7A		
.	–		
SINGLE STEP	200A.22		Resume single stepping at this point
,	200d 93.		
.	–		Terminate single step mode
SUBST MEM 2017,	2017 7A.		verify contents of OPR1
,	2018 00.		
.	–		
GO	200d.93		Resume full speed execution at this point
.	– 80 85		Return to monitor after RST 1 is executed
SUBST MEM 2019,	2019 EA.		Verify contents of OPR2
,	201A FF.		
.	–		Return to monitor

Note: ** represents unpredictable values.

Figure 12-5   Example of depositing, single-stepping and executing an SDK-85 program.

programs, and data.   Diskettes may provide up to 720K bytes of storage. Many development systems include a hard disk, which increases mass storage capacity substantially.

SYSTEM CONSOLE—A console provides a means of communication between the user and the system.   Typically, a CRT terminal is used as the system console to bring up the system, input commands, and create programs.   Results are displayed on the screen at a speed of up to approximately 1000 characters per second (9600 baud).

PRINTER—A printer is needed to produce a hard copy of the program or data.

PROM PROGRAMMER—A PROM programmer allows the user to program PROMs through the development system under software control.

EMULATOR—An emulator is a real-time debugging facility.   With the accompanying software, it is an efficient development tool for microprocessor-based hardware development as well as software development.

PROM programmers and emulators will be discussed in Sections 12-7 and 12-8.

The operating system for the development system consists of a monitor and a group of system programs that are stored on a mass storage device.   When the system is turned on, the monitor becomes resident in the memory and supervises the operation of the system.   The main functions of the monitor are to manage both the hardware and software resources and to provide an interface between the user and the system.   The monitor recognizes the user's commands from the system console and then performs the requested tasks by executing the appropriate system routines.   In addition, the monitor includes file management routines and I/O handlers.   This allows the user to simplify the I/O programming and to create, manipulate, and delete files.   The system programs normally include a text editor for creating and modifying source programs and other ASCII files, an assembler, one or more interpreters and compilers (typical high-level languages for microcomputers are BASIC, Fortran, PL/M, and Pascal), a linker, and a set of utility routines.   Two utility routines that are frequently available are a real-time debugging routine, which is used in conjunction with an emulator, and a routine for controlling a PROM programmer.

All development systems are interactive systems in which commands, source code, and data are entered through a terminal.   When interactive processing is employed, the user may add, delete, or change source text by giving the proper commands to the text editor and then, in the case of adding or changing text, typing in the desired text string.   The text editor may also be used to store newly created or modified source modules as files on a storage device or recall them from a storage device for further editing.

A text editor includes a working area in memory called a *text buffer,* which is used to store the text while it is being edited.   It also includes a position identifier, called a *buffer pointer*, which points to that part of the text buffer that is currently being manipulated.   A line of text is the text between any two ASCII-coded carriage return/line feed combinations, and most text editors have commands to move the pointer between lines and within lines.   Once the pointer is properly

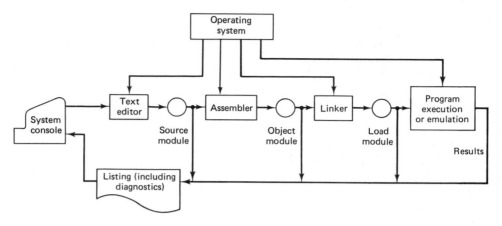

Figure 12-6 Flowchart of creating and verifying a program using a development system.

positioned, new text can be added or old text can be changed or deleted. New files can be created by adding the desired text to an empty text buffer, naming it as a file, and then transferring it to a storage device. The entire process for creating and executing a program on a development system is shown in Fig. 12-6.

12-5 HP64000 DEVELOPMENT SYSTEM

A development system manufactured by a microprocessor vendor only supports the microprocessors designed by the same company. The HP64000 system offered by Hewlett-Packard is more universal in this respect. It supports the software and hardware development for most of the commonly used microprocessors, not just for one microprocessor family made by a particular vendor. Among the microprocessors it supports are the 8080/8085, 6800/6809, Z80, 8088/8086, 68000, and Z8000.

Although an HP64000 development station (model 64100A) can operate as a standalone system, up to six of them can be tied together through the high-speed HP-IB bus to provide for team development. As shown in Fig. 12-7, these stations can share the hard disk and printer with one station (any one) being designated as the master station. An HP64000 system may also link to a minicomputer, such as an HP3000 or a Digital Equipment Corporation (DEC) VAX, or to another HP64000 system via RS-232-C serial lines.

Each station is based on a Hewlett-Packard's proprietary 16-bit microprocessor and is equipped with 32K ROM and 64K RAM. Therefore, the HP64000 is a multiprocessing system with all stations operating simultaneously except when accessing the hard disk or printer. As an option, a station may include a dual 5¼ diskette drive or cartridge drive to provide local storage. A station also has a

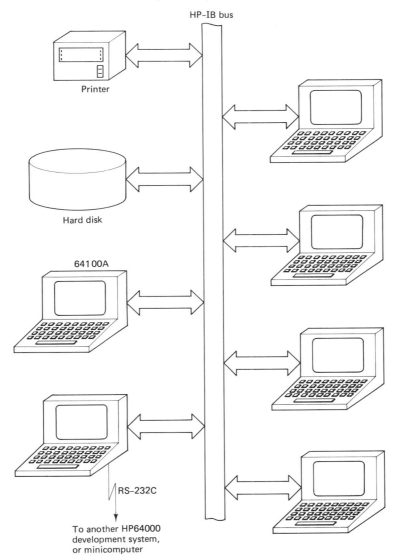

Figure 12-7   Typical HP64000 development system.

space to plug in a PROM programmer module and has 10 card slots for optional development tools, such as a state analyzer, a timing analyzer, a software performance analyzer, and various emulators.

Each user can create a separate account, either protected or unprotected. However, within one account no subdirectory can be created. The keyboard has eight soft keys and four function keys, in addition to regular alphanumeric and cursor movement keys. The four function keys are CLR LINE, RECALL, CAPS LOCK, and RESET. The CLR LINE key causes the current line to be cleared. This key is useful when aborting a command before it starts to execute. The work station saves previous commands on a stack. Pressing the RECALL key allows the user to recall the previous command for execution. The RESET key is for returning to the monitor and for holding the display on screen. When it is pressed once, the system pauses and freezes the screen until any key except RESET is depressed. Pressing the RESET key twice causes the termination of current operation and returns to the monitor.

The eight soft keys make the HP64000 very easy to use. By using these keys, the user can enter keywords or options in a command with single-key strokes. On the bottom of the screen, there is a soft key label line that constantly displays all allowable entries. As each soft key is pressed, the soft key label line changes accordingly to reflect the next expected syntax choices in a command. Therefore, if the user follows the soft key label line at each step, the resulting command is always free of syntax errors. To illustrate how soft keys are used to enter a command, the actual display of the soft key label line for an assemble command is shown in Fig. 12-8.

Note that the first line of the source file must identify the microprocessor for which the source code is written. For example, an 8085 program must include "8085" as the first line. If a sequence of commands is to be executed again and again, a command file can be set up to eliminate much of the required instruction between the user and the system. The command file can be created either by the text editor or by the "log-commands to filename" command. This command saves all further commands to a file designated by the given file name until a "log-commands off" command is entered. For example, assume that a file COMSEQ is created to include the following lines (comments for each line are given in parentheses):

```
PARMS &SOURCE               (pass a parameter to command sequence)
assemble &SOURCE listfile printer options list xref
                            (assemble the given program, print
                             a listing, and select options)
link                        (link)
&SOURCE                     (object file name to be linked)
a blank line                (no library files to be linked)
02000H,00000H,00000H        (specify beginning addresses for
                             PROG, DATA, and COMMON areas)
yes                         (more object files to be linked)
SUBPROG                     (object file name)
a blank line                (no library files to be linked)
03000H,00000H,00000H        (specify beginning addresses for
                             PROG, DATA, and COMMON areas)
```

```
Note that in the parentheses are added comments.   The initial soft
key label line appears as:

edit compile assemble link emulate prom_prog run --ETC--
(--ETC-- key is to display the next set of soft key labels.)
```

After "assemble" key is depressed, the soft key label appears as:

```
<FILE>
(File name to be assembled.)
```

After a filename TEST and "return" key are entered, the soft key
label appears as:

```
listfile options
(listfile: specify the output device for assembly listing.
 options: allow user to override listing options specified in the
          source file.)
```

After "listfile" key is depressed, the soft key label appears as:

```
<FILE> display printer null
(<FILE>: specify a disk filename to store the listing.
 display: display the listing on screen.
 printer: print out the listing.
 null: none.)
```

After "printer" key is depressed, the soft key label appears as:

```
options
```

After "options" key is depressed, the soft key label appears as:

```
list nolist expand nocode xref
(list: force listing of all lines.
 nolist: force no listing of all lines except errors.
 expand: list all source and macro generated codes.
 nocode: suppress object code generation.
 xref: generate a cross-reference table.)
```

After "list", "xref" are depressed, the command line appears as:

```
assemble TEST listfile printer options list xref
```

After "return" key is depressed, file TEST is assembled, listing is
printed, and the soft key label line returns to its initial state:

```
edit compile  assemble  link  emulate prom_prog run --ETC--
```

Figure 12-8   An example of using soft keys.

```
no                          (no more object files to be linked)
a blank line                (select default options)
&SOURCE                     (use parameter as absolute file name)
```

Then, to assemble any file, TEST, and link it with SUBPROG only requires the
command

```
COMSEQ TEST
```

The HP64000 system provides cross-assemblers/linkers and cross Pascal and C compilers for the commonly used 8-bit as well as 16-bit microprocessors. The system does not provide simulators. Therefore, to verify and debug a program, the appropriate emulator must be installed.

One unique software tool provided by the HP64000 is the software performance analyzer. Operated in conjunction with an emulator, this tool is used to analyze the characteristics of the user's software and thereby assist the user in optimizing the performance of his software. The software performance analyzer allows the user to measure and display six major program characteristics. Each measurement is displayed in both event count and bar graph forms. The six measurements are

1. Program activity—Displays the processor activities in each of the given (up to 12) modules or program segments. This measurement is valuable in identifying the modules that create the bottlenecks. For example, Fig. 12-9 reveals that module E is responsible for over 50 percent of the CPU activity. Therefore, improving this module would be the most effective way of optimizing the performance of the entire software system.

2. Memory activity—Displays memory access activities for given memory regions. It is useful in allocating available memory efficiently.

3. Module duration—Displays the time distribution during execution of a selected module or code segment. This indicates to the user whether or not a module is operating within its expected bounds.

4. Module usage—Displays the time distribution between successive accesses to a selected module or code segment. This indicates the intensity of demand

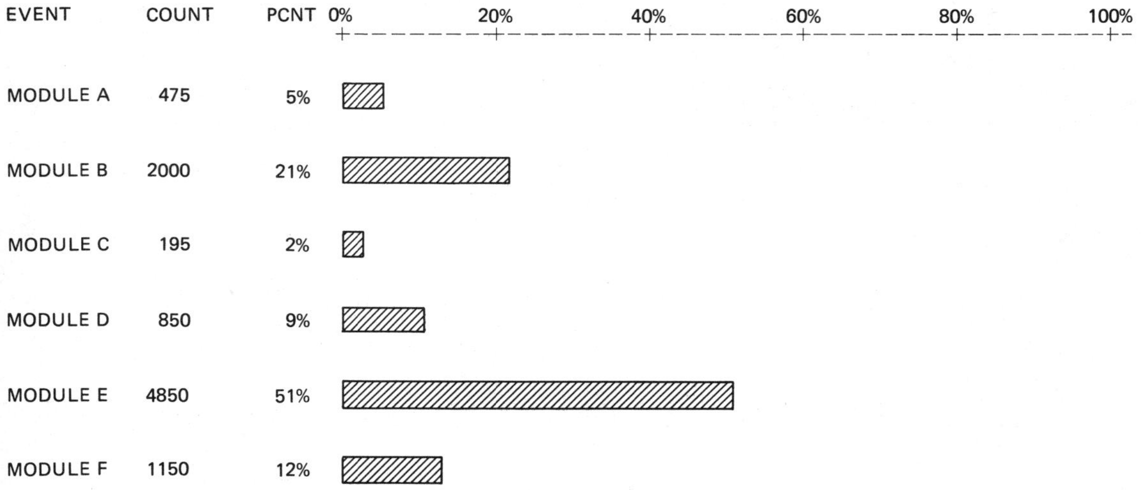

EVENT	COUNT	PCNT	0% 20% 40% 60% 80% 100%
MODULE A	475	5%	
MODULE B	2000	21%	
MODULE C	195	2%	
MODULE D	850	9%	
MODULE E	4850	51%	
MODULE F	1150	12%	

Figure 12-9 Sample display of program activities.

for the services of a module.   One possible application is in comparing different scheduling policies.

5. Intermodule duration—Displays the time distribution of transitions between two selected modules.   A transition time is the time between leaving a module and entering another module.

6. Intermodule linkage—Displays the number of direct transfers between two selected modules.   Up to six pairs of modules may be selected.   This measurement reveals the intensity of the various program flow paths.

12-6 INTEL DEVELOPMENT SYSTEMS

Intel produces a series of development systems, consisting of the iPDS portable system, the Intellec family, and the NDS II network system, to support a variety of Intel microprocessors and microcontrollers.   The low end is the Personal Development System (iPDS), which is designed to be a low-cost portable development system.   Compared to other Intel development systems, it has rather limited hardware and software facilities and fewer add-on options.   The system is based on a 5 MHz 8085 and mainly provides development support for the 8085.   It can also be used for the development of 8088 and 8-bit microcontroller systems.

The Intellec family has several models, the latest being the Series IV development system.   In a standalone configuration, an Intellec is designed for use as a single-terminal system.   With the addition of a communication board, a member in the Intellec family can be converted to a work station in an NDS II network system.

The network development system is a sophisticated multistation, multiuser system.   The heart of the system is an 8086-based network resource manager that runs under the iNDX multitasking operating system.   An NDS II system includes several work stations, with each being an Intellec development system.   The network resource manager allocates shared resources and dispatches tasks among the work stations.

Figure 12-10 shows the hardware organization of a Series IV system.   To improve its performance, it uses two microprocessors: an 8085 and an 8088.   The central processors and I/O (CPIO) board is 8088-based.   It runs the system software and controls the peripheral devices.   The ISIS execution unit (IEU) board is based on a 5 MHz 8085 and, therefore, supports software developed under the ISIS operating system (which was used in earlier Intellec development systems).   As an option, the user may also install a third processor board based on the 8086.   Each processor board includes memory, interrupt management, and bus interface logic.   Because of the dual-processor architecture, the system provides execution environments for both the 8085 and 8088 and can support development for all Intel microprocessors and microcontrollers.

A typical Series IV system is equipped with a 640 Kb 5 1/4-in. diskette drive and a 10 Mb hard disk for mass storage, a printer, and, as an option, a PROM

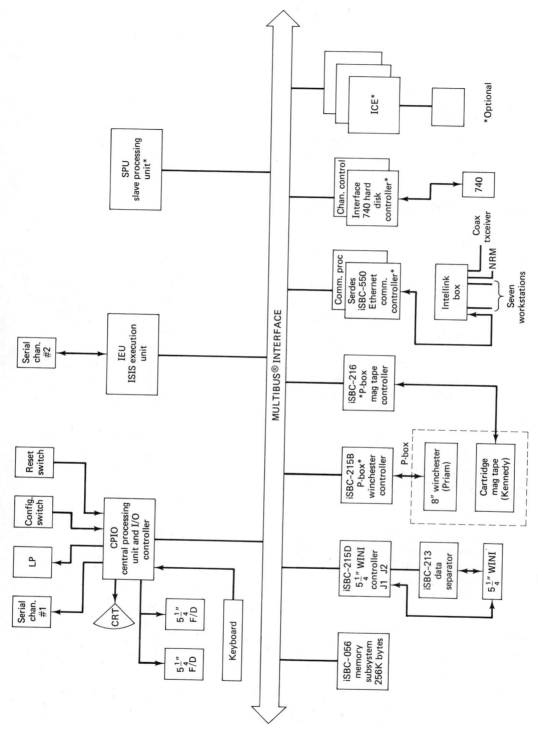

Figure 12-10 Functional block diagram of an Intel Series IV. (Reprinted by permission of Intel Corporation, Copyright 1983.)

444

programmer.   The system also provides four slots for expansions.   There are in-circuit emulators for the 8048, 8051, 8080, 8085, 8088, and 8086.   To support 16-bit microprocessors, the system can work with their corresponding integrated instrumentation in-circuit emulators (I^2ICE).   Using an I^2ICE, the user can debug programs in a high-level language without referring to the translated assembly mnemonics.   In addition I^2ICE can operate with an optional logic timing analyzer.

The system runs under the iNDX (network distributed executive) operating system, which allows the Series IV to operate in the 8086/8088 mode.   By entering the ISIS-IV, a subsystem of iNDX, the user can execute ISIS commands and 8080/8085 operations.   The Series IV development system can run a foreground job and a noninteractive background job simultaneously.   For example, the user might edit a file in the foreground while the system is compiling a program in the background.

The system uses a hierarchical directory structure that can be thought of as a tree.   The leaves correspond to files, and the branches are the paths to access the files.   For example, assume that file SAMPLE.MAC is in the subdirectory PROJECT, which, in turn, is in the current directory's subdirectory DEPTA.   Then file SAMPLE.MAC is accessed by using its path name: DEPTA/PROJECT/SAMPLE.MAC.   With a hierarchical file structure, user files can be divided into convenient groups of files.   Any one directory can contain any reasonable number of files as well as other directories (referred to as subdirectories).   This provides an organized handling of a large number of files for the users and reduces the time required by the system to search for a given file.   In addition, a tree structure provides better file protection and, therefore, is commonly used in multiuser systems.

The Series IV also has eight soft keys to make the system easier to use.   A command can be entered by depressing the corresponding soft key.   The command associated with a soft key may change and its definition is always accessible through the on-line HELP facility.

Major software facilities and options provided by the Series IV are listed below:

1. Text editor—The text editor, AEDIT, is a full screen editor.   The keyboard provides cursor keys so that the places to be modified can be quickly located.   A unique feature of the AEDIT is that it can edit two files simultaneously.   The user may open two files for editing and switch between the two at any time.

2. Assemblers—The system provides macro assemblers for Intel's 8-bit and 16-bit microprocessors and microcontrollers.

3. Compilers—The system supports PL/M, Pascal, C, Fortran and BASIC high-level languages for both 8080/8085 and 8088/8086.

4. Debugger—For a conventional debugger, debugging commands, such as setting break points, stepping, and code patching, must be performed at machine code level.   Therefore, it is rather time consuming and inconvenient to use

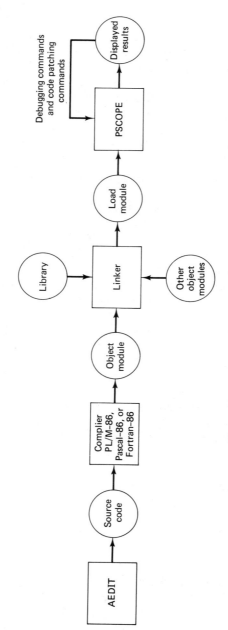

Figure 12-11 Using a high-level language debugger.

when the source program is in a high-level language. To make changes and then resume debugging, the user must go through the editing, compiling, and linking processes. Series IV provides an advanced debugger called PSCOPE, which allows the user to debug programs written in Pascal, PL/M, or Fortran in addition to assembler language. However, PSCOPE only supports the 16-bit Intel microprocessors (the 8088, 8086, 80186, and 80286), not the 8085 or the 8-bit microcontrollers. As illustrated in Fig. 12-11, once the load module has been created, the user can debug and modify the program without leaving PSCOPE. This debugging tool allows the user to set break points or to step through by high-level language statements, procedures, or functions instead of machine instructions. In addition, modifications (code patching) can be made in PSCOPE and then the user can immediately resume debugging. The PSCOPE can also operate in conjunction with an appropriate I²ICE to provide real-time debugging, which is important for time-dependent code.

5. Program management tools—The Series IV provides a set of program management tools to support complex software development projects. Frequently, such a software project involves a large number of program modules developed by several people. The program management tools can maintain a change history of each module, prevent simultaneous modifications to the same module, and automatically generate complete, up-to-date versions of the software. Therefore, with these tools, the tracking of program changes and administration of software modules are significantly simplified.

12-7 PROM PROGRAMMERS

A PROM programmer is a device for installing programs into PROM memory chips, and when used with a development system, it may be placed under software control. The front panel of a PROM programmer includes one or more sockets for inserting the PROM chips that are to be programmed or examined. There must be a separate socket for each of the possible PROM pin configurations that may be plugged into the programmer.

The control signals for programming a specific PROM are not TTL-compatible, and they vary, depending on the memory device being programmed. To accommodate these varying electrical requirements, some programmers are built to accept circuit modules that provide customized electrical outputs. Each module is called a *personality card* and provides all the electrical signals needed for programming a given type of memory chip. In addition to personality cards for the various PROMs, a PROM programmer may have a control module that includes a microprocessor. The control module permits a block of data from a development system to be written into a PROM with a single command. A programmer may also include a display for verifying the contents of a PROM. In conjunction with a development system, a typical PROM programmer can perform the following operations:

1. Loading the data to be programmed from a selected input device (disk file, paper tape, or system console) into the memory of the development system.
2. Displaying or changing data in the memory of the development system.
3. Programming a segment of a PROM with the data that are stored beginning at a specified address in the memory of the development system.
4. Transferring a block of data in a PROM into memory so that the contents of the PROM may be examined through the system console or used to produce a duplicate PROM.
5. Transferring a block of data from a PROM into a disk file.
6. Comparing a block of data in a PROM with the contents of a segment of memory (program verification).

Because the contents of an EPROM (erasable PROM) are determined by charge distribution, an external energy source can be used to reduce its contents to their initial state (i.e., to erase the EPROM). Usually, the external source is an ultraviolet light and the initial state is for all bits to be set to 1. The length of time required to erase an EPROM depends on the type of device and varies from 10 to 50 minutes. EPROM erasers are commercially available and are inexpensive. Once erased, an EPROM can be programmed using a PROM programmer, assuming the necessary personality card is installed.

12-8 EMULATORS

After the hardware and software have been developed, both are integrated into the prototype system for testing and debugging. At this stage, additional hardware and software are necessary to provide efficient diagnostic features. For a simple system, very likely this will cost much more than the product itself. An *emulator* is a device that can be used in conjunction with a development system to provide a powerful debugging tool that eliminates the need to add expensive diagnostic logic and equipment to the prototype hardware. The emulator is substituted for the prototype's microprocessor and executes the microprocessor instructions in the environment of the prototype system under the control of the development system. Therefore, most of the hardware and software resources of the development system can be shared with the prototype system during the debugging stage. A program can be executed step by step while the status is being displayed, just as if the program were being run in the development system. In addition, prototype hardware items such as memory modules, I/O interfaces, and interrupt management modules can be tested and debugged individually by programs stored in the development system. Once the prototype system is completely debugged, the emulator is removed and replaced by the prototype's microprocessor.

Figure 12-12 is a block diagram showing an 8085 emulator connected to the development system and an 8085-based prototype system.   The emulator consists primarily of an 8085 microprocessor to emulate the prototype's processor, the control logic needed to trace and monitor the emulation, and the emulator memory that can be used to store the program to be emulated.   In debugging the prototype system, the 8085 is removed from its socket and a 40-pin connector that is attached

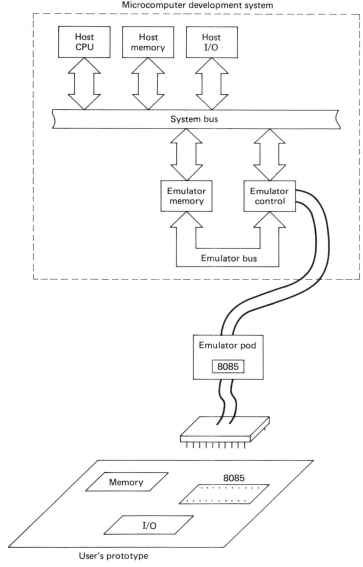

Figure 12-12   Connection of an emulator.

to the emulator is substituted for the 8085. The connector is interfaced to the emulator through a flexible cable and driver circuits. The interface between the development system and the emulator allows the system hardware to be shared by the prototype system and allows the user to control the emulation via the development system. Note that because it has an 8085 microprocessor, an 8085 emulator can be operated without being connected to the user's prototype system. This feature facilitates software development even before the user's hardware is available.

Under the software provided with the emulator, the program to be emulated can be stored entirely in the emulator memory, entirely in the prototype's memory, or divided between the two. This allows the user to test the memory modules of the prototype system individually. Also, the peripherals of the development system can be loaned to the prototype system by substituting the I/O ports of the development system for those of the prototype system. Under the full emulation mode, the emulator runs the program stored in the prototype's memory using the prototype's memory and I/O system. All control signals, data, and addresses are supplied by the prototype hardware; consequently, the prototype operates as if its 8085 were being used.

Emulator commands are available to allow the user to control and monitor the emulation. After an emulation has been terminated, selected portions of its log may be displayed. Among the commands for a typical emulator are:

1. Go—Starts emulation until a break condition is satisfied and allows the user to specify the starting point and breakpoints. A break condition can be specified on address values, data values, and/or bus status.
2. Step—Allows the user to single-step through the program from a given starting address.
3. Trace—Allows the user to specify the conditions for enabling and disabling trace data collection during real-time and single-step emulation. Trace information includes register contents, memory contents, flags, and input pins.
4. Display—Displays trace data and emulation conditions. Various forms, including binary, hexadecimal, and symbolic, can be chosen for display.
5. Clock—Specifies whether the internal clock (the one in the emulator) or an external clock (provided by the prototype) is used to run the emulator processor during an emulation.
6. Memory map—Displays and declares what user memory is to be accessed and the range of memory to be borrowed from the development system.

12-9 LOGIC STATE ANALYZERS

The role of the logic state analyzer in digital hardware design is as important as that of the oscilloscope in troubleshooting analog circuitry. An oscilloscope may simultaneously display up to four voltage signals as a function of time. However,

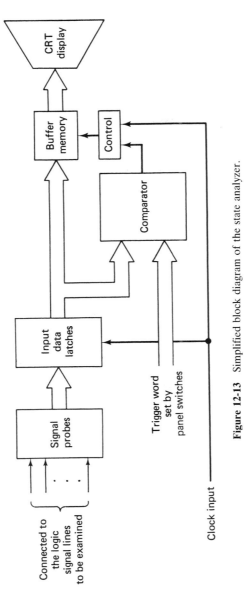

Figure 12-13 Simplified block diagram of the state analyzer.

451

to debug a digital circuit, normally many signal lines need to be examined at the same time (e.g., all address lines or data lines may need to be monitored while debugging an I/O interface). Also, the exact voltage is often not important; only the state of each signal is of interest. A *logic state analyzer* simultaneously samples the states of several input channels, typically 16, each time it detects a clock pulse, and stores the input states in its internal memory. The sampled input data may then be displayed in a 0/1 format on the screen of the analyzer to provide the user with a snapshot of the circuit activity.

A simplified block diagram of a logic state analyzer is given in Fig. 12-13. The logic signals to be examined are fed into the logic state analyzer through multiconductor cables and external probes. The probes have high input impedance to reduce the loading on the circuit being tested. The input signals are sampled under the control of the clock input, either by positive-going transitions or by negative-going transitions. The internal buffer memory allows the analyzer to continuously retain the most recent segment of data. Many analyzers permit the user to select data just before and just after a specific event. This is done by means of triggering. When the incoming data match the trigger conditions, or *trigger word*, the data just before and after this point are frozen in the analyzer's memory. This feature allows the user to analyze the state transition both leading up to and after a preselected input combination. As opposed to a logic state analyzer, a conventional oscilloscope can only display the signal after it has been triggered.

If an analyzer has an internal clock to sample the input at a high clock rate and can display the signals as timing diagrams, it is called a *logic analyzer*. The capability to sample data asynchronously and to display the inputs as timing diagrams is useful in debugging handshaking and other control signals. A logic analyzer can also detect unexpected voltage spikes. A typical logic analyzer has the ability to record data with frequency up to 200 MHz and to detect spikes as narrow as 5 nS.

BIBLIOGRAPHY

1. *SDK-85 System Design Kit User's Manual* (Santa Clara, Calif.: Intel Corporation, 1978).
2. *Intellec Series IV Operating and Programming Guide* (Santa Clara, Calif.: Intel Corporation, 1984).
3. *Intellec Series IV ISIS-IV User's Guide* (Santa Clara, Calif.: Intel Corporation, 1982).
4. *HP64000 Logic Development System Software Reference Manual* (Colorado Springs, Colo.: Hewlett-Packard Co., 1980).
5. RATIQUZZAMAN, MOHAMED. *Microprocessors and Microcomputer Development Systems—Designing Microprocessor-Based Systems* (New York: Harper & Row, 1984).

EXERCISES

1. Give three examples of tasks that could be done by either hardware or software and discuss the trade-offs.
2. Determine the load module produced by the cross-assembler in Section 12-1 for the following sample program:

```
START:      LDA     DATA
            ADI     12H
            STA     RESULT
            LDA     DATA+1
            ACI     23H
            STA     RESULT+1
            HLT
DATA:       DW      025H
RESULT:     DW      0H
            END
```

3. Assume that the program given in Exercise 2 is simulated by the simulator discussed in Section 12-2. Determine the simulation results after the following two commands:
    (a) DUMP 0, 0, 15
    (b) DUMP 10, 0, 15
4. Discuss the applications of the following simulator commands:
    (a) DISTRIBUTION
    (b) ADDRESS STOP
    (c) OPERAND STOP
    (d) PATCH
5. Give two examples in which an error cannot be detected through simulation.
6. Write a program that will input a key from the SDK-85 and display that digit on its rightmost display unit.
7. Enter the following program into the SDK-85 with load address 2000H:

    11 50 20 21 52 20 1A 86 27 12 23 13 1A 8E 27 12 CF

    and deposit 12H, 34H, 56H, and 78H into locations 2050H, 2051H, 2052H, and 2053H, respectively. Then execute the program beginning at 2000H and determine the contents of locations 2050H and 2051H after execution is complete.
8. Use an SDK-85 to step through the program in Exercise 2 (with ORG 2000H being inserted) and trace the contents of the A register.

Appendix A

8085 Instruction Set

The following table gives a summary of the 8085 instruction set. The first column in the table lists the instruction mnemonics, and the second and third columns provide verbal and symbolic descriptions of the instructions, respectively. The fourth, fifth, and sixth columns give the machine code, the flags affected, and the minimum number of clock cycles required to execute the instructions. The abbreviation and symbol definitions are given in Section 6-1. The conditional branch instructions have two numbers of clock cycles associated with them. The first number applies when the branch is not taken and the second number applies when there is a branch. Detailed definitions of the instructions are given in the figures in Chapters 6, 7, and 8.

SUMMARY OF 8085 INSTRUCTION SET

Mnemonic	Description	Symbolic description	Machine code	Affected flags	Clock cycles
MOV r1, r2	Move register to register	(r1) ← (r2)	01DDDSSS	None	4
MOV r, M	Move memory to register	(r) ← ((H)(L))	01DDD110	None	7
MOV M, r	Move register to memory	((H)(L)) ← (r)	01110SSS	None	7
MVI r,data	Move immediate register	(r) ← (byte 2)	00DDD110 data	None	7
MVI M, data	Move immediate memory	((H)(L)) ← (byte 2)	00110110 data	None	10
LXI rp, data 16	Load immediate register pair	(rh) ← (byte 3) (rl) ← (byte 2)	00RP0001 Low data High data	None	10
LDA addr	Load A direct	(A) ← ((byte 3)(byte 2))	00111010 Low addr High addr	None	13
STA addr	Store A direct	((byte 3)(byte 2)) ← (A)	00110010 Low addr High addr	None	13
LHLD addr	Load HL direct	(L) ← ((byte 3)(byte 2)) (H) ← ((byte 3)(byte 2) + 1)	00101010 Low addr High addr	None	16
SHLD addr	Store H and L direct	((byte 3)(byte 2)) ← (L) ((byte 3)(byte 2) + 1) ← (H)	00100010 Low addr High addr	None	16
LDAX rp	Load A indirect (rp ≠ HL)	(A) ← ((rp))	00RP1010	None	7
STAX rp	Store A indirect (rp ≠ HL)	((rp)) ← (A)	00RP0010	None	7
XCHG	Exchange DE, HL register pairs	(H) ↔ (D) (L) ↔ (E)	11101011	None	4
ADD r	Add register to A	(A) ← (A) + (r)	10000SSS	Z, S, P, CY, AC	4
ADD M	Add memory to A	(A) ← (A) + ((H)(L))	10000110	Z, S, P, CY, AC	7
ADI data	Add immediate to A	(A) ← (A) + (byte 2)	11000110 data	Z, S, P, CY, AC	7
ADC r	Add register to A with carry	(A) ← (A) + (r) + (CY)	10001SSS	Z, S, P, CY, AC	4
ADC M	Add memory to A with carry	(A) ← (A) + ((H)(L)) + (CY)	10001110	Z, S, P, CY, AC	7

SUMMARY OF 8085 INSTRUCTION SET (Continued)

Mnemonic	Description	Symbolic description	Machine code	Affected flags	Clock cycles
ACI data	Add immediate to A with carry	$(A) \leftarrow (A) + (\text{byte 2}) + (CY)$	11001110 data	Z, S, P, CY, AC	7
SUB r	Subtract register from A	$(A) \leftarrow (A) - (r)$	10010SSS	Z, S, P, CY, AC	4
SUB M	Subtract memory from A	$(A) \leftarrow (A) - ((H)(L))$	10010110	Z, S, P, CY, AC	7
SUI data	Subtract immediate from A	$(A) \leftarrow (A) - (\text{byte 2})$	11010110 data	Z, S, P, CY, AC	7
SBB r	Subtract register from A with borrow	$(A) \leftarrow (A) - (r) - (CY)$	10011SSS	Z, S, P, CY, AC	4
SBB M	Subtract memory from A with borrow	$(A) \leftarrow (A) - ((H)(L)) - (CY)$	10011110	Z, S, P, CY, AC	7
SBI data	Subtract immediate from A with borrow	$(A) \leftarrow (A) - (\text{byte 2}) - (CY)$	11011110 data	Z, S, P, CY, AC	7
INR r	Increment register	$(r) \leftarrow (r) + 1$	00DDD100	Z, S, P, AC	4
INR M	Increment memory	$((H)(L)) \leftarrow ((H)(L)) + 1$	00110100	Z, S, P, AC	10
DCR r	Decrement register	$(r) \leftarrow (r) - 1$	00DDD101	Z, S, P, AC	4
DCR M	Decrement memory	$((H)(L)) \leftarrow ((H)(L)) - 1$	00110101	Z, S, P, AC	10
INX rp	Increment register pair	$(rh)(rl) \leftarrow (rh)(rl) + 1$	00RP0011	None	6
DCX rp	Decrement register pair	$(rh)(rl) \leftarrow (rh)(rl) - 1$	00RP1011	None	6
DAD rp	Add register pair rp to HL pair	$(H)(L) \leftarrow (H)(L) + (rh)(rl)$	00RP1001	CY	10
DAA	Decimal adjust A		00100111	Z, S, P, CY, AC	4
ANA r	AND register with A	$(A) \leftarrow (A) \wedge (r)$	10100SSS	Z, S, P, CY, AC	4
ANA M	AND memory with A	$(A) \leftarrow (A) \wedge ((H)(L))$	10100110	Z, S, P, CY, AC	7
ANI data	AND immediate with A	$(A) \leftarrow (A) \wedge (\text{byte 2})$	11100110 data	Z, S, P, CY, AC	7
XRA r	Exclusive OR register with A	$(A) \leftarrow (A) \veebar (r)$	10101SSS	Z, S, P, CY, AC	4
XRA M	Exclusive OR memory with A	$(A) \leftarrow (A) \veebar ((H)(L))$	10101110	Z, S, P, CY, AC	7
XRI data	Exclusive OR immediate with A	$(A) \leftarrow (A) \veebar (\text{byte 2})$	11101110 data	Z, S, P, CY, AC	7
ORA r	OR register with A	$(A) \leftarrow (A) \vee (r)$	10110SSS	Z, S, P, CY, AC	4
ORA M	OR memory with A	$(A) \leftarrow (A) \vee ((H)(L))$	10110110	Z, S, P, CY, AC	7
ORI data	OR immediate with A	$(A) \leftarrow (A) \vee (\text{byte 2})$	11110110 data	Z, S, P, CY, AC	7

Mnemonic	Description	Operation	Encoding	Flags	Cycles
CMP r	Compare register with A	$(A) - (r)$	10111SSS	Z, S, P, CY, AC	4
CMP M	Compare memory with A	$(A) - ((H)(L))$	10111110	Z, S, P, CY, AC	7
CPI data	Compare immediate with A	$(A) - (byte\ 2)$	11111110 / data	Z, S, P, CY, AC	7
RLC	Rotate A left	$(A_{n+1}) \leftarrow (A_n); (A_0) \leftarrow (A_7)$ / $(CY) \leftarrow (A_7)$	00000111	CY	4
RRC	Rotate A right	$(A_n) \leftarrow (A_{n+1}); (A_7) \leftarrow (A_0)$ / $(CY) \leftarrow (A_0)$	00001111	CY	4
RAL	Rotate A left through carry	$(A_{n+1}) \leftarrow (A_n); (CY) \leftarrow (A_7)$ / $(A_0) \leftarrow (CY)$	00010111	CY	4
RAR	Rotate A right through carry	$(A_n) \leftarrow (A_{n+1}); (CY) \leftarrow (A_0)$ / $(A_7) \leftarrow (CY)$	00011111	CY	4
CMA	Complement A	$(A) \leftarrow (\overline{A})$	00101111	None	4
CMC	Complement carry	$(CY) \leftarrow (\overline{CY})$	00111111	CY	4
STC	Set carry	$(CY) \leftarrow 1$	00110111	CY	4
JMP addr	Jump unconditional	$(PC) \leftarrow (byte\ 3)(byte\ 2)$	11000011 / Low addr / High addr	None	10
Jcondition addr	Conditional jump	$(PC) \leftarrow (byte\ 3)(byte\ 2)$ if condition is true	11CCC010 / Low addr / High addr	None	7/10
CALL addr	Call unconditional	$((SP) - 1) \leftarrow (PCH)$ / $((SP) - 2) \leftarrow (PCL)$ / $(SP) \leftarrow (SP) - 2$ / $(PC) \leftarrow (byte\ 3)(byte\ 2)$	11001101 / Low addr / High addr	None	18
Ccondition addr	Conditional call	$((SP) - 1) \leftarrow (PCH)$ / $((SP) - 2) \leftarrow (PCL)$ / $(SP) \leftarrow (SP) - 2$ / $(PC) \leftarrow (byte\ 3)(byte\ 2)$ if condition is true	11CCC100 / Low addr / High addr	None	9/18
RET	Return	$(PCL) \leftarrow ((SP))$ / $(PCH) \leftarrow ((SP) + 1)$ / $(SP) \leftarrow (SP) + 2$	11001001	None	10
Rcondition	Conditional return	$(PCL) \leftarrow ((SP))$ / $(PCH) \leftarrow ((SP) + 1)$ / $(SP) \leftarrow (SP) + 2$ if condition is true	11CCC000	None	6/12
RST n	Restart	$((SP) - 1) \leftarrow (PCH)$ / $((SP) - 2) \leftarrow (PCL)$ / $(SP) \leftarrow (SP) - 2$ / $(PC) \leftarrow 8 \cdot (NNN)$	11NNN111	None	12

SUMMARY OF 8085 INSTRUCTION SET (Continued)

Mnemonic	Description	Symbolic description	Machine code	Affected flags	Clock cycles
PCHL	HL to program counter	$(PCH) \leftarrow (H)$ $(PCL) \leftarrow (L)$	11101001	None	6
PUSH rp	Push	$((SP) - 1) \leftarrow (rh)$ $((SP) - 2) \leftarrow (rl)$ $(SP) \leftarrow (SP) - 2$	11RP0101	None	12
PUSH PSW	Push A and flags on stack	$((SP) - 1) \leftarrow (A)$ $((SP) - 2)_0 \leftarrow (CY), ((SP) - 2)_1 \leftarrow 1$ $((SP) - 2)_2 \leftarrow (P), ((SP) - 2)_3 \leftarrow 0$ $((SP) - 2)_4 \leftarrow (AC), ((SP) - 2)_5 \leftarrow 0$ $((SP) - 2)_6 \leftarrow (Z), ((SP) - 2)_7 \leftarrow (S)$ $(SP) \leftarrow (SP) - 2$	11110101	None	12
POP rp	Pop	$(rl) \leftarrow ((SP))$ $(rh) \leftarrow ((SP) + 1)$ $(SP) \leftarrow (SP) + 2$	11RP0001	None	10
POP PSW	Pop A and flags from stack	$(CY) \leftarrow ((SP))_0$ $(P) \leftarrow ((SP))_2$ $(AC) \leftarrow ((SP))_4$ $(Z) \leftarrow ((SP))_6$ $(S) \leftarrow ((SP))_7$ $(A) \leftarrow ((SP) + 1)$ $(SP) \leftarrow (SP) + 2$	11110001	Z, S, P, CY, AC	10
XTHL	Exchange top of stack and HL	$(L) \leftrightarrow ((SP))$ $(H) \leftrightarrow ((SP) + 1)$	11100011	None	16
SPHL	HL to stack pointer	$(SP) \leftarrow (H)(L)$	11111001	None	6
IN port	Input	$(A) \leftarrow (port)$	11011011 port	None	10
OUT port	Output	$(port) \leftarrow (A)$	11010011 port	None	10
EI	Enable interrupts		11111011	None	4
DI	Disable interrupts		11110011	None	4
RIM	Read interrupt masks		00100000	None	4
SIM	Set interrupt masks		00110000	None	4
HLT	Halt		01110110	None	5
NOP	No operation		00000000	None	4

Register Addr. (DDD or SSS)	Register Name	Register Pair Address (RP)	Register Pair	CONDITION	CCC
000	B	00	BC	NZ – not zero (Z = 0)	000
001	C	01	DE	Z – zero (Z = 1)	001
010	D	10	HL	NC – no carry (CY = 0)	010
011	E	11	SP (One 16 bit register)	C – carry (CY = 1)	011
100	H			PO – parity odd (P = 0)	100
101	L			PE – parity even (P = 1)	101
111	A			P – plus (S = 0)	110
				M – minus (S = 1)	111

Appendix B

Z80 Instruction Set

This appendix summarizes the instruction set of the Zilog Z80 and has been re-produced by permission of Zilog, Inc., © 1986. This material shall not be repro-duced without the written consent of Zilog, Inc.

8-BIT LOAD GROUP

Mnemonic	Symbolic Operation	S	Z	H	P/V	N	C	76	543	210	Hex	No. of Bytes	No. of M Cycles	No. of T States	Comments
LD r, r'	r ← r'	•	•	X	•	X	•	•	•	01	r	r'		1	1	4	r, r' Reg.
LD r, n	r ← n	•	•	X	•	X	•	•	•	00	r	110		2	2	7	000 B
									← n →							001 C
LD r, (HL)	r ← (HL)	•	•	X	•	X	•	•	•	01	r	110		1	2	7	010 D
LD r, (IX + d)	r ← (IX + d)	•	•	X	•	X	•	•	•	11	011	101	DD	3	5	19	011 E
									01	r	110					100 H
									← d →							101 L
LD r, (IY + d)	r ← (IY + d)	•	•	X	•	X	•	•	•	11	111	101	FD	3	5	19	111 A
									01	r	110					
									← d →							
LD (HL), r	(HL) ← r	•	•	X	•	X	•	•	•	01	110	r		1	2	7	
LD (IX + d), r	(IX + d) ← r	•	•	X	•	X	•	•	•	11	011	101	DD	3	5	19	
									01	110	r					
									← d →							
LD (IY + d), r	(IY + d) ← r	•	•	X	•	X	•	•	•	11	111	101	FD	3	5	19	
									01	110	r					
									← d →							
LD (HL), n	(HL) ← n	•	•	X	•	X	•	•	•	00	110	110	36	2	3	10	
									← n →							
LD (IX + d), n	(IX + d) ← n	•	•	X	•	X	•	•	•	11	011	101	DD	4	5	19	
									00	110	110	36				
									← d →							
									← n →							
LD (IY + d), n	(IY + d) ← n	•	•	X	•	X	•	•	•	11	111	101	FD	4	5	19	
									00	110	110	36				
									← d →							
									← n →							
LD A, (BC)	A ← (BC)	•	•	X	•	X	•	•	•	00	001	010	0A	1	2	7	
LD A, (DE)	A ← (DE)	•	•	X	•	X	•	•	•	00	011	010	1A	1	2	7	
LD A, (nn)	A ← (nn)	•	•	X	•	X	•	•	•	00	111	010	3A	3	4	13	
									← n →							
									← n →							
LD (BC), A	(BC) ← A	•	•	X	•	X	•	•	•	00	000	010	02	1	2	7	
LD (DE), A	(DE) ← A	•	•	X	•	X	•	•	•	00	010	010	12	1	2	7	
LD (nn), A	(nn) ← A	•	•	X	•	X	•	•	•	00	110	010	32	3	4	13	
									← n →							
									← n →							
LD A, I	A ← I	‡	‡	X	0	X	IFF	0	•	11	101	101	ED	2	2	9	
									01	010	111	57				
LD A, R	A ← R	‡	‡	X	0	X	IFF	0	•	11	101	101	ED	2	2	9	
									01	011	111	5F				
LD I, A	I ← A	•	•	X	•	X	•	•	•	11	101	101	ED	2	2	9	
									01	000	111	47				
LD R, A	R ← A	•	•	X	•	X	•	•	•	11	101	101	ED	2	2	9	
									01	001	111	4F				

NOTE: IFF$_1$, the content of the interrupt enable flip-flop, (IFF$_1$), is copied into the P/V flag.

16-BIT LOAD GROUP

Mnemonic	Symbolic Operation	S	Z		H		P/V	N	C	76	543	210	Hex	No. of Bytes	No. of M Cycles	No. of T States	Comments
LD dd, nn	dd ← nn	•	•	X	•	X	•	•	•	00	dd0	001		3	3	10	dd Pair
											← n →						00 BC
											← n →						01 DE
LD IX, nn	IX ← nn	•	•	X	•	X	•	•	•	11	011	101	DD	4	4	14	10 HL
										00	100	001	21				11 SP
											← n →						
											← n →						
LD IY, nn	IY ← nn	•	•	X	•	X	•	•	•	11	111	101	FD	4	4	14	
										00	100	001	21				
											← n →						
											← n →						
LD HL, (nn)	H ← (nn + 1)	•	•	X	•	X	•	•	•	00	101	010	2A	3	5	16	
	L ← (nn)										← n →						
											← n →						
LD dd, (nn)	dd$_H$ ← (nn + 1)	•	•	X	•	X	•	•	•	11	101	101	ED	4	6	20	
	dd$_L$ ← (nn)									01	dd1	011					
											← n →						
											← n →						
LD IX, (nn)	IX$_H$ ← (nn + 1)	•	•	X	•	X	•	•	•	11	011	101	DD	4	6	20	
	IX$_L$ ← (nn)									00	101	010	2A				
											← n →						
											← n →						
LD IY, (nn)	IY$_H$ ← (nn + 1)	•	•	X	•	X	•	•	•	11	111	101	FD	4	6	20	
	IY$_L$ ← (nn)									00	101	010	2A				
											← n →						
											← n →						
LD (nn), HL	(nn + 1) ← H	•	•	X	•	X	•	•	•	00	100	010	22	3	5	16	
	(nn) ← L										← n →						
											← n →						
LD (nn), dd	(nn + 1) ← dd$_H$	•	•	X	•	X	•	•	•	11	101	101	ED	4	6	20	
	(nn) ← dd$_L$									01	dd0	011					
											← n →						
											← n →						
LD (nn), IX	(nn + 1) ← IX$_H$	•	•	X	•	X	•	•	•	11	011	101	DD	4	6	20	
	(nn) ← IX$_L$									00	100	010	22				
											← n →						
											← n →						
LD (nn), IY	(nn + 1) ← IY$_H$	•	•	X	•	X	•	•	•	11	111	101	FD	4	6	20	
	(nn) ← IY$_L$									00	100	010	22				
											← n →						
											← n →						
LD SP, HL	SP ← HL	•	•	X	•	X	•	•	•	11	111	001	F9	1	1	6	
LD SP, IX	SP ← IX	•	•	X	•	X	•	•	•	11	011	101	DD	2	2	10	
										11	111	001	F9				
LD SP, IY	SP ← IY	•	•	X	•	X	•	•	•	11	111	101	FD	2	2	10	
										11	111	001	F9				qq Pair
PUSH qq	(SP − 2) ← qq$_L$	•	•	X	•	X	•	•	•	11	qq0	101		1	3	11	00 BC
	(SP − 1) ← qq$_H$																01 DE
	SP → SP − 2																10 HL
PUSH IX	(SP − 2) ← IX$_L$	•	•	X	•	X	•	•	•	11	011	101	DD	2	4	15	11 AF

NOTE: (PAIR)$_H$, (PAIR)$_L$ refer to high order and low order eight bits of the register pair respectively. e.g., BC$_L$ = C, AF$_H$ = A.

462

16-BIT LOAD GROUP (Continued)

Mnemonic	Symbolic Operation	S	Z	Flags H		P/V	N	C	Opcode 76	543	210	Hex	No. of Bytes	No. of M Cycles	No. of T States	Comments
	$(SP-1) \leftarrow IX_H$								11	100	101	E5				
	$SP \rightarrow SP-2$															
PUSH IY	$(SP-2) \leftarrow IY_L$	•	•	X	• X	•	•	•	11	111	101	FD	2	4	15	
	$(SP-1) \leftarrow IY_H$								11	100	101	E5				
	$SP \rightarrow SP-2$															
POP qq	$qq_H \leftarrow (SP+1)$	•	•	X	• X	•	•	•	11	qq0	001		1	3	10	
	$qqL \leftarrow (SP)$															
	$SP \rightarrow SP+2$															
POP IX	$IX_H \leftarrow (SP+1)$	•	•	X	• X	•	•	•	11	011	101	DD	2	4	14	
	$IX_L \leftarrow (SP)$								11	100	001	E1				
	$SP \rightarrow SP+2$															
POP IY	$IY_H \leftarrow (SP+1)$	•	•	X	• X	•	•	•	11	111	101	FD	2	4	14	
	$IY_L \leftarrow (SP)$								11	100	001	E1				
	$SP \rightarrow SP+2$															

EXCHANGE, BLOCK TRANSFER, BLOCK SEARCH GROUPS

Mnemonic	Symbolic Operation	S	Z	Flags H		P/V	N	C	Opcode 76	543	210	Hex	No. of Bytes	No. of M Cycles	No. of T States	Comments
EX DE, HL	$DE \leftrightarrow HL$	•	•	X	• X	•	•	•	11	101	011	EB	1	1	4	
EX AF, AF'	$AF \leftrightarrow AF'$	•	•	X	• X	•	•	•	00	001	000	08	1	1	4	
EXX	$BC \leftrightarrow BC'$	•	•	X	• X	•	•	•	11	011	001	D9	1	1	4	Register bank
	$DE \leftrightarrow DE'$															and auxiliary
	$HL \leftrightarrow HL'$															register bank
																exchange
EX (SP), HL	$H \leftrightarrow (SP+1)$	•	•	X	• X	•	•	•	11	100	011	E3	1	5	19	
	$L \leftrightarrow (SP)$															
EX (SP), IX	$IX_H \leftrightarrow (SP+1)$	•	•	X	• X	•	•	•	11	011	101	DD	2	6	23	
	$IX_L \leftrightarrow (SP)$								11	100	011	E3				
EX (SP), IY	$IY_H \leftrightarrow (SP+1)$	•	•	X	• X	•	•	•	11	111	101	FD	2	6	23	
	$IYL \leftrightarrow (SP)$								11	100	011	E3				
LDI	$(DE) \leftarrow (HL)$	•	•	X	0 X	① ‡	0	•	11	101	101	ED	2	4	16	Load (HL) into
	$DE \leftarrow DE+1$								10	100	000	A0				(DE), increment
	$HL \leftarrow HL+1$															the pointers and
	$BC \leftarrow BC-1$															decrement the
																byte counter
																(BC)
LDIR	$(DE) \leftarrow (HL)$	•	•	X	0 X	② 0	0	•	11	101	101	ED	2	5	21	If BC ≠ 0
	$DE \leftarrow DE+1$								10	110	000	B0	2	4	16	If BC = 0
	$HL \leftarrow HL+1$															
	$BC \leftarrow BC-1$															
	Repeat until															
	$BC = 0$															

NOTE: ① P/V flag is 0 if the result of BC − 1 = 0, otherwise P/V = 1.
      ② P/V flag is 0 only at completion of instruction.

EXCHANGE, BLOCK TRANSFER, BLOCK SEARCH GROUPS (Continued)

Mnemonic	Symbolic Operation	S	Z	Flags H	P/V	N	C	Opcode 76	543	210	Hex	No. of Bytes	No. of M Cycles	No. of T States	Comments
LDD	(DE) ← (HL) DE ← DE − 1 HL ← HL − 1 BC ← BC − 1	•	•	X 0 X	① ↕	0	•	11 10	101 101	101 000	ED A8	2	4	16	
LDDR	(DE) ← (HL) DE ← DE − 1 HL ← HL − 1 BC ← BC − 1 Repeat until BC = 0	•	•	X 0 X	② 0	0	•	11 10	101 111	101 000	ED B8	2 2	5 4	21 16	If BC ≠ 0 If BC = 0
CPI	A − (HL) HL ← HL + 1 BC ← BC − 1	↕	③ ↕	X ↕ X	① ↕	1	•	11 10	101 100	101 001	ED A1	2	4	16	
CPIR	A − (HL) HL ← HL + 1 BC ← BC − 1 Repeat until A = (HL) or BC = 0	↕	③ ↕	X ↕ X	① ↕	1	•	11 10	101 110	101 001	ED B1	2 2	5 4	21 16	If BC ≠ 0 and A ≠ (HL) If BC = 0 or A = (HL)
CPD	A − (HL) HL ← HL − 1 BC ← BC − 1	↕	③ ↕	X ↕ X	① ↕	1	•	11 10	101 101	101 001	ED A9	2	4	16	
CPDR	A − (HL) HL ← HL − 1 BC ← BC − 1 Repeat until A = (HL) or BC = 0	↕	③ ↕	X ↕ X	① ↕	1	•	11 10	101 111	101 001	ED B9	2 2	5 4	21 16	If BC ≠ 0 and A ≠ (HL) If BC = 0 or A = (HL)

NOTE:
① P/V flag is 0 if the result of BC − 1 = 0, otherwise P/V = 1.
② P/V flag is 0 only at completion of instruction.
③ Z flag is 1 if A = HL , otherwise Z = 0.

8-BIT ARITHMETIC AND LOGICAL GROUP

Mnemonic	Symbolic Operation	S	Z	Flags H	P/V	N	C	Opcode 76	543	210	Hex	No. of Bytes	No. of M Cycles	No. of T States	Comments
ADD A, r	A ← A + r	‡	‡	X	‡	X	V	0	‡	10	[000]	r		1	1	4	r Reg.
ADD A, n	A ← A + n	‡	‡	X	‡	X	V	0	‡	11	[000]	110		2	2	7	000 B
										← n →						001 C
																010 D
ADD A, (HL)	A ← A + (HL)	‡	‡	X	‡	X	V	0	‡	10	[000]	110		1	2	7	011 E
ADD A, (IX + d)	A ← A + (IX + d)	‡	‡	X	‡	X	V	0	‡	11	011	101	DD	3	5	19	100 H
										10	[000]	110					101 L
										← d →						111 A
ADD A, (IY + d)	A ← A + (IY + d)	‡	‡	X	‡	X	V	0	‡	11	111	101	FD	3	5	19	
										10	[000]	110					
										← d →						
ADC A, s	A ← A + s + CY	‡	‡	X	‡	X	V	0	‡		[001]						s is any of r, n,
SUB s	A ← A − s	‡	‡	X	‡	X	V	1	‡		[010]						(HL), (IX + d),
SBC A, s	A ← A − s − CY	‡	‡	X	‡	X	V	1	‡		[011]						(IY + d) as
AND s	A ← A > s	‡	‡	X	1	X	P	0	0		[100]						shown for ADD
OR s	A ← A > s	‡	‡	X	0	X	P	0	0		[110]						instruction. The
XOR s	A ← A⊕s	‡	‡	X	0	X	P	0	0		[101]						indicated bits
CP s	A − s	‡	‡	X	‡	X	V	1	‡		[111]						replace the
																[000] in the
																ADD set above.
INC r	r ← r + 1	‡	‡	X	‡	X	V	0	•	00	r	[100]		1	1	4	
INC (HL)	(HL) ←																
	(HL) + 1	‡	‡	X	‡	X	V	0	•	00	110	[100]		1	3	11	
INC (IX + d)	(IX + d) ←	‡	‡	X	‡	X	V	0	•	11	011	101	DD	3	6	23	
	(IX + d) + 1									00	110	[100]					
										← d →						
INC (IY + d)	(IY + d) ←	‡	‡	X	‡	X	V	0	•	11	111	101	FD	3	6	23	
	(IY + d) + 1									00	110	[100]					
										← d →						
DEC m	m ← m − 1	‡	‡	X	‡	X	V	1	•			[101]					

NOTE: m is any of r, (HL), (IX + d), (IY + d) as shown for INC. DEC same format and states as INC. Replace [100] with [101] in opcode.

GENERAL-PURPOSE ARITHMETIC AND CPU CONTROL GROUPS

Mnemonic	Symbolic Operation	S	Z	Flags H	P/V	N	C	Opcode 76	543	210	Hex	No. of Bytes	No. of M Cycles	No. of T States	Comments
DAA	@	‡	‡	X	‡	X	P	•	‡	00	100	111	27	1	1	4	Decimal adjust accumulator.
CPL	A ← Ā	•	•	X	1	X	•	1	•	00	101	111	2F	1	1	4	Complement accumulator (one's complement).
NEG	A ← 0 − A	‡	‡	X	‡	X	V	1	‡	11	101	101	ED	2	2	8	Negate acc. (two's complement).
										01	000	100	44				

NOTES: @ converts accumulator content into packed BCD following add or subtract with packed BCD operands.
IFF indicates the interrupt enable flip-flop.
CY indicates the carry flip-flop.
★ indicates interrupts are not sampled at the end of EI or DI.

465

Mnemonic	Symbolic Operation	S	Z		H		P/V	N	C	76	543	210	Hex	No. of Bytes	No. of M Cycles	No. of T States	Comments
CCF	CY ← CY	•	•	X	X	X	•	0	‡	00	111	111	3F	1	1	4	Complement carry flag.
SCF	CY ← 1	•	•	X	0	X	•	0	1	00	110	111	37	1	1	4	Set carry flag.
NOP	No operation	•	•	X	•	X	•	•	•	00	000	000	00	1	1	4	
HALT	CPU halted	•	•	X	•	X	•	•	•	01	110	110	76	1	1	4	
DI ★	IFF ← 0	•	•	X	•	X	•	•	•	11	110	011	F3	1	1	4	
EI ★	IFF ← 1	•	•	X	•	X	•	•	•	11	111	011	FB	1	1	4	
IM 0	Set interrupt mode 0	•	•	X	•	X	•	•	•	11	101	101	ED	2	2	8	
										01	000	110	46				
IM 1	Set interrupt mode 1	•	•	X	•	X	•	•	•	11	101	101	ED	2	2	8	
										01	010	110	56				
IM 2	Set interrupt mode 2	•	•	X	•	X	•	•	•	11	101	101	ED	2	2	8	
										01	011	110	5E				

NOTES: @ converts accumulator content into packed BCD following add or subtract with packed BCD operands.
IFF indicates the interrupt enable flip-flop.
CY indicates the carry flip-flop.
★ indicates interrupts are not sampled at the end of EI or DI.

16-BIT ARITHMETIC GROUP

Mnemonic	Symbolic Operation	S	Z		H		P/V	N	C	76	543	210	Hex	No. of Bytes	No. of M Cycles	No. of T States	Comments
ADD HL, ss	HL ← HL + ss	•	•	X	X	X	•	0	‡	00	ss1	001		1	3	11	ss Reg. 00 BC
ADC HL, ss	HL ← HL + ss + CY	‡	‡	X	X	X	V	0	‡	11	101	101	ED	2	4	15	01 DE
										01	ss1	010					
SBC HL, ss	HL ← HL − ss − CY	‡	‡	X	X	X	V	1	‡	11	101	101	ED	2	4	15	10 HL
										01	ss0	010					11 SP
ADD IX, pp	IX ← IX + pp	•	•	X	X	X	•	0	‡	11	011	101	DD	2	4	15	pp Reg. 00 BC
										01	pp1	001					01 DE 10 IX 11 SP
ADD IY, rr	IY ← IY + rr	•	•	X	X	X	•	0	‡	11	111	101	FD	2	4	15	rr Reg. 00 BC
										00	rr1	001					01 DE
INC ss	ss ← ss + 1	•	•	X	•	X	•	•	•	00	ss0	011		1	1	6	10 IY
INC IX	IX ← IX + 1	•	•	X	•	X	•	•	•	11	011	101	DD	2	2	10	11 SP
										00	100	011	23				
INC IY	IY ← IY + 1	•	•	X	•	X	•	•	•	11	111	101	FD	2	2	10	
										00	100	011	23				
DEC ss	ss ← ss − 1	•	•	X	•	X	•	•	•	00	ss1	011		1	1	6	
DEC IX	IX ← IX − 1	•	•	X	•	X	•	•	•	11	011	101	DD	2	2	10	
										00	101	011	2B				
DEC IY	IY ← IY − 1	•	•	X	•	X	•	•	•	11	111	101	FD	2	2	10	
										00	101	011	2B				

ROTATE AND SHIFT GROUP

Mnemonic	Symbolic Operation	S	Z	Flags H	P/V	N	C	Opcode 76	543	210	Hex	No. of Bytes	No. of M Cycles	No. of T States	Comments
RLCA	[CY]←[7←0]←	•	•	X	0	X	•	0	↕	00	000	111	07	1	1	4	Rotate left circular accumulator.
RLA	[CY]←[7←0]←	•	•	X	0	X	•	0	↕	00	010	111	17	1	1	4	Rotate left accumulator.
RRCA	→[7→0]→[CY]	•	•	X	0	X	•	0	↕	00	001	111	0F	1	1	4	Rotate right circular accumulator.
RRA	→[7→0]→[CY]	•	•	X	0	X	•	0	↕	00	011	111	1F	1	1	4	Rotate right accumulator.
RLC r		↕	↕	X	0	X	P	0	↕	11 00	001 [000]	011 r	CB	2	2	8	Rotate left circular register r.
RLC (HL)		↕	↕	X	0	X	P	0	↕	11 00	001 [000]	011 110	CB	2	4	15	
RLC (IX + d)	r,(HL),(IX + d),(IY + d)	↕	↕	X	0	X	P	0	↕	11 11 ←d→ 00	011 001 [000]	101 011 110	DD CB	4	6	23	
RLC (IY + d)		↕	↕	X	0	X	P	0	↕	11 11 ←d→ 00	111 001 [000]	101 011 110	FD CB	4	6	23	
RL m	[CY]←[7←0]← m = r,(HL,(IX + d),(IY + d)	↕	↕	X	0	X	P	0	↕		[010]						
RRC m	→[7→0]→[CY] m = r,(HL),(IX + d),(IY + d)	↕	↕	X	0	X	P	0	↕		[001]						
RR m	→[7→0]→[CY] m = r,(HL),(IX + d),(IY + d)	↕	↕	X	0	X	P	0	↕		[011]						
SLA m	[CY]←[7←0]←0 m = r,(HL),(IX + d),(IY + d)	↕	↕	X	0	X	P	0	↕		[100]						
SRA m	[7→0]→[CY] m = r,(HL),(IX + d),(IY + d)	↕	↕	X	0	X	P	0	↕		[101]						
SRL m	0→[7→0]→[CY] m = r,(HL),(IX + d),(IY + d)	↕	↕	X	0	X	P	0	↕		[111]						

r	Reg.
000	B
001	C
010	D
011	E
001	H
101	L
111	A

Instruction format and states are as shown for RLCs. To form new opcode replace [000] or RLCs with shown code.

ROTATE AND SHIFT GROUP (Continued)

Mnemonic	Symbolic Operation	S	Z	H	P/V	N	C	76	543	210	Hex	No. of Bytes	No. of M Cycles	No. of T States	Comments
RLD	[7-4][3-0] A ← [7-4][3-0] (HL)	‡	‡	X	0	X	P	0	•	11	101	101	ED	2	5	18	Rotate digit left and right between the accumulator and location (HL).
										01	101	111	6F				
RRD	[7-4][3-0] A → [7-4][3-0] (HL)	‡	‡	X	0	X	P	0	•	11	101	101	ED	2	5	18	The content of the upper half of the accumulator is unaffected.
										01	100	111	67				

BIT SET, RESET AND TEST GROUP

Mnemonic	Symbolic Operation	S	Z	H	P/V	N	C	76	543	210	Hex	No. of Bytes	No. of M Cycles	No. of T States	Comments
BIT b, r	Z ← r_b	X	‡	X	1	X	X	0	•	11	001	011	CB	2	2	8	r Reg.
										01	b	r					000 B
BIT b, (HL)	Z ← $(HL)_b$	X	‡	X	1	X	X	0	•	11	001	011	CB	2	3	12	001 C
										01	b	110					010 D
BIT b, (IX + d)$_b$	Z ← $(IX+d)_b$	X	‡	X	1	X	X	0	•	11	011	101	DD	4	5	20	011 E
										11	001	011	CB				100 H
										← d →							101 L
										01	b	110					111 A
																	b Bit Tested
BIT b, (IY + d)$_b$	Z ← $(IY+d)_b$	X	‡	X	1	X	X	0	•	11	111	101	FD	4	5	20	000 0
										11	001	011	CB				001 1
										← d →							010 2
										01	b	110					011 3
SET b, r	r_b ← 1	•	•	X	•	X	•	•	•	11	001	011	CB	2	2	8	100 4
										[11]	b	r					101 5
SET b, (HL)	$(HL)_b$ ← 1	•	•	X	•	X	•	•	•	11	001	011	CB	2	4	15	110 6
										[11]	b	110					111 7
SET b, (IX + d)	$(IX+d)_b$ ← 1	•	•	X	•	X	•	•	•	11	011	101	DD	4	6	23	
										11	001	011	CB				
										← d →							
										[11]	b	110					
SET b, (IY + d)	$(IY+d)_b$ ← 1	•	•	X	•	X	•	•	•	11	111	101	FD	4	6	23	
										11	001	011	CB				
										← d →							
										[11]	b	110					
RES b, m	m_b ← 0 m≡r, (HL), (IX + d), (IY + d)	•	•	X	•	X	•	•	•	[10]							To form new opcode replace [11] of SET b, s with [10]. Flags and time states for SET instruction.

NOTE: The notation m_b indicates location m, bit b (0 to 7).

468

JUMP GROUP

Mnemonic	Symbolic Operation	S	Z	H	P/V	N	C	76	543	210	Hex	No. of Bytes	No. of M Cycles	No. of T States	Comments	
JP nn	PC ← nn	•	•	X	• X	•	•	11	000	011	C3	3	3	10	cc	Condition
								← n →							000	NZ (non-zero)
								← n →							001	Z (zero)
JP cc, nn	If condition cc	•	•	X	• X	•	•	11	cc	010		3	3	10	010	NC (non-carry)
	is true PC←nn,							← n →							011	C (carry)
	otherwise							← n →							100	PO (parity odd)
	continue														101	PE (parity even)
JR e	PC ← PC + e	•	•	X	• X	•	•	00	011	000	18	2	3	12	110	P (sign positive)
								← e – 2 →							111	M (sign negative)
JR C, e	If C = 0,	•	•	X	• X	•	•	00	111	000	38	2	2	7	If condition not met.	
	continue							← e – 2 →								
	If C = 1,											2	3	12	If condition is met.	
	PC ← PC + e															
JR NC, e	IF C = 1,	•	•	X	• X	•	•	00	110	000	30	2	2	7	If condition not met.	
	continue							← e – 2 →								
	If C = 0,											2	3	12	If condition is met.	
	PC ← PC + e															
JP Z, e	If Z = 0	•	•	X	• X	•	•	00	101	000	28	2	2	7	If condition not met.	
	continue							← e – 2 →								
	If Z = 1,											2	3	12	If condition is met.	
	PC ← PC + e															
JR NZ, e	If Z = 1,	•	•	X	• X	•	•	00	100	000	20	2	2	7	If condition not met.	
	continue							← e – 2 →								
	If Z = 0,											2	3	12	If condition is met.	
	PC ← PC + e															
JP (HL)	PC ← HL	•	•	X	• X	•	•	11	101	001	E9	1	1	4		
JP (IX)	PC ← IX	•	•	X	• X	•	•	11	011	101	DD	2	2	8		
								11	101	001	E9					
JP (IY)	PC ← IY	•	•	X	• X	•	•	11	111	101	FD	2	2	8		
								11	101	001	E9					
DJNZ, e	B ← B – 1	•	•	X	• X	•	•	00	010	000	10	2	2	8	If B = 0	
	If B = 0,							← e – 2 →								
	continue															
	If B≠0,											2	3	13	If B≠0.	
	PC ← PC + e															

NOTES: e represents the extension in the relative addressing mode.
   e is a signal two's complement number in the range < – 126, 129 >.
   e – 2 in the opcode provides an effective address of pc + e as PC is incremented by 2 prior to the addition of e.

CALL AND RETURN GROUP

Mnemonic	Symbolic Operation	S	Z	Flags H	P/V N	C	Opcode 76	543	210	Hex	No. of Bytes	No. of M Cycles	No. of T States	Comments
CALL nn	$(SP-1) \leftarrow PC_H$	•	•	X • X	• •	•	11	001	101	CD	3	5	17	
	$(SP-2) \leftarrow PC_L$							$\leftarrow n \rightarrow$						
	$PC \leftarrow nn,$							$\leftarrow n \rightarrow$						
CALL cc,nn	If condition cc is false	•	•	X • X	• •	•	11	cc	100		3	3	10	If cc is false.
	continue,							$\leftarrow n \rightarrow$			3	5	17	If cc is true.
	otherwise same as CALL nn							$\leftarrow n \rightarrow$						
RET	$PC_L \leftarrow (SP)$	•	•	X • X	• •	•	11	001	001	C9	1	3	10	
	$PC_H \leftarrow (SP+1)$													
RET cc	If condition cc is false	•	•	X • X	• •	•	11	cc	000		1	1	5	If cc is false.
	continue, otherwise same as RET										1	3	11	If cc is true.
RETI	Return from interrupt	•	•	X • X	• •	•	11	101	101	ED	2	4	14	
							01	001	101	4D				
RETN[1]	Return from non-maskable interrupt	•	•	X • X	• •	•	11	101	101	ED	2	4	14	
							01	000	101	45				
RST p	$(SP-1) \leftarrow PC_H$	•	•	X • X	• •	•	11	t	111		1	3	11	
	$(SP-2) \leftarrow PC_L$													
	$PC_H \leftarrow 0$													
	$PC_L \leftarrow p$													

cc	Condition
000	NZ (non-zero)
001	Z (zero)
010	NC (non-carry)
011	C (carry)
100	PO (parity odd)
101	PE (parity even)
110	P (sign positive)
111	M (sign negative)

t	p
000	00H
001	08H
010	10H
011	18H
100	20H
101	28H
110	30H
111	38H

NOTE: [1]RETN loads $IFF_2 \rightarrow IFF_1$

INPUT AND OUTPUT GROUP

Mnemonic	Symbolic Operation	S	Z	H	P/V	N	C	76	543	210	Hex	No. of Bytes	No. of M Cycles	No. of T States	Comments
IN A, (n)	$A \leftarrow (n)$	•	•	X	•	X	•	•	•	11	011	01	DB	2	3	11	n to $A_0 \sim A_7$ Acc. to $A_8 \sim A_{15}$
										$\leftarrow n \rightarrow$						
IN r, (C)	$r \leftarrow (C)$ if r = 110 only the flags will be affected	↕	↕	X	↕	X	P	0	•	11 01	101 r	101 000	ED	2	3	12	C to $A_0 \sim A_7$ B to $A_8 \sim A_{15}$
	①																
INI	$(HL) \leftarrow (C)$ $B \leftarrow B - 1$ $HL \leftarrow HL + 1$	X	↕	X	X	X	X	1	X	11 10	101 100	101 010	ED A2	2	4	16	C to $A_0 \sim A_7$ B to $A_8 \sim A_{15}$
	②																
INIR	$(HL) \leftarrow (C)$ $B \leftarrow B - 1$ $HL \leftarrow HL + 1$ Repeat until B = 0	X	1	X	X	X	X	1	X	11 10	101 110	101 010	ED B2	2 2	5 (If B≠0) 4 (If B = 0)	21 16	C to $A_0 \sim A_7$ B to $A_8 \sim A_{15}$
	①																
IND	$(HL) \leftarrow (C)$ $B \leftarrow B - 1$ $HL \leftarrow HL - 1$	X	↕	X	X	X	X	1	X	11 10	101 101	101 010	ED AA	2	4	16	C to $A_0 \sim A_7$ B to $A_8 \sim A_{15}$
	②																
INDR	$(HL) \leftarrow (C)$ $B \leftarrow B - 1$ $HL \leftarrow HL - 1$ Repeat until B = 0	X	1	X	X	X	X	1	X	11 10	101 111	101 010	ED BA	2 2	5 (If B≠0) 4 (If B = 0)	21 16	C to $A_0 \sim A_7$ B to $A_8 \sim A_{15}$
OUT (n), A	$(n) \leftarrow A$	•	•	X	•	X	•	•	•	11	010	011	D3	2	3	11	n to $A_0 \sim A_7$ Acc. to $A_8 \sim A_{15}$
										$\leftarrow n \rightarrow$						
OUT (C), r	$(C) \leftarrow r$	•	•	X	•	X	•	•	•	11 01	101 r	101 001	ED	2	3	12	C to $A_0 \sim A_7$ B to $A_8 \sim A_{15}$
	①																
OUTI	$(C) \leftarrow (HL)$ $B \leftarrow B - 1$ $HL \leftarrow HL + 1$	X	↕	X	X	X	X	1	X	11 10	101 100	101 011	ED A3	2	4	16	C to $A_0 \sim A_7$ B to $A_8 \sim A_{15}$
	②																
OTIR	$(C) \leftarrow (HL)$ $B \leftarrow B - 1$ $HL \leftarrow HL + 1$ Repeat until B = 0	X	1	X	X	X	X	1	X	11 10	101 110	101 011	ED B3	2 2	5 (If B≠0) 4 (If B = 0)	21 16	C to $A_0 \sim A_7$ B to $A_8 \sim A_{15}$
	①																
OUTD	$(C) \leftarrow (HL)$ $B \leftarrow B - 1$ $HL \leftarrow HL - 1$	X	↕	X	X	X	X	1	X	11 10	101 101	101 011	ED AB	2	4	16	C to $A_0 \sim A_7$ B to $A_8 \sim A_{15}$
	②																
OTDR	$(C) \leftarrow (HL)$ $B \leftarrow B - 1$ $HL \leftarrow HL - 1$ Repeat until B = 0	X	1	X	X	X	X	1	X	11 10	101 111	101 011	ED	2 2	5 (If B≠0) 4 (If B = 0)	21 16	C to $A_0 \sim A_7$ B to $A_8 \sim A_{15}$

NOTES: ① If the result of B − 1 is zero, the Z flag is set; otherwise it is reset.
② Z flag is set upon instruction completion only.

SUMMARY OF FLAG OPERATION

Instructions	D7 S	Z		H		P/V	N	D0 C	Comments
ADD A, s; ADC A, s	‡	‡	X	‡	X	V	0	‡	8-bit add or add with carry.
SUB s; SBC A, s; CP s; NEG	‡	‡	X	‡	X	V	1	‡	8-bit subtract, subtract with carry, compare and negate accumulator.
AND s	‡	‡	X	1	X	P	0	0	Logical operation.
OR s, XOR s	‡	‡	X	0	X	P	0	0	Logical operation.
INC s	‡	‡	X	‡	X	V	0	•	8-bit increment.
DEC s	‡	‡	X	‡	X	V	1	•	8-bit decrement.
ADD DD, ss	•	•	X	X	X	•	0	‡	16-bit add.
ADC HL, ss	‡	‡	X	X	X	V	0	‡	16-bit add with carry.
SBC HL, ss	‡	‡	X	X	X	V	1	‡	16-bit subtract with carry.
RLA; RLCA; RRA; RRCA	•	•	X	0	X	•	0	‡	Rotate accumulator.
RL m; RLC m; RR m; RRC m; SLA m; SRA m; SRL m	‡	‡	X	0	X	P	0	‡	Rotate and shift locations.
RLD; RRD	‡	‡	X	0	X	P	0	•	Rotate digit left and right.
DAA	‡	‡	X	‡	X	P	•	‡	Decimal adjust accumulator.
CPL	•	•	X	1	X	•	1	•	Complement accumulator.
SCF	•	•	X	0	X	•	0	1	Set carry.
CCF	•	•	X	X	X	•	0	‡	Complement carry.
IN r (C)	‡	‡	X	0	X	P	0	•	Input register indirect.
INI; IND; OUTI; OUTD	X	‡	X	X	X	X	1	•	Block input and output. Z = 1 if B ≠ 0, otherwise Z = 0.
INIR; INDR; OTIR; OTDR	X	1	X	X	X	X	1	•	Block input and output. Z = 1 if B ≠ 0, otherwise Z = 0.
LDI; LDD	X	X	X	0	X	‡	0	•	Block transfer instructions. P/V = 1 if BC ≠ 0, otherwise P/V = 0.
LDIR; LDDR	X	X	X	0	X	0	0	•	Block transfer instructions. P/V = 1 if BC ≠ 0, otherwise P/V = 0.
CPI; CPIR; CPD; CPDR	X	‡	X	X	X	‡	1	•	Block search instructions. Z = 1 if A = (HL), otherwise Z = 0. P/V = 1 if BC ≠ 0, otherwise P/V = 0.
LD A; I, LD A, R	‡	‡	X	0	X	IFF	0	•	IFF, the content of the interrupt enable flip-flop, (IFF$_2$), is copied into the P/V flag.
BIT b, s	X	‡	X	1	X	X	0	•	The state of bit b of location s is copied into the Z flag.

SYMBOLIC NOTATION

Symbol	Operation	Symbol	Operation
S	Sign flag. S = 1 if the MSB of the result is 1.	‡	The flag is affected according to the result of the operation.
Z	Zero flag. Z = 1 if the result of the operation is 0.	•	The flag is unchanged by the operation.
P/V	Parity or overflow flag. Parity (P) and overflow (V) share the same flag. Logical operations affect this flag with the parity of the result while arithmetic operations affect this flag with the overflow of the result. If P/V holds parity: P/V = 1 if the result of the operation is even; P/V = 0 if result is odd. If P/V holds overflow, P/V = 1 if the result of the operation produced an overflow. If P/V does not hold overflow, P/V = 0.	0	The flag is reset by the operation.
		1	The flag is set by the operation.
		X	The flag is indeterminate.
		V	P/V flag affected according to the overflow result of the operation.
		P	P/V flag affected according to the parity result of the operation.
		r	Any one o the CPU registers A, B, C, D, E, H, L.
H*	Half-carry flag. H = 1 if the add or subtract operation produced a carry into, or borrow from, bit 4 of the accumulator.	s	Any 8-bit location for all the addressing modes allowed for the particular instruction.
N*	Add/Subtract flag. N = 1 if the previous operation was a subtract.	ss	Any 16-bit location for all the addressing modes allowed for that instruction.
		ii	Any one of the two index registers IX or IY.
C	Carry/Link flag. C = 1 if the operation produced a carry from the MSB of the operand or result.	R	Refresh counter.
		n	8-bit value in range < 0, 255 >.
		nn	16-bit value in range < 0, 65535 >.

*H and N flags are used in conjunction with the decimal adjust instruction (DAA) to properly correct the result into packed BCD format following addition or subtraction using operands with packed BCD format.

MC6809 Instruction Set

This appendix summarizes the instruction set of the Motorola MC6809 and has been reprinted from the *Motorola Microprocessors Data Manual* through the courtesy of Motorola, Inc.

Addressing Modes

Instruction	Forms	Immediate Op	~	#	Direct Op	~	#	Indexed Op	~	#	Extended Op	~	#	Inherent Op	~	#	Description	H	N	Z	V	C
ABX														3A	3	1	B + X → X (Unsigned)	•	•	•	•	•
ADC	ADCA	89	2	2	99	4	2	A9	4+	2+	B9	5	3				A + M + C → A	↕	↕	↕	↕	↕
	ADCB	C9	2	2	D9	4	2	E9	4+	2+	F9	5	3				B + M + C → B	↕	↕	↕	↕	↕
ADD	ADDA	8B	2	2	9B	4	2	AB	4+	2+	BB	5	3				A + M → A	↕	↕	↕	↕	↕
	ADDB	CB	2	2	DB	4	2	EB	4+	2+	FB	5	3				B + M → B	↕	↕	↕	↕	↕
	ADDD	C3	4	3	D3	6	2	E3	6+	2+	F3	7	3				D + M:M + 1 → D	•	↕	↕	↕	↕
AND	ANDA	84	2	2	94	4	2	A4	4+	2+	B4	5	3				A Λ M → A	•	↕	↕	0	•
	ANDB	C4	2	2	D4	4	2	E4	4+	2+	F4	5	3				B Λ M → B	•	↕	↕	0	•
	ANDCC	1C	3	2													CC Λ IMM → CC					7
ASL	ASLA													48	2	1	A ⎫	8	↕	↕	↕	↕
	ASLB													58	2	1	B ⎬ ← 0	8	↕	↕	↕	↕
	ASL				08	6	2	68	6+	2+	78	7	3				M ⎭ c b7 ... b0	8	↕	↕	↕	↕
ASR	ASRA													47	2	1	A ⎫	8	↕	↕	•	↕
	ASRB													57	2	1	B ⎬	8	↕	↕	•	↕
	ASR				07	6	2	67	6+	2+	77	7	3				M ⎭ b7 ... b0 c	8	↕	↕	•	↕
BIT	BITA	85	2	2	95	4	2	A5	4+	2+	B5	5	3				Bit Test A (M Λ A)	•	↕	↕	0	•
	BITB	C5	2	2	D5	4	2	E5	4+	2+	F5	5	3				Bit Test B (M Λ B)	•	↕	↕	0	•
CLR	CLRA													4F	2	1	0 → A	•	0	1	0	0
	CLRB													5F	2	1	0 → B	•	0	1	0	0
	CLR				0F	6	2	6F	6+	2+	7F	7	3				0 → M	•	0	1	0	0
CMP	CMPA	81	2	2	91	4	2	A1	4+	2+	B1	5	3				Compare M from A	8	↕	↕	↕	↕
	CMPB	C1	2	2	D1	4	2	E1	4+	2+	F1	5	3				Compare M from B	8	↕	↕	↕	↕
	CMPD	10 83	5	4	10 93	7	3	10 A3	7+	3+	10 B3	8	4				Compare M:M + 1 from D	•	↕	↕	↕	↕
	CMPS	11 8C	5	4	11 9C	7	3	11 AC	7+	3+	11 BC	8	4				Compare M:M + 1 from S	•	↕	↕	↕	↕
	CMPU	11 83	5	4	11 93	7	3	11 A3	7+	3+	11 B3	8	4				Compare M:M + 1 from U	•	↕	↕	↕	↕
	CMPX	8C	4	3	9C	6	2	AC	6+	2+	BC	7	3				Compare M:M + 1 from X	•	↕	↕	↕	↕
	CMPY	10 8C	5	4	10 9C	7	3	10 AC	7+	3+	10 BC	8	4				Compare M:M + 1 from Y	•	↕	↕	↕	↕
COM	COMA													43	2	1	$\bar{A}$ → A	•	↕	↕	0	1
	COMB													53	2	1	$\bar{B}$ → B	•	↕	↕	0	1
	COM				03	6	2	63	6+	2+	73	7	3				$\bar{M}$ → M	•	↕	↕	0	1
CWAI		3C	≥20	2													CC Λ IMM → CC Wait for Interrupt					7
DAA														19	2	1	Decimal Adjust A	•	↕	↕	0	↕
DEC	DECA													4A	2	1	A − 1 → A	•	↕	↕	↕	•
	DECB													5A	2	1	B − 1 → B	•	↕	↕	↕	•
	DEC				0A	6	2	6A	6+	2+	7A	7	3				M − 1 → M	•	↕	↕	↕	•
EOR	EORA	88	2	2	98	4	2	A8	4+	2+	B8	5	3				A ⊻ M → A	•	↕	↕	0	•
	EORB	C8	2	2	D8	4	2	E8	4+	2+	F8	5	3				B ⊻ M → B	•	↕	↕	0	•
EXG	R1, R2													1E	8	2	R1 → R2[2]	•	•	•	•	•
INC	INCA													4C	2	1	A + 1 → A	•	↕	↕	↕	•
	INCB													5C	2	1	B + 1 → B	•	↕	↕	↕	•
	INC				0C	6	2	6C	6+	2+	7C	7	3				M + 1 → M	•	↕	↕	↕	•
JMP					0E	3	2	6E	3+	2+	7E	4	3				EA[3] → PC	•	•	•	•	•
JSR					9D	7	2	AD	7+	2+	BD	8	3				Jump to Subroutine	•	•	•	•	•
LD	LDA	86	2	2	96	4	2	A6	4+	2+	B6	5	3				M → A	•	↕	↕	0	•
	LDB	C6	2	2	D6	4	2	E6	4+	2+	F6	5	3				M → B	•	↕	↕	0	•
	LDD	CC	3	3	DC	5	2	EC	5+	2+	FC	6	3				M:M + 1 → D	•	↕	↕	0	•
	LDS	10 CE	4	4	10 DE	6	3	10 EE	6+	3+	10 FE	7	4				M:M + 1 → S	•	↕	↕	0	•
	LDU	CE	3	3	DE	5	2	EE	5+	2+	FE	6	3				M:M + 1 → U	•	↕	↕	0	•
	LDX	8E	3	3	9E	5	2	AE	5+	2+	BE	6	3				M:M + 1 → X	•	↕	↕	0	•
	LDY	10 8E	4	4	10 9E	6	3	10 AE	6+	3+	10 BE	7	4				M:M + 1 → Y	•	↕	↕	0	•
LEA	LEAS							32	4+	2+							EA[3] → S	•	•	•	•	•
	LEAU							33	4+	2+							EA[3] → U	•	•	•	•	•
	LEAX							30	4+	2+							EA[3] → X	•	•	↕	•	•
	LEAY							31	4+	2+							EA[3] → Y	•	•	↕	•	•

Legend:

OP	Operation Code (Hexadecimal)	$\bar{M}$	Complement of M
~	Number of MPU Cycles	→	Transfer Into
#	Number of Program Bytes	H	Half-carry (from bit 3)
+	Arithmetic Plus	N	Negative (sign bit)
−	Arithmetic Minus	Z	Zero result
•	Multiply	V	Overflow, 2's complement
		C	Carry from ALU

↕	Test and set if true, cleared otherwise
•	Not Affected
CC	Condition Code Register
:	Concatenation
V	Logical or
Λ	Logical and
⊻	Logical Exclusive or

Instruction	Forms	Immediate Op	~	#	Direct Op	~	#	Indexed[1] Op	~	#	Extended Op	~	#	Inherent Op	~	#	Description	H	N	Z	V	C
LSL	LSLA													48	2	1	(A, B, M shift left)	•	↕	↕	↕	↕
	LSLB													58	2	1		•	↕	↕	↕	↕
	LSL				08	6	2	68	6+	2+	78	7	3					•	↕	↕	↕	↕
LSR	LSRA													44	2	1	(A, B, M shift right)	•	0	↕	•	↕
	LSRB													54	2	1		•	0	↕	•	↕
	LSR				04	6	2	64	6+	2+	74	7	3					•	0	↕	•	↕
MUL														3D	11	1	A × B → D (Unsigned)	•	•	↕	•	9
NEG	NEGA													40	2	1	$\overline{A}$ + 1 → A	8	↕	↕	↕	↕
	NEGB													50	2	1	$\overline{B}$ + 1 → B	8	↕	↕	↕	↕
	NEG				00	6	2	60	6+	2+	70	7	3				$\overline{M}$ + 1 → M	8	↕	↕	↕	↕
NOP														12	2	1	No Operation	•	•	•	•	•
OR	ORA	8A	2	2	9A	4	2	AA	4+	2+	BA	5	3				A V M → A	•	↕	↕	0	•
	ORB	CA	2	2	DA	4	2	EA	4+	2+	FA	5	3				B V M → B	•	↕	↕	0	•
	ORCC	1A	3	2													CC V IMM → CC	7				
PSH	PSHS	34	5+[4]	2													Push Registers on S Stack	•	•	•	•	•
	PSHU	36	5+[4]	2													Push Registers on U Stack	•	•	•	•	•
PUL	PULS	35	5+[4]	2													Pull Registers from S Stack	•	•	•	•	•
	PULU	37	5+[4]	2													Pull Registers from U Stack	•	•	•	•	•
ROL	ROLA													49	2	1	(A, B, M rotate left)	•	↕	↕	↕	↕
	ROLB													59	2	1		•	↕	↕	↕	↕
	ROL				09	6	2	69	6+	2+	79	7	3					•	↕	↕	↕	↕
ROR	RORA													46	2	1	(A, B, M rotate right)	•	↕	↕	•	↕
	RORB													56	2	1		•	↕	↕	•	↕
	ROR				06	6	2	66	6+	2+	76	7	3					•	↕	↕	•	↕
RTI														3B	6/15	1	Return From Interrupt					7
RTS														39	5	1	Return from Subroutine	•	•	•	•	•
SBC	SBCA	82	2	2	92	4	2	A2	4+	2+	B2	5	3				A - M - C → A	8	↕	↕	↕	↕
	SBCB	C2	2	2	D2	4	2	E2	4+	2+	F2	5	3				B - M - C → B	8	↕	↕	↕	↕
SEX														1D	2	1	Sign Extend B into A	•	↕	↕	0	•
ST	STA				97	4	2	A7	4+	2+	B7	5	3				A → M	•	↕	↕	0	•
	STB				D7	4	2	E7	4+	2+	F7	5	3				B → M	•	↕	↕	0	•
	STD				DD	5	2	ED	5+	2+	FD	6	3				D → M M + 1	•	↕	↕	0	•
	STS				10 DF	6	3	10 EF	6+	3+	10 FF	7	4				S → M M + 1	•	↕	↕	0	•
	STU				DF	5	2	EF	5+	2+	FF	6	3				U → M M + 1	•	↕	↕	0	•
	STX				9F	5	2	AF	5+	2+	BF	6	3				X → M M + 1	•	↕	↕	0	•
	STY				10 9F	6	3	10 AF	6+	3+	10 BF	7	4				Y → M M + 1	•	↕	↕	0	•
SUB	SUBA	80	2	2	90	4	2	A0	4+	2+	B0	5	3				A - M → A	8	↕	↕	↕	↕
	SUBB	C0	2	2	D0	4	2	E0	4+	2+	F0	5	3				B - M → B	8	↕	↕	↕	↕
	SUBD	83	4	3	93	6	2	A3	6+	2+	B3	7	3				D - M:M + 1 → D	•	↕	↕	↕	↕
SWI	SWI[6]													3F	19	1	Software Interrupt 1	•	•	•	•	•
	SWI[6]													10 3F	20	2	Software Interrupt 2	•	•	•	•	•
	SWI[6]													11 3F	20	1	Software Interrupt 3	•	•	•	•	•
SYNC														13	≥ 4	1	Synchronize to Interrupt	•	•	•	•	•
TFR	R1, R2													1F	6	2	R1 → R2[2]	•	•	•	•	•
TST	TSTA													4D	2	1	Test A	•	↕	↕	0	•
	TSTB													5D	2	1	Test B	•	↕	↕	0	•
	TST				0D	6	2	6D	6+	2+	7D	7	3				Test M	•	↕	↕	0	•

Notes:

1. This column gives a base cycle and byte count. To obtain total count, add the values obtained from the INDEXED ADDRESSING MODE table, Table 2.
2. R1 and R2 may be any pair of 8 bit or any pair of 16 bit registers.
   The 8 bit registers are: A, B, CC, DP
   The 16 bit registers are: X, Y, U, S, D, PC
3. EA is the effective address.
4. The PSH and PUL instructions require 5 cycles plus 1 cycle for each **byte** pushed or pulled.
5. 5(6) means: 5 cycles if branch not taken, 6 cycles if taken (Branch instructions).
6. SWI sets I and F bits. SWI2 and SWI3 do not affect I and F.
7. Conditions Codes set as a direct result of the instruction.
8. Vaue of half-carry flag is undefined.
9. Special Case — Carry set if b7 is SET

Branch Instructions

Instruction	Forms	Relative OP	~9	#	Description	5 H	3 N	2 Z	1 V	0 C
BCC	BCC	24	3	2	Branch C=0	•	•	•	•	•
	LBCC	10 24	5(6)	4	Long Branch C=0	•	•	•	•	•
BCS	BCS	25	3	2	Branch C=1	•	•	•	•	•
	LBCS	10 25	5(6)	4	Long Branch C=1	•	•	•	•	•
BEQ	BEQ	27	3	2	Branch Z=1	•	•	•	•	•
	LBEQ	10 27	5(6)	4	Long Branch Z=0	•	•	•	•	•
BGE	BGE	2C	3	2	Branch ≥ Zero	•	•	•	•	•
	LBGE	10 2C	5(6)	4	Long Branch ≥ Zero	•	•	•	•	•
BGT	BGT	2E	3	2	Branch > Zero	•	•	•	•	•
	LBGT	10 2E	5(6)	4	Long Branch > Zero	•	•	•	•	•
BHI	BHI	22	3	2	Branch Higher	•	•	•	•	•
	LBHI	10 22	5(6)	4	Long Branch Higher	•	•	•	•	•
BHS	BHS	24	3	2	Branch Higher or Same	•	•	•	•	•
	LBHS	10 24	5(6)	4	Long Branch Higher or Same	•	•	•	•	•
BLE	BLE	2F	3	2	Branch ≤ Zero	•	•	•	•	•
	LBLE	10 2F	5(6)	4	Long Branch ≤ Zero	•	•	•	•	•
BLO	BLO	25	3	2	Branch lower	•	•	•	•	•
	LBLO	10 25	5(6)	4	Long Branch Lower	•	•	•	•	•

Instruction	Forms	Relative OP	~9	#	Description	5 H	3 N	2 Z	1 V	0 C
BLS	BLS	23	3	2	Branch Lower or Same	•	•	•	•	•
	LBLS	10 23	5(6)	4	Long Branch Lower or Same	•	•	•	•	•
BLT	BLT	2D	3	2	Branch < Zero	•	•	•	•	•
	LBLT	10 2D	5(6)	4	Long Branch < Zero	•	•	•	•	•
BMI	BMI	2B	3	2	Branch Minus	•	•	•	•	•
	LBMI	10 2B	5(6)	4	Long Branch Minus	•	•	•	•	•
BNE	BNE	26	3	2	Branch Z=0	•	•	•	•	•
	LBNE	10 26	5(6)	4	Long Branch Z≠0	•	•	•	•	•
BPL	BPL	2A	3	2	Branch Plus	•	•	•	•	•
	LBPL	10 2A	5(6)	4	Long Branch Plus	•	•	•	•	•
BRA	BRA	20	3	2	Branch Always	•	•	•	•	•
	LBRA	16	5	3	Long Branch Always	•	•	•	•	•
BRN	BRN	21	3	2	Branch Never	•	•	•	•	•
	LBRN	10 21	5	4	Long Branch Never	•	•	•	•	•
BSR	BSR	8D	7	2	Branch to Subroutine	•	•	•	•	•
	LBSR	17	9	3	Long Branch to Subroutine	•	•	•	•	•
BVC	BVC	28	3	2	Branch V=0	•	•	•	•	•
	LBVC	10 28	5(6)	4	Long Branch V=0	•	•	•	•	•
BVS	BVS	29	3	2	Branch V=1	•	•	•	•	•
	LBVS	10 29	5(6)	4	Long Branch V=1	•	•	•	•	•

SIMPLE BRANCHES

	OP	~	#
BRA	20	3	2
LBRA	16	5	3
BRN	21	3	2
LBRN	1021	5	4
BSR	8D	7	2
LBSR	17	9	3

SIMPLE CONDITIONAL BRANCHES (Notes 1-4)

Test	True	OP	False	OP
N = 1	BMI	2B	BPL	2A
Z = 1	BEQ	27	BNE	26
V = 1	BVS	29	BVC	28
C = 1	BCS	25	BCC	24

SIGNED CONDITIONAL BRANCHES (Notes 1-4)

Test	True	OP	False	OP
r > m	BGT	2E	BLE	2F
r ≥ m	BGE	2C	BLT	2D
r = m	BEQ	27	BNE	26
r ≤ m	BLE	2F	BGT	2E
r < m	BLT	2D	BGE	2C

UNSIGNED CONDITIONAL BRANCHES (Notes 1-4)

Test	True	OP	False	OP
r > m	BHI	22	BLS	23
r ≥ m	BHS	24	BLO	25
r = m	BEQ	27	BNE	26
r ≤ m	BLS	23	BHI	22
r < m	BLO	25	BHS	24

Notes:

1. All conditional branches have both short and long variations.
2. All short branches are 2 bytes and require 3 cycles.
3. All conditional long branches are formed by prefixing the short branch opcode with $10 and using a 16-bit destination offset.
4. All conditional long branches require 4 bytes and 6 cycles if the branch is taken or 5 cycles if the branch is not taken.

Index